The Great State of
White and High

The Great State of White and High

Buddhism and State Formation in Eleventh-Century Xia

RUTH W. DUNNELL

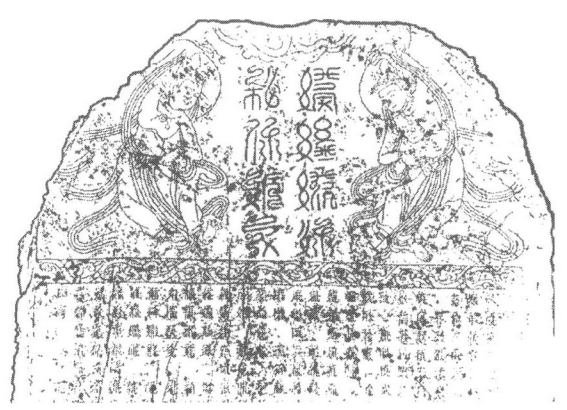

UNIVERSITY OF HAWAI'I PRESS, HONOLULU

© 1996 University of Hawai'i Press
All rights reserved
Printed in the United States of America

96 97 98 99 00 01   5 4 3 2 1

Library of Congress Cataloging-in-Publication Data

Dunnell, Ruth W., 1950–
The great state of white and high: Buddhism and state formation in eleventh-century Xia / Ruth W. Dunnell
p. cm.
Includes bibliographical references and index.
ISBN 0–8248–1719–2 (alk. paper)
1. Buddhism—China—History—960–1644. 2. Buddhism and state—China. 3. China—History—Hsi Hsia dynasty, 1038–1227. 4. Tangut—History. I. Title.
BQ640.D86 1996
322'.1'09517509021—dc20   95–31978
                                  CIP

University of Hawai'i Press books are printed on acid-free paper and meet the guidelines for permanence and durability of the Council on Library Resources

Frontispiece: State Preceptor Bai Zhiguang presiding over a session of the sūtra translation bureau, with Empress Dowager Liang and Huizong in attendance, ca. 1085. Blockprint engraving in the first chapter of the "Sūtra on the Thousand Buddha Names of the Present Bhadra Kalpa," Yuan woodblock edition in the Beijing Municipal Library. Courtesy of the Beijing Municipal Library.

Designed by Kenneth Miyamoto

To Charles and Eileen

Contents

Preface   *ix*
Conventions   *xiii*
Xia Rulers and Reign Era Titles   *xvii*
Genealogy of Eleventh-Century Xia Dynastic Alliances   *xx*
Brief Chronology of the Main Events in Xia History   *xxi*

PART 1. BUDDHISM IN ELEVENTH-CENTURY XIA

1   Introduction   *3*
2   Buddhism and Monarchy in the Early Tangut State   *27*
3   Buddhism under the Regencies (1049–1099)   *50*

PART 2. THE 1094 STELE INSCRIPTIONS FROM LIANGZHOU

4   A History of the Dayun (Huguo) Temple at Liangzhou   *87*
5   Annotated Translation of the 1094 Stele Inscriptions   *118*
6   Reading between the Lines: A Comparison and Analysis of the Tangut and Han Texts   *133*
7   Conclusion   *157*

APPENDICES

A. Photoreproductions of Rubbings of the 1094 Gantong Stūpa Stele Inscriptions   *163*
B. Chronology of Sources Recording or Discussing the Inscriptions on the Gantong Stūpa Stele   *173*

Abbreviations *179*

Notes *181*

A Select Glossary of Chinese Names and Terms *243*

Bibliography *253*

Index *271*

Preface

THIS BOOK grew out of an appendix to my doctoral dissertation, "Tanguts and the Tangut State of Ta Hsia," containing a translation of the Chinese text of a stele inscription in both Tangut and Chinese, dated 1094, from a Xia temple in Wuwei, Gansu. The dissertation relied mainly on Chinese sources and Russian translations of Tangut materials to reconstruct the history of the Xia state from its beginnings through the twelfth century. It did not address the topic of Buddhism. After completing the dissertation in 1983, I decided to undertake the study of both the Tangut language and Buddhism so that I could use the extant primary sources in Tangut, which are mostly Buddhist. Both of these undertakings have proved every bit as daunting as I suspected they might be, and my ongoing apprenticeship has not been as systematic and comprehensive as I would wish. This work is a measure of the distance I have come and also of the distance I have yet to travel.

Many kind and knowledgeable people have aided and encouraged me over the years. To my colleagues in "Tangut studies" I owe special debts of gratitude. Evgenii Ivanovich Kychanov and Ksenia Borisovna Kepping welcomed me into this enterprise in 1980–1981, in what was then called Leningrad, and have remained loyal pillars of support. Kychanov's lifelong labors in translating key Tangut documents in the Khara-khoto archive in St. Petersburg and the voluminous publications on Tangut history resulting therefrom have shaped my own work in many ways. Kepping's meticulous and groundbreaking studies of the Tangut language have refined our understanding of the documents that both of these Russian scholars have brought into the public domain. Support by the International Research and Exchanges Board (IREX) made possible my research trips to Russia in 1980–1981 and 1993–1994. Kenyon College supported a trip in the summer of 1991.

A grant from the Committee on Scholarly Communication with China enabled me to spend 1987–1988 in Beijing, working at the Institute of Nationality Studies of the Chinese Academy of Social Sciences with Shi Jinbo, Bai Bin, Huang Zhenhua, and Nie Hongyin. My first systematic study of Tangut language began under Shi Jinbo, who, although pressed for time, devoted his Friday mornings for over three months to my education. We discovered a large area of shared interest in Xia Buddhism and history, and his vast corpus of published works forms a critical foundation for my own research. Unfortunately the translation of the twelfth-century Xia law code into Chinese by Shi Jinbo, Huang Zhenhua, and Nie Hongyin was published in 1994 and reached me too late to be used here. Instead I have used the text and Russian translation of E. I. Kychanov (see below).

During 1987–1988 and, thanks to the generosity of Kenyon College, in the summers of 1990 and 1992, I traveled to old Tangut territories in Ningxia, Gansu, and Inner Mongolia. There I made many friends at museums, institutes, and universities. Their unfailing kindness in part expressed gratitude and amazement that a foreigner, for apparently unaccountable reasons, should take such an interest in so remote and unprofitable a corner of the world. In equal part it conveyed a sense of urgency about the difficult task of preserving what remains of that distant time and place, both on (or under) the ground as well as in the minds and priorities of policy makers. Among others I wish to thank Wu Fengyun, Li Fanwen, Niu Dasheng, Luo Maokun, Chen Bingying, Li Wei, Liang Xinmin, Liu Yuquan, Lu Sixian, and Li Yiyou. Many of their names can be found in the bibliography. My occasional arguments with the scholars acknowledged here as well as those not so acknowledged in no way diminishes my debt to them.

Earlier drafts of various chapters of this book were presented as papers or published as separate articles. In 1990 I presented a version of Chapter 2 at the China Colloquium of the University of Washington, and at the University of Hawai‘i. Parts of chapters 3 and 5 appeared in *Central and Inner Asian Studies* 7 (1992). A revised and annotated translation of the Chinese text of the 1094 stele inscription was published in the 1988 festschrift to Professor Tatsuo Nishida of the University of Kyoto. A summary of Chapter 4 was given at the 1992 annual meeting of the American Association of Chinese Studies in Novi, Michigan.

Preface

In the winter and spring of 1993, the Program for Inter-Institutional Collaboration in Area Studies at the University of Michigan supported a semester's leave in Ann Arbor, where I completed five of the book's seven chapters. Donald S. Lopez, T. Griffith Foulk, and Luis Gómez read chapters 3 and 4, and offered useful suggestions and corrections. Don Lopez also read several other chapters, and his editorial comments improved the internal coherence of those parts of the book.

Daniel Stevenson suggested solutions to several Buddhological mysteries in the Tangut text of the inscription. Robert N. Linrothe read the entire manuscript with a critical eye to style, argument, and sources. His extensive comments were the best gift a scholar can receive, and I have incorporated many of his suggested changes and rephrasings. Two careful readers for the University of Hawai'i Press have corrected obvious errors and suggested ways to make the book more appealing to its likely readers.

It was my fortune to write my dissertation under James T. C. Liu at Princeton University. James Liu combined a profound knowledge of his own cultural tradition and its history with a cheerful willingness to challenge its dearest assumptions. He encouraged my interest in "barbarians" and enthusiastically supported my endeavors. I regret that this work arrives too late for his scrutiny. Liu's student and my first mentor, Hok-lam Chan at the University of Washington, has remained a loyal and generous supporter from the very beginning. I will be pleased if he takes satisfaction in this book.

I have adopted Ksenia B. Kepping's proposed translation of the Tangut's own name of their state for the title of this book and throughout; linguistically it is impeccable. Her elaborate and ingenious etymology of the name, however, remains to be tested against the available evidence (see Kepping 1994 in the Bibliography).

Finally, I wish to thank my friend and former student, Jennifer Johnston, whose musings on ancient Greeks and on recreating from scattered bits the histories of people long gone have enlivened my faith in this work and in myself as historian.

Conventions

Use of the Words "Tangut" and "Xia"

The ethnonym "Tangut" first appeared in the Orkhon Turkic runic inscriptions of 735 (see Dunnell, "Who Are the Tanguts?" for details). It remained the North Asian term of reference to a people called Dangxiang in the Chinese histories from the seventh century on. Various forms of the name "Tangut" appear in Chinese histories of the Liao, Jin, and Yuan dynasties; in Ming and Qing writings it refers to people living in the Kokonor and Gansu border areas. Western explorers and writers passed on the term, and it has become the standard referent in Russian, Euro-American, and Japanese scholarship.

The Tibetans referred to these same people, or at least an important segment of them, as Mi-nyag, a term close to one of the Tanguts' own ethnonyms, Mi-niah (or Mi). Mi is the most common self-appellation used in Tangut writings; Xia authors generally render Mi into Chinese as Fan. As far as we know, the Xia Tanguts never referred to themselves as Tanguts, yet that term has become standard in Western (especially Russian) scholarship, reflecting the persistence of Northern Asian elements in the ethnolinguistic complexion of the Sino-Tibetan borderland.

I use the words "Tangut" and "Xia" in a fashion analogous to the terms Mongol/Mongolian and Yuan. Tangut, like Khitan, may be used as a noun or as an adjective. It narrowly refers to a specific ethnic group or federation, its culture, and its language. More broadly it points to the people who lived and the things they produced under the Xia state (1038–1227) ruled by the Tangut royal clan. Finally, it may also designate their descendants after the Mongolian conquest of 1226–1227, whose origins in postconquest literature are most often described as "Hexi" ("west of the [Yellow] River"). When I refer to Tangut or Chinese sources of Xia, I mean documents written either in Tangut or in Chinese, as both languages and scripts were in common use in the Xia state; Tangut continued to be used after the conquest as well.

Xia is temporally and spatially specific; it denotes the period from roughly the early eleventh century (or from 982) up to 1227 and the territories ruled over by the dynasty. The date 1038 marks the formal commencement of the Xia state and Tangut imperial history. Xia (or Great Xia) is analogous to Yuan (Great Yuan) in the sense that it is the formal Chinese name of the Tangut state. The founders also gave it a Tangut name, the Great State of White and High (as K. B. Kepping reads it; translated into Chinese as Gao Bai Da [Xia] Guo, or in Chinese word order, Bai Gao Da Xia Guo), which is the only form used in Tangut-language sources of the Xia period. Xia sources in Chinese refer to the state by both names, as do Tangut sources written after 1227, in the Mongol period.

Xi Xia, or "Western Xia," is an informal name used mainly by Chinese scholars of the Song and later periods up to the present day. In fact, Song and Jin writers most often referred to the Tangut state as simply Xia *(Xia guo)*. "Xi Xia" seems to have gained currency from Ming times onward and is standard in contemporary Chinese scholarship.

Translating to and from Tangut

Translating from Tangut requires several stages. For better or for worse, in the first stage I find it natural to produce a literal Chinese rendering of the Tangut passage. Many Tangut words have Chinese equivalents, especially if they are loanwords or calques; many do not. This intermediate stage is not yet a translation, properly speaking; it is a tool for identifying and establishing any relationship between the Tangut text and a hypothetical or real Chinese analog. In the second stage I try to establish the meaning of the passage through an English translation. If, to cite a simple example, a Tangut text is a translation of a Buddhist sūtra from a known Chinese version, then the latter will help immensely in arriving at a meaningful translation. The 1094 stele inscription, in contrast, presents bilingual texts that are not translations of each other or of a hypothetical original.

In this book, I often give a literal Chinese rendering of a Tangut term rather than romanize it. Tangut romanization would be meaningless to 99 percent of my readers, whereas many of them will recognize the Chinese. If I say that Tangut term X translates literally into Chinese term Y, I am referring to stage one in the translation process; meaning has not yet been established.

It gets even more complicated, however. Xia documents in Chinese and Tangut teem with multiple transliterations and translations of terms from both languages. Chapter 6 attempts to sort out the hybrid language of the stele inscription and to establish its possible meanings.

Chinese, Han, Fan

Xia documents usually refer to Chinese people and China as "Han." When quoting or paraphrasing from them, I, too, often use "Han" to mean "Chinese." Likewise, "Fan" usually means Tangut, but as I explain in Chapter 6, it can have other meanings depending on context. The terms "Han" and "Fan" should not be considered to be analytical categories; rather, as highly charged constructs, they become proper objects of analysis themselves.

Temple or Monastery?

Throughout this work I have translated the Chinese word *si* as temple. In many if not most cases, the context requires that we understand the *si* in question to be a monastic complex, with resident monks and an assemblage of buildings.

Liangzhou, Wuwei, Xiliang, the Five Liang

The names "Liangzhou," "Wuwei," and "Xiliang" all refer to the same region of Gansu, the town today called Wuwei (anciently called Guzang) and its surrounding area. Wu Liang (the Five Liang) was also an epithet of this region, deriving from the five regimes that governed the Gansu corridor in the fourth and fifth centuries: Former Liang (301–376) and Later Liang (386–403) were both headquartered at Guzang; Southern Liang (397–414) also eventually took over Guzang; Northern Liang (397–460) was headquartered at Zhangye (Ganzhou); and Western Liang (400–421) had its seat at Jiuquan (Suzhou).

Transcriptions and Romanizations

I use the *pinyin* system of Chinese romanization, despite its alleged inferiority to Wade-Giles in rendering phonetic values. Its great virtue is keyboard facility. The reader need only remember that *q* renders a sound like "ch" followed by the vowels i, umlauted u, and the diphthongs ia, iao, ie, io, iu, and umlauted ua and ue. X renders the sound "hs" followed by the same vowels and diphthongs. C is pronounced like "ts" in the English word "its" and z like unaspirated "ts." *Zh* sounds like the "j" of English "jug," and *j* like the "j" of English "jingle."

No standard romanization of Tangut yet exists. I follow the system devised by M. S. Sofronov in his *Grammatika tangutskogo iazyka* (1968), which, one hopes, will soon be revised and updated. For Tibetan I use the Wylie system and do not capitalize any but the first letter of a word. I render Sanskrit terms not appearing in dictionaries of American English, as well as proper names and titles, according to the system laid out in Macdonell's grammar. Diacritics are retained for all words; most are italicized. In transliterating Russian I use a modified version of the Library of Congress system.

I have not tried to reconstruct the forms of Tangut or other names appearing in the Chinese sources. In some cases where the Chinese original transcribes a foreign term or name of uncertain origin or special interest, I cite Edwin Pulleyblank's recent reconstructions of Early Mandarin (Yuan period) pronunciation. The reconstruction of non-Chinese names and terms in Song sources, although of critical importance, is a perilous and unrewarding exercise for a nonspecialist. Thus, medieval names are rendered here, for the most part, in modern Chinese romanization.

References to the Texts of the 1094 Inscriptions

Throughout the work I refer to lines of the Chinese (Han) and Tangut texts of the 1094 stele inscription translated in Chapter 5 as, for example, H2 and T4, respectively. H2 refers to line 2 of the Han text and T4 to line 4 of the Tangut text, which the reader may want to skip over to Chapter 5 and read.

Xia Rulers and Reign Era Titles

THE MAIN SOURCE for Xia dynastic titulature is *Song shi*, 485–486. Li Fanwen, in *Xi Xia yanjiu lunji* (1983), 76–99, has tabulated Tangut honorary titles not found in *Song shi* or other non-Xia Chinese sources, including a special set of short honorifics ending with the element "wall" (cheng). (See Shi Jinbo and Huang Zhenhua, "Xi Xia wen zidian 'Yin tong' di banben yu jiaokan" [1986], 22, for a more accurate reading of the title that Li Fanwen wrongly attributes to Li Deming.) Unless otherwise indicated, the last reign year is also the year of death.

Taizu, Li Jiqian (963–1004). *Honorary title:* Yingyun fatian shenzhi rensheng zhidao guangde xiaoguang. *Posthumous title:* Shenwu.

Taizong, Li Deming (b. 983?, r. 1004–1032), son of Li Jiqian and Yeli shi (titled Shuncheng yixiao huanghou). *Posthumous title:* Guangsheng.

Jingzong, Li Yuanhao (Weiming Nangxiao) (b. 1003, r. 1032–1048), eldest son of Li Deming and Weimu shi (titled Huici dun'ai huang hou). *Honorary titles:* Shengwen yingwu chongren zhixiao, Shizu shiwen benwu xingfa jianli renxiao. *"Wall" title:* Fengjiao cheng. *Posthumous title:* Wulie.

    Xiandao 1 (1032)
    Guangyun 1 (1035; originally Kaiyun)
    Daqing (1036–1038)
    Tianshou lifa yanzuo (1038–1048)

Yizong, Weiming Liangzuo (b. 1047, r. 1048–1067), son of Yuanhao and Mocang shi. *Posthumous title:* Zhaoying.

Yansi ningguo (1049)
Tianyou chuisheng (1050–1052)
Fusheng chengdao (1053–1056)
Chandu (1057–1062)
Gonghua (1063–1067)

Huizong, Weiming Bingchang (b. 1061, r. 1068–1086), son of Liangzuo and Liang shi (Gongsu zhangxian huanghou). *Honorary title:* Chengde guozhu shengfu zhengmin daming. *"Wall" titles:* Mianbi cheng, *zhenling cheng*. *Posthumous title:* Kangjing.

Qiandao (1068–1069)
Tianci lisheng guoqing (1069–1073)
Da'an (1074–1084)
Tianan liding (1085–1086?)

Chongzong, Weiming Qianshun (b. 1084, r. 1086–1139), son of Bingchang and Liang shi (Zhaojian wenmu huang hou). *Honorary title:* Shengong shenglu dejiao zhimin renjing. *"Wall" titles:* Bai cheng, Ming cheng. *Posthumous title:* Shengwen.

Tianyi zhiping (1086?–1089)
Tianyou min'an (1090–1097)
Yongan (1098–1100)
Zhenguan (1101–1113)
Yongning (1114–1118)
Yuande (1119–1126)
Zhengde (1127–1134)
Dade (1135–1139)

Renzong, Weiming Renxiao (b. 1124, r. 1139–1193), son of Qianshun and Cao shi. *Honorary titles:* Tianli dazhi zhixiao guangjing xuande jinzhong yongping, Fengtian xiandao yaowu xuan wen shenmou ruizhi zhiyi quxie dunmu yigong. *"Wall" titles:* Zhu cheng, Hu cheng shengde zhiyi. *Posthumous title:* Shengde.

Daqing (1140–1143)
Renqing (1144–1148)
Tiansheng (1149–1169)
Qianyou (1170–1193)

Huanzong, Weiming Chunyou (b. 1177, r. 1193–1206), son of Renxiao and Luo shi (Zhangxian qinci huang hou). *Posthumous title:* Zhaojian.

    Tianqing (1194–1206)

Xiangzong, Weiming Anquan (b. 1169?, r. 1206–1211), grandson of Qianshun and cousin of Chunyou, usurped the throne from the latter. *Posthumous title:* Jingmu.

    Yingtian (1206–1209)

    Huangjian (1210–1211)

Shenzong, Weiming Zunxu (b. 1162?, d. 1226, r. 1211–1223), son of Weiming Yanzong, the Zhongwu Prince of Qi (Qi guo zhongwu wang), usurped the throne, abdicated in 1223. *Posthumous title:* Yingwen.

    Guangding (1211–1223)

Xianzong, Weiming Dewang (b. 1180?, r. 1223–1226), son of Zunxu.

    Qianding (1223–1226)

Weiming Xian (b. ?, r. 1226–1227), Prince of Nanping, son of the Commandery Prince of Qingping (Qingping junwang).

    Baoyi[?] (1226–1227)

Genealogy of Eleventh-Century Xia Dynastic Alliances

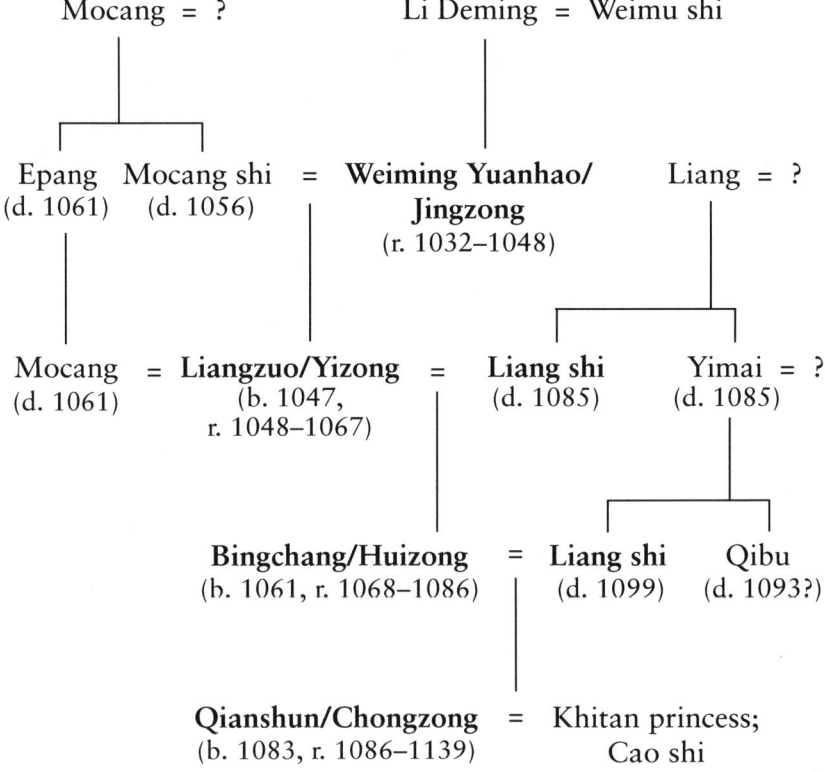

= denotes marital relationship
Names of Tangut emperors and their Liang spouses appear in boldface

Brief Chronology of the Main Events in Xia History

Adapted from Wu Tianchi, *Xi Xia shigao*, appendix 3; and Shi Jinbo, *Xi Xia fojiao shilüe* (1988), appendix 2. Shi's dating of Xia reign eras corrects the errors in Wu's.

983   (Song, Taiping xingguo 7; Liao, Qianheng 4) Li Jiqian launches an Ordos independence movement.

1002   (Song, Xianping 5; Liao, Tonghe 20) Jiqian's forces conquer Song outpost of Lingzhou on the Yellow River.

1004   (Song, Jingde 1; Liao, Tonghe 22) Jiqian dies of wounds sustained in the first Tangut takeover of Liangzhou; son Li Deming succeeds. Boluozhi, Tibetan ruler of Liangzhou, killed by local Tangut allies; his brother, Siduodu, succeeds, enfeoffed by Song as military governor *(jie du shi)* of Shuofang Commandery. Liao enfeoffed Li Deming as Prince *(wang)* of Xiping.

1006   (Song, Jingde 3; Liao, Tonghe 24) Deming negotiates treaty with Song; Song recognizes de facto independence of the Tangut state, enfeoffs him as military governor of Dingnan Commandery and Prince of Xiping.

1020   (Song, Tianxi 4; Liao, Kaitai 9) Liao attacks Liangzhou in retaliation for Deming's obstruction of Tibetan envoys from Kokonor to Liao; Deming establishes site of Xia capital at Xingzhou.

1028   (Song, Tiansheng 6/Liao, Taiping 8) Yuanhao conquers Ganzhou.

1031   (Song, Tiansheng 9; Liao, Jingfu 1) Yuanhao reconquers Liangzhou; Deming dies, succeeded by Yuanhao. First request for Song Buddhist canon.

1032	(Xia, Xiandao 1; Song, Mingdao 1; Liao, Chongxi 1) Liao enfeoffs Yuanhao as Xia *guo wang* (king of Xia state); Song enfeoffs Yuanhao as Prince of Xiping.
1033–1039	Yuanhao implements reforms, wars with Qingtang Tibetans, further conquests in Hexi. Second request (1035) for Song Buddhist canon.
1038	(Xia, Daqing 3/Tianshou lifa yanzuo 1; Song, Baoyuan 1; Liao, Chongxi 7) Liao envoy protests death of Yuanhao's royal Khitan wife. Yuanhao suppresses dissent in royal clan, carries out enthronement as first emperor of Great Xia, sends envoys to Song court.
1039	Hostilities with Song commence.
1044	(Xia, Tianshou lifa yanzuo 7; Song, Qingli 4; Liao, Chongxi 13) Defection to Xia of Dangxiang tribes along Liao border leads to Khitan attack on Xia, repulsed by Yuanhao. Song and Xia conclude negotiations, ending hostilities and establishing protocol governing their mutual relations; they do not delineate a common border.
1046	Khitans again attack Xia, relations with Liao hit nadir.
1048	Yuanhao dies in first month from wounds inflicted by his eldest son of the demoted Yeli empress; bastard infant son Liangzuo succeeds him, by decision of tribal council dominated by Mocang Epang, now controlling Xia government with his sister, Liangzuo's mother.
1051	(Xia, Tianyou chuisheng 2; Song, Huangyou 3; Liao, Chongxi 20) Hostilities with Liao end, relations still cool.
1053	(Xia, Fusheng chengdao 1) Formal relations with Liao restored, but Khitans refuse subsequent Tangut requests to renew marriage alliance.
1055	(Song, Zhihe 2; Liao, Qingning 1) Mocang empress inaugurates Chengtian Temple in capital; third request for Song Buddhist canon. Quye River border dispute with Song.
1056	(Song, Jiayou 1) Assassination of Mocang empress; Mocang Epang consolidates power in his own hands, marries daughter to Liangzuo.
1058	(Xia, Chandu 2) Fourth request for Song Buddhist canon.

Brief Chronology of Xia History *xxiii*

1061	Assassination of Epang; Liangzuo in power, marries ally Liang shi, confirms her brother Yimai as new minister. Settles Quye border dispute with Song. Replaces "Fan" rites with "Han" rites.
1065	(Xia, Gonghua 3; Song, Zhiping 2) Qingtang Tibetan leader Gusiluo dies; son Dongzhan succeeds.
1067	(Liao, Xianyong 3) Song border commander Chong E obtains surrender of Tangut military commander Weiming Shan, captures Xia outpost of Suizhou. Tanguts seek revenge; Liangzuo dies.
1068	(Xia, Qiandao 1; Song, Xining) Seven-year-old Bingchang succeeds Liangzuo under regency of Empress Dowager Liang and Liang Yimai. Song Shenzong comes to throne.
1072–1074	Song official Wang Shao active in Tao River valley.
1081	(Xia, Da'an 8; Song, Yuanfeng 4; Liao, Dakang 7) Bingchang's plot with Xia Chinese commander Li Qing uncovered; Bingchang incarcerated; civil war imminent; Song armies invade.
1081–1084	Song war effort met by unified resistance; Song captures Lanzhou, defeated at Yongle fortress; overall losses heavy on both sides; Qingtang Tibetans also attack Xia; Xia begins pressing for return of captured border territories.
1085	Xia minister Liang Yimai dies, succeeded by son Qibu. Song Shenzong dies; Song-Xia relations partially normalized; Empress Dowager Liang dies.
1086	(Xia, Tianan liding 2; Song, Yuanyou 1) Bingchang dies, succeeded by three-year-old son Qianshun under regency of his mother Empress Dowager Liang (niece of her predecessor) and her brother Liang Qibu. Qingtang ruler Dongzhan dies, succeeded by adopted son Aligu (from Khotan); Liang Qibu subsequently forms alliance with Aligu.
1094	(Xia, Tianyou min'an 5; Song, Shaosheng 1; Liao, Da'an 10) Stele erected at Huguo Temple in Liangzhou; assassination of Liang Qibu by Weiming allies (possibly in 1093).

1096–1099 Song-Xia border hostilities resume; Xia repeatedly seeks Liao intervention. Aligu's death in 1096 leads to turmoil in Kokonor; Song intervenes.

1099 (Xia, Yongan 1; Song, Yuanfu 2; Liao, Shouchang 5) Empress Dowager Liang dies; Qianshun seeks reconciliation with Song; Tanguts resist Song armies' advance to Qingtang.

1101 (Liao, Qiantong 1) Qianshun initiates reforms.

1102 (Xia, Zhenguan 1; Song, Chongning 1) Xia court establishes marriage alliance with Kokonor Tibetan ruler.

1103–1106 Xia resists Song efforts to assert control over Kokonor; seeks Liao intervention to persuade Song to return Xia territories; Liao renews marriage alliance with Xia.

1114–1119 Song renews war against Xia; Jurchens attack Khitans.

1123 (Xia, Yuande 4; Song, Xuanhe 5; Liao, Baoda 3) Qianshun offers sanctuary to fleeing Liao emperor, who recognizes Xia ruler as "emperor."

1124–1125 Qianshun recognizes Jurchen Jin suzerainty; Jurchens capture Liao emperor.

1126–1136 Xia takes advantage of Jin conquest of North China to recover territories lost to Song; takes Qingtang.

1139 (Xia, Dade 5; Song, Shaoxing 9; Jin, Tianjuan 2) Qianshun dies; son Renxiao succeeds.

1141 (Xia, Daqing 2; Jin, Huangtong 1) Jin and Xia open border markets; Jin and Song conclude peace. Internal uprisings and natural disasters in Xia.

1145–1146 (Xia, Renqing 2–3) Renxiao establishes university, cult of Confucius; Jin delineates border with Xia.

1149–69 (Xia, Tiansheng 1–21) Tiansheng era. Tiansheng legal code compiled; surrendered Chinese commander Ren Dejing climbs to power and threatens to split the country; Renxiao presides over reediting and printing of Xia Buddhist canon, establishes office of Buddhist imperial preceptor (*dishi*), and invites Tibetan monks to court.

1170 (Xia, Qianyou 1; Jin, Dading 10) Jin Shizong protests Xia minister Ren Dejing's attempt to divide Xia; Ren Dejing and his followers assassinated.

Brief Chronology of Xia History

1189	(Xia, Qianyou 20; Jin, Dading 29) Jin Shizong dies; Renxiao celebrates his fiftieth enthronement anniversary with lavish Buddhist ceremonies and distribution of sūtras.
1193	Renxiao dies; succeeded by son Chunyou; border conflicts with Jurchens on the rise.
1205	(Xia, Tianqing 12) Temüjin leads first attack on Hexi.
1206	(Xia, Yingtian 1) Weiming Anquan usurps throne; Chunyou dies. Song attacks Jin. Temüjin becomes Chinggis Qan.
1207	Mongols attack Xia border post at Uraqai (Wulahai).
1208	(Jin, Taihe 8) Tanguts seek Jin aid against Mongols; Song-Jin war ends in Song defeat; Jin Zhangzong dies.
1209–10	(Xia, Yingtian 4/Huangjian 1) Third Mongolian attack, Xia capital besieged; Xia agrees to become Mongol vassal and render aid to Chinggis Qan.
1211	(Xia, Guanding 1; Jin, Da'an 3) Weiming Zunxu replaces Anquan on throne. Mongols open campaign against Jin.
1212–1223	Xia-Jin hostilities; Mongols surround Xia capital in 1217; Tanguts refuse to assist Chinggis' Central Asian campaign.
1223	(Jin, Yuanguang 2) Jin emperor dies; Xia emperor abdicates to son Dewang, who begins peace negotiations with Jin, seeks allies against Mongols.
1226–1227	Final Mongol campaign against Xia; under duress Xia and Jin conclude treaty as "brother states." Too late.

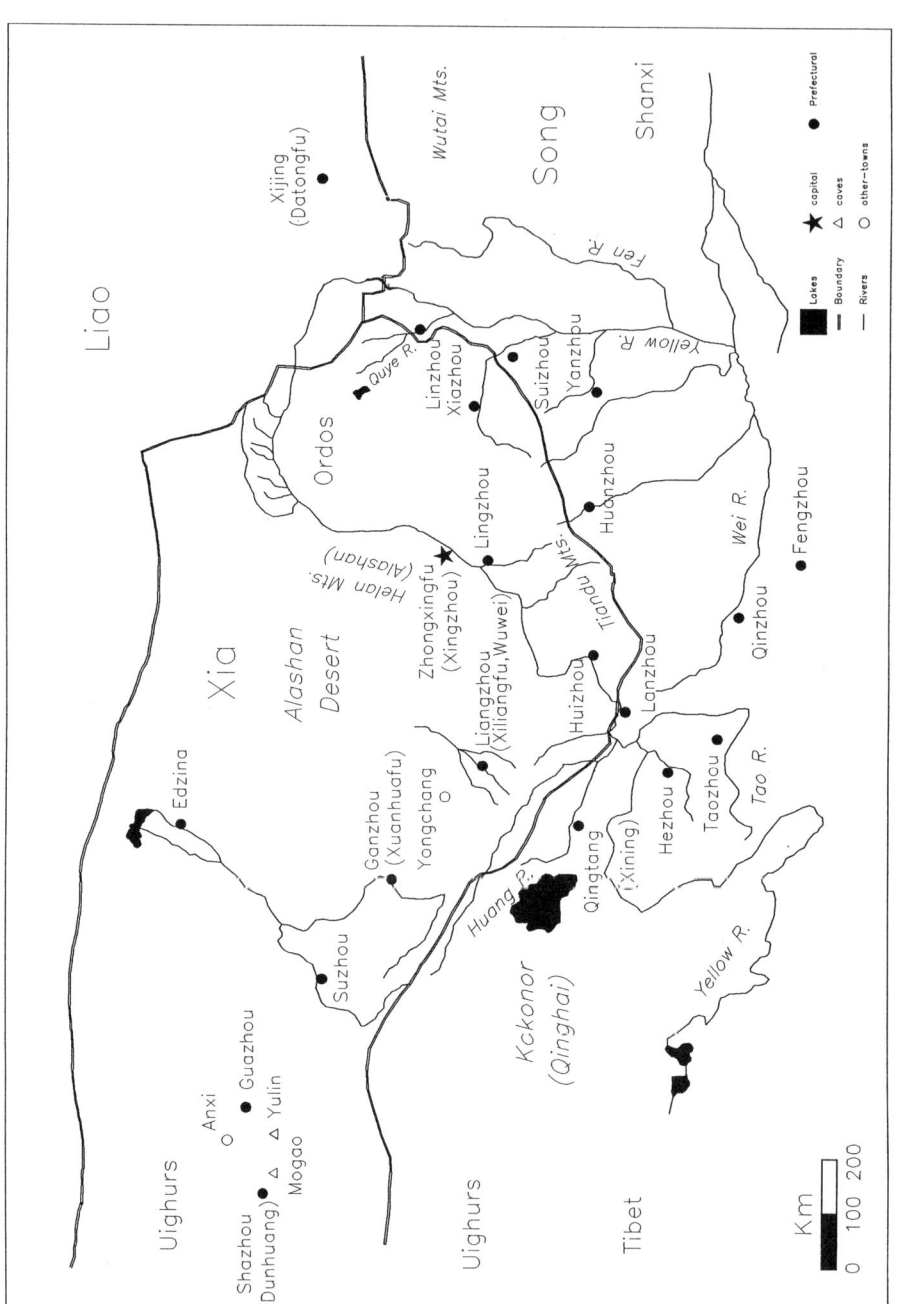

Xia State and Neighbors (1094)

PART 1
Buddhism in Eleventh-Century Xia

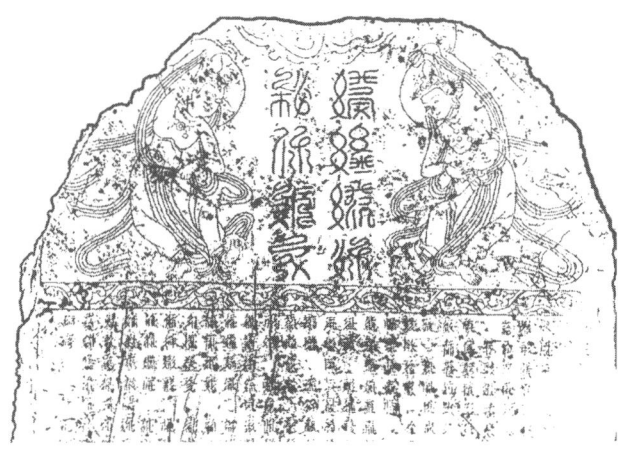

CHAPTER 1
Introduction

IN THE LATE TENTH and early eleventh centuries a group of people, known in Western and Japanese scholarship as Tangut and in Chinese as Dangxiang Qiang, established an independent regime in the Ordos (the steppe region within the loop of the Yellow River, present-day Ningxia, Shaanxi, Gansu, and Inner Mongolia). It quickly grew into the empire of Xia, or, as they called it in their own language, the Great State of White and High.[1] Xia was a formidable neighbor of the Song, Liao, and Jin states to the south and east, of the Tibetans to the southwest, and of the Central Asian kingdoms to the west (see map). The ruling group, who spoke a language related to Tibetan, called themselves Mi (Tib. Mi-nyag) and became renowned throughout Asia as devout Buddhists. An imperial state was formally born in 1038, and it chronicled its existence up to 1227, when it was finally crushed in Chinggis Qan's last campaign. State records have all but disappeared, and, unlike Liao and Jin, no Chinese-style dynastic history was compiled for Xia.[2]

In the past century imperialism and archeology have vastly expanded the body of primary source materials for Xia history, the largest and most important of which is housed in the St. Petersburg branch of the Russian Institute of Oriental Studies (referred to as the Khara-khoto or Kozlov collection, after the place where they were found or the man who found them) and the State Hermitage Museum.[3] Most of these materials date to the twelfth century or later, and approximately 80 percent of the Khara-khoto collection is Buddhist in nature. Xia materials are also housed in Beijing and other cities in China, and in London, Paris, Berlin, Stockholm, Delhi, and Kyoto, among other places. For several decades scholars in Russia, China, and Japan, primarily, have been working to bring this material into the public realm and to restore to history this little known but pivotal corner of Inner Asia.[4]

This book examines the native sources for early imperial Tangut history and interprets them in the light of the state's political vicissitudes up to the end of the eleventh century. By native sources I mean documents generated within the Xia state itself, by Tanguts, Chinese, or others, in the Tangut script or in Chinese. Contemporary Song, Liao, and Jin records are treated as secondary sources and later Chinese chronicles as tertiary. Nevertheless, given the paucity of native sources for the eleventh century, I do not ignore the secondary and tertiary record, and I rely heavily on it when the discussion goes outside the main temporal framework.

Because the overwhelming majority of extant Xia sources are Buddhist and products of imperial patronage, it became apparent to me that no real understanding of Tangut history could proceed without dealing with those sources and the place of Buddhism at the court and in society. One could argue that the survival of these Buddhist sources was an accident of history and that an interpretation based exclusively on them would inevitably be distorted. Thus, for example, I may be faulted for underemphasizing Confucian influence on the Xia state, although Confucian influence may have been considerably stronger in the twelfth century than in the eleventh. Furthermore, despite its merits, that argument leaves one with the option of ignoring the extant evidence and constructing an interpretation based on normative assumptions and Chinese accounts. I would rather err on the side of the existing native record, which is undeniably Buddhist.

My thesis is simply that the history of early Tangut Buddhism is so intertwined with Xia state formation and the needs of the throne that analysis of the relationship between the two is a prerequisite to understanding one or the other.[5] Moreover, this mutual relationship characterized the East Asian political landscape, such that the Buddhism constituent in early Song and Liao state building was probably far more significant than has hitherto been appreciated. The Buddhist activities of the first four Song emperors in particular (about whom we have more information than their Liao counterparts) shaped the environment in which Tangut Buddhism emerged and began developing. Furthermore, as tensions between Song and Xia intensified throughout the eleventh century, the diplomatic and political weight of Buddhist symbols and Buddhist monks, at least along the frontier and in Xia, likewise heightened. A distinctive Tangut

Buddhism, heavily influenced by Tibetan Tantric Buddhism, matured later in the twelfth and early thirteenth centuries, and the abundant textual and visual sources for that period allow us to analyze the important Himalayan contributions and the development of local artistic styles and cult practices. For that later time it may even be possible to speak of the internal dynamics of Tangut Buddhism, keeping in mind that the imperial court, as the principal source of wealth and patronage, was one of those "dynamics." Defining what is distinctive about Tangut Buddhism must take account of Buddhism's political role at the Xia court and in Inner Asian affairs.[6] My present research encompasses these topics in their twelfth- and thirteenth-century settings.[7]

The principal Xia source for the eleventh century, and the piece around which this book is organized, is a unique bilingual stele inscription dated to 1094 from the Dayun (Huguo) Temple in Liangzhou (present-day Wuwei, Gansu). Liangzhou was a frontier town important throughout imperial Chinese history and a major oasis on the eastern end of the trading route linking China and Central Asia through the Gansu Corridor. Both sides of the stele were carved, one in Tangut and the other in Chinese, with a text celebrating restoration of the temple by the Xia throne. The texts are long and detailed, and provide a rare glimpse into Tangut affairs and thinking. Part 2 of this book focuses on the temple at Liangzhou and the inscription, and presents annotated translations and an analysis of the Tangut and Chinese texts. Although the inscription does not directly answer questions about the power struggles at the Tangut court examined in Part 1, it does shed light on some important issues pertinent to those struggles.

One crucial issue for Xia elites was the construction of a "national" identity and of policies to promote it, as tasks inseparable from securing and governing the state. To a large extent that identity was shaped by the cultural and ethnic self-conceptions of the dynasty, which I call "Tangut," as opposed to "Chinese" or "Tibetan," although Chinese and Tibetan elements were important ingredients in that identity. Heavily implicated in this complex and troublesome endeavor were dynastic politics, patronage of Buddhism, and relations with Han Chinese and Chinese culture, especially in the hostile environment of the eleventh century. The reformulation of diverse tribal affinities (ethnic, genealogical, and linguistic) into a national identity or identities accompanied the transformation of early Tangut military elites into a mostly literate and lettered Xia aristocracy. Written texts and architectural monuments produced throughout the entire Xia period up to the thirteenth century testify to this ongoing process and the concerns and frictions that it engendered.

My aim is to elicit the "voices" in the Xia sources studied here, yet I do not believe that "facts speak for themselves," and even under the best of circumstances the voices I am able to bring to the surface resist translation. Part 1 of the book therefore establishes the contexts (or background) for reading and understanding the 1094 inscriptions with an exploration of the two major motifs of Xia history that interest me here: state formation and Buddhism. Chapters 2 and 3 trace, more or less chronologically, the history of Buddhism in the eleventh century in the context of the political fortunes of the Xia state.

By state formation I mean dynastic politics and the evolution of the imperial institution, although it is not my purpose here to analyze the structures of the Xia government. To be sure, a medieval state was often more than the royal institution, but without the throne there would be only tribal confederations, no state. The devolution of the Tangut state into a tribal confederation seemed a real possibility in the crisis-ridden years of the late eleventh century. In particular, therefore, I am interested in Tangut conceptions, representations, and practice of sovereignty and monarchy, and the implications of these "imaginings" for the Xia state. But any substantive ruminations on these questions must await an analysis of the more abundant twelfth-century sources, in particular the Tiansheng law code.[8] This book lays the groundwork for those explorations.

Because it is likely to be the first volume in English on the subject of Tangut Xia history, it is necessary to state clearly what this book does *not* treat. It does not provide a comprehensive introduction to all the literature in the field or to all the issues that have taxed scholars' brains over the decades. It pretends no mastery of the linguistic and philological puzzles that any use of Chinese, Tangut, or Tibetan materials presents. It tries to be responsible Buddhologically but is not primarily about Buddhism. Most regrettably it does not take up the stunning Tangut art featured in the catalogue *Lost Empire of the Silk Road,* and it offers only one reproduction of a black-and-white blockprint engraving (see frontispiece). Nor does it linger in much detail on Tangut temple and tomb architecture or artifacts, although the rich remains of Xia material culture are certainly relevant to my theme. Finally, it makes references to but does not unravel the fasci-

Introduction

nating and complicated history of the Kokonor Tibetans, with whom Tanguts had ancestral, linguistic, cultural, political, and economic ties.[9]

In the following pages I will sketch out the terrain over which my understanding of the issues of state formation and Buddhism ranges. My discussion is not a systematic review of the literature on these topics, which would require a separate book. Rather it is a selective exposition of the ideas and concerns that have animated this study, whose central thesis is the inseparability of Xia Buddhism and state formation, their shared characteristics, their fate, and ultimately their significance for Chinese and Inner Asian history.

State Formation and Rulership: Some Theoretical Considerations

Social scientists hotly debate when, how, and why the "state" emerged and what made it a "state" rather than a kingdom, empire, dynasty, feudatory, or node in the world system. My use of the word to denote a medieval Asian polity might be contentious. Although it is clear that I am not talking about the modern nation state, the handy and concise word "state" is both justified and appropriate in contexts predating 1500. Looking at how some European historians or world-system theorists analyze the rise of the modern nation state or the world system can usefully contextualize this inquiry, enlarge the possibilities of its significance, and overcome the limitations of Europocentric and sinocentric interpretations.[10]

Relations with Song China overshadowed the first one hundred years of Tangut state-building activity, and from 1039 to 1115 these relations were often hostile, punctuated by episodes of bloody warfare, and predicated on an economic interaction in the form of an annual exchange of Tangut tribute and Song subsidy (during years of peace), official border trade, and mutual raiding along the frontier. Traditionally the Chinese have regarded the northern "nomads" (or western "barbarians") as simply greedy for Chinese riches. Western scholars have also emphasized the economic incentives behind "nomad" raids, Sino–Inner Asian relations, and the rise of nomadic states.[11] The notion that economic incentives operated on the Chinese side as well tends to get smothered by the assumption that "nomads" needed the Chinese but the Chinese did not need the "nomads," a comforting cultural prejudice that world-system theory nullifies.

Properly speaking, the Tanguts were not nomads, although many of the groups living in the Ordos and the Gansu Corridor practiced transhumance. The ecology of their polity was a complex mix, perhaps even more so than that of their contemporaries, the Khitans (a true nomadic people of the Mongolian steppe who founded the Liao state) or the Jurchens (a forest-dwelling, horse-breeding people of Manchuria whose Jin state conquered Liao and north China, forcing the Song to retreat south of the Huai River).[12] While accumulating economic surplus was usually a concern of rulers, it was only one, and not necessarily the primary, cause of the rise of the Tangut state or the friction between Song and Xia. As Sechin Jagchid has observed, "As a rule, when the power of a nomadic people and a Chinese state was nearly equal, there was a better chance for peace."[13] Chinese power vastly overwhelmed that of the Tanguts, although not on the battlefields in the northwest, given the unfavorable logistics for the Chinese. So although the Tanguts could fend off conquest from the south and the east, and expand west into Hexi, they were too weak to bargain for or to impose a peaceful demarcation of the frontier with Song China. Military considerations therefore loomed large in the eleventh century for both the Chinese and the Tanguts, and influenced the state-building processes in both empires.

One recent essay on military studies in European history addresses some of the broader issues I touch on and therefore offers ways of looking at them in a comparative context.[14] Reviewing five recent works of comparative European history, John Lynn argues for "placing the history of warfare and military institutions at the center of our understanding of European history—most notably in describing the creation, character, and dominance of the state."[15] One need not follow Lynn in his enthusiasm to find his perspective a useful corrective to the antimilitary bias of most scholars. Charles Tilly traces the interaction between coercive power (state-conducted warfare) and economic development (urbanization) to account for differing patterns of state formation in Europe and Russia from the early modern period through the present.[16] According to Lynn,

> Tilly sees the national state emerging from a process of bargaining between the rulers and competing power blocks in society. Standing armies were both a product of and an influence on this bargaining process.... The increased demands of warfare gave advantages to the power blocks within societies, allowing them to extract concessions from rulers—concessions that created or reinforced representative institutions. (p. 85)

Lynn is willing to concede the last point only because Tilly's book covers a period down to 1990. For our purposes, we can see similar pressures brought to bear on Xia rulers by the military elites. The rulers' "concessions" were, in part, law codes that enshrined the privileges of the hereditary aristocracy, a function that law codes also played in China and elsewhere, even while rulers used these same codes to try to curb the "power blocks" in society.

We can also read the eleventh-century Song-Xia wars as the surface manifestations of pervasive civil conflicts: in Xia among various "power blocks" including the throne, regency, military elites, and frontier chiefs; in Song among reformist factions, the throne, and various regional military-commercial interests.[17] Thus the enormously costly 1081 Song invasion of Xia was not precipitated by any tangible Tangut threat to Song security, but by the logic of political struggle at the Song court. "Religious unity" became an important tool of the Tangut throne and regency in strengthening its authority, as it did for the Song court and for European monarchs,[18] although this "unity" did not denote anything so well defined and institutionalized as the Neo-Confucian "orthodoxy" of later Chinese history (fourteenth century onward) whose roots go back to this period. Indeed, the factional battles at the Song court take on the contours of religious inquisition in the 1080s and 1090s.

Just as Meiji Japan, Petrine Russia, late Qing China, or the late Ottoman empire felt compelled to adopt Western technologies to avoid European political domination,[19] many tribal groups and border dynasties in East Asia have used similar strategies to avoid Chinese political domination, although the armaments they borrowed were more likely to be the instruments of imperial bureaucracy than of war. The Tanguts are a good example, provoking the following questions: Is westernization (sinicization) inevitable? Is the alternative a silencing of the "native"?[20]

A world-system response to this question might be "not necessarily," because change in any one part of the system affects all its parts, and the term "westernization" (or "sinicization") only denotes the greater or lesser integration of any given part into the larger system, rather than analyzing the sociocultural change that takes place in consequence of that integration. In the case of "westernization" or "sinicization" most people assume that integration into the larger system irresistibly forces the integrating element to undergo radical systemic change in alignment with the cultural and political values of the powers dominating the system. This assumption remains problematic on several grounds.

For one thing, it presupposes an irresistible, lineal progression in which everyone and everything inevitably becomes absorbed into a dominant political and cultural system by virtue of participating in a linked economy, a process leading to the "end of history." Further, it overlooks the transformations taking place or that have taken place in the system itself as a result of the participation of new members, transformations that may or could mount a successful challenge to the currently dominant powers through their own "technologies." Third, it underestimates the strength, diversity, and implications of resistance to the dominant system, resistance not located purely on the geographic peripheries of the "developed" world. In all of these respects, the presumption of inevitable alignment with the dominant political-cultural power is on one level profoundly *ahistorical,* a frozen moment, not movement through time.

The assumption in European history that "modern" and "early modern" have fixed and singular chronological boundaries in recent centuries obscures the interesting possibilities of a nonlinear and multicentered perspective on history.[21] World-system theory moves toward the latter by shifting the focus from parts (the "state") to the system as a whole, which may develop numerous centers and change in many apparently contradictory directions and at diverse rates.[22] The role that revolutionary changes in military technology and organization played in state formation, for example, is not limited to early modern Europe, although it may very well account for the rise of European hegemony from the sixteenth century.

The sinocentric perspective, which inevitably colors much Euro-American historiography on China, not to mention the writings of the Chinese themselves over many centuries, has only vaguely perceived that China was part of a larger world that mattered in any intrinsic way to China's internal development until the last century or so.[23] When we look at the world through sinocentric glasses, the unification of "China" (always through war) is good and desirable, its division into separate polities always bad, and border dynasties appear as security threats rather than as manifestations of China's participation in "an Inner Asian continuum" and a dynamic cultural give-and-take that shaped China as much as Inner Asia.[24] Although Marxist historiography made serious inroads into the sinocentric perspective, certain features have resisted change.

In particular, the ideological requirements of defining "Chineseness" and the Chinese polity, whether the imperial state or its modern successors, have imposed unities and uniformities over the most diverse phenomena. Linguistics provides a good example. In the same way that the group of related "Chinese" spoken languages have for political reasons been considered dialects of one language, so too the Sino-Tibetan language family is considered by some scholars an arbitrary hypothesis kept alive for largely political purposes.[25] The proposed affiliation of Tangut with this language family, as an ancient member of its Tibeto-Burman branch,[26] along with other factors, has meant that "Tangut" (Xi Xia or Dangxiang, in Chinese) has become a subset of the politicized category "Tibet" in contemporary Chinese discourse. More sophisticated and well-trained Chinese scholars are able to work around such constraints, but a larger problem intervenes: defining what it means to be or to have been "Chinese." The role that so-called minority nationalities, the "native" or "other" of the Chinese, play in this process is both culturally and politically strategic, and is systematically imposed on the past through the use of a modern political vocabulary and its categories.

Without denying the significance of Chinese contributions, the problem with such an approach lies in its exclusivity, on the one hand (if "a" then not "b"), and simultaneously, on the other hand, in its hierarchical subordination (if "b" then part of "a"). These apparently mutually exclusive propositions lie at opposite ends of an analytical spectrum along whose middle reaches lurk complicated and ambiguous combinations. Take, for example, Pamela Crossley's discussion of our understanding of Chinese emperorship in the Qing period.

> Narratives of the emergence of Qing power in the seventeenth century frequently follow the evolution of the emperorship from the khanship created by Nurgaci (r. 1616–1626). The primary themes have been the movement from corporate, consultative governance to autocracy, the maturation of bureaucratic influence, the diminution of the civil and military authority of the Manchu aristocracy, and the increasing symbolic expression of imperial universalism toward the end of the Qianlong reign. *The idea that khanship in growing Inner Asian regimes metamorphoses irresistibly into emperorship* was fundamental to the work of Joseph Fletcher, who considered the Mongol great khans as ancestors, though not exclusive ancestors, of the Qing, Ottoman, and Timurid regimes.[27]

Without rejecting Fletcher's conclusions for the seventeenth-century Ottomans, Crossley nevertheless insists that "in the case of the Qing, it is clear that while the khan became an emperor, he also remained a khan." In particular, he remained a khan to members of the Liaodong elite and population who joined Nurgaci's cause after 1616 primarily, Crossley suggests, because he "publicized himself as a champion of regional concerns. Moreover, this Liaodong population was given a special identity in the Eight Banners by the Qing court, which continued to address it in the terms of khanal relationships—master to slave—for its entire history" (p. 1475).

I propose to examine the evolution of the Xia state and the Tangut monarchy from this inclusive, ambiguous middle ground. Moreover, we are well served to keep in mind the much better documented history of the early Japanese state (sixth to tenth centuries), which formed on the sinitic periphery and, to defend and promote itself, self-consciously adopted all the latest cultural technologies and administrative innovations from a recently reunified Chinese empire. It is precisely the *differences* between Nara/Heian Japan and Xia that make comparison so enlightening: Japan is still here today, and however one chooses to characterize it, it did not become "Chinese" nor has it become "American."

Xia State Formation: Some Historical Considerations

The Xia state was more than a kingdom; like its Chinese and Khitan contemporaries, Song and Liao, it was an empire that claimed and sought to legitimate its dominion over far-flung lands and numerous peoples. Although the main model and perhaps the impetus for creating a state came from China, it bears emphasizing that the goal of state making was not originality, but success, that is, durability. Nevertheless, the practical results of state making necessarily reflected the different social (kinship) structures, livelihoods, customary laws, religious beliefs, historical and geographic circumstances, and political needs or aspirations that the Tanguts and their partners had to negotiate.

Motivation for state formation was threefold: (1) to preserve the privileged economic and political gains that the elite had garnered over several centuries, (2) to protect Tanguts (and other non-Han frontier residents) from the depredations of Chinese border officials, and (3) to guard against displacement by the Han population during periods of an expansive Chinese empire and against absorption and denaturing by the Chinese imperium. Hence, although the organizers of the state certainly stood to benefit by institutionalizing their power, the historical narratives reveal years (centuries) of exploitation by Chinese border officials as a precipitating factor in Tangut state formation, especially in the unstable years following the collapse of Tang authority (most of the ninth and tenth centuries).[28] As in the case of the Manchu chieftain Nurgaci, regional concerns made possible the emergence of the Tangut state and created new identities for its participants.

Protecting themselves meant not only resisting Chinese pressures, but, more important, stabilizing the ecological frontier where the two societies, Han and Inner Asian, agrarian and herding, overlapped. After the collapse of Tang authority, the Tanguts moved into the power vacuum and began to assert their economic paramountcy in the Ordos, which they had already established in the eighth century, as a fulcrum from which to build up political supremacy, by serving as loyal guardians of Tang imperial interests.[29] As long as Tang was weak, these interests served their own; defending Tang allowed them to enhance their own authority.

The gradual reconstitution of central authority in north China during the tenth century was closely watched by Tangut leaders, who successfully resisted the efforts of north Chinese courts to reassert power over the region. Tangut leaders, although wary of it, ultimately benefited by the formation of a state in the northeast under the Khitans, which prevented the north Chinese courts from concentrating their resources on reincorporation of the Ordos. However, as the north China court grew much stronger under the Song regime and began to conquer the other regional kingdoms, Tangut chieftains eventually had to choose between defending their autonomy in the new world that was emerging from the 960s on and joining the Song establishment.

Prompted by strong ethnic and economic pressures to remain autonomous, the more daring Tangut leaders found in their past abundant models for action. Thus the Tangut state emerged first as a strategy for resisting absorption by the centralizing Chinese state (and perhaps the Khitan Liao as well). Those elements of the leadership who wavered on the issue of autonomy surrendered to the Song court in the 981–982 succession crisis at Xiazhou, the Tanguts' Ordos base; they accepted the Song emperor's cup of wine and retired.

Every state has its founding or charter myths, which legitimize the enterprise. At first the Song regime must have looked to everybody like one more Tang successor state. But it eventually managed to outlive the others, and it began to act like Tang in its political pretensions. To lay full claim to the charter myth of the imperial

Chinese state, Song had to reunify as much of the former empire as possible. Its inability to do so completely in the north fostered a disjuncture between myth and reality, the source of a nervous and creative insecurity.

Song insecurity nourished political idealism and experimentation; it also stoked imperial ambitions to prove and assert the throne's legitimacy on the battlefield. Conventional assessments of the Song military do not convey the offensive and expansive nature of Song military operations from the late 1060s through the twelfth century. Song Shenzong's fixation on conquering the Xia state, passed on to his son Zhezong, may be directly responsible for the events that led to the fall of northern Song. It is important to stress that Shenzong's failure to achieve his objective was not a result of the inefficiency or inadequacy of Song military strength and organization. Liao could not defeat the Tanguts in battle, either, much less conquer its neighbor. Shenzong was aware of this, and it worried him, as his recorded conversations with Wang Anshi reveal. Although some Chinese statesmen and commanders appear to have been reasonably well informed about the workings of the Tangut state, others seemed to speak or act according to stereotypical analyses of "barbarian" groups.[30] The usual divide and conquer, carrot and stick strategies backfired over time, and only reinforced and validated the Tanguts' own charter myth.

To wonder why Song policymakers did not make adjustments in their expectations and conduct vis-à-vis Xia, however, as lone figures like Su Che and Sima Guang argued, is analogous to wondering why the United States has not yet (in 1994) extended diplomatic recognition to Cuba. Such criticisms challenge but cannot dislodge the potent ideological self-conceptions and legitimating myths to which each regime must lay claim in a particular and compelling set of historical circumstances.

The first element I have identified in the charter myth of Tangut state formation, defense against China, was not merely a negative external pressure. Its corollary was a positive internal pressure taking shape in a strong sense of identity as a people self-consciously distinct from the Chinese in culture, language (although many were "bilingual"), and livelihood, an identity that Chinese domination threatened to eradicate. We may call this ethnicity. Not all Tanguts clung to their ethnicity; over the centuries many willingly or perforce gave it up in exchange for "citizenship" in China or Tibet. Not surprisingly, this occurred on a large scale after the Mongolian conquest of the Xia state in 1227. That the Tanguts did not survive as an entity capable of reconstituting a polity at a more propitious time resulted from historical and geographic circumstances more than any supposed weakness of ethnic integrity. To the contrary, one must marvel at the tenacity that Tangut identity displayed in the face of overwhelming odds in the political and ecological environment of the eleventh and early twelfth centuries.

That such a profusion of materials written in the dense and cryptic Tangut script survives to this day testifies to a powerful determination and need. The Tanguts' own exposition of their mythic origins is foreshadowed in eleventh-century sources and emerges fully articulated in late twelfth-century courtly verses. Owing to the loss of all historical records kept by the Xia court, these twelfth-century compositions serve as our main sources for the Tanguts' charter myths. Although examination of this material lies outside the scope of the present work, we can see the Tangut text of the 1094 stele inscription as introducing stylistic elements and thematic concerns that the later compositions elaborate in greater detail.

Other critical factors shaping Tangut state formation were socioeconomic and military. The flourishing (via the horse trade with north China) and expansion of the Ordos population in the ninth and tenth centuries meant the growth of tribal armies, which Tangut rulers needed to mobilize or restrain in order to achieve such goals as control over access to and profits of trade. Tribal/military chiefs jockeyed to maintain or enhance their power vis-à-vis the Tangut leadership (the Tuoba/Li/Weiming clan). Early Tangut leaders and even the later emperors were never really more than primus inter pares, like early Japanese emperors. Unlike early Japanese emperors, however, eleventh-century Tangut leaders were also, by necessity, warriors. This was one fundamental distinction between the Chinese imperial institution in its Song manifestation and the Tangut, Khitan, Jurchen (to a lesser extent), and Yuan monarchies.

Tangut tribal and social structure is not as well documented as the Jurchen or Khitan, but it is important to note that most Tangut tribals were not nomads, like the Khitans, but pastoralists. That Tanguts had a peculiar social structure quite distinct from the Chinese becomes obvious with even a cursory reading of the Song dynastic history's chapters on Xia. Yet Chinese and Western scholars have not confronted the implications of these differences and in fact have "read" Tangut social history and vocabulary through "Chinese" translations, assuming an equivalent content or weight for terms signifying similar categories of things. For the Chinese (and for all of us), then as now, it was easy and comforting to translate strange things into familiar shapes. Unfortunately, those familiar shapes often do not correspond to Tangut realities.

In spite of a certain quantity of circumstantial evidence in Song and Xia sources, Tangut social structure, especially in a comparative context, remains unstudied.[31] My own analysis could benefit from critical work in that area, but the focus of this work lies elsewhere. One area of acute relevance is marriage politics and the structure of the Tangut tribal and imperial marriage systems. Until we understand how these worked we cannot really comprehend the political roles of Tangut empresses and their brothers, who dominate eleventh-century narratives.

For example, one reason why the Fujiwara clan could dominate the Heian court from the late ninth to eleventh centuries was that child rearing remained the primary responsibility of the mother's relatives. Hence, the offspring of Fujiwara empresses were raised by the Fujiwara, not the imperial clan, and were therefore more easily controlled by them, persuaded to retire young, married to a Fujiwara, and so forth.[32] There are some indications that in eleventh-century Xia maternal relatives also played a vital role in child rearing, as the origins of the second emperor, Weiming Liangzuo (Yizong, see Chapter 3), suggest. Did the participation of paternal relatives in a child's upbringing expand in Xia, as it did in late Heian Japan, accounting in part for the decline of Fujiwara power?[33] If so, for what reasons, apart from the obvious example of Chinese custom?

The prominence of female regents in eleventh-century Xia was by no means an isolated phenomenon. Song empresses too asserted significant political influence as regents throughout the eleventh century and into the twelfth. Liao empresses, like their Tangut counterparts, also exercised active military leadership. In fact, in eleventh-century Song, as in Xia, "three emperors began their reigns under the regencies of empress dowagers," while altogether the northern Song court set up five regencies.[34] The operational dynamics of succession under the Song and the role of empresses (mothers and wives) need to be kept in mind for two reasons: (1) to avoid anachronistic assessments of Tangut dynastic politics as somehow messier or more aberrant than Song politics, and (2) to understand better Song Chinese attitudes toward the dowager-regents of Xia.

Succession based on primogeniture, although an established principle in China, in contrast to Inner Asia, did not operate automatically or smoothly in the Song. The consequences of Song experience have important implications for this study. Song Taizu, the founding emperor, was succeeded by his brother (Taizong), who set aside Taizu's son and himself took the throne.³⁵ Zhenzong's mental state also invited suspicion, and by the end of his reign (997–1022) his growing incapacity had made his empress Liu the effective ruler. Zhenzong's sixth and only surviving son succeeded to the throne at age twelve, under the regency of his foster mother, the empress dowager Liu. She ruled until her death in 1033, and even left a will specifying that her friend, Lady Yang, should succeed as regent. Song statesmen, led by Fan Zhongyan, successfully opposed the perpetuation of the regency.³⁶

Yingzong (1063–1067), the adopted son of Renzong (1022–1063), shared rule with his adopted mother, Renzong's principal wife. Shenzong's (r. 1068–1085) mother, empress dowager Gao, opposed his policies, and when he died, leaving a nine-year-old heir, she promptly reversed them.

Supreme empress dowager Gao ruled actively as regent for Zhezong from 1085 until her death in 1093, resisting calls for her retirement in 1092. She came from a family with a long record of military service to the Song court. Anti–Wang Anshi statesmen and eunuchs alienated by Wang's hostility to them served her willingly. Although Chinese historians have praised the empress dowager's rule as enlightened (she restricted her relatives' access to power and reversed the reform policies), Zhezong idolized his father, resented the conservatives, and disliked his grandmother's choice of consort for him. After her death he restored the reform policies and reactivated the aggressive northwest frontier campaign against Xia.

Song statesmen and elites, thus, had firsthand and continuous experience with empressorial regencies. They did not have to reach back into history for cautionary tales. Therefore, when they responded to, commented on, and made policy in regard to the Tangut regencies, they proceeded from a specific and immediate set of assumptions about how regents and empresses operated or should operate. The Tangut regencies, however, clearly operated in a different manner, on different sets of assumptions, and in different sociopolitical and kinship structures. We do not know very much about those structures and dynamics, but Jennifer Holmgren's studies of marriage and succession in the non-Han regimes throughout Chinese history have demonstrated that we cannot assume that they were the same as the Chinese.³⁷

Ironically, female regents, even powerful ones, were tolerated in Chinese history precisely because it was generally understood, after the Tang experience, that they could not themselves become emperor. No male could be trusted with the regent's job, the Duke of Zhou notwithstanding. Heian Japan poses the interesting exception, where Fujiwara clan chiefs dominated the regency, marrying Fujiwara girls to juvenile emperors. Chinese insistence on primogeniture, moreover, legitimated a prolonged regency while a young son grew to maturity.[38] Ambitious and skillfull Tangut clans could readily appreciate the usefulness of this Chinese practice. Yet the political role of imperial agnates (Weiming princes) was only partially attenuated during the eleventh-century regencies and reemerged stronger than ever by the last decade of the century. If there was a tendency in Xia for maternal uncles—the empresses' brothers—to strive for the position of regent, the empresses' counterclaims to this position presumably would have been supported by the imperial clan as less threatening to its monopoly on the throne.

Other questions arise in this connection: Did the centralization of power provide more opportunities for certain women to exercise power even as it sought to constrain them? To what degree was power actually centralized? And how did property and inheritance rights and practices, intimately linked with marriage and child-rearing customs, change over time? These questions and others concerning the basic economic and fiscal structures of the state indicate avenues of inquiry that will shed light on the nature of Tangut state formation.

From a world-system perspective, the Tanguts helped to set the stage for the Mongolian explosion into the world's primary centers of production and accumulation. As they first resisted and were then absorbed into the Mongolian empire, the Tanguts and their Tibetan partners also brought with them a rich cultural resource, Tibetan Buddhism.

Buddhism and Monarchy in Chinese History

We have become comfortable with the notion that non-Han dynasties, particularly in the later imperial period (the eleventh century onward), found Buddhism an attractive religion to patronize for largely cultural reasons, the principal one being that Buddhism had no ingrained prejudices against barbarians, as Confucianism supposedly did.[39] Although this argument has some truth to it, the reasons why emperors of non-Chinese or Chinese dynasties turned to Buddhism are quite complex. And, early on, Buddhism became intimately associated with the Chinese model of sovereignty inherited and refined by all dynastic founders and their descendants.

Scholars have acknowledged that Buddhism could be useful in governing states or empires with a significant population of believers, and Arthur Wright even asserted that Sui and Tang emperors "relied heavily on an alien religion to augment the credenda and miranda of their power."[40] According to Howard J. Wechsler's analysis in his *Offerings of Jade and Silk: Ritual and Legitimation in the T'ang Dynasty*, Buddhism played a minor supporting role in Tang legitimation.[41] Nevertheless, Buddhism defined an important arena of public imperial activity during the Tang, because, as Stanley Weinstein remarked, even the most unenthusiastic Tang monarch "could not but be aware of the political advantages that accrued from using Buddhist monasteries to strengthen the tie between the Buddhist populace and the imperial family."[42] Weinstein argues, moreover, that Tang Xuanzong (r. 712–756) became the first imperial promoter of Esoteric Buddhism precisely because of his interest in Daoism and its magical repertoire.[43] I will return to the question of Esoteric Buddhism and Tang imperial patronage below.

Several publications of the 1970s have examined earlier and later imperial approaches to Buddhism, advancing the analysis along political and historical rather than cultural lines. Antonino Forte's *Political Propaganda and Ideology in China at the End of the Seventh Century* (1976) shows how Empress Wu (late seventh century) cultivated Buddhist sources of legitimation for her rule, resulting in "a striking conflation of Indian and Chinese notions of sovereignty. ... It was in her splendid Ming-t'ang, designed by court ritualists, that Wu Chao carried out the Pañcavarṣika ceremonies that confirmed her in the role of a Buddhist Cakravartin."[44] It was a unique event, as far as we know, and its implications have apparently been deemed of limited significance owing to the subsequent repudiation of Wu Zhao's reign in Confucian historiography.

In a 1978 article, "Emperor as Bodhisattva in the Governance of the Ch'ing Empire," David M. Farquhar explores the Qing emperors' manipulation or management of their Buddhist personae, their identification with the bodhisattva Mañjuśrī, patronage of Mañjuśrī's cult sites at Mount Wutai, and other practices with roots in earlier dynasties.[45] Farquhar's concluding suggestion that the political component of the Qing monarch's various public images was of paramount importance does not simply repeat the cliché that rulers cynically manipulated religion for political purposes. Rather, evolving Buddhist theories and practices of sovereignty and universal community are a political phenomenon inseparable from both local religious developments and the evolving emperorship, unquestionably the supreme religious (and political) institution of China. Farquhar, unacquainted with Forte's study, turned from Sui Wendi to Qubilai, passing over Wu Zhao in silence. Probing the testimony of the intervening centuries is critical to understanding the relationship between Buddhism and the imperial institution.[46]

The early Buddhist conception of rulership in the figure of the *cakravartin* (the "wheel-turning" monarch) was a problematic and unstable model, because of the *cakravartin*'s theoretical subordination to the Buddha and dharma, symbolized by his wheel. A *cakravartin* could lose his wheel in roughly the same way that a Chinese emperor could lose the mandate of Heaven.[47] And he was even less able than his Chinese counterpart to command the unquestioned allegiance of adherents of the Way (dharma). Different solutions to these difficulties emerged.

In the late fourth century, the imperial cleric Faguo went so far as to identify the Northern Wei ruler as the Tathāgata ("Thus-Come-One," i.e., the Buddha). Efforts to break down the duality or separateness of the monastic community and secular society, however, particularly as expressed in popular prophecies and sectarian movements, never appealed greatly to the Chinese Buddhist establishment. After the Northern Wei, emperors apparently did not again attempt to project themselves, at least not publicly, as the Buddha or the Tathāgata.

Northern Wei rulers also seem to have absorbed from Liangzhou, which they conquered in the late fourth century, the cult of the bodhisattva Maitreya, the future Buddha, and emperor-worship, whereby "the emperor of the Northern Wei, as a living Maitreya, became the object of all the hopes and expectations of a future salvation, then, after death, was placed in the role of a Buddha protecting the state and the nation."[48] Sixth-century monarchs Liang Wudi (r. 502–549, in south China) and Sui Wendi (r. 581–605, who unified north and south China) allowed or encouraged identification of self with both the *cakravartin*, Aśoka in Wudi's case, and the bodhisattva, symbolizing in Wendi's case his claims to preeminence in both sacred and secular realms.[49] Wu Zhao, in the late seventh century, strengthened her *cakravartin* credentials by identifying with the potent bodhisattva Maitreya, the future Buddha. Yet, as Forte notes, a bodhisattva was above all a compassionate being, and this requirement too could be used to constrain an ambitious ruler.⁵⁰ Hence there was no necessary connection between Buddhism and authoritarianism per se, as Wright might have it.⁵¹ Yet the bodhisattva-*cakravartin* partnership remained a powerful image or emblem of sovereignty.

After Wu Zhao's successful Buddhist legitimation, and very likely because of it, apparently no subsequent native Chinese emperor "experimented" so aggressively with Buddhist identities. Evidence exists, however, that later emperors did not shun attempts to foster or suggest identification with the Buddha. Tang Xuanzong decreed that all Daoist temples and Buddhist monasteries, later including the state-supported network of Kaiyuan monasteries, celebrate the imperial birthday. Further, "to emphasize the relationship between the K'ai-yüan monasteries and the imperial person, the former were ordered in 744 to install images of the Buddha in the likeness of the emperor."⁵²

Ming founder Zhu Yuanzhang may have flirted with Maitreyan symbolism in naming his dynasty, but by the fourteenth century the antiestablishment messianic associations of Maitreya limited its imperial usefulness.⁵³

From the eleventh century onward in Tibet and the non-Han dynasties, Buddhists developed and propagated theories of incarnation and sovereignty that had a distinct impact on the Chinese monarchical institution. Tibetan Buddhism, which exerted considerable influence in ruling circles both Chinese and non-Chinese throughout the later imperial period, offered enhanced opportunities to rulers for bodhisattvahood through incarnation and, occasionally, reincarnation. The specific bodhisattva who became associated with the throne of China was Mañjuśrī, in part following the Tang dynastic house's patronage of the Mañjuśrī cult sites at Mount Wutai in the mid–eighth century.⁵⁴ According to Raoul Birnbaum,

> By the mid and late-T'ang, the cult of Mañjuśrī had a distinctly fourfold character. The Bodhisattva was perceived as a mountain deity, a national (and personal) protector, a prince of penetrating wisdom, and a cosmic lord. . . . Its [Mount Wutai's] location less than one hundred miles from the ancestral homeland of the T'ang imperial family is a factor of some significance in considering the rise and establishment of the Mañjuśrī cult centered at Wu-t'ai shan during the T'ang.⁵⁵

It may be no coincidence that the Mañjuśrī cult acquired intensified royal patronage, especially through the activities of the Tantric master Amoghavajra (705–774), after the restoration of the Tang house following Wu Zhao's reign and more immediately the An Lushan rebellion. Noting the rising popularity of Mañjuśrī in the wake of the An Lushan rebellion, Birnbaum also speculates that Amoghavajra interpreted the manifestation of Mañjuśrī at Wutai shan as "a sign that the temporal ruler of this vast land could become a *cakravartin,* a great 'wheel-turning' king who would assist in promulgating and propagating the Buddhist Dharma throughout the realm.... It appears that Amoghavajra sought to transform his rulers, especially Tai-tsung, into *cakravartin*s."[56] In this spirit Amoghavajra referred to Daizong (r. 762–779) as "the earthly representative of the Buddha."[57] Tang rulers seem not to have benefited substantially from these efforts, but later monarchs, up through the Qing and including the Tangut rulers, all patronized the cult sites at Wutai shan.

Farquhar identifies three strands converging in the late Yuan (fourteenth century): the Tibetan theory of bodhisattva reincarnation, the Chinese cult to Mañjuśrī at Wutai shan, and the ancient Chinese notion of the king as "destined by Heaven."[58] With these developments, Tang Taizong, Chinggis Qan, and Qubilai Qan were constituted as a lineage of reincarnated *cakravartin* emperors. After Qubilai's reign, Pamela K. Crossley argues, "emperors in China thereafter were 'wheel-turning,' that is, *cakravartin* (*zhuanlun*) kings," and occasionally also bodhisattvas.[59] Mongols, however, were conservative in attributing bodhisattvahood to their past rulers, and Manchus were conservative in asserting the bodhisattvahood bestowed on them by the Fifth Dalai Lama.[60] But the *cakravartin* model was more readily assimilable into the evolving Chinese imperial institution.[61]

A critical aspect of this matter is the dynamic interplay between a ruler's perceptions and projections of his imperial persona and the efforts of other people, potential or actual subjects or even later historians, to influence those perceptions or mold that persona in order to promote their own interests. This dimension of state formation is an ongoing process, not something achieved once and for all at the beginning of a dynasty. Carrying out rituals of legitimation gives expression to or "enacts" the state, which is identified with the imperial institution. So does raising troops and engaging in war. In popular stereotype, renunciant Buddhists prefer to live by themselves in remote retreats, but in real life their membership in and social interaction with larger communities and the state indelibly shaped everyone involved.

As a pan-Asian religion with well-developed apotropaic functions, Mahāyāna Buddhism was historically and politically a natural choice for patronage by the Xia state at this time and place. Although the Tanguts had surely come into contact with Buddhism before the eleventh century, it is not clear to what degree they or their elites had become committed to the religion before their expansion westward out of the Ordos from the late tenth century on. The geography of Xia gave it direct access to the early Buddhist traditions of Central Asia, Tibet, and north China. Embedded in the very sand, rock, and lore of the Gansu localities that the Tanguts conquered and absorbed in the eleventh century, these traditions conferred important advantages and sources of strength upon the state. By the same token, the founding of Xia may have revitalized local Buddhists, who since the Tang collapse had had to rely principally on Khotan for royal patronage. As the Central Asian oasis kingdoms came under increasing Muslim pressure from the late tenth century onward, the Tangut expansion filled a regional religious vacuum and soon would embrace the Tibetan Buddhist renaissance.[62]

Herbert Franke has argued that Buddhism was attractive to non-Han rulers of China and its border areas not merely because it was non-Chinese in origin, but rather because it offered an alternative conception of kingship and community that was more inclusive and universal. It "transcended the sinocentric and monocultural idea which had been the basis for Chinese speculations about the role of the emperor in All-under-Heaven."[63] Given the diversity of local practice and adaptations, we should not assume that Buddhism ipso facto became a monolithic, unifying force, overriding local allegiances. Surely, though, Tangut rulers promoted it in part as a common cultural "heritage" unifying the diverse elements in the social polity (as Sui Wendi had done). Another of its attractions, the important link between Buddhists and interregional trade, was likewise of paramount interest to Tangut rulers, as it was to their Mongol successors.[64]

All this does not deny that Tangut rulers also patronized the Confucian tradition and its carriers. There can be no doubt that Buddho-Confucian elites, if we may use this term, had more in common with each other than either had with the unlettered masses, while the practices and beliefs of the latter were as "mixed" and indifferent to scholars' categories as they were anywhere in the world. Let me put it this way: There were very few, if any, subjects of Xia educated in the Confucian classics who were not also devout practicing Buddhists. How would they have described themselves?

There is a tendency among many modern scholars, notably E. I. Kychanov, Shi Jinbo to a lesser extent, and most other Chinese, to characterize the mature twelfth-century Tangut state (i.e., government) as basically "Confucian" in spirit and practice, primarily on the basis of the "Confucian"-inspired reforms, including imperial promotion of the cult to Confucius, carried out under the reign of Renzong (1139–1193) and recorded in the Song dynastic history.[65] According to Chinese sources, the Tanguts also introduced an examination system, and one imperial prince later took the throne to become the first (and only) East Asian emperor with a *jinshi* ("presented scholar") degree.[66] Scholars rarely define what they mean by a "Confucian" state, and the assumption is that a cult to Confucius and Chinese-style bureaucratic structures suffice to constitute a "Confucian" state. But do they? Was Heian Japan a "Confucian" state? Even if these attributes suffice, in some eyes, to label a state "Confucian," that labeling does not necessarily reveal what is most important or interesting about the state.

Significantly, the Tiansheng law code issued early in the reign of Renzong makes no mention of an examination system and spells out in considerable detail procedures for recruitment to government office through inheritance and family background. It seems unlikely that the examination system later adopted played any substantial role in official recruitment, although it may have improved the quality of some candidates' preparation. Thus it probably functioned more like the Yuan examination system, which was a late and short-lived departure from dynastic procedure, used "to advance the careers of Mongols and Western and Central Asians to the detriment of the advancement of Chinese, Jurchens, and Khitans."[67]

We know nothing about the Tangut examination system; it has left no traces in the extant native record.[68] Moreover, the extensive Buddhist activities of the throne and the elite, to which we owe the vast majority of extant Xia materials, find no echo in Song or Jin Chinese sources for twelfth- and thirteenth-century Xia history. In spite of this, Kychanov has argued that the Tanguts had to choose between Confucianism and Buddhism as the ideological basis of their state, and ultimately chose Confucianism:

> Having created their state and founded a national dynasty, the Tanguts soon confronted the dilemma of selecting an ideological direction for the development of that state, acknowledging themselves between Tibet and China. . . . Who would they follow? The Tibet-

ans, who had already made Buddhism the ideological basis of their society and governing regime, or the Chinese, for whom Confucianism was the ideological foundation of society and state?[69]

Kychanov's exposition of the issue ("if 'a' then not 'b' ") seems overly deterministic and somewhat anachronistic. Tangut rulers, generals, clerics, and statesmen probably did not frame the pressing issues of their day in such a fashion. Song Chinese thinking and realities were not so simple: Buddhism was even more socially and economically entrenched in Song than in Tang China.[70] And the situation in eleventh- to twelfth-century Tibet was hardly so well defined as Kychanov paints it.

Equally problematic is the widely drawn distinction between religious and political "ideologies," in which the former is made subordinate to the latter. Kychanov asserts that the Tanguts eventually put Confucianism in the latter position and Buddhism in the former, in service to the dynasty's spiritual needs only.[71] He, among others, supposes that because the state controlled Buddhist ordinations and monasteries, it could therefore not be a true Buddhist state, and hence was instead Confucian. We need a far more flexible understanding of ideology and politics, in which religion and ritual are not set apart from them but viewed as their very substance; in which ideology is not a holistic worldview, nor "a coherent set of ideas, statements, or attitudes imposed on people who dutifully internalize them," but rather "a strategy of power, a process whereby certain social practices or institutions are depicted to be 'natural' and 'right.' "[72] As I have observed elsewhere, the matter was far more complex than simply choosing between Confucianism or Buddhism, and that for a solution we must look into the muddled middle reaches between "a" and "b."[73]

It may be helpful to pose the issue in terms of the specific activities or appeals through which a state or social group legitimated itself. A Confucian state, beginning with the Tang, strove for inclusivity, the emperor acting for all his subjects, not just his family, in ritual intercession with Heaven and Earth. It developed the notion of a particular reciprocal relationship between the ruler and people, on the one hand, and between the ruler and Heaven, on the other, summed up in the phrase "mandate of Heaven" *(tianming)*. Further, for the Chinese state the legitimating importance of political ancestry, not biological (or genealogical, as in Japan), was articulated in the extended notion of *zhengtong*, or the orthodox (correct) line of political succession that linked together all regimes from the past to the present. Finally, ideally the emperor was a unique figure, the "One Man," who from Tang times on mediated between one Heaven and his earthly empire.⁷⁴ Just as there was one sun and one Heaven, so too there was only one emperor, one Son of Heaven. This requirement was perforce reinterpreted in the eleventh and twelfth centuries in such a way that each state in East Asia became its own "all under Heaven."⁷⁵

The Tanguts adapted some, or parts of, these legitimating strategies, giving them a greater or lesser twist to suit their own needs and combining them with other Inner Asian and Buddhist notions and rituals to develop a distinctive ideology, or practice, of legitimation. Tangut ideology, moreover, evolved continuously over the life of the dynasty in tandem with the power struggles among the elite. So far there is no evidence that the Xia court engaged in the kind of discussions on legitimate succession that began at the Jin court in 1194 under Zhangzong and continued in 1214 under Xuanzong, although the Mongol crisis provoked other kinds of political contention.⁷⁶ Not unrelated to the Jin concern with legitimation as a Chinese dynasty, in 1191 the Jin court forbade the use of the word *fan* to refer to the Jurchen people or language,⁷⁷ in stark contrast to the honored place that Fan occupied in Xia as the Chinese equivalent of Tangut!

Because Xia did not occupy any core areas of the Chinese heartland and because the Tangut elite was not a tiny minority in a sea of Han Chinese, the Chinese terms of legitimation were less relevant to them and could be freely recombined without concern for the *zhengtong* (the line of legitimate succession of all Chinese emperors, as embodied, for example, in the Taiwan-published reference book for converting Chinese dates, *A Sino-Western Calendar for Two Thousand Years 1–2000 A.D.*). Nevertheless, the most successful foreign rulers of China, even when they did position themselves within the Confucian line of legitimate succession, also reached beyond it to a larger, Buddhist-inspired conception of the world and China's place in it.

In the next chapter I examine the relationship between the early Xia state and Buddhism, and the Tangut legitimating formulations framed during the emergence of the imperial institution as a formal entity in the 1030s under the celebrated warrior and first emperor, Weiming (Li) Yuanhao. I also sketch in a general way the larger context, noting the Sino-Indian Buddhist contacts that flourished at the early Song court and Liao imperial interest in Buddhism. This subject, however, requires a much fuller treatment than I can give it here.

CHAPTER 2

Buddhism and Monarchy in the Early Tangut State

TANGUT IMPERIAL HISTORY formally begins with the reign of Li (Weiming) Yuanhao (Jingzong, r. 1032–1048), the third ruler of the autonomous Ordos state founded in 981 by his grandfather Li Jiqian. In the winter of 1038 the Tangut ruler was enthroned as the first emperor of the Great State of White and High (Bai Gao Da Guo), or Great Xia (Da Xia, its Chinese name), and sent a letter to the Song court demanding due recognition as the sovereign of an independent neighboring state. The Song ruler could not countenance this challenge to the established order, in part owing to compromises already made to accommodate the Khitan Liao, whom the Tanguts regarded at once as protector, rival, and model. Thirty years of peaceful trade between Song China and its Ordos vassal gave way to an era of intermittent, escalating hostilities along the northwestern frontier, punctuated by brief lulls, until the Jurchen conquest of north China separated the two states.

For the Tanguts, prolonged military and political crises strained the structures of centralized government erected by Yuanhao (Jingzong),[1] intensified factional struggles for power and control of the throne, sapped the economic resources of the state, and menaced its very survival. For nearly forty years (1061–1099), one clan, the Liang, dominated the court in the Fujiwara style, acting as regents and marrying daughter or niece to an underaged emperor. During these same decades, however, when Song sources on Xia are filled with nothing but warfare and intrigue, the entire Buddhist canon was translated into Tangut.

Most if not all Tangut rulers were devout Buddhists who sought to harness religious faith in support of the throne; yet there is little evidence that the Tangut state ever achieved the degree of centralization, nor its monarch the degree of absolute power, enjoyed by the contemporary Song states and their rulers. Hence the notion, affirmed by Shi Jinbo, that the promotion of the Buddha Śākyamuni led to a demotion of native Tangut deities in the same way that the rise of the Tangut imperial institution led to the subordination of tribal leaders to the throne may reflect the hopes of the Tangut emperor but probably oversimplifies the real state of affairs.²

The spread of Buddhism among the populace in earlier centuries did not replace or appreciably weaken native religious beliefs. Deity cults, spirit worship, fertility rites, and shamanistic practices persisted and are attested in Tangut sources like the dictionary *Wenhai*.³ Such beliefs permeated all levels of society, and a number of non-Buddhist rituals became enshrined in Xia court ceremonials. One was the annual animal sacrifice to Heaven conducted by shamans in the old imperial palace on the third day of the fourth month, described in the twelfth-century law code.⁴

In Tibet, China, and Japan, competition and accommodation between pre-Buddhist (Bon, Daoist, Shinto) religious technicians and newly introduced Buddhists enjoying royal patronage played a prominent part in the history of state formation. A similar process may have occurred in Xia, especially before the eleventh century, though the meager sources make it virtually impossible to reconstruct. The Tanguts' long exposure to Buddhism before the rise of the Xia state probably minimized the conflict occasioned by the emergence of a state-sponsored Saṅgha in the eleventh century.

From the founding of the state to the end of the eleventh century, through the era of the regency, a Buddhist establishment grew under imperial patronage and became a significant feature of the political and cultural landscape. The Weiming restoration of 1099, when the death of the second Empress Dowager Liang ended the nearly forty-year dominance of her clan, marks a turning point in the fortunes of both the throne and the Buddhist establishment, which seemed to go into temporary eclipse. In the few sources available to us, the level of recorded Buddhist activity drops and does not resume until the reign of the great twelfth-century monarch Weiming Renxiao (Renzong, r. 1139–1193). This gap in the record may reflect an actual decline in Buddhist influence and imperial patronage, or simply incomplete data, or both. The overall paucity of sources for the early twelfth century and specifically the Jurchen conquest period may account for the impression of a Buddhist retreat. Yet we cannot discount a court reaction against the Saṅgha long under the empress dowager's control.

In this period a number of salient domestic developments converge around issues of gender, religion, war, and legitimation: the Liang empresses' struggle to legitimate and secure their authority; the Weiming emperors' attempts to assert and sustain theirs; the Buddhists' efforts to promote their own agenda; and the military aristocracy's determination to preserve its privileges. How was survival of the state accommodated to these often sharply conflicting interests? In the 1090s, at the peak of Northern Song military offense against Xia and Kokonor, it is clear that several compromises were worked out to prevent the collapse of the state and central authority.

Before turning to these questions, it will be useful to sketch the larger Buddhist world of the tenth and eleventh centuries.

Inner Asian Buddhism in the Late Tenth and Early Eleventh Centuries

Early Song emperors adopted a liberal Buddhist policy, sent Chinese monks and pilgrims to India, patronized visiting Indian monks, supported new translation activities, and sponsored the printing and dissemination of the Buddhist canon throughout East Asia.[5] From the 960s up to 1036, through the early part of Song emperor Renzong's reign (1023–1064), Song sources record a steady stream of cultural exchanges with India.[6] Indian monks and scholars in the eleventh and twelfth centuries fled Muslim invaders to seek refuge in Central Asia and China. For many of them the route of travel passed through the Gansu Corridor and what were to become Tangut territories; beyond Dunhuang the Buddhist kingdom of Khotan at this time was facing Kharakhanid conquest.

According to a later account, some of these Indian monks settled in Xia for varying lengths of time and traveled from there to the Song capital at Kaifeng, or in one case to Sichuan. Yu Qian's *Xin xu gaoseng zhuan siji* records the biographies of several such "Xi Xia" monks,[7] who, like the other Indian monks in Kaifeng, composed and translated principally Esoteric Buddhist works, many of which then entered the Song canon, some with imperial prefaces. Jan Yün-hua states that Chinese monks at the Song court remained indifferent to these new translations and uninterested in Esoteric Buddhism.[8] This was not true of the Tanguts and other East Asians. A closer look at the activities of these monks suggests ways in which Xia Buddhists, with their significant Esoteric Buddhist inclinations, engaged in and become enriched from exchanges with Song and Central Asian Buddhists, and also how Tangut rulers may have responded to and competed with the example set by the Song emperors (the Liao case is considered below).

One prominent Indian monk, Fatian,[9] made his way first to Fuzhou in Shaanxi, just south of Yan'anfu and the Ordos prefectures of the Tanguts, and began translating texts that he brought with him or composed there with Fajin, a Shaanxi monk studying Sanskrit.[10] The local administrator informed the court, and Song Taizu summoned Fatian to Kaifeng and awarded him the purple robe.[11] Until his death in 1001 he worked under three emperors to translate over forty works in the Bureau for Canonical Translations (Yijing yuan), established by Song Taizong at the Taiping Xingguo Temple,[12] and received several honorary titles. One of Fatian's many works appears to be the ninth title in a Xia list of eleven Buddhist texts forming the examination curriculum for Tangut and Tibetan candidates for ordination, but it does not appear in the curriculum for Chinese ordination candidates.[13]

In approximately 980 the Kashmiri monk Tianxizai (d. 1001), given the name Faxian in 987, and the Indian monk Shihu joined Fatian at the Bureau for Canonical Translation, renamed the Dharma Transmission Bureau (Chuanfa yuan) in 983–984.[14] Fatian, Faxian, and Shihu among themselves accounted for over one hundred new titles entering the Chinese Tripiṭaka. In Xianping 1 or 2 (998–999), Song Zhenzong wrote a preface to one of Faxian's new translations.[15]

Another monk, Fahu, reached Kaifeng from northern India in 1004 and took up residence in the Dharma Transmission Bureau, working along with several Chinese students of Sanskrit. He lived to the age of ninety-six, passing away in 1058.[16] Early in the Qingli period (1041–1049), during the unsuccessful war with Xia, civil officials again proposed to abolish the Dharma Transmission Bureau (also referred to by its old name, Bureau for Canonical Translation). Song Renzong demurred, citing his ancestors' precedent and the valuable knowledge of foreign languages the monks possessed, compared to officials in its parent agency, the Honglu si or Court of State Ceremonial, which oversaw the reception of foreign visitors.[17]

In fact, it appears that strategic concerns in part motivated the Song emperors' patronage of Indian monks and commitment to retaining the Dharma Transmission Bureau long after some of its inmates, now virtual hostages, felt they had any useful work left to do.[18] Renzong was not about to allow Indian monks to travel back home through Central Asia during the Song war with Xia in the

1040s. Moreover, Buddhist exchanges had become an instrument of diplomacy and spying as well as an important element in international protocol and the discourse of imperial legitimacy for all parties to the East Asian order. A ruler did not spurn the gifts of monks, regardless of how tiresome his officers found these occasions. And even if most Chinese intellectuals, Buddhist and Confucian, had no use for "Tantric" texts, can we pronounce so confidently on the religious tastes of the imperial family, Daoists, and others? Finally, as we shall see, the Song edition of the Buddhist canon became a highly prized export. Its production and dissemination, moreover, was strictly controlled, as Richard Bowring has argued, and the Song emperors' fascination with the Tantric texts being translated by Indian monks in Kaifeng remained a private affair.[19]

Religious interest and concern with legitimizing their rule also prompted early Song emperors' patronage of Indian monks and translation activities. Huang Chi-chiang demonstrates that Song emperors invested great energy in expounding as well as collecting and printing the dharma, and in supervising the saṅgha, even to the point of personally testing a monk's knowledge of sūtras. The "Buddhist mission" of the first four Song emperors "enabled them to create for themselves the image of a universal king so useful to their rulership."[20] Bernard Faure has observed that relic worship was "a powerful instrument of monastic and imperial legitimacy."[21] Indian monks traveling to the Northern Song court frequently presented Buddha relics to the throne.[22] Like the translation of Indian Esoteric texts, such gifts, even if dispassionately received, carried weight with Song emperors, for they were part of what Russell Kirkland has called Song Taizong's "holistic vision" of the world and his desire to reconstitute and give expression to the unity of culture and human affairs.[23] Xia and Liao rulers welcomed Buddha relics for perhaps slightly different reasons, although the political implications for each remained equally vital.

According to Yu Qian, another group of monks associated with the cleric Fa Jixiang were probably Indian or Central Asian in origin but came to be known as "Xi Xia monks": "Some say that Dharma Jixiang was an Indian who traveled to Xi Xia and settled there a while before first coming to the central land (*zhongtu*, China). Therefore people called him a Xi Xia monk."[24] Jixiang and five companions presented Sanskrit texts to the Song court in Tiansheng 5 (1027–1028) and were assigned to the Translation Office of the Dharma Transmission Bureau. Jinzongchi, also called a "Xi Xia" monk by Yu

Qian, traveled and settled together with Jixiang at Kaifeng, and translated the *Mañjuśrī-nāma-saṃgīti (Wenzhu pusa [suo shuo] zuisheng mingyi jing)*.[25] Significantly, this title appears second on a list of eleven texts forming the examination curriculum for Tangut and Tibetan candidates for ordination in twelfth-century Xia, but not on the otherwise similar list of eleven texts for Chinese candidates.[26] Evidently these texts were incorporated into a Song edition of the Tripiṭaka that the Tanguts received a few years later. Jinzongchi enjoyed an improbably long career, as he was reported still to be translating in 1113.[27]

Another "Xi Xia" monk, Richeng, apparently also traveled to China around the same time as Jixiang, or a few years later, in Qingli 6 (1046).[28] Richeng made contributions to the canon into the reign of Song Shenzong (r. 1068–1085).[29]

Most intriguing of Yu Qian's "Xi Xia" monks is an Indian monk called Budong, whose undated biography is translated below.[30]

Shi Budong's Sanskrit name is Akṣobhya *(a shan pie)*[31] Woziluo *(Skt. vajra)*, in Chinese Budong Jingang (Unshakable Vajra), called Budong for short. Originally an Indian, when he first left home he traveled widely around India, thoroughly mastered the revealed and Esoteric doctrines, and completely understood nature and its phenomenal expression. His reputation spread to neighboring lands. Then he came to Xi Xia and stayed at the Huguo Temple [in Wuwei]. He translated Esoteric teachings and disseminated widely the prajña Vajra teaching called Yoga. It has five parts *(bu)*: one is the Buddha *(fo)* part; the second is the Vajra *(jingang)* part; the third is the Ratnasambhava *(baosheng)* part; the fourth is the Lotus *(hualian)* part; the fifth is the Karma *(kamo)* part.[32] Budong only transmitted the Vajra part, so he was named Vajra Supreme Master *(jingang shangshi)*. This name was given to him at the time of his consecration. As for Akṣobhya, it means at the very beginning relying on the law of the Akṣobhya part[33] and practicing it. Budong diligently practiced the five repentances *(wuhui)* and broadly demonstrated the three maṇḍalas *(dan)*. He once took "The Text of the Penitential Offering to the Sūtra on the Thirty-five Buddhas' Names,"[34] translated by Tang Tripiṭaka Amoghavajra (705–774), and before it added fifty-three Buddhas' [names?], and after [it] inserted ten great vow-gāthās of Samantabhadra,[35] in all making 108 periods of worship *(baiqi)* to cut off the 108 defilements.[36] Later [Budong] moved to Mengshan, Sichuan, where he took the Yoga rite of bestowing food [on monks and ghosts] of Vajrabodhi[37] of the Tang and gave it the translated descriptive name of "flaming mouth." Further he preached the small rite of bestowing food, calling it the "Mengshan law." Because he sustained his life solely on the "ambrosial truth" *(ganlu)*, he was also given the title Master of the Sweet Dew Dharma. His disciple Lebu transmitted this teaching and it was again transmitted by Bao'an; yet a third transmission [was carried out] by Weide Zhuang. Now the transmissions are especially numerous.... It is not known when Budong died.

Thus we learn that Budong was a Tantric master of considerable renown and accomplishment in western China (Gansu, Sichuan). This biography provides no dates. It may be a conflation of several stories, for the *Song huiyao* mentions a Ganlu dashi (Sweet Dew Master) active at Mengshan in the 1180s.[38] The Huguo Temple was located at Wuwei, and this territory came under Tangut control in 1031. Undoubtedly one of Yu Qian's sources was the supplement to the seventeenth-century Jiaxing (Jingshan) canon, which includes a "flaming mouth" text, identified as translated by Amoghavajra, newly collated by Dharma Preceptor Budong Jingang of the Xi Xia Huguo Temple, and arranged by Shoudeng of the early Qing.[39]

The biography states that Budong's Sanskrit (or Brahman) name was "Ashanpie [Akṣobhya] Woziluo, in Chinese Budong Jingang [Unshakable Vajra]." New evidence recovered from a ruined temple in the Helan Mountains outside of Yinchuan confirms the existence of a Xia cleric by that name.[40] Sūtra fragments in Tangut preserve the names and titles of several high clerics involved in producing the texts. One is a state preceptor Unshakable Vajra Preceptor (Chin. *guo shi ... budong jingang shi*). Since this material very likely dates to the late twelfth century, as probably does the Budong of Yu Qian's sources, they may well be the same person, perhaps even the *Song huiyao*'s Sweet Dew Master of Mengshan.

Mengshan was situated in Yazhou, southwest of Chengdu and northwest of Emei shan, near Lushan and fifteen *li* west of Mingshan. According to one account: "Mengshan has five peaks. The highest is called Shangqing [Supreme Purity] Peak. At its crest is a rock as big as a pavilion chamber. There are seven tea plants growing on top of the rock, but no cracks [in the rock]. Tradition has it that it was Sweet Dew Great Master (Ganlu dashi) who planted [them]."[41]

Although not mentioned in the more common Buddhist sources, some recent works on Buddhist practice refer to Budong and his Xia connection.[42] Since we have proof of a historical Budong active in Tangut Buddhist court circles, probably in the late twelfth century, we may speculate on the existence of active Buddhist networks in the Sichuan-Gansu region, spanning political boundaries.[43]

Budong falls outside the timeframe of this book and will appear again in its sequel. In regard to tales of traveling monks, however, there is one story in circulation that should be retired. According to Wu Guangcheng's early-nineteenth-century chronicle, in 1036 Yuanhao detained at Xiazhou a group of Indian monks who were returning home from a visit to the Song court.[44] The Indian monks' visit to Kaifeng is recorded in *Song shi* and *Xu zizhi tongjian changbian,* but with no mention of their detention by the Tanguts on their way home.[45] A close examination of the Song history account shows that Wu conflated two passages, one describing the journey to Kaifeng in the 980s of an Indian and Persian pair and one several lines (or columns) later relating the 1036 embassy. Wu's version appears to be an embroidering and expansion of the later account with details from the former to explain why, in the author's eyes, after this time no more Indian monks traveled to Song China. Modern scholars often repeat this story in their publications, but its historicity must be doubted.[46]

India and Song China were not the only forces shaping the East Asian Buddhist landscape. Active Khitan Liao propagation of Buddhism from the tenth century on helped to spread the religion throughout the Khitans' Inner Asian domains.[47] Moreover, during Liao Xingzong's reign (1031–1055) the Khitans produced an edition of the Buddhist canon regarded as superior to the Northern Song (Kaibao or Sichuan) edition. Although the Koreans received a copy of the Liao canon circa 1063, no evidence exists of a Tangut request for it during those decades of the eleventh century when the Xia court repeatedly sought copies of the Song canon.[48] Of the few notices concerning Xia-Liao Buddhist relations, one dated to 1067 (Liao Xianyong 3/11) relates that Xia sent to Liao Uighur monks, golden Buddhas (statues), and a Sanskrit sūtra on enlightenment *(fan jue jing).*[49] Systematic research on the Tangut canon may yet show that the Tanguts had access to the Liao Tripiṭaka, for later Tangut sources state that twelfth-century redactions of Buddhist texts were made in consultation with "sūtras of south and north," which may be an allusion to the Khitan canon.[50]

Buddhism and the Emerging Xia State, 1007–1032

Upon Li Jiqian's death in 1004, his son Li Deming (d. 1032) assumed leadership of the expanding Tangut confederation. Li Deming's main interests were to protect the favorable trade relations he worked out with the Song court and to assuage Liao anxieties over Tangut military expansion into the Gansu Corridor, targeting Liangzhou and territories farther west. His son and heir, Yuanhao, took over command of Tangut armies in the 1020s and achieved a wide reputation for his warrior skills and inclination to overturn the status quo nurtured by his father.[51]

The earliest recorded Tangut Buddhist activities of this era date to 1007. In that year Li Deming's "mother," Lady Wang,[52] died, and he requested permission from Song authorities to make offerings at ten temples on Wutai shan in Shanxi. Permission was granted, and an officer was sent to escort the Tangut offerings.[53] Li Deming's act following the death of Lady Wang suggests that, if he was not a practicing Buddhist, she was, and that she had requested that he make offerings at Wutai shan on her behalf. Although Wutai shan had long been a renowned Buddhist pilgrimage site for Chinese and foreigners alike, Tangut interest in the place assumes added significance given the associations of this sacred mountain site with the cult to Mañjuśrī and that bodhisattva's state-protecting functions, both prominent features of the evolving Xia state Buddhist cult (see Chapter 4). Establishing a presence at or patronage of Wutai shan was therefore an important step in state building and in legitimating the emerging state in domestic as well as foreign eyes.

Some thirty-one years later, in the first month of 1038 (Song, Baoyuan 1; Xia, Tianqing 3), in preparation for his formal enthronement, Yuanhao submitted another request to send offerings to Wutai shan. The Song court blocked it on the grounds that the Tangut ruler really just wanted an opportunity to spy on Song defenses in Shanxi.[54] Genuine religious motivation may have prompted Yuanhao's desire to seek the protection and blessing of the guardian bodhisattva on Wutai shan, whatever other opportunities the pilgrimage offered.

Lacking ready access to the Shanxi cult center, the Tanguts in time created their own Wutai shan complex in the Helan Mountains to the west of their capital city, Zhongxing (present-day Yinchuan),[55] calling it "Northern Five-Terrace Mountain" or just Wutai Mountain Temple.[56] Moreover, the Qingliang si, one of the five main temples of the Shanxi Wutai shan, had its Tangut counterpart, as we learn from two native inscriptions attesting to the Helan Wutai shan. One, a Xia period graffito in Chinese from cave 444 at the Mogao cave complex outside of Dunhuang, reads: "Northern Wutai Mountain Great

Qingliang Temple monk śra[mana]...."⁵⁷ The other, a Xia *dhāraṇī* text in the Taishō Tripiṭaka with a preface dated to 1200, names one of its compilers as Northern Wutai Mountain Great Qingliang Temple *chujia tidian* ("superintendent of those who have left home [i.e., monks]"), the *śramana* Huizhen.⁵⁸

These indications span a period from the later eleventh century (the earliest Xia date found at Dunhuang is 1070) to the early thirteenth century and give us little clue as to when the Tanguts began construction of their local Wutai shan temple complex. They do, however, demonstrate devotion to the cult of Mañjuśrī, which enjoyed imperial sponsorship from the very beginning.

Conquest of Hexi and acquisition of the classical Buddhist lands—Ganzhou in 1028, Liangzhou in 1031–1032, Gua and Shazhou (Dunhuang) somewhat later⁵⁹—brought new religious obligations and opportunities to the Tangut rulers. It also intensified Tangut rivalries with the Kokonor Tibetan regime of the Amdo prince Gusiluo (*rgyal-sras*, "son of Buddha, prince"), which relocated to Qingtang (near present-day Xining) around 1032, the year that Yuanhao came to power. Refugees from Hexi flocked to Qingtang, as did merchants and agents from all over Asia, whose routes now skirted the Gansu Corridor. Yuanhao attacked the Song-supported Kokonor regime on both military and ideological fronts, the latter perhaps more successfully.⁶⁰

Buddhism and Imperial Ideology under Weiming Yuanhao

The first Tangut ruler to promote himself and his family publicly to imperial status manipulated a variety of ideas and symbols to legitimate his claim to emperorship. Although Buddhism is the focus of this book, all the significant components of the evolving ideology of Tangut kingship will be examined in the documents generated by Yuanhao (Jingzong, r. 1031–1048). Despite their diverse origins, prominent themes will emerge.

Yuanhao's education included the study of Chinese and Tibetan (Fan) literature, Buddhism, and law.⁶¹ This means that some members of the ruling strata (Tanguts, Chinese, and others) had private libraries stocked with many of the standard classical texts and Buddhist works in Chinese and Tibetan. It is also likely that Yuanhao's mother, Lady Weimu, was a practicing Buddhist and encouraged her son's education in this area as well as others. Yuanhao may have urged his father to request a copy of the Tripiṭaka from the Song court. In the twelfth month of Tiansheng 9 (1031–1032), the last year of his reign, Li Deming sent an envoy with seventy gift horses and a petition to request one set of canonical texts.[62] Yuanhao renewed the request (evidently yet unfulfilled) in the twelfth month of 1035 (Song, Jingyou 1; Xia, Guangyun 1),[63] and at that time received the promised volumes, which became the basis of the project he launched to translate into Tangut the entire Buddhist canon. The Tangut ruler did not thank the Song court for its gift until after negotiating the treaty that concluded the 1039–1044 war with Song. When in the summer of 1045 Tangut envoys traveled south to express gratitude for the Song decree investing the Weiming emperor as the lord (zhu) of Xia, the monk Jiwaiji Fazheng went along to express gratitude for the Buddhist sūtras,[64] evidently those presented in 1035, as there is no mention of another such bestowal at this time.

Promulgation of a native script was one in a series of major reforms carried out between 1032 and 1038, culminating in Yuanhao's elevation to the throne. He also enforced a national hairstyle; adopted independent reign names, an imperial title (wuzu), and revised ritual codes; changed the royal surname to Weiming (pronounced something like Ngweimi; in the Yuan it was transcribed Yumi) and his personal name to Nangxiao; and reorganized the army and government, bringing both under greater central control.[65] The new script, graphic like Chinese rather than alphabetic like Tibetan, came into use around 1036, and soon thereafter the translation of Buddhist sūtras began, using Kaibao editions of the canon.

Invention of a script was an act of state creation as well as a creation of the state. It was a politically charged event that asserted cultural claims, met strategic needs, and advanced dynastic legitimacy. Even the decision to adopt a graphic script, following the Chinese model, rather than the more linguistically suitable Tibetan alphabetic script was political.[66] China was the dominant power of East Asia, the principal source of statecraft strategies and symbols, the main military threat and economic benefactor. Later, in the twelfth century, probably circa 1162, an ode in praise of the inventor of the Tangut script, "the honored teacher" Yeli, was composed. It was copied on the reverse side of two pages in an extant collection of court odes printed in 1185.[67] After affirming a common source ("mother") but different development in the languages of Tibetans, Chinese, and Tanguts, the ode lauds Iri (Yeli), the "honored teacher" of the Tangut country, and his 3700 disciples who spread learning throughout the land, enabling the Tanguts and their long-lived imperial clan to prevail over the Tibetans and the Chinese, culturally and politically. Thus the ode acknowledges a link to China, yet also takes pride in the Tanguts' independent achievements. It is not clear who the disciples of Iri were, if they were Buddhists, or why there were 3700 of them.

The Tanguts created an enormously complex and dense graphic system, rather than a variation on the reduced stroke combinations of the Khitan and later Jurchen scripts. One reason was to make their writing distinctive. Another was to make it impenetrable to outsiders, a veritable secret code. Thus it was unlikely that any Song Chinese or Liao Khitans, except those living in Xia, could easily break the code and read Tangut documents. (The Khitan script itself was and still is a puzzle to scholars, largely because so little of it remains.) The apotropaic aspects of the script-as-amulet testify to a major preoccupation of the Tanguts: protection against enemies of both the physical and the spirit realms.

Shi Jinbo is right to affirm significant religious motives, in addition to more secular ones, behind the invention of the Tangut script around this time.[68] In fact, the distinction between the secular and sacred functions of writing disappears here: Translating the Buddhist canon consecrated the new state, announced its patronage of and protection by the Law (Dharma), enhanced its authority in the eyes of the Buddhist population within and without its borders, and served as a vehicle for importing up-to-date technologies. The Buddhist project, therefore, met a wide range of needs and offered something to nearly everyone.

In addition to an interest in the cults associated with Wutai shan in Shanxi, further evidence for Tangut devotion to relics and stūpa worship comes from a 1038 inscription in Chinese eulogizing the burial of 150 relic fragments, including a finger and a head bone of the Buddha presented by an Indian monk.[69] The timing of this eulogy also makes it a significant political act; it constituted one of Yuanhao's accession rituals.

Dated to the eighth month, tenth day of 1038 (Daqing 3), two months before Weiming Yuanhao's public enthronement, the text was composed by Vice Director of the Right and Concurrent Vice Director of the Secretariat and Manager of Affairs *(you puye jian zhongshu shilang pingzhang shi)* Zhang Zhi and inscribed by Right Grand Master of Remonstrance *(you jianyi dafu)* Yang (personal name illegible).[70] After summarizing the life of the Buddha, it extols Yuanhao as the "Sage of Culture, Hero of War, Esteeming Humaneness and Perfectly Filial Emperor,"[71] whose talent and valor surpass those of Tang Yao (the ancient Chinese sage emperor) and the Han progenitors *(Han zu)*;[72] who reveres the Buddha path (dharma) and has disseminated the Tangut script, lavishly furbished the temple wherein these precious relics will lie, and with folded hands upholds and protects the Diamond Vehicle (Vajrayāna) and the Treasure Realm.

Further, the text describes the richly appointed coffin for the 150 pieces of Buddha relics, presented by an Indian adept. The many-layered burial chamber included a silver outer coffin and a gold inner coffin, inside of which was an iron casket containing a stone chest, in which lay the relics wrapped in precious materials. The coffin was protected by Vaiśravaṇa, guardian king of the North, probably depicted on the outer surface.[73] Below, it communicated with an underground spring; above, it reached to the cloud-spiraling stūpa. A prayer follows for the protection of the state and the longevity of imperial posterity, for sincere officials and a peaceful populace, for a cessation of border fighting, and for the overflowing of granaries. The temple and stūpa honored by receipt of these relics are not named (the text is incomplete), but presumably they were located in the capital at Xingzhou (present-day Yinchuan). This text and the deed it records bear out Faure's observation on the legitimating functions of relic worship mentioned above.

In this document the Tangut ruler, already named emperor, is lauded for virtues exceeding those of the great Chinese monarchs of yore and also for the qualities of a *cakravartin,* "a wheel-turning monarch; a great king who rules the world according to Dharma," a *dharmarāja.*[74] The text does not so much claim for him a place within the lineage of Chinese sage rulers as assert his equality with them. A Chinese text, full of Chinese imperial symbols and allusions, this inscription was surely directed to a domestic Chinese audience as much as to a Tangut one. Unfortunately no Tangut version survives, for a comparison would be revealing; it would also be the earliest composition in the Tangut language.

Li Tao records Weiming Yuanhao's formal enthronement in the tenth month of 1038: "Yuanhao built an altar and received appointment; he falsely calls [the country] Great Xia, [and himself] Originator of Literature, Hero of Might, Giver of Law, Founder of Ritual, Humane and Filial Emperor. He changed the reign era from Tianqing second [*sic*] year to Tianshou lifa yanzuo first year."[75] As will become clear, most of the details in Li Tao's account come from the letter Yuanhao sent to Song Renzong's court. The *Song shi* account preserves other critical elements of Yuanhao's accession rituals:

> [Yuanhao] together with his braves smeared blood on their lips and took an oath first to attack Fuyan, desiring to enter [Song territory] simultaneously from three routes out of Dejing, Saimen fort, and Chicheng. Then [he] built an altar, received appointment, and assumed the imperial position *(ji huangdi wei)*. At that time [he] was thirty *sui*.[76]

Sealing his imperial promotion with the military aristocrats required a blood oath sworn around the promise of a raid on Song territory, or, more than a raid, a promise to launch a preemptive attack, in expectation of Song retaliation upon receipt of Yuanhao's letter to the Song court.

Finally, Yuanhao's accession rituals concluded, as they had begun, with a religious act. In the eleventh month the new emperor traveled to Xiliangfu (Liangzhou or Wuwei) to make sacrifices to the spirits *(cishen);* the term indicates ancestral spirits but probably also included ceremonies at the Buddhist temples of Liangzhou, which were to play a vital role in the state religious establishment. In 1039 Yuanhao sent envoys with a letter to the Song court.

The Tangut ruler's letter to Song Renzong contains no overt Buddhist allusions but merits a close analysis for what it can tell us about Tangut conceptions of monarchy and legitimation, and their manipulation of Chinese ideas of the same. I have numbered the principal sections:

1. Your servant's ancestors were originally emperors of Later Wei, and the old state of Helian [Bobo] is the legacy of the Tuoba.[77]

2. During the Tang [my] distant ancestor [Tuoba] Sigong led troops to rescue [the court] from hardship and was granted the [imperial] surname [Li].

3. Your servant's grandfather Jiqian deeply grasped the requirements of strategy, held fast to Heaven's omen, grandly raised the righteous banner, and completely subdued all the tribes. The five districts by the Yellow River submitted at once; the seven prefectures along the border all [sent deputies?] to surrender.

4. [My] father Deming inherited and served the great undertaking [i.e., Jiqian's autonomous state], perforce following the [Song] court's orders. [The name of a true king formerly made itself

felt through widespread promulgation; an insignificant fief was explicitly received in an act of severing and sharing.]⁷⁸

5. Your servant has by chance violated elegance to create a humble Fan script, altered the great Han official dress, changed the five musical tones to one tone, reduced the ritual bow from nine prostrations to three. Now that the dress [regulations] are completed, the script put into effect, the rites and music made manifest, the vessels and implements prepared, of the Tibetans (Tufan), Tatars, Zhangye (Uighurs), and Jiaohe (Gaochang), there are none who have not followed to submit.

6. Not pleased with the title of king *(wang)*, [they] would follow only that of emperor. Converging without end until the mountains rang with their assembly, humbly they begged for a land of one border, to establish a country of ten thousand chariots. At that [I] repeatedly refused, but the assembled crowd kept pressing, until the matter could not but be carried out.⁷⁹

7. Therefore on the eleventh day of the tenth month, an altar was erected and the ceremony completed, [I] was enthroned as Shizu, Originator of Literature, Rooted in Might, Giver of Law, Founder of Ritual, Humane and Filial Emperor. The country is called Great Xia, the reign era Tianshou lifa yanzuo ("Heaven-Conferred Rites, Law, and Protracted Blessings").⁸⁰

8. [I] humbly look to Your Majesty the Emperor, in your profound wisdom and perfection, whose benevolence extends to all things, to permit [me] to be invested in this western land as the ruler facing south.⁸¹

9. [I] dare to exert my humble merits and will always esteem our good relations. As the fish come and the birds go, so will be transmitted the sounds of our neighboring states; as the earth is old and the heavens spacious, so long will [we] subdue disturbances along the border. In utmost sincerity do [I] beseech [you], humbly awaiting the imperial affirmation.⁸²

10. [I] have respectfully sent the envoys Nushe Eji, Nisimen, Wopu Lingji, and Weiyaini to submit this message.⁸³

The first statement establishes the Tanguts' historical and genealogical claim to a piece of the Chinese imperial legacy, in the spirit of what S. A. M. Adshead calls the "afterglow of Tang cosmopolitanism".⁸⁴ A link to the Tuoba Wei also alerts us to the possible significance of the Northern Wei Buddhist legacy in the formation of Xia imperial institutions and ideology. But certainly Yuanhao did not look to the Wei rulers for strategies of accommodation to Chinese culture; far from mandating Tuoba adoption of Chinese surnames, for example, he mandated use of a Tangut surname for the imperial clan. Helian Bobo's fourth-century Ordos regime of Da Xia supplied an obvious precedent for the Chinese name of the Tangut state. But did invocation of the Northern Wei also imply a comparison of Song with the short-lived courts of the south China of that period?

Second, Yuanhao cites rewards received for loyal service to the great Tang dynasty, which, besides appealing to imperial precedent, served also to remind the Song of its vulnerability and potential dependence on friendly border forces. In the third statement Yuanhao develops this theme by affirming the justice of his grandfather's cause and the skill with which he brought it to fruition. Heaven stood behind the Tangut drive to unify and pacify Hexi. Implicitly Yuanhao contrasts Jiqian's unification of all the tribes with the Song failure to reunify the Tang realm, an uncomfortable reminder, to say the least. (The fact that numbers of tribes resisted the Tangut unifiers is beside the point.) Furthermore, insofar as physical unification constituted a qualification for legitimate rule, Yuanhao drives home the unassailable point that the Tanguts are more qualified to rule this territory than the Chinese.

Next, Yuanhao suggests that his father's filial service to the ancestral Tuoba legacy was vitiated by Song pressure on him to accept vassal status, thus implicating the Chinese in a breach of that fundamental virtue filial piety. The passage in brackets that follows occurs only in the *Song shi* text of the 1038 letter and seems to refer to Song Zhenzong's recognition of de facto Tangut sovereignty over the Ordos prefectures and Lingzhou, through his 1006 enfeoffment of Li Deming.

In the fifth statement Yuanhao summarizes his cultural and ritual reforms, whereby his fame and reputation as a true ruler have won the willing submission of all the Tanguts' neighbors. This recital poses yet another challenge to Song universalist claims as well as to Chinese cultural norms, which Yuanhao has rejected in favor of native forms. In effect asserting cultural equality with the Chinese, Yuanhao injects a relativism into Chinese hierarchical conceptions of human society that is extremely subversive.

The sixth statement emphasizes Yuanhao's legitimacy by describing popular recognition of his mandate to rule. His election to emperorship invokes both a steppe military tradition of rule by acclamation as well as an established Chinese tradition of dynastic transfer, most recently practiced in Zhao Kuangyin's founding of the Song itself.

Having established his imperial status, Yuanhao proceeds to announce the Chinese version of his official insignia, imperial title, reign era name, and state's official name, so that the Song court can now apply the appropriate etiquette in their mutual dealings. He has unilaterally assumed the right to titles that the Song yielded to the mightier Khitans only after close encounters on the battlefield.

In the eighth statement Yuanhao indulges in what appears to be a mock humility far more insulting than his previous protestations. He praises Song Renzong's benevolence and innocently begs the emperor to invest him as a friendly western ruler "facing south," an orientation reserved for the "One Man" occupying the pinnacle of the Chinese political-cosmological hierarchy. The ninth statement promises the best of intentions in preserving mutually beneficial relations. Implicit in these promises, however, lies the threat of hostile border activity should the Song court fail to comply. It was unthinkable for the Song emperor to acknowledge such a document, and surely all parties realized this.

The rhetoric of this letter plays with all the traditional Confucian claims to rulership. Yet Yuanhao's argument subverts the Confucian logic of Chinese imperial rule by the simple means of multiplying the pinnacles of the hierarchy. There are many active bodhisattvas in the Buddhist pantheon but only one living sage ruler in the Confucian one.

Even though the Chinese had advance notice of Yuanhao's intentions (his New Year's envoys failed to appear), the Tangut missive produced a stir in Kaifeng. After some court debate over the merits of executing the Tangut envoys, Renzong extended the usual courtesies but returned the gift of horses and camels. Likewise, the Xia embassy declined the Song emperor's edict and presents, and was escorted back to the border.[85] Then Renzong promptly revoked all of his erstwhile subject's titles and ranks, and closed all frontier markets. Yuanhao returned the Song paraphernalia of office with another "insulting" letter: "The Fan and the Han are each different countries, and their lands are vastly dissimilar. This is not a case of usurpation; why is your resentment so deep? Moreover, [I] was elevated by the throng and in accordance with ancient Tuoba tradition became emperor. Where is the harm in that?"[86] Besides his renewed emphasis on Tuoba precedent, here Yuanhao also argues that geography and custom are sufficient bases for legitimating a separate but equal sovereignty. A significant stratum in early Tangut imperial ideology, therefore, appears to be a firm belief in the ecological, ethnic, and cultural distinctions that mandated and legitimated a separate state in the territories occupied by the "Fan."[87] These considerations received further support from historical precedents established by earlier Xianbei-Tuoba state building. Why indeed was Song "resentment so deep"?

A Song conceptualization of the issues involved is systematically laid out in Fan Zhongyan's eloquent and unauthorized letter to Yuanhao during the early stage of the war that followed, when Fan (989–1052) served as assistant pacification commissioner of Shaanxi and prefect of Yanzhou in 1040–1041.[88] Fan asks, since Yuanhao has followed his "country's custom" *(guo zhi su)* in costume, language, and the like, why does he want to use the Chinese imperial title? Why not use the steppe titles of *shanyu* or *qan*, which command great respect? The reason Yuanhao covets the title of Son of Heaven, Fan concludes astutely, is that the Khitans use this title. Yet, Fan explains, the Khitans are different; they earned their emperorship "a long time ago" and became a brother state with Song. The Tanguts, however, do not have the same "merit" or accomplishments and should be content to serve as Song's border wardens.

But Yuanhao had modern ambitions that went beyond securing autonomy for the Tangut realm. Fiercely proud of his and his people's accomplishments and desiring recognition of them, he evidently decided that the Tangut state could only maintain its integrity by gaining parity with the other powers dominating the East Asian world. His "insult" to the Song court challenged Khitan pretensions as well, as Fan Zhongyan implied. The Tangut ruler's claim to descend from the Tuoba Wei rulers implied a superior ancestry to the Khitans, who traced their descent from tribes who submitted to the Northern Wei.[89] Thus the Liao presence figured as importantly as the Song in Yuanhao's calculations. Song records, unfortunately, vastly outnumber Khitan ones, forever skewing our understanding of this era. The Tanguts were engaged in immediate and more serious competition with the Khitans, their dynastic alliance notwithstanding. Equally important, the Xia elite included a significant Chinese component, as did the Liao, and it was vital for these groups to validate their position and status at home and abroad (vis-à-vis each other).

Fan Zhongyan also tried to dismiss the appeal to Tuoba precedent by pointing out that if every descendant of a former ruling house in China were to advance a claim to the imperial title, then China would be full of emperors! Moreover, what about the other powerful Tangut clans who could also claim Xianbei descent?[90] This was a somewhat disingenuous rhetorical ploy, if rather clever. To be sure, another clan could, on the basis of Tuoba connections alone, claim the mantle of leadership. Yet the Weiming had long ago emerged as the leading clan, and the others had already acknowledged its paramountcy. Multiple genealogical claims to the Tuoba legacy, in fact, strengthened rather than diluted the Tanguts' argument.

Eventually a solution was reached whereby Yuanhao agreed to refer to himself as *chen*, "servant," in correspondence with the Song court, while reserving his imperial title for domestic use. The same protocol applied in relations with Liao. Although Song suffered heavy losses in the war, it gained its primary goal, principally through intense negotiations carried out between battles. For this compromise it paid a moderate sum in annual "gifts" to the Tangut ruler.[91]

After concluding a treaty with Song in 1044, Yuanhao spent his remaining years (d. 1048) repelling Khitan invasions and building summer palaces and temples in the Helan and Tiandu mountains (southeastern Ningxia), where he retired to play with his concubines. One, the mother of the next emperor, was a woman of the powerful Mocang clan and formerly the wife of Yuanhao's Yeli empress' brother Yeli Yuqi. Yeli Yuqi and his brother, heads of the right and left wings of the army, had been executed by Yuanhao (in 1045?) on suspicion of plotting a coup.[92] Yuanhao later regretted his deed and allowed the Yeli empress to bring her Mocang sister-in-law out of hiding to the palace, where he began having an affair with her. Unwilling to kill Mocang, the empress sent her to live as a nun in the capital's Jietan Cloister, where she became known (ironically?) as Mocang dashi (Great Master Mocang).[93] The emperor continued to see her, and she bore him a son, some say early in 1047, some say three months after the emperor's death by his eldest son's hand early in 1048.[94] Yuanhao left a will naming a cousin as his successor, but the Mocang clan leader persuaded the other members of the tribal council to accept his sister's bastard son by the deceased emperor as the new ruler, thus assuring his own position as the power behind the throne.

Local gazetteers for Ningxia and Gansu refer to many temples and palaces built during the eleventh century under Yuanhao and his successors.[95] Most lack inscriptions and precise datings, and are best examined collectively. Contemporary Song sources say nothing about the Tangut ruler's Buddhist activities, nor can much be found in the meager Liao record. Tangut archives from this period have not survived, but a few later sources do refer back to the great founder, notably in prefaces to Buddhist sūtras.

One is the preface to a Tangut translation of the *Miaofa lianhua jing* (*Saddharmapuṇḍarīka-sūtra*, "Lotus Sūtra"), probably written between 1048 and 1056, or in the early 1070s.[96] The author, Wang Puxin (evidently a Tangut), was a high official in the Bureau of Military Affairs with several honorary titles. After summarizing the history of the "Lotus Sutra," Wang comes to the present era:

> The Fengjiao cheng emperor, using the country's native language, established Tangut rites, created a script, and translated sūtras. His military prowess was outstanding, his virtuous deeds most remarkable. In ruling the people, none can compare. The previous court [Yuanhao's?] translated a great many sūtras, but this Lotus law was not included. Now the imperial child and mother have taken the throne, revere and have faith in the Three Treasures [Buddha, dharma, saṅgha], rule the country and practice virtue, causing the rites of the ancestors to flourish.

Wang affirms Yuanhao's deeds on behalf of the faith as important elements in his legacy as a great ruler. "Fengjiao cheng" was one of a series of posthumous imperial titles containing the graph translated as the Chinese word *cheng* (wall; perhaps a tomb enclosure and hence a posthumous title).[97] Such titles have been identified for four Xia emperors, and at least some seem to have had Buddhist significance (see table of Xia Rulers and Reign Eras).[98]

Likewise, the preface to a later text in the Tangut canon gives credit to the Feng emperor (a shortened form of Yuanhao's wall title) for initiating the translation of the Buddhist canon into Tangut.[99] Reference to the first Tangut emperor also appears in a Yuan era Buddhist text. A 1312 preface to the Tangut translation of the *Guoqu zhuangyan qie qian foming jing* ("Sūtra on the Thousand Buddha Names of the Past Ornamented Kalpa") notes: "The Feng emperor of the Xia state newly implemented rites and virtuous examples. In the *xuyan* year [1038] the State Preceptor *(guoshi)* Bai Faxin, the...[?] official Zhiguang, et al., in all thirty-two people, were put in charge of translating [sūtras] into Tangut."[100] This important notice provides our earliest glimpse of a state Saṅgha, or official Buddhist establishment. It suggests that State Preceptor Bai Faxin and the other clerical officials had already been in office for some time before 1038, but whether before 1032, that is, in Li Deming's reign, remains uncertain.

Thus we learn that by the time of Yuanhao's enthronement, a regular Buddhist establishment headed by a state preceptor, Bai Faxin, had emerged to direct the labor of translating sūtras. Later Tangut sources yield substantial information about the official Buddhist establishment.[101]

Wu Guangcheng's chronicle says that in 1047 Yuanhao made his birthday (the fifth day of the fifth month) a day of celebration and also designated the first day of each of the four seasons a holy day on which officials and the people were supposed to pay homage to the Buddha.[102] Further, according to Wu, Yuanhao built the Gaotai Temple fifteen *li* east of the capital, to house the Tripiṭaka presented by Song, and assigned Uighur monks to translate the sūtras into Tangut. I have not found contemporary evidence to corroborate this account, and scholars have debated the degree and import of Uighur participation in translating Tangut sūtras.[103] That Uighur Buddhists were active in Xia cannot be doubted, however, as will be seen.

In sum, during the first phase of state building, Tangut rulers showed interest in the cults at Wutai shan and the worship of stūpas and relics, engaged in temple and stūpa building and reconstruction, patronized Indian monks, collected copies of texts and the Buddhist canon to translate into their own newly invented script, appointed monks to Buddhist offices overseeing translation work, and starting with Yuanhao began to portray themselves as great patrons and defenders of the dharma. Our material points to an interest in Esoteric Buddhist texts and rituals, which among other things supplied potent weapons against enemies. Yet almost all of the solid evidence for Esoteric Buddhist activity dates to the twelfth century, and so it is difficult to argue that in the earlier period the Tanguts had already expressed a clear preference for one particular school or style of Buddhism. They appeared to have been open to everything at first, and the commitment to Esoteric Buddhism, so strongly expressed in material from the twelfth and thirteenth centuries, emerged gradually after a long period of incubation.

We can affirm, however, that the Buddhist concerns and activities sketched above were closely intertwined with evolving Tangut notions of kingship and community, of the sovereign and the state. The *dharmarāja* and *cakravartin*-conqueror swore a blood oath with his chieftains and appealed to geography and ethnohistorical genealogy to buttress his claim to rule.

We have no direct evidence that the first Weiming emperor achieved the status of his Khitan counterpart, Liao Xingzong

(r. 1031–1055), who was celebrated in a Buddhist inscription as a bodhisattva and *cakravartin* of the highest order in the critical year 1044.[104] At this time Liao-Xia relations deteriorated to a state of war; a rebellion of Tangut tribes dwelling within the Liao border provided the pretext for a Khitan invasion of Xia in the summer of 1044. Equally important, Xingzong, who had ascended the Liao throne at age fifteen under the regency of his mother, had since then been engaged in a domestic struggle to preserve his position and assert his authority over the powerful Jin'ai empress dowager. He never completely succeeded, owing to the "complex pattern of divided authority" at the Liao court.[105] But shortly before the empress dowager returned to court in 1039 after a five-year exile for plotting to replace Xingzong with his brother, the Liao emperor took Buddhist vows, and later he had monks visit his mother's residence to expound Buddhist doctrines.[106] Xingzong continued his devotions and is recorded to have visited Buddhist temples in 1042 (with his mother), 1043, 1047 (probably with his mother), 1052, and 1054.[107]

In the fourth month of Chongxi 13 (1044), just as the Khitans launched their ill-fated campaign into Xia, a stele inscription was erected at the Badaling Stūpa of the Luohan Cloister (northeast of Yanjing), likening the Liao sovereign to a bodhisattva of unbounded powers, who had inherited the wisdom of the Golden Wheel, highest *cakravartin,* and whose powers had subdued a myriad dependent peoples.[108] Xingzong, however, proved unable to subdue the Tanguts. After humiliating the Liao armies, the Weiming emperor hastened in person (to what place is not specified) to atone for the breach.[109] The Khitans exacted revenge after Yuanhao's death in 1048, and Xia-Liao relations remained strained for some time after.

If the extant Xia record does not make the same claims for Yuanhao as we find in Liao sources for the Khitan emperor, what about the testimony left behind in his burial? The tombs of the Tangut monarchs west of Yinchuan in the foothills of the Helan Mountains (Mong. Alashan) are key sources in the study of Tangut imperial ideology and its Buddhist components, for the grave mounds *(lingtai)* are quite distinctive in their location behind, not over, the burial chamber and in their unmistakable stūpa shape and function.[110] Yuanhao probably had his grandfather and father reburied in the first two tombs identified among the nine that remain in the complex; his appears to be the third, in the first north-south row. It is the largest and most elaborate, with several characteristics distinguishing it from the others. Systematic desecration of the Xia royal tombs by

Buddhism and Monarchy 49

the conquering Mongolian armies can be understood as an effort to cut off and neutralize the charisma of the Tangut Buddhist emperors.[111] Nevertheless, these monuments remain today evocative reminders of the Tangut monarchy and its complex identity.

The next chapter examines the "complex pattern of divided authority" that emerged at the Tangut court following the death of Weiming Yuanhao and the rise to power of the maternal-regent clans, first the Mocang and then the Liang. Surely it was no coincidence that the Mocang and Liang empresses championed the project of translating the Buddhist canon into Tangut and building up the official Saṅgha.

CHAPTER 3

Buddhism under the Regencies (1049–1099)

AFTER WEIMING YUANHAO'S death the vital role of Tangut empresses in promoting Buddhism emerges in sharper focus. Owing largely to the youth of later emperors, their mothers occupied prominent political and military positions. Three empresses, a Mocang and two Liang, along with their male kin and allies dominate the historical records to the end of the eleventh century. Like the Yeli before them, the Mocang and the Liang were two prominent clans in the Tangut elite that supplied military leadership and royal consorts to the Xia court. During the second half of the eleventh century, the throne requested and received four more copies of the Buddhist canon from the Song court.[1] By the end of the century the Xia court had produced a roughly complete translation of the canon into Tangut, an act with profound cultural and political implications.

Any discussion of Xia history in the latter half of the eleventh century must take note of Song expansion along its northwest frontier from 1067 onward.[2] Officials under the Song emperor Shenzong (r. 1067–1085) and his successors (with a pause during the regency of the Empress Dowager Gao for Zhezong from 1086 to 1093) pursued an aggressive border policy in the northwest that aimed to "pacify" the Tibetans, occupy Kokonor and adjacent areas, assert Chinese control over trade with Central Asia, and if possible conquer Xia. Systematic implementation of Song policy began with Wang Shao's establishment of Xihe Circuit in 1072–1074, in the Huang and Tao river valleys west and north of Qinfeng Circuit (see map).[3]

At the same time, during the 1070s, in the Xia state Liang Yimai and his sister, the first Liang empress dowager, consolidated their control over the military, excluding or banishing uncooperative Weiming princes and their supporters. Perhaps the Liang felt justified in their grip on power by the threat posed by Song advances along the Tanguts' southern perimeter and redoubled Chinese efforts to enroll Tibetans in espionage and military actions against Xia. From Chinese accounts one can deduce that the Liang saw the Weiming as too willing to compromise with Song in an effort to stabilize and strengthen royal power. The Song exploited these tensions fully by, among other things, trying to make separate deals with powerful Tangut chieftains.

As in Liao, however, the lines of dissension in eleventh-century Xia did not so much divide Liang and Weiming as cut across these and other clan groups. Despite alleged attempts by the maternal clan chief ministers to set aside the "legitimate" emperor, the real issue at stake was not who was going to occupy the throne, but how power was going to be delegated. Moreover, rivalry and division arose within the consort clan, as they did within the royal clan and between the two. Like their Liao counterparts, Xia empresses sought to promote (and control) their imperial offspring as a way to preserve their own personal influence, and this brought them into conflict with their own clan, specifically with their brothers, the chief ministers.[4]

Patronage of Buddhism allowed the Xia empress dowager to cultivate a wide range of allies across clan lines and outside the military elite. Through her Buddhist activities and Saṅgha allies, the empress dowager expressed personal piety, gained support for her rule on behalf of the Weiming emperor, and defended the throne against domestic and foreign threats, real and perceived. For the latter she also relied on and guarded her access to military power. Like her Liao counterparts, she probably promoted and employed distant Weiming (Li) princes over the emperor's agnates. With the death of the second Liang empress dowager in 1099, however, the Weiming clan elders closed ranks around the young emperor Chongzong (r. 1086–1139) and sponsored a series of reforms in the early twelfth century to strengthen the central government's authority over the military aristocracy. The Weiming Restoration marked a turning point in the fortunes of the Xia state, and these changes must also have affected the Buddhist establishment, although our evidence for this period remains spotty.

Historians of Xia, myself included, have generally understood Yuanhao's accomplishments as the founding emperor to have given the state its characteristic institutions and administrative apparatus. Yet the reforms carried out during the Weiming Restoration in the early part of the twelfth century, leading up to and culminating in the publication of the Tiansheng law code, probably circa 1150, were equally significant and have not yet been systematically analyzed. Scholars often credit Yuanhao with a degree of centralization greater than subsequent events warrant us to posit. Throughout the eleventh century, the confederate structure of the Xia polity remained substantially intact and produced both negative and positive effects. On the one hand, it challenged and fractured the center's authority; on the other hand, it allowed the "state" to make a strategic retreat and leave the defense of the country in the hands of strong regional military powers.[5] In the course of this process, the struggle over central authority devolved for a time upon regional military alliances. In the 1090s the process gradually reversed itself, for in the face of rapidly deteriorating conditions, the Weiming were able to recover sufficient authority to reconstitute the state.

From the Mocang Clan to the Liang

Yuanhao's successor, Weiming Liangzuo (Yizong, r. 1048–1067), came to the throne an infant under his mother's rule. The Mocang empress dowager and her brother, Mocang Epang, assumed the reins of power in the midst of a foreign crisis. In 1049 and 1050 Liao troops invaded Xia, penetrated the imperial Tangut retreats in the Helan Mountains, captured a wife of Yuanhao, threatened the capital, and raided the environs of Liangzhou.[6] As in the 1044–1045 invasion, the Khitans suffered serious losses, and the Liao court accepted the empress dowager's petition to normalize relations.

In the third month of 1050, at the height of the Liao campaign, the empress dowager celebrated the construction of a new temple in the capital, Chengtian si (Received from Heaven Temple), to house Buddha relics. The extant and dated Chinese text of a stele inscription recording the events may have had a now lost Tangut version.[7] It opens with a Buddhist encomium:

> The Xia state empress dowager newly constructs the Chengtian Temple to bury the casket containing relics of the Buddha's skull bone.
>
> The original enlightened August's responsive traces[8] [are like] the moon[light] submerged in the myriad waters; the holy teachings overflow in brilliance, [like] stars arrayed in the surrounding vault of Heaven. [. . .][9] regularly displayed the utmost transformation in accord with inherent capabilities, manifested great compas-

sion, and saved living beings.¹⁰ Passing unhindered through *kalpa*s as innumerable as dust particles, [the Buddha-truth] increasingly made itself known in form. By esteeming temples and monasteries, past and present form a seamless continuity. By reverencing the blessings of this Indian relic, near and far are not discriminated.

The gist of this passage is that through enshrining these Indian relics of the Buddha in this temple, the Tanguts transcended time and space and established direct contact with the historical Buddha and with his homeland. These were powerful "connections" to have. There follows mention of the Xia state's prosperity and expansion. Then,

> The empress dowager received from Heaven *(chengtian)* the late emperor's will and has been appointed to preside at court. She orders the myriad beings so as to promote peace; disciplining the various officials, [she] follows the proper pattern. As the present emperor ascended the throne in infancy, [she] reverently holds firm the imperial plan. Sharing the seried brilliance of the fourth reign, [she] harmonizes the three efficacies¹¹ and nurtures [them]. On behalf of the concealed dragon's throne [she] received the order of investiture. It behooves [her] to continue the Sages' celebrated foundations and extend the empire's superior lands. [She] greatly venerates spiritual dwellings, and throughout [the land] erects Buddhist stūpas to ensure that the Sage's life will be without limit and to perpetuate the royal lineage.¹²

Several themes stand out here. First, the empress dowager took this occasion to assert and legitimize her direct rule as regent for Yizong, using the appropriate Chinese phraseology. As in the case of later bilingual texts, especially the 1094 Gantong Stūpa stele inscriptions, the manipulation of the Chinese rhetoric of legitimacy suggests that the empress had a significant sinophone audience to reach with her appeals for recognition and loyalty. It is not clear how effective her appeals were, nor can we assume the existence of a Chinese constituency as a monolithic community with a set agenda. The use of such rhetoric might, however, satisfy the need of Chinese to validate their service to the Xia court, and it would not be lost on literate Tanguts ("political" literacy in East Asia at this time, excepting Tibet, would include a knowledge of literary Chinese).¹³

Second, the occasion was a Buddhist one, and the text draws a direct connection between the welfare of the royal family (hence, the state) and its promotion of Buddhism, specifically the building of stūpas. Moreover, naming the temple Chengtian ("Received from

Heaven") reinforces the association of legitimate (empressorial) rule with service to the Buddha and the good fortune secured thereby. Here is further evidence of a cult of stūpa worship, about which I say more in the next chapter, being employed, in Bernard Faure's phrase, as a "powerful instrument of monastic and imperial legitimacy."[14]

The question of Uighur involvement in the Buddhist establishment arises in connection with the Chengtian episode. Wu Guangcheng's *Xi Xia shushi* (ca. 1826) dates the opening of the Chengtian Temple to the tenth month of 1055, explaining that,

> Lady Mocang was fond of Buddhism; since China presented [to Xia] the Tripiṭaka, [she] raised several tens of thousands of soldiers and people, on the western side of Xingqingfu built a great temple, stored the sūtras in it, and named it Chengtian. [She] had Uighur monks ascend to sit [in the temple] and lecture on the sūtras. Lady Mocang and Liangzuo on occasion went there to listen to [their lectures]. (19:11b)

The Song court did present another set of sūtras to Xia in the fourth month of 1055,[15] presumably at the empress dowager's request. Evidently, however, Wu Guangcheng did not have access to either the *Jiajing Ningxia xin zhi* (1540) or the 1780 edition of the *Ningxia fuzhi*, which record the text of the inscription of 1050, for surely he would have made an appropriate entry under this date in his chronicle. Instead, he has apparently dated the construction of the Chengtian Temple to the tenth month of 1055 on two bases: (1) the earlier *Ningxia xin zhi* (1501) notice that the Chengtian si was built under Liangzuo and (2) the assumption that the Chengtian si was built to house a Buddhist canon received from Song earlier in 1055, perhaps based on a Song edict to Xia preserved in Ouyang Xiu's complete works and dated to 1058.[16] Yet we know from the inscription cited above that initially the Xia empress dowager had the temple built to house Buddha relics, not sūtras (although the latter may have found a home there too).

The reference to Uighur monks here raises some questions, for Uighurs constituted diverse groups who played important but ill-documented roles in both Liao and Xia state formation. Were they refugees from Central Asian Muslim rulers or ambitious emigrants from Shazhou (Dunhuang) anxious for employment?[17] Or were they local Alashan (i.e., Helan shan) Uighurs?[18] Different groups of Uighurs moved throughout the region in the tenth through twelfth centuries, some entering the Liao elite and some the Xia elite; some settling inside the Song border; and many maintaining traditional trading connections with Tibet, Qinghai, and Central Asia. The cultural influence of the Gansu Uighurs is especially well documented at the Dunhuang and Yulin Buddhist caves.[19]

If the empress dowager was cultivating allies among the Uighur Buddhists, it would be appropriate to ask where they hailed from and what role they played in translation activity or in the power struggles at the Xia court. Song sources on the Gaochang Uighurs and on the Ganzhou Uighur regime absorbed in the 1030s by Xia describe a political culture in which empresses and their minister brothers exercised powerful influence at court, sent their own embassies to China, used monks and nuns as envoys, and in which Buddhism generally was an integral component.[20] Likewise, among the Qingtang Tibetans, Buddhist monks and women moved prominently across the political landscape. According to a contemporary Song source, Lady Qiao, the mother of Gusiluo's successor Dongzhan, dwelled apart at the walled town of Lijing, had sixty to seventy thousand followers in her "tribe" *(bu)*, went by the title of *ling (yan) ming*, and earned the fear and respect of all.[21] Similar phenomena observed for the Tanguts highlight the presence of Central and Inner Asian elements in Tangut political culture and alert us to possible sources of tension in the evolution of the Tangut state and monarchy.

In 1056 the Mocang empress dowager was assassinated. Li Tao's record of the affair reveals that her older brother, palace minister and strongman Mocang Epang, manipulated a sexual intrigue to get rid of the empress dowager and one of her intimate allies, who opposed Epang's colonization of some fertile border territories claimed by the Chinese. The Song historian's first entry notes that on the *jia zi* day of the twelfth month of 1056 the Xia ruler Liangzuo (i.e., Mocang Epang) sent envoys to announce the death of his mother. It continues:

> Originally a certain Li Shougui had taken care of accounts for Yuege [Yeli Yuqi, one of Yuanhao's great generals whom the latter put to death]. Baixi Qitejile had served Nangxiao (Yuanhao) and Lady Mocang at the Jietan Cloister. Therefore [Baixi] could come and go from Lady Mocang's place without impediment. After Lady Mocang began an intimate liaison with [Li] Shougui, she also became intimate with Qitejile. Shougui grew enraged and thereupon killed Qitejile and Lady Mocang. Etepeng (Mocang Epang) slew Shougui and reared Liangzuo. Subsequently he married his daughter to [Liangzuo]. At that time Liangzuo was nine *sui*.[22]

This account paints Mocang Epang as the emperor's rescuer, with no part in the intrigue, and thus probably derives from a letter by Epang (written in the emperor's name), that the Xia embassy delivered to the Song court. Baixi Qitejile represents a Qing transcription of the name written in the other Song account of the event as Baobaoxi Jiduoji;[23] it may transcribe a Tibetan or Uighur name rather than a Tangut one (*duoji* renders Tib. *rdo-rje* or Dorje, *"vajra,"* "thunderbolt," a common name or title of respect). Baixi/Baobaoxi may, moreover, represent the title *bağşi/pakshi/baksi,* "learned one, religious teacher, scribe," believed to derive from Chinese *boshi* (scholar of wide learning) and to have been transmitted by the Uighurs to the Tibetans, and then to the Mongols in the thirteenth century.[24] At this time it was already in wide use among the Uighurs (and Tibetans), strengthening the possibility that Empress Mocang's intimate was either a Uighur or a Tibetan.[25]

Events culminating in the murder of the Mocang empress go back no later than Yuanhao's purging of the mighty Yeli generals, the brothers Yuqi and Wangrong, sometime in 1045 or 1046. Yuanhao's Yeli empress was their sister. Lady Mocang was Yuqi's wife and the sister-in-law of the empress, who retained enough influence to shelter Mocang in the palace after the slaying of her relatives. Yuanhao soon began an affair with Mocang and continued to visit her after his empress moved her out to the Jietan Cloister in the suburbs of the capital. Around the time that Mocang bore Liangzuo, Yuanhao demoted his Yeli empress to install as empress another woman, originally the intended bride of his son and heir by his Yeli wife. This unlucky youth, the last surviving son of the Yeli empress, took revenge by trying to assassinate his father. After stabbing Yuanhao in the nose (a fatal wound, it turned out), he sought refuge in the home of his presumed ally Mocang Epang, who instead had him arrested and executed.[26] Exit the Yeli, enter the Mocang. In an interlinear note, Li Tao gives an alternate version of the story about the empress' assassination:

> In that year [1056], tenth month, *dingmao* [day], in the Veritable Records it is written that the Huanqing Pacification Office said that Weimi Liegui, the paternal uncle *(a shu)* of the Xia state little great king *(xiao da wang),* and Mizang Etepeng [Mocang Epang] killed their empress and minister *(xianggong)* Baixi. Then when Etepang seized the little great king and put him under the supervision of his own clan, [Huanqing] tightened precautions at all border forts. Comment: The so-called little great king is Liangzuo.

Baixi *xianggong* is Qitejile. Weimi Liegui perhaps is Li Shougui. Yet the affair is different from what the official history [says].²⁷

This report suggests that a younger brother or cousin of Yuanhao, who claimed the royal surname of Weiming but also went by its predecessor, Li, conspired with Mocang Epang to rid the palace of the powerful empress and her lover-ally, Baixi Qitejile. Mocang Epang outmaneuvered the prince and took over control of the young emperor. Although this report does not mention the fate of Weimi Liegui, most likely Epang cut short the activities of such a potentially dangerous royal rival, as he had done before in the case of Yuanhao's son. The probable identity of Li Shougui and Weimi Liegui means that this prince perhaps nourished a strong grudge against Yuanhao, who had killed his benefactor and lord, Yeli Yuqi, and demoted Yuqi's sister (we do not know the ultimate fate of the former Yeli empress).²⁸ Passed over in the succession to Yuanhao, Liegui/Shougui may also have believed that he had a stronger claim to the throne than the Mocang clan's protégé and so tried to insinuate his way to the seat of power by cooperating with Mocang Epang to eliminate the empress and her minister. His failure marks the first documented attempt by a Weiming clansman to recover power following Yuanhao's death.

Another critical piece of the affair comes to light in Li Tao's chronicle of the Tanguts' illegal colonization of some fertile lands on the Song side of the Quye River, which flows into the Yellow River in northwest Hedong Circuit (Shaanxi, see map). This longstanding border dispute was being manipulated by Mocang Epang. Li Tao, following Sima Guang's record of the dispute, reports under the second month of 1057:

> Thus the enemy have encroached and plowed [the disputed land] for a long time, happily considering it their own fields. Further, the income obtained therefrom all goes back to their chieftain Mizang Etepeng. Therefore when [Zhang] Anshi and others have pressed them, they become belligerent; when [Anshi et al.] treat them gently, they refuse to leave. The Pacification Office has repeatedly marked the old border and notified [the Xia] to cause them to return the seized fields. Etepeng's younger sister sent her personal trusted retainer Jiayike to come and inspect them. Returning, he reported that the plowed land was all Han territory, so it was ordered to return [the land]. Just as Etepeng was about to return the seized lands, Jiayike created a disturbance and was executed, while the empress died. Etepeng luckily was able to relax [and not return the land].²⁹

What a coincidence that Jiayike, who must be Qitejile/Jiduoji, and the empress should be eliminated just as Epang was about to lose his lucrative Quye properties. The implication of this passage is clear: The empress had the authority and the means to make her brother comply with her demands, so that his only recourse was to have her and her ally killed. Wu Guangcheng, drawing upon an unknown source (which probably reflects popular traditions) or his imagination, relates that one day the empress and Jiduoji went hunting in the Helan Mountains. Upon their return to the capital that evening, they were ambushed and slain by several dozen mounted tribesmen.[30]

The death of the empress dowager left the border dispute alive and nine-year-old Liangzuo at the mercy of his uncle, who married his daughter to the young monarch to secure his position as the power behind the throne. In 1057 his attacks on Song border outposts led to a suspension of frontier markets in Shaanxi and Hedong and heightened tensions between the two states. Yet, at the same time the Tangut court evidently requested another copy of the Tripiṭaka.

A Song edict dated to the twelfth month of the second year of Jiayou (early 1058) informed the Xia court that its request for a copy of the Buddhist canon would be fulfilled at the next New Year celebration in Jiayou 4 (a year later).[31] The Tangut court sought this copy of the canon, the edict reveals, on behalf of a newly built monastery (possibly, but not necessarily, the Chengtian Temple). As Buddhist institutions expanded in Xia, demand for access to the Tripiṭaka intensified, and the Song court was still the only source. An interesting question is, Who initiated the 1058 request? Mocang Epang, as the apparent power at court? Or the youthful emperor, acting in concert with Buddhist allies (of his mother)?[32] It seems likely that Yizong resented his domineering uncle and was marshaling support for a palace coup.

That coup took place early in 1061, when Yizong (I will now refer to Liangzuo as Yizong to distinguish him from the Liangs) was fifteen. Befriending the unhappy wife of Epang's son, Lady Liang, and allying himself with other disgruntled courtiers, Yizong raised a force to murder Epang and exterminate his clan, including the daughter Epang had married to him. Lady Liang became his new wife, and her brother Liang Yimai took Mocang Epang's place.[33] Exit the Mocang, enter the Liang.

Shen Kuo, an eleventh-century Song scholar and statesman who served as military commissioner of Fuyan Circuit, Shaanxi, from 1080 to 1082, claims that the Liang was a Chinese clan.[34] But the Liang name was also attached to the ruling Dangchang clan, sixth-century ancestors of the Tanguts in the Kokonor region, and to seventh-century Tuyühun princes, and there is no reason to suppose that the eleventh-century Liang were anything but Tangut in culture, language (which does not preclude a knowledge of Chinese), and identity.[35]

Lady Liang's devotion to Buddhism is relatively well documented for the reign of Yizong's successor, her son, but not before then, as the sources focus exclusively on Yizong as historical actor. Yizong's recorded actions, until his death at the end of 1067, reveal a passionate ambition to enhance the prestige of the dynasty and to consolidate the power of the throne. No doubt the Liangs were also concerned with the prestige of Xia abroad, but their ambition lay in consolidating their own power, which led them to champion different conceptions of the "state." Buddhism played an important role in these various struggles and in the cultural life of the court.[36]

The Song court agreed to print a fifth copy of the Tripiṭaka for the Tanguts in 1062.[37] Yizong submitted the 1062 request with a series of other demands presented to the Song court, clearly aiming to fortify his power vis-à-vis Tangut tribal-military elites, whose leader he had just eliminated, and to raise the prestige of Xia vis-à-vis Liao and the Tanguts' bitter rivals the Kokonor Tibetans. Snubbing a Xia request of 1054 to renew their marital alliance, in 1058 the Khitans instead married a princess to Dongzhan, the third son and eventual successor of Tibetan leader Gusiluo.[38] A year later the Song court elevated the seating of Tibetan envoys at court banquets to match that of the Tanguts.[39] Yizong tried to cultivate closer ties with Liao as leverage over Song, and simultaneously to compete at the Song court for diplomatic parity with Liao (which would have elevated Xia above the recently promoted Tibetans). Liao protocol after 1055 dictated that all Khitan officials wear Chinese dress for major events; thus Yizong's move in 1061 to replace Tangut with Chinese costume at his court may have been a step in his program to catch up with Liao.[40] Yizong's 1061–1062 wish list to the Song court therefore included permission to use Han rites and dress to greet Song envoys (granted), permission to buy Chinese official clothing (granted) and books (the classics, Tang histories, *Cifu yuan gui,* and so on [some granted]), an imperial princess in marriage (denied owing to surname exogamy, for Song had formally given the Tangut royal family the Zhao surname), permission to change his surname (denied), and skilled artisans (denied).[41] Besides the Buddhist canon, Song sent copies of the nine classics, commentaries, *Mengzi,* and some medical books.[42]

If Yizong's various reforms, campaigns, and foreign policy initiatives all strove to bolster the prestige of his court in one way or another, what about his Buddhist activities? The record is sparse. Later gazetteers list temples that tradition attributes to his reign.[43] We know that just a month before Yizong's death at the end of 1067, the Liao court (then at the Southern Capital, Yanjing) received a Xia embassy that presented Uighur monks, a golden Buddha (statue), and a "Sanskrit sūtra on enlightenment" *(fan jue jing)*.[44] As discussed above, relations with the Khitans had been cool. We can view the presentation of Buddhist treasures in 1067 as placing the Xia throne in the position of a generous patron (as well as an ambitious vassal) bestowing valuable gifts. Perhaps these Uighur monks came from Central Asia and were escorted by Tangut envoys to the Liao court; the statue and sūtra may in fact have been "obtained" from them for offering to the Khitan emperor. Such authentic Indian Buddhist treasures, then, served as a form of political capital.

Yizong died, probably of battle wounds, at the end of 1067 or early in 1068, at age twenty-one *sui*, and was succeeded by his seven-*sui*-old son, Bingchang (Huizong, r. 1068–1086).[45] In the eighth month of 1069 the empress dowager Liang petitioned Song, in the new emperor's name, to restore Tangut *(fan)* rites.[46] In so doing, did Yizong's widow signal that she and her allies identified with and resolved to uphold Yuanhao's legacy, as opposed to Yizong's "revisionism"? What did this legacy mean to the Liang empress dowager, to her clan, and to the court? Both Yuanhao and his son fought for strong central authority under Weiming control. Yizong's adoption of Han rites, in a departure from his father's policy, was clearly prompted by the need to reassert Xia's declining standing in the international arena.

Yuanhao initiated the use of Tangut court rituals, costumes, and hairstyle, the translation of Buddhist sūtras, and so on, as part of a program to define a cultural identity independent from and often in defiance of Song/Chinese prescriptions, to which the Tanguts were self-consciously indebted. In the process of promoting his nativizing and centralizing measures, he made numerous enemies. Many members of the ruling clan, in particular, resented Yuanhao's autocratic exercise of power and cavalier treatment of noble women; they saw their best interests served by cultivating good relations with Song. They did not view the use of Han rites as compromising their cultural identity if it assured their preeminence. But these inclinations met stiff resistance among other sectors of the Tangut military elite, whom Yuanhao had assuaged by challenging and defeating both Song and Liao on the battlefield. After the great founder's death, use of Tangut, as opposed to Han, rites came to signal a power-sharing arrangement that subordinated the Weiming to consort clan control and gave significant autonomy to the military elites in return for their loyalty (to the Weiming throne? the Liang regency? the Xia "state"?). Yizong and his successor, Huizong, expressed their desire to alter this arrangement by replacing Tangut with Han rites.

Huizong's attempts at self-assertion confirmed the regency's fears of independent Weiming initiative. Chafing against Liang domination, sometime in 1080 eighteen-year-old Huizong insisted on reinstating Han rites, against the strong opposition of his mother, the chief minister, and other Liang allies.[47] Aside from court costume and so forth, we are not sure what these rites involved or who objected to which particular detail of protocol and why. At one level, they pitted the youthful (although legally of age) and isolated Weiming emperor against his Liang relatives. But this was not all.

In 1081, the young emperor precipitated a massive Song invasion of Xia when word leaked out of his alleged plotting with a Chinese favorite to kill Liang Yimai and turn over the southern Ordos to Song. Liang Yimai moved first, and the young monarch barely escaped an ambush at a banquet.[48] A certain symmetry exists between Huizong's actions and those of his father twenty years earlier, although the outcomes diverged dramatically. Huizong bungled his bid for power and ended up in a dungeon. Temporary incarceration of the emperor rallied the loyal opposition and gave Song armies a long-awaited excuse to march north and punish the usurpers of legitimate Xia authority in the war of 1081–1085, which I call the Yuanfeng campaign, after the Song era name.

However divided, the Tanguts nevertheless foiled the invaders' assumptions of easy victory and effectively cooperated to defend their land against the devastation wreaked by Song armies from 1081 to 1083. Song actions in the war lent historical as well as cosmological resonance to the protective powers of the Gantong Stūpa described in the 1094 stele inscription. When one Song army reached Lingzhou in midwinter of 1081, an officer remarked that only several hundred monks and Daoist priests *(seng dao)* remained in the city, implying that it would be easy to take.[49] But perhaps these religious technicians were chanting potent spells as they busied themselves dismantling the Yellow River dikes to flood the Song camps, forcing the Chinese to retreat in icy disarray.

The Xia court, under the empress dowager Liang, presented its sixth and final request for a copy of the Song Buddhist canon in 1073 (the twelfth month of Xining 5).[50] The Tanguts, like the Koreans, sought expanded and updated versions of the canon, containing the new Esoteric works translated by the Indian monks described in the previous chapter. Revisions of the original Kaibao canon, for which blocks were carved between 971 and 983, were made in the Xianping era (999–1004), the Tianxi era (1017–1022), and the Xining era (1069–1078).[51] In 1073 the Tanguts requested the most recent version: "An edict to the Xia ruler: [I] have perused your memorandum 'requesting to receive at exchange value one set of Buddhist canon, along with markers, cases, and wrappings *(qian zhi fu pa)* and altogether the new and old translated sacred texts.'"[52] This text of the Xia letter and Song response goes on to quote another concern of the Tanguts: "And [we] fervently hope that Your Majesty will be compassionate and specially issue a decree ordering the responsible officials to verify that no listed volumes have been omitted." Missing titles may have been another reason why the Xia court repeatedly requested copies of the Song canon.

The year 1073 is interesting in several other connections. Diplomatic exchanges with Song, although wary, remained regular throughout the early 1070s. It is not clear when the requested Buddhist texts were delivered, but later in 1073 the Tanguts tightened the fortifications at Liangzhou, purportedly fearing attack by Song armies. This information on the Tangut defenses was gleaned from two Tangut soldiers who had defected across the border and conveyed to Song Shenzong, whose conversation with Wang Anshi on preparing for a campaign against the "Western people" indicates that Tangut fears of a planned Song invasion were well founded as early as 1073.[53] The eventual attack on Liangzhou in 1082, part of the Yuanfeng campaign discussed above, was successfully repelled owing, of course, to the protective powers of its local guardian, the Gantong Stūpa.

The first Xia inscriptions from the Yulin caves, south of Anxi and east of Dunhuang, are also dated to 1073. This site, not the more famous Mogao caves at Dunhuang, became the center of Tangut devotional activity in the dedication, carving, and decoration of Buddhist shrines. Caves 15 and 16 preserve two identical inscriptions in Chinese, each twenty-one lines long.[54] Sponsored by a Chinese monk from the Ayuwang (Aśoka) Temple, with a group of disciples and lay donors, the inscription is dedicated to Maitreya, a large statue of whom graces the cave to this day, and to rebirth in Tuṣita Heaven, over which this future buddha presides. These inscriptions provide some of our earliest evidence of the Tangut presence in the Dunhuang area and affirm the interest of Xia Buddhists in the Aśokan legacy and in Maitreya. Although the inscription does not reveal the location of this particular Ayuwang Temple, it does indicate that the sponsor had some connection with the official Buddhist establishment. Line 13 prays for long life to the emperor and the empress dowager, blessings to the officials, contentment of the masses in their occupations, and so on. Tangut patronage of Buddhism and local Buddhists may have played a key role in the extension and acceptance of Xia authority over Dunhuang. By 1073 this process was in full swing. At the same time, it is significant that Xia Buddhists chose the Yulin caves and not those at Dunhuang as the focus of their religious initiatives, a choice perhaps born of necessity, given the long-established Uighur presence at Dunhuang and the Mogao caves.

Translation of Buddhist texts into Tangut proceeded systematically throughout the latter half of the century and by 1094 had produced 3,579 rolls (*juan*), about two-thirds the size of the Song canon, according to the 1312 vow attached to the Yuan publication in Tangut of the *Guoqu zhuangyan qie qian foming jing* ("Sūtra on the Thousand Buddha Names of the Past Ornamented Kalpa"), quoted in Chapter 2.[55] Although the throne sponsored the production of a Tangut Tripiṭaka, "private" editions of sūtras in Chinese and Tangut also appeared in Xia, with prefaces composed by monks or officials.[56] Since the most intense phase of translation occurred during the last three decades of the eleventh century, the dowager empresses Liang emerge as key sponsors of the work. This sponsorship is reflected in extant colophons to Tangut sūtras or on the title page of sūtra chapters, where typically the title and name of the empress dowager appear first, followed by the title and name of the emperor, and finally in many cases the title and name of the emperor Renzong (r. 1139–1193), who later oversaw the editing and revision of many earlier translations.[57]

The Saṅgha under the Regency

Several Tangut documents from the period shed light on the development of the official Buddhist establishment and the throne's relationship to it. The mid-twelfth-century Tangut law code outlines the bureaucratic structures of the official Buddhist establishment, but a *gongde si* (Office of Merit, or Saṅgha Office, as I call it) is first attested in the 1094 inscription (T2; see Chapter 5), and must already have been in existence for some time.

From the undated Tangut preface to the *Cibei daochang chanfa* ("Method for [Conducting] Repentance in a Ritual Site of Compassion")[58] composed by Huizong (r. 1068–1086) and his mother we learn:

> A ruler must forbear the people's comings and goings, and because they are his subjects, instruct and restrain [them]. [Yet] in governing evil arises, [so] the Buddha appeared and by means of compassion guided, saved, and uplifted [beings]. From India the dharma of the first sage [i.e., Śākyamuni] appeared and was transmitted throughout the world, and reaching the eastern countries, holy monks translated and disseminated religious texts. I have observed all kinds of people; owing to avarice, anger, and ignorance, desires arise everywhere; [people] fail to distinguish real and empty, and grasp at the phenomenal and noumenal. Because [they] stubbornly do not relinquish [their desires], they die and are reborn in the stream of transmigration of this world and constantly dwell in a sea of vexations. None enjoys any peace, yet [they] say that this is real happiness. Not cultivating virtuous attainments, they do not realize that they will have cheated themselves in the life after. I cause this "Repentance" to be recited; having compassion for sentient beings, [I] established a Canonical Institute, summoned monks [to it], and among all the dharma [texts] to be translated, choose this "Repentance of Sin" text first among all the other dharmas. A sage of eloquence[59] harmonized the meanings, and produced [a work of] ten chapters. Its awesome import is outstanding, its parables on the merit of grace are subtle. As when the sun sends forth rays of light, there is no place where the dew does not melt. When one confesses relying on compassion, are there any karmic deeds that are not destroyed? Desiring to cultivate the tree's roots, in no case is having water not beneficial to growth; desiring to achieve the true path, in no case does surrendering the heart [to the dharma] not achieve it. The merit of the confession method is broad, and the explication of meaning in this preface does not illuminate it [i.e., does not do it justice]. Now [I] urge sentient beings not to neglect the cultivation of good works and to transmit this dharma constantly.[60]

The royal author of this preface (using the imperial pronoun "I") takes credit for the translation of the text. I am not sure how we should understand the claim that he (or she) established a Canonical

Institute (Chin. *jingyuan*), since presumably the institutional apparatus for translating texts already existed. Perhaps, however, the empress dowager was speaking through her son here and publicizing her patronage of the Saṅgha, formalizing and expanding its activities. If so viewed, the piece may date to the early part of Huizong's reign (early 1070s), when the empress assumed full power as regent following Yizong's death. Her institutional measures may have regularized previously informal arrangements and brought the translation of texts under the direct supervision of the court, rather than of individual temples or monasteries, as earlier evidence has suggested. Thus, this text points to a key development in the centralization of the Buddhist establishment under the empress dowager Liang. It is also a nice expression of the throne's concerns for the spiritual welfare of its subjects.

A wider window on the empress dowager's Buddhist activities and the evolving institutional framework for them survives in a blockprint illustration to the Yuan woodblock edition of the Tangut translation of *Xianzai xian qie qian foming jing* ("Sūtra on the Thousand Buddha Names of the Present Bhadra Kalpa"), portraying the attendance of the emperor and his mother at a session of the sūtra translation bureau, perhaps the very agency mentioned above (see frontispiece).[61] Eleven of the twenty-five persons depicted in the blockprint are identified in cartouches. The emperor and the empress dowager, each flanked by three attendants, sit in the foreground, at the bottom of the picture, on either end of an altar laden with offerings. A figured textile lies across the center of the altar, its end draping down the front over two layers of ruffled material cascading from the altar's edge. In front of the altar a small black dog chases a diminutive white lion-like creature, providing a further decorative element in this elaborate composition.

Above and behind the imperial pair four monks to the left and four to the right sit cross-legged before benches on which lie pens, paper, and texts. Behind each monk stands a lay assistant, among whom the upper left hand figure wears different attire from the others. The opening of his robe crosses in a V-shape in front, as do the robes worn by the imperial figures, whereas the other lay figures all display rounded collars and a seam down the center front of their robes. Moreover, the monk behind whom he stands, Cao Guangzhi, also wears distinctive robes. At the very least we can suppose that these figures ranked above their fellows. The eight monks are all highly individualized in features.

In the upper central portion of the picture, facing the altar, the presiding monk sits in lotus posture; a cartouche above his head identifies him as the Anquan ("Calm and Complete"?) State Preceptor *(guoshi)* Bai Zhiguang.[62] Behind him stands a tripartite screen, its two wings folded back, with a Chinese-style landscape painting across its panels. The tiny floral print of the drapery hanging across the top corners of the illustration is repeated in Bai Zhiguang's short sleeved robe. In front of him is a bench equipped with pens, ink, and a text. Between his work bench and the altar stands another table draped with an intricately patterned textile, on which sit five piles, each resting on a lotus base and surrounded by a mandorla. Three piles are unquestionably sacred texts; the other two piles look like leaves, one of which has two thongs encircling it.

Fortunately, we can say more about this high prelate. In the preceding chapter I quoted a 1312 preface to the Tangut translation of the *Guoqu zhuangyan qie qian foming jing* ("Sūtra on the Thousand Buddha Names of the Past Ornamented Kalpa"), which reads: "The Feng emperor of the Xia state newly implemented rites and virtuous examples. In the *xu yan* year [1038] the State Preceptor *(guoshi)* Bai Faxin, the . . . [?] official Zhiguang, et al., in all thirty-two people were put in charge of translating [sūtras] into Tangut."[63] It is certain that the Zhiguang mentioned here as a monastic official charged with supervising the translation of Buddhist texts went on to become a state preceptor and perhaps head of the Saṅgha or Buddhist establishment. The preface to a 1247 Tangut edition of the *Jin guangming zuisheng wang jing* (*Suvarṇaprabhāsottamarāja-sūtra*, "Sūtra on the Golden Light All-Conquering King") lists Bai Zhiguang as the first to translate this sūtra from Chinese into Tangut at the order of Huizong and the first empress Liang, with whom he is depicted in the blockprint.[64] In the "Sūtra on the Golden Light All-Conquering King" his title appears as Anquan State Preceptor of the Liberation Tripiṭaka (Chin. *dujie sanzang anquan guoshi*). Bai Zhiguang's full title in the blockprint includes the designation of "chief translation officer" (Chin. *duyi gouguan zuozhe*). His prominence is highlighted by his portrayal as the largest figure in the composition; the eight seated monks are somewhat smaller, the emperor and the empress dowager and eight lay attendants are smaller still, and the imperial attendants are the smallest figures in the picture. State Preceptor Bai Zhiguang thus dominates the proceedings, while the imperial visitors occupy only a modest position at the bottom of the illustration. He appears to be in the act of praying, expounding, or translating; some of the attending monks have their pens poised for composing.

The cartouches containing the imperial titles identify the pair as the "mother empress dowager Liang" and "her son" (Huizong), here referred to by his shortened honorary title of *daming huangdi* ("emperor of great enlightenment").[65] The emperor appears as a young man with a beard, suggesting that the blockprint was executed sometime in the early 1080s, after his twentieth birthday, either before or after the disastrous events of 1081–1082.

This rare imperial portrait testifies to the piety of the empress dowager, just as the 1094 stele inscription expresses the piety of her niece and successor, the second Empress Liang, wife of Huizong and mother of Chongzong (r. 1086–1139). These sources suggest further that the empresses and their imperial sons received consecration and took the bodhisattva vows, which do not require entrance into a monastic community and hence are available to lay persons. For instance, line 13 of the Tangut text of the 1094 inscription tells us that in undertaking repairs to the Gantong Stūpa, the throne acted in accordance with the six *pāramitās* (perfections enabling one to cross over to the other shore, i.e., achieve salvation) and the "four great vows," which were taken by all bodhisattvas.[66] Hence, in the preface to the *Cibei daochang chanfa* quoted above, the throne expresses its concern to foster conditions for the salvation of all sentient beings, the first great vow of a bodhisattva, through the translation and dissemination of this text.

Available evidence indicates that the eleventh-century Saṅgha was already sizable and ethnically diverse, and in the twelfth century it was to grow much larger. Of the eight monks named in the engraving to the *Xianzai xianqie qian foming jing*, four bear Tangut surnames (Beique, Weiming, Xiyu, Lubu) and four may be Chinese (Zhao, Hao, Cao, Tian).[67] We saw how in 1081 Lingzhou was evacuated but for several hundred monks. In the 1094 ceremonies at the Gantong Stūpa thirty-eight monks were ordained (T17/H13); a hundred years later at a ceremony commemorating Renzong's death, three thousand monks were ordained.[68] Most numerous, probably, were Chinese and Tanguts, although Uighur, Tibetan, and Indian monks also appear, especially in twelfth-century materials.

Only a few texts with names and dates survive from the earlier period. The earliest-dated printed sūtra in the St. Petersburg collection is a Tangut translation *Foshuo Amituo jing* (*Sukhāvatīamṛtavyūha-sūtra*, or the "Smaller Sukhāvatīvyūha Sūtra"), with a colophon dated to the eighth month of the eleventh year of Da'an (1084) of "the Great State of White and High," which mentions two monks and two woodblock engravers.[69] The lesser-ranked of the two monks was Liang Zhihui. Zhihui is a common enough clerical name; his clan name of Liang suggests that this monk-scribe may have been a relative of the empress dowager (who died two months later).

A blockprinted edition of *Weimoji suo shuo jing* (*Vimalakīrtinirdeśa-sūtra*, "The Sūtra Spoken by Vimalakīrti"), dated to 1106, about which see below lists the names and titles of the first Empress Liang, Huizong, and two monks.[70] One, the translator Guangzhi, must be the same Cao Guangzhi who appears as one of the eight monks depicted and named in the blockprint illustration of the translation bureau.

What kind of relations developed between monks and the emperor? The hieratic scale of figures depicted in the woodblock illustration discussed above and reproduced as the frontispiece to this book suggests an attitude of imperial reverence toward the leading cleric in the Saṅgha, and that the Saṅgha occupied a relatively high status in relation to its patrons, the highest-ranking personages in the state. Perhaps here we see again the hand of the empress dowager, yet this attitude of imperial reverence also characterizes the later-twelfth-century materials. Thus the high status and close relationship with the emperor that clerics enjoyed in the later twelfth and early thirteenth centuries have roots in the earlier, formative period.

We know from the 1094 stele inscription that the emperor had one or more clerical tutors, an association that surely began no later than at age seven. At the same time, the emperor's education must also have included military training, probably under his mother or her closest lieutenants. Aside from the ritual and educational activities of the throne, high-ranking monks at the capital played a vital role in imperial preparations for military campaigns or defense against attacks by foreign armies (T11). Possibly clerical officials also had a hand in bestowing on the regent and emperor the honorary titles preserved on the title pages of many sūtra chapters.

From the preface of the repentance text, *Cibei daochang chanfa*,[71] the following titles represent a literal Chinese rendering of the Tangut, in order of appearance: (1) *tiansheng quanneng fanlu fashi guozheng huang taihou Liang shi* ("born of Heaven, all-capable, securing prosperity for the Tanguts, taking the Law [or Dharma] as pattern, rectifying the state Empress Dowager Liang"); (2) *decheng guozhu fusheng minzheng mingda huangdi Weiming* ("accomplished virtue, lord of the state, multiplying merit, rectifying the people, great illumination Emperor Weiming)." A slighly longer version of these titles appears in the Tangut translation of *Foshuo yueguang pusa jing* (*Candraprabha-bodhisattvacaryāvadāna-sūtra*, "The Sūtra of Moonlight Bodhisattva").[72] Again I offer a literal Chinese rendering of the Tangut, highlighting the variations: (1) *tiansheng quanneng fanlu* sheng you *fashi* beihe *guozheng huang taihou* ("born of Heaven, all-capable, securing prosperity for the Tanguts, *sagely support*, taking the Law as pattern, *in accord with compassion*, rectifying the state empress dowager"); (2) *decheng guozhu* zhiguang fusheng minzheng shouyi *mingda huangdi* ("accomplished virtue, lord of the state, *broad wisdom*, multiplying merit, rectifying the people, *extending life*, great illumination emperor").

Empress Dowager Liang's honorifics lay claim to some rather special qualities that clearly place her in a superior position relative to her son. Particularly interesting is the phrase *fanlu*, which I have rendered "securing prosperity for the Tanguts." The Tangut graph corresponding to *fan* is one of two common ethnonyms used by the Tanguts (the other is the better-known *mi*, also translated by Chinese *fan*). This phrase acknowledges that the empress dowager and her policies benefit and protect the Tangut peoples and their Weiming ruler, implicitly from encroachments mainly by Chinese and Chinese culture. Her restoration of Tangut court ritual was one of those policies. Where Xia Chinese fit in here is not clear. It is clear that the empress dowager saw herself as a champion of Tangut interests, and that her supporters at court bestowed this title on her in recognition of her service to those interests. It is also likely that not all Tanguts agreed with her vision of the Tangut enterprise.

In many senses the religious and political connotations in the titles are inextricable, and literate contemporaries would not miss the nuances of meanings conveyed. In the longer title of the empress, *beihe* evokes the pity or compassion that an aspiring bodhisattva feels for all beings in distress. The emperor's corresponding title adds the phrase *zhiguang*, broad wisdom, evoking the other key characteristic of a bodhisattva.

In the emperor's title, we note that he "rectifies the people" *(minzheng)* while his mother "rectifies the state" *(guozheng)*; in other words, the emperor set a moral example for the people while his mother took care of state affairs, a role properly played by a sage minister, in the Confucian scheme of things. For the emperor moral perfection had another dimension and goal: the achievement of enlightenment and the fulfillment of his Buddhist vows. Thus he must accomplish virtue *(decheng)*, make abundant merit or good works *(fusheng)*, strive for broad wisdom *(zhiguang)*, extend life to all sentient beings *(shouyi)*, and become greatly illuminated *(mingda)*.

Compared with these titles, those recorded for Huizong's son and successor, Chongzong (r. 1086–1139), and Chongzong's mother, Huizong's wife and Liang Yimai's daughter, seem somewhat subdued. This generation came to power in 1085–1086, following the deaths in 1085 of first Liang Yimai, who as chief minister was succeeded in office by his son Qibu, and then his sister, who was succeeded by her niece, Qibu's sister. Huizong died in 1086, completing the transition (see Genealogy of Eleventh-Century Xia Dynastic Alliances). The Tangut translation of *Bijuzhi pusa yibaiba ming jing* ("Sūtra on the One Hundred Eight Names of Bhṛkutī Bodhisattva"[73]) lists the following titles: (1) *zhisheng luguang minzhi liji desheng huang taihou* ("surpassing in wisdom, expanding prosperity, ordering the people, assembling [completing] ritual,[74] abundant in virtue empress dowager"); (2) *shengong shenglu dejiao minzhi renjing huangdi* ("divine merit, surpassing prosperity, transforming by virtue, ordering the people, humane and pure emperor"). We do not have a longer variant of these titles. Little here suggests the Buddhist ardor or military exploits of the regent and the monarch, which are elaborated in the 1094 Gantong Stūpa inscription. Since that inscription cites the short form of these titles, *desheng huang taihou* (T10, graphs 45–46) and *renjing huangdi* (T10, graphs 52–53), we can assume that the titles were bestowed before 1094. On the same basis we can date the publication of this sūtra to the late 1080s or early 1090s.

All of these titles reveal a desire to be seen (read) and acknowledged (remembered) as being concerned with bringing order and material (as well as spiritual or moral) well-being to their subjects, challenging tasks under the prevailing circumstances of political infighting, military emergency, and economic stringency. The preface to the *Cibei daochang chanfa*, cited above, hints strongly at these preoccupations of the throne and its responses to the challenges.

The *Cibei daochang chanfa* remained a prominent text in the second Liang regency. It may have featured in the ceremonies commemorating completion of repairs to the Gantong Stūpa at Liangzhou in 1094.[75] The Tangut edition of this text has a blockprint depicting the Liang emperor Wudi (r. 502–550) conducting a repentance ceremony based on this text, which was compiled at his court and is hence popularly known as "Emperor Liang's Precious Repentance" *(Lianghuang baochan)*.⁷⁶ Liang Wudi was undoubtedly the most famous Chinese emperor who pursued a public career as a bodhisattva, which would make him an appealing figure for later like-minded rulers and the Buddhist monks at their court. The coincidental identity of surname might have tickled the vanity of Empress Dowager Liang, but the prefatory explanation of the text's origins may have impressed her even more. When Wudi's empress Xi died, in punishment for killing someone in a jealous rage she sank on the ladder of transmigration to the level of a snake. To rescue his suffering wife from such a bitter rebirth, Wudi summoned his dharma masters to compile a repentance text as an offering of merit. The offering was received and secured a raise in Lady Xi's karmic status, thus confirming the potency of the text and its salvific powers. Devotion to and spread of this dharma will turn evil into blessings, provide escape from a bad rebirth, dispel darkness, and benefit all sentient beings with its immeasurable merit.⁷⁷ What could have been more apposite to a regent and throne in crisis?

The Monarchy in Political and Spiritual Crisis

The empresses dowager Liang, protectors of the throne and its juvenile occupants, must have felt a strong need for all the spiritual potency they could muster. Relentless foreign subversion and encroachment on their border fortifications, invasions by Song and allied armies, mounting economic devastation left in the wake of war, a suffering and restive populace, fractious military chiefs, and overbearing older brothers defined the world they moved in. The second regent had strong reason to fear that she might be made to pay the price for Tangut afflictions.

In the beginning she enjoyed a brief normalization of relations with Song, including a resumption of annual subsidies and trade, and the return of several forts. Most important, the second empress dowager–regent Liang, evidently a young woman in her twenties, inherited the military prerogative and army commands of her aunt and was trained and determined to exercise them, for her own sake, but also to protect her three-year-old son, the new emperor Chongzong.⁷⁸ In part over this issue, open disagreement soon split the Liang regency.

One sign of the growing power struggle was the Xia court's failure to send an envoy to thank Song for its certificate of investiture for

Chongzong until early in 1089, two years after receipt of the Song investiture envoys.[79] From the late 1080s through the early 1090s, moreover, the Tanguts kept raiding key sites to vent frustration with the Song refusal to settle the border and return certain territories recently captured by Song, especially around Lanzhou. During these years the Song was expanding border defenses and intelligence operations against Xia, trying to determine when Liang Qibu would fall, and taking over the "good fields of the westerners."[80] At the Tanguts' repeated requests, border talks did take place on several occasions in 1090–1091, albeit without conclusive results.[81] In winter of 1091 the Song decided to use the annual Xia subsidy to fund rewards for border troops in Hedong and Shaanxi, and a Song officer led troops on a raid in Tangut territory.[82] Repeated warnings to border officials in 1092 to restrain their soldiers suggests mounting support for the Song military to go on the offensive again.[83] The surrender, defection, or capture of Tangut warriors and tribespeople swelled alarmingly. Repeatedly the Tangut court sent envoys to Liao requesting Khitan intercession with Song to negotiate peace.[84] In the tenth month of 1092 the empress dowager herself led troops into Huanzhou.[85]

By the end of 1091 border dispatches back to the Song court were already reporting the death of Liang Qibu,[86] but his name was still circulating in 1092. The fate of Liang Qibu is intertwined with the inscription to the Gantong Stūpa, erected in the first month of 1094. At some point in 1093 or 1094 Qibu was finally assassinated by a coalition of Weiming supporters, with at least the tacit cooperation of the empress dowager, whose power he was challenging. His cruelty, vanity, and belligerence, we are told, made him intolerable to just about everyone.[87] But when exactly did he die? Standard histories of Xia follow Wu Guangcheng's account of Qibu's death in the tenth month of 1094.[88] In the absence of credible sources and based on a close reading of the stele inscription, my sense is that his demise predated 1094.

Both texts of the 1094 inscription (T 16–17, H22) refer to a high official, director of the Secretariat Liang Xingzhenie, holder of the rank *huai wo le* ("completed [precepts]"),[89] equivalent to that of great prince (Chin. *da guowang*, Tang. *ling ning ling*; see H22). Shen Kuo reports that Liang Qibu was called *mo ning ling*, which he glosses as *tian dawang* (heavenly great prince).[90] The differences in names and titles alone, however, make it difficult to treat these two figures as one and the same. I am more inclined to see in Liang Xingzhenie the successor to Liang Qibu (if the latter ever even held the office of director of the Secretariat). Further, I can imagine the empress dowager appointing as her brother's successor not a nephew, but a more distant relative, one amenable to her court and to the Weiming. He probably did not exercise much more than ceremonial power.

The restoration of the Gantong Stūpa at the Huguo Temple in Liangzhou occurred during a brief lull in the hostilities with Song, during which for roughly two years (1093–1094) regular tribute and gift exchanges with the Song court resumed.[91] Despite the stringent circumstances of the times, there must have been other similar undertakings, perhaps on a smaller scale, although only the record in the 1094 inscriptions has by chance survived. The restoration of a stūpa renowned for its salvational qualities benefiting local residents as well as the entire country constituted a dramatic expression of compliance with the bodhisattva vows taken by the empress dowager and the emperor. It also expressed the empress dowager's ability to mobilize economic and spiritual capital to demonstrate and affirm the throne's legitimacy. Yet it cannot have been a unique event.

The public display of imperial piety took a variety of specific forms in the ceremonies celebrating completion of the restoration project, in the religious service and feast, in the amnesty of criminals and the ordination of new monks, in the gifts to the monastery of gold and silver, silk, cash, grain, and bonded households, in rewards to the workers and officers (H 13–14, T 16–18), and finally in the very carving of the inscriptions to perpetuate the record of these admirable deeds. Further, in 1094 the empress dowager and the emperor decreed the printing and distribution of ten thousand copies of a Tangut edition of the *Dacheng sheng wuliangshou jing* (*Amitābha-vyūha*, "Sūtra of the Buddha of Limitless Life"). In a postscript ostensibly written by the young emperor himself, the imperial author describes his vow to have the text translated from Tibetan and carved (on printing blocks).[92]

This sūtra narrates the origins of Amitābha and the forty-eight vows he made while still a bodhisattva, one being to establish a Pure Land. It thus elaborates the notion of the transferability of merit from one person (or bodhisattva, in Amitābha's case) to another struggling to achieve salvation.[93] It was a fitting text to distribute in 1094, in connection with the throne's merit-making activities at the Gantong Stūpa. The 1094 inscription, however, alludes not to Amitābha's Pure Land, but to Maitreya's Tuṣita Heaven (T 20: "From the eighteen hells guilty beings obtain release; to the forty-nine stories [in the heavenly palace] of the happy Maitreya [they] hasten in eagerness"). Evidently the cult of Maitreya coexisted peaceably with worship of Amitābha and his Pure Land. The more heavens one patronized, the better; it increased the odds of a better rebirth for people carrying a heavy load of bad karma.

Whether it occurred before or after the unveiling of the 1094 stele, the destruction of Liang Qibu and his family did not mark the end of Liang influence. The empress dowager still remained a powerful figure, but it appears that she rid herself of her embarrassing and dangerous brother at the cost of cultivating or tolerating a greater Weiming role in government. The names of Weiming and allied Renduo clansmen occur in Li Tao's *Changbian* with greater frequency from the late 1080s onward, indicating that they were active in the military and diplomatic initiatives of these years. Weiming and others were no happier than Liang warriors to surrender territory to Song without a fight; nor did Xia's problems with Song go away following Liang retirement from the scene. The campaign to exterminate Xia that Zhezong's court renewed from 1096 to 1099 posed the gravest threat yet to Tangut survival.

Renewed warfare with Song broke out in 1096; in that year the empress dowager and the emperor together led forces in a retaliatory raid on a Song border fort.[94] In 1097 the Tanguts lost many key towns and forts to Song armies while domestic conditions grew precarious. The defection or capture of several of the Tanguts' most renowned generals threatened the country's defenses. At the end of 1098, shortly after a Song general took by ruse two key Tangut commanders, Chongzong proclaimed an amnesty in response to the appearance of a comet *(huixing)*.[95] The Xia court repeatedly sent envoys to Liao requesting intercession with Song.[96] In 1098–1099 the Khitans were preoccupied with pacifying some distant subject peoples and in fact early in 1099 directed the Tangut emperor to attack one group, the Basimu, perhaps in return for intervening with Song on the Tanguts' behalf.[97] The empress dowager Liang led armies against the Song until her death in the beginning of 1099, but apparently neither she nor any other military leader at court responded to the Liao demand. Rumor had it that she was poisoned by a Liao agent; if she did not die of wounds sustained in battle, she almost certainly fell victim to a palace coup.[98]

By 1099 the Song had pushed its defense perimeter deep enough into Tangut territory to halt and make concessions to possible Liao fears of excessive Song encroachment on its client state.[99] The death of the empress dowager at the beginning of the year also signaled the end of an era. Two of her closest officers were executed upon Song demand; other Liang allies probably met a similar fate or may have numbered among the Xia defectors recorded in Song sources at this time.

What did all of this mean to the Buddhist establishment? In the midst of these mortal crises, we recall that the Saṅgha was completing a first "draft" translation of the Buddhist canon into Tangut, surely its most notable contribution to defending the state. Meanwhile, relations with the Qingtang Tibetans, under the pressure of the Song advance into Kokonor, had shifted from open hostility to a complex set of competing alliances among the various political factions in both Qingtang and Xia. Dongzhan died in 1086 and was succeeded by his adopted son, Aligu (d. 1096), who allied himself with Liang Qibu and was not popular in Qingtang. Trade and cultural exchanges flourished, and Tangut translations of Buddhist texts were made from Tibetan as well as Chinese versions. In the twelfth century when the Tangut canon underwent revision and expansion, it absorbed many new texts translated from Tibetan. Surely some of these texts and their translators passed through Kokonor on the way to Xia. Without going into detail about the intricate relationships that developed between Xia and the Kokonor Tibetans from the 1070s onward, it is nevertheless possible to shed light on the situation at Qingtang as revealed in Chinese sources documenting the Song conquest of the main settlements along the Huang River.

The Qingtang Nexus

Song armies marched up the valley of the Huang River in 1099 to secure the surrender of the towns of Miaochuan, Tsongkha, and Qingtang (subsequently renamed Shanzhou, then Xining in 1104); Tibetan resistance (with Tangut backing) made occupation and control virtually impossible.[100] Aligu's successor in Qingtang became the Miaochuan candidate Longcan, who contracted a marriage alliance with the Tangut royal house in 1102. Chinese accounts of the 1099 and 1104 surrender of Qingtang afford an intriguing glimpse of the complexion of the city.

In 1099, "the bogus ruler *(weizhu)* of Qingtang, Longcan, and the great chieftains ... led all the tribal chieftains and all the various Han and Fan groups *(buluozi),* the Uighurs, and the Khitan, Tangut, and Uighur princesses, and so on, together and came out of the town to tender submission."[101] In 1100 Longcan, his rival Xiazheng

(Aligu's son by the Tangut princess? see below), and the various princesses and chieftains were all presented at court in ranked order, the Khitan princess preceding the Tangut princess, and so on. After interrogation, this group was escorted back to Kokonor. As Dongzhan's wife, the Khitan princess was a senior political figure at Qingtang. Next ranked the Tangut princess, Jinshan, who was first married to Dongzhan's son.[102] When her husband died, she became the wife of Aligu, Dongzhan's adopted son. Aligu's mother was a Khotanese woman who served Dongzhan is some unspecified manner, possibly as a secretary in charge of correspondence with Song, Xia, Khotan, Liao, and others.[103]

In 1104 Qingtang again surrendered to Song:

> Wang Hou and Tong Guan led a great army to Shanzhou. When the army was five *li* east of the city wall, the Kuchean princess..., Qingyijiemou, and the tribal leader Li Awen led the Uighurs and Khotanese *panci* [tribute bearers], and the great and lesser chieftains of all the tribes, and, opening the gates, came out to surrender, and Shanzhou was pacified.[104]

Here we have also a princess from Kucha, said to be the mother of Longcan's younger brother.[105] The warehouses and temples at Qingtang contained a fortune in gold, precious stones, and other goods, some perhaps the wares of Khotanese, Uighur, and Tangut merchants residing in the city. Much of it was looted by the Song commander Wang Dan in 1099.

A short contemporary account, *Qingtang lu* ("Chronicle of Qingtang"), records the observations of Song officer and military expert Li Yuan, who apparently accompanied the Song army in 1099:[106]

> On the sides [of the Qingtang city wall] eight gates open up. In the center lies a separately walled enclosure where the bogus ruler lives. On the city gates two series of watchtowers have been erected; behind the watchtowers is the Central Gate and behind [the Central Gate] lies the Yi Gate. East of the Yi Gate is the residence of the Khitan princess; at its western extremity lies the residence of the Xia princess.
>
> Passing through the Yi Gate [going] north at a distance of over two hundred paces stands the great hall. Its pillars on the north [i.e., behind the dias] are painted yellow, the steps ascend eight feet and are situated over ten feet from the throne. Turquoise-hued glazed tiles encompass it [the throne], and the Qiang call it the "Forbidden Enclosure" *(jinwei)*. All the chieftains who ascend the

hall to make reports stand beyond the glazed tiles; anyone who trespasses is killed.

Next to [the hall] stands a statue of Buddha cast in bronze, several dozens of feet tall, decorated with real gems [lit. "pearls," *zhu*] and a feather canopy. To its west is the site where state ministers conduct business; to its east is the site where the king and his retinue conduct business. West of the great boulevard that extends south of [the great hall] is a three-tiered altar over a *mou* in breadth. Every three years solemn sacrifices to Heaven are made atop of it.

... West of the city is the Qingtang River, which flows into the Zong River. West of the river on a distant plain stands a Buddhist shrine, five or six *li* in expanse, whose twisting walls follow the ridges [of the hills], with cells numbering over a thousand. [They have] made a great statue [of Buddha?] and covered its body with gold. In addition, [they have] made a thirteen-tiered[107] stūpa to protect it. [When] Aligu taxed people to build that statue, people began to express disaffection.

The Tufan esteem monks. Whenever there is important business, they are sure to assemble the monks to reach a decision. When a monk violates the law,[108] there are none who do not get away with it. Of the dwellings in the city, Buddhist hermitages account for half. Only the state hall and Buddhist hermitages [may be decorated with] tiles; as for the rest, even the roof of the ruler's mansion is made of packed earth.

Buddhism was embedded in the political infrastructure of Qingtang and those relations that it cultivated with Song, Xia, Liao, and Central Asia.[109] Despite the momentarily successful Song effort to disrupt the regional network of exchanges centered at Qingtang, a long-standing ecological and cultural logic knit together northern Sichuan, northeastern Qinghai, and southeastern Gansu,[110] and this logic reasserted itself in the twelfth century following the northern Song collapse. We can imagine that Buddhist monks traveled throughout the region, some as spies, diplomats, traders, and consultants; others as teachers and scholars. Many of them most likely ended up at the Tangut court for varying lengths of time. One sign of continued contacts with northern India, central Tibet, and Central Asia in the late eleventh century showed up in an offering of palm leaf sūtra(s) made by the Tangut court to Liao at the end of 1095.[111] Such an item must have been considered quite rare and hence of special value, and recalls earlier (e.g., 1067) Tangut gifts to the Liao court of precious religious objects.

End of an Era

No evidence indicates that any Tangut emperor ever rebelled against or persecuted Buddhism or Buddhist monks as a form of asserting Weiming prerogative.[112] The Buddhists offered tools too potent to disregard. Moreover, the Saṅgha was eager to participate in the imperial project of producing a Xia canon (in Tangut and in Chinese), quite apart from the regent's or emperor's motives in the matter. With the death of the empress dowager Liang in 1099, the Saṅgha lost a powerful patron. Her sixteen-year-old son Chongzong, now ruling under the direct guidance of his clansmen, must have felt deep concern for the state of his maligned mother's progress through the wheel of transmigration, and so carried out on her behalf numerous meritorious deeds. Possibly under his direction, a large block-printed edition of the *Vimalakīrtinirdeśa-sūtra* was published in 1106.[113] Far more intriguing are accounts of the origin of a certain temple in Ganzhou.

Wu Guangcheng's chronicle enters under the year 1103 (Xia, Zhenguan 3) the following item:

> Ever since his mother Lady Liang had died, Qianshun had been making regular offerings to Buddha for his mother's welfare. In Ganzhou a monk, Fajing, saw at night a glow in the foothills of the Ganling Mountains southwest of old Zhangye prefecture. He went digging around and found three old Buddha [images], all reclining Buddhas, and presented them to Qianshun. Qianshun ordered a temple to be erected as an offering to them, and named it Recumbent Buddha.[114]

This is the Wofo si (Recumbent Buddha Temple), or Dafo si (Great Buddha Temple), still standing in Zhangye, with its thirty-five-meter-long reclining Buddha intact and largely unaltered since its construction under Xia, the largest reclining clay Buddha statue in China.[115] The Ganzhou gazetteer gives a somewhat different version of the story, one based on several Ming stele inscriptions dedicated to repairs of the temple in the fifteenth and sixteenth centuries.[116] It preserves an inscription of the Xuande period (1426–1436, the exact year is not specified), composed in the name of the Ming emperor himself, a summary of which follows.

After an opening homage to the Buddha and to Ganzhou as the gateway for the Indian faith's entry into China, the text relates that in the time of Li Qianshun (Weiming Qianshun, Chongzong, r. 1086–

1139), there was a monk surnamed Weimi (Weiming), with the clerical name of Sineng, who was a disciple of State Preceptor Yandan (Yandan guoshi). Sineng achieved a marvelous understanding of the true vehicle; he earned the respect of high and low, feeble and sturdy, and was also called "State Preceptor" (officially? informally? the text is ambiguous). One day while sitting quietly, Sineng sensed something strange and perceived a pure light; he listened closely and, hearing a sound not far away, arose to seek its source. He found it in the nearby foothills (of the Ganling Mountains). After digging in the ground, Sineng eventually unearthed some old images of the Buddha in nirvana. At this point the monk's excellent reputation brought other monks flying to witness this prodigy, proof that Sineng had "buddha-karma." Sineng now referred to as Wei shi (Preceptor Wei), vowed to build a great temple for the images, and the task was accomplished within a year. On the day of completion, a large crowd assembled to admire and pay homage to Sineng's magnificent act of merit.

At that time Yandan, who had gone to India seeking the dharma, came to the border of Bati (?) and saw a stone stele that recorded a past prophecy about the Tathāgata (i.e., the Buddha). It related:

> At Ganquan ["Sweet Springs," said to be a former name of Ganzhou in a preceding passage][117] are remaining traces of Kāśyapa,[118] who will in the coming world of Śākyamuni's dharma realm[119] meet a bodhisattva of the eighth stage,[120] who will manifest the true rites for Kāśyapa's [remains] and carry out great deeds. From this point on, if moreover there be sincere persons of excellent faith who are able with a single flower and a single incense [offering] to revere and worship him to the utmost, they will certainly attain the Buddha fruit and will be reborn in a heavenly realm.[121]

Yandan memorized this text and set out to the east for home. On the way he heard that Preceptor Wei had obtained a resonant prodigy *(ganying)* and knew that it must be the traces of Kāśyapa and that Sineng must be the bodhisattva of the eighth stage. After Sineng died, his temple grew ever grander over time, in many respects resembling Tuṣita Heaven (the paradise over which Maitreya presides).[122] The temple was named Recumbent Buddha *(wofo)*.

The text continues in the voice of the Ming emperor ("I" [zhen]), who, having inherited the great legacy of his ancestors, must pacify the myriad countries and repair old temples, especially one at the crossroads of Buddhist traffic from India to China where a Buddha transformation had occurred. The emperor had the main buildings restored and gave the temple a new name, Baojue ("Treasure Enlightenment"), in the pious hope that it would contribute to the blessings, peace, and stability of the country and people. To record its origins, he ordered a stele inscribed. (Here my summary ends.)

Before receiving the name Baojue from the Xuande emperor, the temple was known as the Hongren si. A few years earlier, in Yongle 9 (1411), the temple underwent repair, from which only a bronze plaque survives. Unfortunately it was inaccessible for my scrutiny when I visited Zhangye in 1988. A third Ming stele still preserved in the temple but not recorded in the gazetteer is dated to Zhengtong 6 (1441), not long after the one summarized above. The first few lines of this small engraved stone refer to the temple as Hongren Baojue si and note that earlier, according to the 1411 plaque, it was called Kāśyapa Rulai si (Kāśyapa Tathāgata Temple). It seems that this may have been another Xia name of the temple, but the relationship between the 1441 inscription, which alas I did not copy in full and was not allowed to photograph, and the Xuande text remains unclear.

From what we do know, it appears that this Weiming monk fulfilled a Buddhist prophecy circulating in Hexi around the end of the eleventh century. This prophecy suggests possible links to Khotan or a familiarity with the Tibetan text about Khotan "The Prophecy of the Li Country." Hubert Durt has described this text as "mostly a chronicle of the foundation of the monasteries in Khotan," in which "the references to the Buddhas of the Past, especially Kāśyapa, are so numerous that one wonders if such a 'patronage' was not a prerequisite for all the important monasteries. The link with the Buddhas of the past is established either by describing the monasteries as possessing their relics or as having previously been headed by such a Buddha."[123] The monastery built by Weiming Sineng meets precisely this criterion. Prophecies of the sort described above circulated throughout Buddhist Asia; Durt describes one associated with the establishment of Buddhism in Silla. As in the case of an Aśokan stūpa, the function of archeological fabrication, Durt points out, is to demonstrate "that the place in question was predestined to become a holy place . . . such a discovery helped to establish a link between a distant past or a famous ancestor and the present. To establish continuity and thus to legitimize a contemporary situation is indeed one of the foremost aims of traditional historiography."[124]

It is not hard to imagine the relationship this affair may have had with events at the Tangut court. Wu Guangcheng's account credits Chongzong with establishing the temple; further, it invites speculation that a monk (of the imperial clan? he only gives the name Fajing, a far cry from Sineng) conveniently found some precious relics to present to the court at a time when the throne direly needed an auspicious augury to boost its dignity. This may represent an alternative memory of the story engraved in the Ming stone inscriptions, but it also indicates that Wu did not have access to the *Ganzhou fuzhi* and was relying on what appear to be less authoritative materials that cast the story in a characteristically Chinese omen tradition, which also served "traditional historiography."

In a different chapter of the gazetteer, the compiler dates the construction of the temple to Yongan 1 (1098), which, being a Tangut reign date, must have come originally from a Xia source by way of an earlier Ming or Yuan inscription.[125] In 1098, however, the empress dowager was not yet dead, so if we accept this date, Wu Guangcheng's explanation of the emperor's part in the temple becomes even more problematic. Yet it is more than likely that there was some connection between the capital and the events unfolding to the west.

A tie between the two Ganzhou monks and the court may have existed in the title of state preceptor ascribed to both. If this title had really been granted by the court and was not merely a later accretion to the tale, then presumably these two figures were members of the official Saṅgha. Further, having as a close relative a famous monk and the transformation of an eighth-stage bodhisattva would not go unremarked by a devout emperor in extreme peril. People in the clerical establishment would make a careful reporting and record of these royal prodigies, for almost certainly the Ming inscription drew on some earlier source, an oral or written tradition passed on through the Yuan, as the Yongan date testifies. It is interesting, however, that the author of the Ming text (the emperor himself?) appears unaware of the connection between Qianshun and Weimi Sineng, who were both of the royal Weiming clan, or has deliberately suppressed the connection. All in all, it is unlikely that a Xia stele from the temple served as a direct source for the Ming composition, for it would not have referred to Chongzong as "Li Qianshun."

Alternatively, later Chinese may have ignored those details so important in eleventh- and twelfth-century Xia, and extracted from the story what served their own purposes. Hence, the early-fifteenth-century Ming emperor embraced a popular local legend to cultivate Ming legitimacy in an area not ruled by a native Chinese regime since the late eighth century and where Mongolian, Turkic, and Tibeto-

Tangut residents possibly outnumbered the Han Chinese.[126] In order not to emphasize the long hiatus in Chinese rule over the region, Ming records simply elided the peculiar details of those earlier regimes. Hence the Tangut reign date of Yongan is not recorded in the same chapter of the gazetteer as the Ming inscription.

The story of Weiming Sineng points to ways in which the Tangut ruler and Xia elites relied on the Buddhist faith and legend as tools of personal salvation and imperial legitimation. It demonstrates how widespread and deeply etched the cult of relics had become in the popular imagination.[127] The comparison of Sineng's temple with Tuṣita Heaven suggests the pervasive influence of Maitreya worship in Xia Buddhist practice, for which we also found evidence in the Tangut text of the 1094 inscription and at Dunhuang. This tale further suggests that Xia monks were traveling freely to India (Yandan's pilgrimage presented no special difficulties), confirming the impression of ongoing exchanges and interaction among Buddhists throughout the region, which left behind abundant traces in twelfth-century Tangut materials. What route or routes of travel they followed poses an interesting question.

Finally, the Ming preservation of the story reinforces the evidence of the next chapter, which testifies to the vital strategic role that Buddhist traditions from the Xia period and earlier continued to play in local and imperial dealings in the Gansu-Ningxia region well into the Qing era.

Today the Dafo si in Zhangye has become associated with legends about the last Song emperor, the last Yuan emperor, and Qubilai.[128] According to a popular travelogue by photographer Jin Bohong: "The Yuan Dynasty changed the temple's name to Shizi Temple. Kublai Khan's mother gave birth to him while she was living here."[129] I have found no evidence to support either of these two assertions. Clearly the tales Jin Bohong records about the last Song emperor being exiled to Zhangye, marrying a daughter of Qubilai, taking refuge in the Dafo Temple as a monk, and fathering a child who became the last Yuan emperor Shundi likewise illustrate the accretion of legend around this particular Buddhist site.

The period of the Liang Regency in Xia history was by no means as black as Weiming and Song propagandists have painted it. It is not at all certain that the constant warfare between Song and Xia from the later eleventh century up to about 1115 can be blamed on the Liang house. No Tangut regime was willing to cede territory to Song, while the seeds for Song expansionism were sown domestically in the

1040s. In fact, the Liang Regency can take credit for accomplishing several difficult tasks: (1) keeping the Xia state intact and independent under intense pressure from both Song and Liao[130] and (2) advancing Tangut cultural and political independence through the translation of the Buddhist Tripiṭaka into Tangut. Available sources amply document both contentions. Economically, militarily, and in other ways, the Tangut people paid a high price for independence. Yet within a few years of Empress Dowager Liang's death in 1099, Song paid an even higher price for its determination to "contain" that independence by losing all of north China. With Song at a safe remove and with the regularization of relations with Jin, Xia entered a long period of relative prosperity and diplomatic stability in the twelfth century.

PART 2
The 1094 Stele Inscriptions from Liangzhou

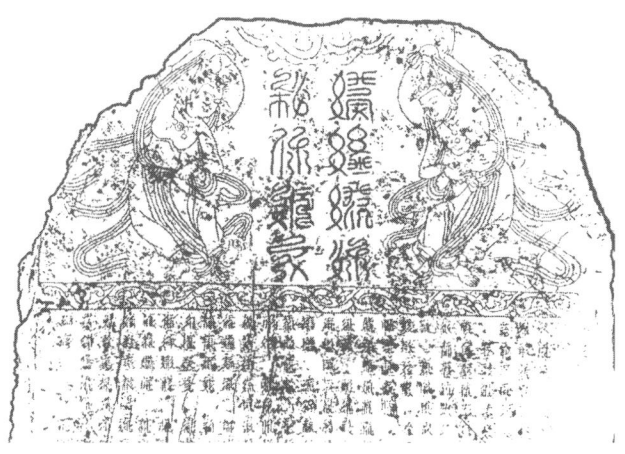

CHAPTER 4

A History of the Dayun (Huguo) Temple at Liangzhou

FIVE STELE INSCRIPTIONS from the Dayun Temple at Liangzhou survive in one form or another today. They date to the years 711, 1094, 1563, 1622 and 1697.¹ All except the 1094 inscription call the temple Dayun ("Great Cloud"); under the Tanguts it became Huguo ("State Protecting"), although throughout the centuries it went by various other names as well. For the nearby Qingying Temple, where the 1094 stele was actually found in the early nineteenth century (described below), three inscriptions survive, dating to 1588, 1672, and 1741.² These sources, along with other notices from the eighth to twentieth centuries, permit us to trace the vicissitudes of the Dayun Temple from at least the Tang dynasty to the eighteenth and even into the twentieth century. Of special concern here is the Gantong Stūpa, to which the 1094 inscription is dedicated, and its relationship with the temples and community throughout the centuries.

At a broader level of significance, these inscriptions allow us to map out the particular spatial and spiritual relationships generated by these temples, which acted as a protective "force field" along the interstices of China and Inner Asia. At these interstices the rival forces of empire met, mingled, and fluctuated; during the Tang, Yuan, Ming, and Qing periods, Liangzhou held or advanced the perimeter of China into Inner Asia; from the late eighth to thirteenth centuries (including the early Mongol period), Liangzhou served Inner Asian interests in confronting or mediating with China, culturally, politically, economically, and militarily.

In this chapter I reconstruct the history of the Dayun Temple, and its relationship with other temples and with the town of Liangzhou. I also trace, in a preliminary way, the rise and practice of the cult of stūpa worship, especially of Aśokan stūpas, as it relates to the Gantong Stūpa and the Liangzhou community. The interest posed by this reconstruction lies not in the uniqueness of this temple, but rather in distinguishing what I suspect are its widely shared properties from its local peculiarities.

The Early History of the Temple

We have a fair idea of the origins of the Dayun temple complex from its earliest source, the inscription of 711. The original stone engraving of this text no longer survives, and the copy that Wang Chang (1725–1806) recorded came from a new engraving, evidently carved during the Ming or Qing (after the mid–fourteenth century), of the older text.[3] Although corrupted and obscure in many places, Wang's text provides a useful starting point. The 711 stele (or a rubbing of it) probably still rested in the temple storeroom in the eleventh century, for it apparently served as a source for the compilers of the 1094 texts.

Wang describes the now lost stele as eight feet three inches seven *fen* high and three feet three inches three *fen* wide. It had sixteen columns with fifty-six characters per column, considerably fewer than the 1094 stele text. The first line following the title records the name of the compiler, the scholar Liu Xiu. Liu informs the reader that the Dayun Temple was founded by Zhang Tianxi, the regional governor *(mu)* of Liangzhou under the Eastern Jin, during the Shengping era (357–362).[4] The first name of the temple was Hongzang (Spacious Repository) si, perhaps alluding to its early character as the site of an Aśokan reliquary, although that claim is not made explicit in the 711 inscription. In 690 Empress Wu decreed that a Dayun Temple be established in every prefecture, and, as was the common practice in such cases, the Hongzang si was simply renamed the Dayun si.[5] Subsequently people also called the temple Tianci an (Heaven Bestowed Hermitage), but in 711 the temple's formal name remained Dayun si.

Liu describes the strategic and scenic situation of the temple, its grounds abutting the borders of four commanderies *(jun)*, its walls encircled by sweeping pines, with auspicious *bailan* (white orchids?) warding off evil.[6] A gnomon (in the courtyard?) announced the morning, noon, and evening sermons. Local and regional officials sponsored the merit-earning refurbishments that occasioned this inscription, which goes on to depict the layout of various buildings comprising the monastery, their decoration, and their wall paintings in some detail.

On the grounds of the Flower Pavilion Hall stood the seven-storied wooden stūpa built by Zhang Tianxi (29b–30a). It was 180 feet high and on each tier one door and two windows faced in each of the four directions, comprising twenty-eight identical faces (jian)[7] altogether. Once, the lower stories started to sag but the community lacked the wherewithal to repair them. Then three faces suddenly collapsed; digging up the foundation, people found a vase of old coins that helped offset the expense of repairs. Later, regional military governor Sima Yi mobilized the labor and resources to renovate the tower and expand or decorate other buildings.

These repairs were recorded in 711 for posterity on a stele at the behest of the new military governor Sima Yi. At just this time the Tang government had begun appointing permanent military governors (jiedu shi) to command frontier garrisons; it established the Liangzhou command for all of Hexi late in Jingyun 1 (710–711).[8] Sima Yi was presumably the first incumbent of this position, although the name remains unattested in Tang sources, indicating possible errors and confusion in the transmission of the text. Three other military officers are also introduced in the text, of whom one or more "understood military strategy and deeply penetrated the Prajñā-pāramitā" (29b). Moreover, the grandson of General An Zhongjing was the temple master (30b). Thus, the production of this inscription in 711 may be regarded simultaneously as a state-sponsored event in the service of Tang Xuanzong's (r. 712–756) frontier policy as well as an expression of religious devotion.

Other structures on the monastery grounds included Southern and Northern Meditation Halls with various narrative murals, and a chamber to translate and copy sacred scripture. The Dayun si, then, comprised a fairly elaborate assemblage of buildings occupying a large landscaped enclosure in a prime location on the outskirts (northeastern, we gather from later data) of the town, near the principal roads connecting Liangzhou with adjacent commanderies.

Most likely the temple's name was changed to Kaiyuan si in 738, when Xuanzong ordered that Buddhist and Daoist temples named Kaiyuan be established in all prefectures and the capitals, just as several decades earlier Empress Wu had ordered that Buddhist and Daoist temples named Dayun be established in every prefecture.[9] Amoghavajra (705–774), the famous Tang monk of north Indian origin and a specialist in Esoteric Buddhism, evidently spent part of his childhood in Liangzhou (called Wuwei from 742).[10] At the request of the powerful military governor of Hexi and Longyou (Gansu), Geshu Han, in 754 Amoghavajra traveled to Liangzhou and stayed in the Kaiyuan Temple. There he performed a public consecration ceremony:

> The Military Governor-General and his subordinates down to the last soul all received *abhiṣeka*. A mob of several thousand gentry and commoners alike all ascended the ordination platform, and along with the clerical disciple Han-kuang, were instructed in the method of the Five Divisions.... On that day, there was a great movement of the earth in the area where the ceremony was held; the master was moved, and said: "This [phenomenon] has been brought about by the trueness of your hearts."[11]

Amoghavajra evidently stayed in Liangzhou until the summer of 756, when an imperial edict summoned him back to Chang'an. An Lushan's rebellion was already over six months in progress.

In the first 350 years of its existence, therefore, the temple at Liangzhou assumed the basic pattern of its spatial and spiritual dynamic: erected by an autonomous frontier ruler defending his realm against powerful forces from the east; repaired by regional commanders defending the Tang realm against incursions from the north and west; revered by the local inhabitants for its miraculous revelations; and site for communal ritual activities on a mass scale. Such ceremonies, given their local cultural and geographic contexts, inevitably were politically charged. Amoghavajra's consecration ceremony took place just months before the outbreak of the An Lushan rebellion, in a town caught up in the Tang struggle with the Turks and the Tibetan empire, which would soon overrun the Gansu Corridor.

The Liangzhou Temple in the Tenth and Eleventh Centuries

From the late eighth century until the Tangut conquest of 1031 or 1032, Liangzhou was occupied and ruled mostly by Tibetans, who in the early eleventh century shared power with Uighurs from the Gansu Corridor. A story from the Five Dynasties period (early to mid–tenth century) relates how the resident garrison commander dispatched from the north Chinese court lost favor with the populace and sought refuge in a certain seven-storied wooden stūpa. When an angry mob gathered below, he threatened them, saying, "If you press me, I'll set fire to myself in here."[12] The people's devotion to their cherished pagoda (our Gantong Stūpa?) led them to compromise and release the hated official. Such representatives, sent intermittently from the court in China at this time, seem to have been isolated and ineffective.

Bent on suppressing the Ordos Tangut independence movement from 980 on, early Song emperors took a keen interest in Liangzhou politics and played off various factions in opposition to Li Jiqian, the Tangut chief. Between 998 and 1005 the local strongmen of Liangzhou took advantage of this situation to obtain from the Song court supplies of gold leaf, paint, and other adornments to build and repair the monastic complex. Local leader Youlongbo personally requested materials in 998 to build a temple.[13] In 1004 Boluozhi,[14] his successor, reported to the Song court that the Hongyuan si had been damaged or destroyed in Li Jiqian's attack the previous winter. He asked for artisans and supplies to repair it. The Song court sent some supplies but replied that it would be too difficult to send artisans. Boluozhi died shortly afterward, and in 1005 his brother and successor, Siduodu, again requested gold lead and colored paints to repair the Hongyuan si.[15] A corresponding entry for 1004 in the Song dynastic history refers to the temple as Hongyuan Dayun si.[16] Either the Dayun Temple was also called Hongyuan, or two temples are meant here, the Hongyuan si and the Dayun si.[17] Hongyuan may be a variant of Hongzang, the first name of the temple.

If Dayun and Hongyuan designated separate establishments, then we might wonder about the relationship between them, whether or not both had seven-storied stūpas and what later became of the Hongyuan si. The 1094 inscription mentions the names of two other temples in conjunction with the Dayun si (now called Huguo), neither called Hongyuan, but since the Tanguts renamed the Dayun Temple, possibly they also changed the name of the Hongyuan.

Development of a Stūpa Cult

The exclusive focus of the 1094 texts on the seven-storied stūpa at the expense of its monastic milieu sets that inscription apart from all the other inscriptions discussed in this chapter. It tells us that the interest of their authors focused on the stūpa, its Aśokan origins, and its miraculous properties, for they are elaborated at great length, whereas very little is said about the temple grounds.

Both texts of the 1094 inscription repeat the history of Zhang Tianxi's construction of the stūpa (H 3–4, T 7) but do not mention the temple under the names of Hongzang or Dayun (or Hongyuan).

The fact that the Xia inscriptions say nothing about the history of the temple after its Later Liang founding up to its incorporation into the Xia state is noteworthy, and I return to that issue in Chapter 6. Instead, the Han text embellishes the story of Zhang Tianxi's deed with pseudohistorical details, including a conversation that discloses the stūpa's special nature deriving from its property as an Aśokan reliquary. An absence of allusions or direct references to Aśokan imagery in the 711 text, excepting the sole occurrence of the number 84,000 (in another context) in the opening lines, suggests that the cult to the seven-storied stūpa as an Aśokan reliquary was not foremost in the minds of the authors of that earlier inscription, although fascination with identifying Aśokan relics had already achieved wide popularity in Chinese Buddhist circles.[18]

By the tenth century, as the tale recited above testifies, the local inhabitants had become firm devotees of their seven-storied wooden stūpa. Liangzhou's new Tangut masters in the eleventh century fully appreciated the prize they had inherited, and their promotion of the cult helped to secure local loyalties.

It may be helpful, at this juncture, to provide a brief sketch of stūpa worship in China.[19] A stūpa is a reliquary for a saint, a mandalic representation of the Buddha's "essential body" *(dharmakāya)* and by extension a symbolic expression of royal authority and power as well as a model of paradise.[20] The references to Aśokan stūpas above ultimately go back to the "Legend of King Aśoka" *(Aśokāvadāna)*,[21] a Buddhist narrative recounting the life and deeds of the third century B.C. Indian emperor Aśoka Maurya. Popularization of this work and its inclusion in the Buddhist canon made Aśoka the model of a Buddhist ruler throughout Asia. Here I quote from John Strong's translation of the legend's account of Aśoka's famous act of stūpa building, which followed his conversion to Buddhism [Aśoka has broken open seven stūpas and taken the Buddha relics from them, replacing each with a new stūpa and a few relics. . . .]:

> Then Aśoka had eighty-four thousand boxes made of gold, silver, cat's eye, and crystal, and in them were placed the relics. Also, eighty-four thousand urns and eighty-four thousand inscription plates were prepared. All of this was given to the yakṣas for distribution in the [eighty-four thousand] dharmarājikās he ordered built throughout the earth as far as the surrounding ocean, in the small, great, and middle-sized towns, wherever there was a [population of] one hundred thousand [persons]. . . . As it is said:

> From those seven reliquaries of old the Mauryan took away the
> relics of the Sage, and built on this earth in one day eighty-four
> thousand stūpas, resplendent as the autumn clouds.

Now when King Aśoka had completed the eighty-four thousand
dharmarājikās, he became a righteous dharmarāja, and thenceforth
was known as "Dharmāśoka." As it is said:

> For the benefit of beings throughout the world
> the noble Maurya built stūpas.
> He has been known as "Aśoka the Fierce;"
> by this act he became "Aśoka the Righteous."[22]

As the concluding verse makes clear, Aśoka demonstrated his personal transformation by performing a great act of merit: constructing 84,000 stūpas throughout the "world" and distributing the relics of the Buddha among them. From the fourth century on, Chinese (and other Asian) Buddhists began claiming to have identified the sites of quite a few of Aśoka's 84,000 stūpas in China, among them our Gantong Stūpa.[23] Building stūpas thus became an exemplary royal act of merit making, mimicked, for example, by the first Sui emperor. As part of his program of nation building and Buddhist revival, Sui Wendi (r. 590–605) had 111 stūpas built to enshrine relics between 601 and 604.[24] One of the most influential of early Mahāyāna texts, the "Lotus Sūtra" *(Saddharmapuṇḍarīka-sūtra),* is "based upon the institution of the stūpa" and sets forth the merit of erecting and worshiping seven-jeweled stūpas.[25]

According to canonical sources, the stūpas of saints should be erected within a monastery, while stūpas for laity (more common in India and Tibet than in China) should be outside the walls of a monastery.[26] Early temple compounds in China featured the stūpa (or pagoda) as the main building, but as temple layout developed and began to conform to native Chinese imperial architecture, one author argues, the icon (or buddha) hall supplanted the stūpa as the dominant structure.[27] In some cases, the stūpa became two structures assimilated to the position of the twin *que* towers, flanking the central axis leading to the main icon hall. At the Yongning Temple in sixth-century Luoyang, however, the lavishly appointed stūpa remained the dominating building.[28]

Both Han and Tangut texts of the 1094 inscription claim that the Gantong Stūpa originated as an Aśokan reliquary (T6, H2–3). This assertion affirms the flourishing of a relic cult in Xia, for which we have already examined earlier evidence in the 1038 inscription eulogizing the burial of 150 Buddha relics from India (Chapter 2). It does not mean that earlier people regarded the Gantong Stūpa as an Aśokan reliquary. We do not know to what extent the layout of the eleventh-century Huguo Temple grounds in Liangzhou resembled that of its eighth-century predecessor, but it seems likely that the Gantong Stūpa was a prominent feature of its landscape. While Tangut rulers performed acts of merit in repairing and maintaining the precious tower, in their eyes the stūpa itself also generated merit through its miraculous deeds of salvation. For example, T12: "Lucky and unlucky prodigal omens being frequent and widespread, in the past [our] forebears reported [them], so as to make clear their distinctions. In thus possessing such mighty merit, this golden stūpa of Liangzhou has passed through many years."

The Gantong Stūpa was not the only Tangut establishment for which an Aśokan connection was claimed. As discussed in Chapter 3, the 1073 inscriptions at Yulin caves 15 and 16 in Anxi name a monk from the Ayuwang si (King Aśoka Temple) and a group of disciples and lay donors.[29] We do not know where this temple was located or when it was built; possibly the Tanguts inherited a monastery of this name or renamed an existing one.

On the Names Huguo Si and Gantong Ta

Only the Han text of the 1094 inscription uses the name Huguo si (title and line 24), instead of Dayun. Later Tangut sources also mention the "State-Protecting Temple."[30] Both Tangut and Han texts name two other associated temples, Shengrong si (Saintly Containment Temple) and Chongsheng si (Exalted Saint Temple), about which I will say more later. Weiming (Li) Yuanhao (r. 1032–1048) must have changed the name of the temple from Dayun to Huguo sometime after his armies occupied Liangzhou in 1031–1032. The Huguo Temple, then, was part of a Tangut imperial cult center located in Liangzhou, where Yuanhao made offerings to the spirits shortly after his enthronement as emperor in 1038.[31]

As the Tanguts faced and fought hostile neighbors to the south (Song China) and the southwest (the Kokonor Tibetans) throughout much of the eleventh century, their decision to rename the monastery "State-Protecting Temple" (Huguo si) requires little explanation. We need only to recall Liangzhou's strategic location along the Tanguts' southwestern frontier (see map) to imagine the role that the stūpa and the temple played in defending the new state. There is more to it than that, however.

The name "Huguo" occurs in the title of an important Chinese Mahāyāna sūtra, *Renwang huguo banruo boluomiduo jing* ("Sūtra on the Perfection of Insight by Which a Humane King Protects the Country").[32] After the outbreak of the empire-shattering rebellions in the mid–eighth century, the eminent Esoteric Buddhist master Amoghavajra made a new translation of this text in 765, to which Tang Daizong (r. 762–779) personally wrote a preface. Daizong sponsored solemn ceremonies to honor the new translation and shortly afterward attributed his victory over the rebel Pugu Huai'en to the potency of the *Renwang jing*.[33]

In 766 Amoghavajra requested imperial permission to assist the monk Daoyuan to complete construction of a temple in the sacred mountains of Wutai, at the behest of the mountain's resident bodhisattva, Mañjuśrī. In most sources this temple is simply called the Jin'ge si, or Golden Pavilion, but its full title was Baomo (*sic*) zhenguo jin'ge si, "Temple of the Golden Pavilion that Protects against Māra [*sic*] and Defends the Nation."[34] At this and the other imperially supported monasteries on Wutai shan, Amoghavajra led the specially ordained monks in one of their principal duties, reciting the "Sūtra on the Perfection of Insight by Which a Humane King Protects the Country."[35]

The name Huguo thus is associated with acutely felt defense needs, with Esoteric Buddhist ritual, and with an imperially sponsored cult to Mañjuśrī at Wutai shan, all of which figure significantly in Xia history.[36] As related in Chapter 2, before his enthronement in 1038 Yuanhao was denied Song permission to send emissaries to Wutai shan to make offerings to the Buddha.[37] Sometime afterward the Tanguts began construction of their own Wutai shan complex in the Helan Mountains.

No source that I have seen, aside from the 1094 inscriptions, records a name for the stūpa tower on the grounds of the Dayun (Huguo) Temple. The Gantong si discussed below in connection with the Shengrong si clearly refers to a separate site some distance from the town of Liangzhou. Judging by the 1094 texts, the Tangut rulers desired both to acknowledge what they perceived as the stūpa's special contributions to the building and defense of their state, and to encourage its continued service to the dynasty. Strategically and ideologically, therefore, the Gantong Stūpa occupied a key position in the eleventh-century Xia state.

The Huguo Temple Compound, Its Affiliates and Its Inhabitants

As noted above, the 1094 inscriptions say little about the temple housing the stūpa. The last section of the inscription (H 22–25, T 24–28) names all the people involved in the restoration project, but even these data leave many unanswered questions. Officials attached to the Chongsheng and Shengrong temples also took part in the effort. To shed some light on the relationships among these establishments, I list all references to them in both Han and Tangut texts of the 1094 inscription:

1. T2: supervisor *(tiju)* of the Shengrong [Temple] . . . Mingwang Qi'e.
2. H23: concurrently supervisor *(tiju)*[38] of monks at both the Shengrong Temple and the Gantong Stūpa, the scarlet-robed monk who understands the scriptures Yaonie Yongquan.
    T24: supervisor of [those attached to] the Shengrong [Temple] and the Gantong Stūpa, the monk who understands the scriptures, the subject Yaonie Yong[quan].
3. H 23–24: [director *(zheng)*] of monks at the Chongsheng Temple, the scarlet-robed monk Lingjie Chengpang.
    T25: director *(zheng)*[39] of monks at the Chongsheng Temple, scarlet-robed monk, the subject Lingjie Chengpang.
4. H24: supervisor of both Fan and Han monks at the Huguo Temple, Gantong Stūpa, scarlet-robed monk Wangna Zhengyu.
    T25: supervisor of both Fan and Han monks at the Gantong Stūpa, scarlet robed monk Wangna Zhengyu.[40]
5. H24: overseer of the various artisans engaged in temple restoration, director *(zheng)* of Han monks at the Gantong Stūpa, scarlet-robed monk Jiu Zhiqing.
    T 25–26: assistant overseer of artisans, director of Han monks at the Gantong Stūpa, scarlet-robed monk Jiu Zhiqing.
6. H24: assistant director of Han monks at the Gantong Stūpa, scarlet-robed monk [Bai Zhixuan].
    T26: assistant director of Han monks at the Gantong Stūpa, scarlet-robed monk Bai Zhixuan.[41]

References to the Shengrong Temple and the Huguo Temple are paired with references to the Gantong Stūpa (except in T2), whereas mention of the Chongsheng Temple occurs alone (number 3 above). Officers of all three took part in the restoration project, although, because it is only mentioned once, one has the impression that the Chongsheng Temple played a less prominent role than the Shengrong

History of the Dayun Temple

and Huguo temples. But why only the single mention of the Huguo Temple, which presumably had the closest tie to the Gantong Stūpa?

From later evidence we know that the Dayun (Huguo) Temple was located in the northeast corner of the town. A recently excavated inscription there sheds light on the history of a Shengrong Temple in the area, although whether it refers to this Shengrong Temple is not certain. In 1979 a stele was unearthed from a corner in the northeast wall of Wuwei, opposite the bell tower (described as occupying the southeast corner of the Tang era Dayun si), with a text of twenty-five lines to which scholars have given the title "Record of the Cause and Condition of the Auspicious Stone Buddha Image at Yushan in Liangzhou."[42] The "Record" was composed in 742 (Baoyuan 1) by a retired scholar named Yang Bo (line 23). Only the lower half of the stele remains legible. Although found in the Wuwei city wall, the "Record" ostensibly describes a temple located some twenty *li* northwest of the Yongchang county seat (72 km northwest of Wuwei).[43]

The origins of this temple built in 561–563 under the Northern Zhou, according to Yang Bo, go back to the appearance of an auspicious stone Buddha image in the mountains north of Liangzhou ("Tiger Head Mountain" in present-day Yongchang County), a tale enshrined in many Dunhuang cave murals. Returning from a campaign in the west, Sui Yangdi visited the monastery in 609 and gave it the new name of Gantong si (or Gantong daochang), by which name it was known up to 742.[44] Under Tibetan occupation, however, sometime in the late eighth or early ninth century the temple's name was changed to Shengrong si, as we learn from an inscription in a surviving stūpa on the mountaintop behind the site of the former temple's main hall.[45]

By the eighteenth century, as recorded in the Yongchang gazetteer, the temple was called Houda si ("Rear Great Temple"), supposedly owing to its proximity to another temple built sometime later. It was apparently destroyed only in the 1950s.[46]

Indirect evidence links this Shengrong si to the temple of that name in the 1094 stele. Line 16 in the "Record" of 742 reports that a monk of a certain Dayun si had gone to live at the Gantong (later Shengrong) Temple, in the hope, fruitless as it turned out, of hearing a mysterious bell sound for which that temple was reputed. If this Dayun si is our monastery in Liangzhou, the episode probably dates to sometime after 690, when the name Dayun was bestowed, and before 742, when the "Record" was composed.[47]

Further indication of a special relationship between the two temples lies in the decision, for reasons not made fully clear, if explained at all, in the half-erased text, to locate the stele of the "Record" (if it was not moved there) in a spot very near if not inside the Dayun monastic compound.[48] Thus, despite the distance separating the Dayun si in Liangzhou and the Shengrong Temple in Yongchang, the latter may be our Shengrong Temple, since no record has come to light of a Shengrong Temple in the town of Liangzhou itself. The Shengrong si kept this name at least through the Xia period, but it had previously gone by the name of Gantong and had a stūpa, still extant, of seven stories. Perhaps this stūpa was (also?) called Gantong in the eleventh century.[49]

The possible existence of two Gantong stūpas might explain why one person in 1094 could hold the title of supervisor of monks at the Shengrong Temple and the Gantong Stūpa and another that of supervisor of Fan (Tangut? Tibetan? Tangut and Tibetan?) and Han monks at the Huguo Temple and the Gantong Stūpa. Otherwise, such cross-staffing indicates a high degree of nested supervision by the central government over what were likely among the largest and richest monasteries in the land. They were public monasteries, closely affiliated with the dynasty. Involvement of the director and assistant director of Han (Chinese) monks at the Gantong Stūpa suggests that many of the artisans working on the project came from the ranks of the Chinese monks living at the stūpa or laymen associated with it. Their skills had perhaps been handed down for generations in this fashion. In any case, it is clear from the inscriptions that the government and monastic officers as well as resident monks closely supervised and participated in the restoration work.

The monks living in these temples were evidently divided into groups according to their ethnic identification; here only Han and Fan groups are named, but Fan could refer to Tangut or Tibetan or both.[50] The Tanguts commonly used the Chinese word *fan* to translate their own ethnonyms, but the twenty-sixth graph in line T25, whose Chinese equivalent in H24 is *fan*, is not one of these specific ethnonyms. It is glossed *zang* (Tibetan) or *qiang* (Qiang) in Tangut dictionaries and in the Tiansheng code refers to Tibetans.[51] Possibly the author or authors used it here in an inclusive sense, distinguishing Tanguts and Tibetans from Chinese. The Tiansheng code refers routinely to Tanguts, Chinese, or Tibetans when discussing qualifications for advancement in the Saṅgha and state bureaucracy, distinguishing Tanguts and Tibetans, on the one hand, from Chinese, on the other.[52]

Twelfth-century vows and postscripts to imperially sponsored publications of scriptures frequently mention Fan and Han editions of so many thousands, which most readers have understood to mean Tangut- and Chinese-language editions.[53] In 1189, to celebrate the fiftieth anniversary of his accession to the throne, Renzong issued several Han and Fan editions, and his vow in one of these Han editions details celebrations that featured readings from Xi (Western) Fan, Fan, and Han scriptures.[54] Xi Fan can only mean Tibetan here. Thus it appears that Fan usually means Tangut, but sometimes may include Tibetans, also glossed Xi Fan in Chinese. The early-thirteenth-century "New Laws" mention Tangut, Tibetan, and mixed Tangut-Chinese communities of monks, but evidently not mixed Tangut-Tibetan communities.[55] If the Fan of our text means only Tibetans, then we must ask why no Tangut monks are mentioned. Surely the temple compound also had a community of Tangut monks who were involved in the restoration project.

Most of the lay and clerical officials named in both inscriptions have Tangut names; monks like Jiu Zhiqing or Bai Zhixuan were probably Chinese, since they were director and assistant director, respectively, of Han monks at the stūpa. The stone carvers listed in T28 and H21 and H25 include both Chinese and Tangut (or Fan, i.e., non-Han) names. In Chapter 6 I look closely at the issue of names and their significance.

Given local demographic patterns, it is not surprising that Liangzhou monasteries housed communities of Tangut, Tibetan, and Chinese monks, distinguished for certain administrative purposes, perhaps even living in separate quarters within the temple grounds. This practice was not confined to Liangzhou. We know that Chinese aspirants to monkhood had to pass an examination on a different set of canonical texts than Tangut or Tibetan candidates.[56] It is difficult to speculate further about the more mundane implications or parameters of ethnic segregation within the Saṅgha. One wants to know what activities they pursued separately, what together; whether this segregation was characteristic of all monastic communities in the Xia state, or only certain ones in particular locales; and to what extent it was a product of local conditions or of state policy.[57]

The Economy of Temple Restoration

A restoration project entails an outlay of resources, mobilization of labor and supplies, fund-raising or politicking for patronage, and the distribution of benefits so acquired, especially in the ceremonies celebrating the completion of restoration work. Our 1094 inscriptions do not stint on this sort of information, although it is never as detailed as one might wish. They do not say, for instance, how many workers spent how many days, at what daily wage, to complete the project.[58] Compared with other inscriptions of this kind, however, we get a remarkable tabulation of participants in the labor and resources distributed or consumed. No doubt this is so because the empress dowager sponsored the repairs and made them an occasion for capitalizing on her pious investments and the high moral ground that she carved out for herself vis-à-vis her political opponents. Thus the stele, especially the Tangut text, in good Mahāyāna fashion collapses the distinction between sacred space and imperial (Tangut) geography. All the people, high and low, whose names appear chiseled in stone on the stele must have felt a certain pride and gratitude in the face of this measure of immortality.

The ceremonies marking completion of the repairs commenced on the fifteenth day of the first month[59] of 1094 and probably lasted several days. They featured all the merit-making activities typical of such occasions: a public vegetarian feast, a confessional service at which texts (unspecified) were chanted, the ordination of thirty-eight monks, the granting of amnesty to fifty-four persons condemned to die, and bequests to the monastery, its officers, and all the artisans (H 13–14, T 15–18). Fifteen ounces of gold and fifty ounces of silver does not sound like very much, but it may have represented a munificent sum, given the straitened circumstances of the state in the early 1090s. In 1091 border trade with Song and the Song annual subsidy had again been cut off, but they were briefly restored in 1093.[60] Moreover, we have few data against which to measure the economic significance of these figures.

The stele does provide some clues as to how the court managed the administration of resources necessary to carry out this project. Several titles of the higher officials named at the beginning of the last section of the inscriptions provide a clue. Mai Majie (H22, T24) held the posts of director of the Fiscal Commission and army supervisor of the military's Right Wing (H22), which was headquartered at the Southern Court (T24), likewise located at Liangzhou. The Fiscal Commission had four directors,[61] who were perhaps responsible for different regions of the country (such as the Southern, Northern, Eastern, and Western courts). Cleric Yaonie Yongquan (H23, T24), supervisor of monks at the Shengrong Temple and the Gantong

Stūpa, held the position of director of the Auxiliary Palace Fiscal Commission, probably a branch office of the central Fiscal Commission that accompanied the throne on its travels or was deputized by the throne for specific duties in conjunction with imperial projects. Possibly a temporary appointment, it gave Yaonie, a local Saṅgha official, authority to make economic decisions in connection with the restoration, such as distributing central government funds to project supervisors.

Three other people were also connected to this office. Wu Modou (H23), a lay official, was supervisor of supplies for the temple restoration and likewise a director of the Auxiliary Palace Fiscal Commission. Yaonie, a "court official overseeing the duties of... *(duda goudang),*" outranked Wu, whose name is not recorded in the Tangut text. Lay officer Liu Quliyai (H23), also not recorded in the Tangut text, served with Wu Modou as assistant supervisor of temple restoration and was a third director of the Auxiliary Palace Fiscal Commission. Was this bureaucratic flexibility (and spreading the largesse), or fiscal checks and balances? Finally, lay officer Muyang Eyi (T25) acted as another assistant supervisor of stūpa repairs and "recipient of edicts" *(chengzhi)* in the Auxiliary Palace Fiscal Commission (he is not mentioned in the Han text). Thus five persons had some direct connection with the government's financial administration, one with the central Fiscal Commission, and four with a branch office. This personnel suggests a major mobilization of resources and finely tuned coordination of authority and supervision over those precious resources.

Reading the Restored Stūpa

If the 1094 stele inscriptions leave us little picture of the temple park surrounding the Gantong Stūpa, they do conjure up the fabulous seven-storied tower, originally situated within the grounds of the old Tang Flower Pavilion (Hualou).

Chapter 11 of the popular "Lotus Sūtra," which was well known to the Tanguts,[62] describes the Buddha's evocation of an immense seven-jeweled (or seven-treasure) stūpa, from which a voice was heard praising the Buddha. When asked for the cause of this apparition, the Buddha replied that the voice belonged to another (earlier) buddha named Many Jewels, who, as he approached nirvana, instructed his followers, "After my passage into extinction, anyone who wishes to make offerings to my whole body must erect a great stūpa." The Buddha goes on to explain that "wherever anyone preaches the Scripture of the Dharma Blossom, his [i.e., Many Jewels'] jeweled stūpa invariably wells up before that person, his whole body in the stūpa giving praise with the words, 'Excellent! Excellent!' "[63]

Building and repairing stūpas, making buddha images, preserving relics, and distributing sūtras all led one to rebirth in a pure land, which was the most widely shared goal of most Mahāyāna Buddhists. Thus, inseparable from its protective functions, such as warding off attacking Tibetan and Chinese armies (H6, T 10–11), the Gantong Stūpa also embodied the promise and striving for spiritual salvation of its devotees.

In metaphorical and physical images, T 14–15 draws a vivid portrait of the newly restored stūpa. The Tangut verses first equate its seven tiers with the seven qualities of *bodhi* (enlightened mind; *qideng juezhi* or *saptabodhyaṅgāni*): (1) mindfulness *(nian, smṛti)*, (2) discrimination of phenomena *(zefa, dharma-pravicaya)*, (3) effort (energy) *(jingjin, vīrya)*, (4) joy *(xi, prīti)*, (5) serenity of body and mind *(qing'an, praśrabdhi)*, (6) concentration *(ding, samādhi)*, and (7) equanimity *(xingshe, upekṣā)*.[64]

In the parallel phrase of this seven-word couplet, "The four sides of the splendid sarcophagus [are like] the order of the four rivers." The power radiating out of the stūpa's four faces flows in all directions, like the mighty rivers of Jambudvīpa (our world), the Ganga, Indus, Oxus, and Śītā, all reputed to arise out of a lake in Tibet and flow, respectively, east, south, west, and north.[65] Śītā is sometimes said to be the Tarim River or the source of the Yellow River, hence the source of the rivers of China. This image underscores the stūpa's universality as a central axis and more subtly its ability to control the unruly Chinese neighbors of Xia.

The stūpa's tile-covered horizontal wooden supports extended out and turned up, so as to resemble a "flying bird." The golden head (disk or crown?) rested securely upon the jade pillar (?). Adornment with the "seven treasures" evokes two possible allusions: (1) to the seven properties of a *cakravartin* (a king who turns the wheel of the law) or (2) to the set of "seven treasures" that includes gold, silver, lapis lazuli, crystal, agate, and rubies or red pearls.[66] Reading the Tangut text, we are invited to imagine a brilliantly arrayed, not to say gaudy, tower, whose virtues reflected and magnified those of its royal patrons.

The "golden light encircling the *bodhi*" (or, "the golden light of the encircling *bodhi*") may refer to a pervasive glow of enlightenment exuded by the divine stūpa, especially the gilt disk crowning it. Complementing this *bodhi* glow in the verse couplet (T15) are the murals of lively bodhisattvas painted on the walls of the stūpa. In the next couplet the meaning of "a dark mist" and the "iron man" adored by the stūpa (or that adores the stūpa) remains elusive. Perhaps the "iron man" refers to a large buddha statue in the buddha or icon hall traditionally situated behind the stūpa on the central axis of a monastic compound. Thus, the tower would stand guard before the icon hall, watching over and "adoring" the image housed therein. Later descriptions of the temple grounds make this supposition plausible. Further, pennants, incense burners, and various religious utensils were apparently displayed in the stūpa, indicating that rituals were carried out inside of it.

Turning to the eulogy text (T19), we enter the realm of prodigy, often expressed in conventional language. At dawn a "five-hued auspicious cloud" shrouds the tower, which emits golden rays (sunrise); at night the divine light atop the stūpa appears and the "myriad buddhas of the Three Times circle around," ostensibly an evocation of the miraculous lamp, standing nocturnal guard against malefactors. A beacon of salvation and hope to all beings, the lamp also illuminates the perimeter of the country and the parameters of belonging to the Tangut/Xia polity: "[The lamp] winks on and off; having obtained the way and land of our forebears, [our] hearts rejoice.... For the black-headed [ones] under Heaven, in both suffering and joy [this is] the place to seek blessings; (T20) for the red-faced [ones] on earth, in both strength and defeat it is the foundation and source." Black-headed and red-faced, common epithets of the Tibetans, occur frequently as tropes in Tangut literature for the Minyag (Tangut) people.[67]

The foregoing passage is absent in the Han text, which devotes no more than two or three general phrases to describing the stūpa's physical appearance (H9). Chapter 6 presents an analysis of these passages.

Our window onto the seven-tiered wooden stūpa closes after 1094, except for a possible allusion to it in a late-twelfth-century court song or ode,[68] and we do not hear of it again until the stele inscription of 1563. At that time we learn that the temple was destroyed at the end of the Yuan and rebuilt early in the Ming. We do not know what miracles it furnished or trials it underwent during the Mongol conquest or the Yuan era. Evidence from later years suggests that the temple and its tower remained objects of local devotion and official concern, for its strategic location and efficacious past record periodically attracted official attention. But neither the 711 text nor any post-Xia inscription records a name for the stūpa, called Gantong ("Spiritual Resonance") in the Xia period. One thing seems certain: Never again would the wooden stūpa figure so prominently and affectionately in the prayers and concerns of a nation and its leaders as it did under the Xia. Yet its survival down to the nineteenth or early twentieth century testifies to its enduring efficacy or *ling*.

The Dayun Temple in the Ming and Qing Periods

According to the 1563 inscription, in the middle of the sixteenth century, the leaders of Liangzhou decided to restore the Dayun Temple, which had suffered pervasive damage in yet another earthquake. The senior official (the "seal keeper") discussed the project with local notables and the temple monk-administrators. Head monk Haishen was delegated to raise funds and supplies, and the town's residents all contributed to the effort. Laborers were hired, and the temple was completely renovated (lines 11–13).[69]

The project leaders then asked a local scholar, Shen Yong, to compose the text for a stele inscription to record the occasion for posterity (lines 17–20). Shen consulted the earlier inscriptions of 711 and 1094, in the form of rubbings, transcriptions, or the steles themselves, and quoted portions of these texts in his composition.

Shen begins by affirming the virtue of restoring the traces of former sages and meritorious works, then summarizes the temple's founding and renaming under Empress Wu, with no mention, however, of Aśoka. Since the "clear traces" of the temple's "meritorious deeds" are all described in detail by the Tang scholar Liu Xiu (composer of the 711 inscription), Shen notes, he will merely sketch the layout of its grounds: a spacious central hall with long side verandas, "marvelous pavilions and precious chambers," carved tile-bearing beams and great rafters, a Vulture Peak and Jeta Garden, a chamber for producing (printing?) sacred texts *(zaojing fang)*, a flower terrace, monks' quarters, a meditation hall, and abbot's chambers. To the north (of these buildings?) stands the seven-storied wooden stūpa *(guxian ta)*, built by Zhang (Tianxi), and here Shen quotes directly from Liu Xiu's description of the stūpa. Behind the stūpa (further north?) stands the buddha hall, to its left and right the bodhisattva and *devarāja* (heavenly kings) halls. One assumes that Shen's account, although quoting earlier sources, describes the temple extant in his day.

Shen then focuses on the stūpa and its record of miracles, quoting extensively from the Han text of the 1094 inscription (lines 6 and 17), but without specifying the referents; for example, he does not explain that "previous court" *(xianhou zhi chao)* refers to the late-eleventh-century Xia court under the empress Liang.

At the end of the Zhiyuan period (1335–1340),[70] we learn, the fires of war completely destroyed the temple. So, the Xia temple and its stūpa perished in the fall of the Yuan dynasty. Some years later, in 1383, a Japanese monk named Zhiman made a vow to gather the necessary funds and rebuild the temple (line 9). Shen does not say how or why this monk came to be in Liangzhou, but thanks to his enterprise, the temple was restored to its previous grandeur.

Zhiman's deed surely merited more than this passing notice, and it is hard to believe that he did not leave behind a commemorative stele. Just such a tantalizing possibility is suggested in the preface to the 1986 publication of Zhang Shu's (1781–1847) gazetteer, *Liangzhou fuzhi beikao*. The preface (p. 3) relates that when Chinese Communist Party Secretary Zhao Ziyang visited Japan in 1983, someone asked about Zhiman's restoration of the Dayun Temple in the early Ming.[71] Zhao relayed the inquiry back to Wuwei, sparking a search through the manuscript of the *Liangzhou fuzhi beikao*. In the *yiwen* section, the preface claims, was found the record of a stele inscription with detailed information about Zhiman's restoration. This information was duly conveyed to the Japanese. Unfortunately, the *yiwen* section of the published version does not contain such a text, as far as I can tell, only the above brief reference and another in the 1622 inscription discussed below. Alas! We will probably never know the tale behind Zhiman's act of devotion.

Shen's text resumes with what must be an erroneous date—Tianyou (min'an) 5 (1094) instead of Tianshun 5 (1461, during Yingzong's reign), at which time the temple was again restored owing to the ravages of wind and rain. The earlier date would reverse the flow of the narrative; in addition, following the (1461) restoration it was decreed that the temple be named Dayun. Certainly this did not happen in 1094. Thus we learn that the temple did not assume its earlier name until the mid–fifteenth century. Perhaps it continued to bear the name Huguo through the Yuan and early Ming eras.

Naming and renaming temples was an imperial prerogative, and the change of name at this particular time is worth exploring. All

Ming emperors had to grapple with policy issues concerning how to handle the Mongols and effectively garrison the northern frontier. Yingzong had been reinstated on the throne in 1457, eight years after his humiliating capture by the Oirat Mongol leader Esen in the notorious Tumu incident of 1449. By the time that Esen released the emperor a year later, Yingzong's stepbrother had taken over and reigned as Jingdi from 1450–1457, isolating and despising the former emperor. A palace coup put Yingzong back on the throne in 1457, but he had some work to do polishing up his imperial image and credentials, not to mention solidifying border defenses.[72]

Surely policy toward religious issues and institutions was intimately bound up with other matters critical to the survival of the dynasty. Questions of dynastic legitimacy perhaps motivated the decision to replace the name Huguo, which otherwise seems most appropriate under the circumstances, with the old name of Dayun. Huguo was, after all, a reminder of a time when Liangzhou and the Ordos had fallen under the rule of lawless foreigners—the Tanguts, who in their time had plagued the Song state (so they may have reasoned) just as the Mongols were now harassing the Ming.[73] Also, if Huguo was the temple's name under the Mongol Yuan dynasty, all the more reason to change it now! Dayun recalled the grandeur and might of the Tang, which had for some time dominated these western regions. Yet, in the next sentence Shen relates that "for over five hundred years up to the present" the temple has illumined this border region, implicitly dating the beginning of the temple's meritorious service to the early Xia period.

Shen's narrative moves on to the events that inspired the most recent restoration, which took place at a time (1550–1566) when the Chahar Mongols under Altan Qan were raiding the Ming border every year and terrorizing Chinese commanders because the Ming government refused to sanction barter trade.[74] Shen again borrows language from the 1094 text (H 9, 20) to describe the artisans' labor, the appearance of the refurbished facade, and the devotion of people of that region (line 14). He also paraphrases the earlier text in reiterating the uniqueness of the stūpa and its prodigies, which demonstrate the Buddha's teaching. A digression on the origins of Buddhist temples and precious pagodas follows, without mention of Aśoka. But there are lacunae in the text at this point where such references might have occurred. Shen explicitly links the divine power of the stūpa to the longevity of the state (line 16), reflecting both contemporary concerns over frontier conditions and the stūpa's fulfillment of its traditional civic duty.

Not many years later, another stele inscription from the Dayun Temple, dated 1622 (Tianqi 2), evokes the gloom and gathering crisis pervading the entire country, especially along the Ming's northern frontier.[75] Historians have considered the Tianqi era (1621–1627) one of the most disastrous in Chinese history, for it saw the rise to power of the vicious eunuch Wei Zhongxian and the debilitating Donglin factional battles at court. Zhao Wanbi, composer of the 1622 text, conveys something of the dismay and confusion of the day.

Zhao states at the outset that the temple's history can be traced from the two Tang and Song (Xia) steles. After its destruction at the end of the Yuan, the Japanese monk Zhiman sponsored the temple's reconstruction in the early Ming (Hongwu 16/1383) but left no record of his deed. Zhao describes two stūpas forming twin towers. One was "of old" a five-tiered stūpa, on which earlier repairs (those begun by Zhiman? or in 1563?) were finally completed in 1592 (thirty years before Zhao penned his text), by Wuwei's (Liangzhou's) vice-commander Lu Guangzu, whose name also appears at the end of this text. This refinished tower was 180 feet high (like the original Gantong tower) and "with the Qingying Temple's stūpa [forms] twin peaks stretching to Heaven," one of the singular sights of the Five Liang (i.e., Liangzhou) (line 4). I will say more about the Qingying Temple below. Originally the Gantong Stūpa had seven stories, and in the 1563 inscription discussed above, Shen Yong also describes a seven-storied stūpa. Is "five" an error here? Did Shen suppress the detail that the reconstructed stūpa really only had five stories? Or when Lu Guangzu completed the repair, did it again rise to seven stories?

Sometime after 1592, Zhao relates, the local people prospered and recovered a thousand *li* of border from the northern tribes. Although this was fate, still, Zhao insists, one could not deny that the potency of the dharma contributed to these successes (line 6). So, to reward the temple for its spiritual assistance, the victorious regional governor *(zongbing)* Da Yun[76] erected a temple to the Dark Emperor (Xuanwu di, Xuan di, also called Zhenwu), a Daoist deity popular during the Ming, in front of the stūpa (line 7).[77] Further, to the left of the temple to the Dark Emperor, the monk-officer Hongkai built a small shrine to Da Yun from the remaining materials. There he burned incense before the image of the governor, more for his military feats than for his construction of the temple to the Dark

Emperor (lines 8–9). Thus the Dayun Temple continued in its role as a locus for the acknowledgment and generation of cosmic power, as a source of the potency that kept enemies at bay, and as an exchange economy of benefactions and merit-making activities, whatever "tradition" they represented.

Further along, Zhao reflects on the origins of Buddhism in China and on Confucian objections to the faith. Zhao observes that Buddhism is effective in reaching the masses and pacifying the cruel and greedy western Hu, who do not practice Chinese customs and are beyond Heaven (lines 20–21). For this reason alone, he boasts bleakly, frontier temples are superior to interior establishments and, moreover, all bear the imperial seal of origin (which is not quite true), including the Dayun and other temples of his native Liang. The inherent superiority and beauty of these temples can instill reverence and faith in the observer and further enlighten the masses and pacify the foreign tribes.

Finally, Zhao says, there are three Buddhist temples in Liangzhou, all in the northeast quadrant of the town.[78] How can one allow the customary pulse of a frontier commandery to collapse into decay without timely repairs? Alas, the stūpa was built and Liangzhou flourished because of it; verandas and hall have been erected and the stūpa will not perish because of them. This (accumulated) merit of recompensing faith, Zhao concludes, is not inferior to that of the Japanese Zhiman (the shadowy benefactor of the 1383 restoration).

It is curious that Zhao returns in the end to the obscure foreign monk's good deed of over two centuries earlier, suggesting that Zhiman had been highly regarded by the community. Equally interesting is Zhao's observation that Liangzhou had only three temples *(futu)* in 1622. This number is hard to square with the long list of temples reported in the late eighteenth century (see below), more than three dated to the pre-Qing period and at least half located within the city walls. The 1622 inscription, like its Tang predecessor, is no longer extant, nor does there appear to be a rubbing, so errors in this version may account for these discrepancies. Alternatively, late Ming Liangzhou may have lacked the resources to keep up its temples or build new ones. With the advent of a new government, the influx of resources to support the Qing effort to extend control over Central Asia, and the prominence of Tibetan Buddhists in Qing affairs, an explosion of Buddhist establishments in early Qing Liangzhou is entirely plausible.

If defending the Liangzhou frontier posed perennial dilemmas to imperial governments throughout history, so did keeping this Buddhist guardian of the frontier in working order. The burden of repairing the temple normally fell on the locality, however. In 1697, local authorities found one solution to this problem and recorded it in a temple inscription of that year (Kangxi 36).[79] Once again the temple had fallen to ruin, probably in the course of the Ming collapse and the Manchu conquest. The commander of the region undertook to rebuild the temple and further organized an Avalambana society *(Yulan foshe)* to meet monthly in the temple, carry out prayer ceremonies, and in general keep the place tidy.[80] These merit-making activities of the society would in turn ensure the continued production of merit by the temple for the community. The short text of this inscription ends with a list of members' names.

We last hear of the Dayun Temple in a list of religious establishments in a local gazetteer of 1775.[81] Its companion, the Qingying Temple, seems to have overshadowed it from the late seventeenth century onward. After all, Zhang Shu reported finding the 1094 stele inside of the Qingying Temple, which suggests that at some point the Qingying Temple occupied land that had formerly been part of the original Dayun monastic compound.[82] Moreover, by the Qing period the cult of stūpa worship appears to have shifted its locus from the Gantong Stūpa of the Dayun Temple to the Qingying Temple.

The Qingying Si and Its Relationship to the Dayun Si

The Finnish general Gustav Mannerheim, acting under orders from the Imperial Russian General Staff, traveled on a reconnaissance mission across Asia in 1906–1908. He notes in his published diary that he reached Liangzhou in January of 1908, saw the 1094 stele pillar, and photographed it:

> The principal sight worth mentioning is an old stone with an inscription said to be in the Sisia language. It stands in the NE part of the town at the foot of two very tall and similar pillar-like towers, visible at a distance of many miles from Lianchow.... When Bonin was here, he was said not to have been able to photograph it or take an impression of it, but an impression is said to have been taken by the Chinese authorities at the request of the French ambassador at Peiping. We tried in vain for two days. It was so cold that everything froze before we could get the cloth into the hollows. Finally I had all the hollows painted with white paint and photographed the stone to-day after working all night. It is possi-

ble that mistakes may have occurred, especially as the work had to be done at night by candle light. Opposite this stone there are two others with inscriptions. These stones seemed to be in an unusually good state of preservation, and on making enquiries I found that at any rate one of them had only been done a few years ago, though the inscription referred to some repairs done in the time of the Emperor T'ang.[83]

"These stones" must refer to the 1563 and 1697 inscriptions; that we have here two new inscriptions executed after 1697 and nowhere recorded seems unlikely. Mannerheim notes that the French scholar Ch.-E. Bonin visited the town at some unspecified earlier time (in fact, 1898–1900)[84] and was not permitted to photograph or take a rubbing of the Tangut stele. But it must have been on that visit that Bonin gathered rubbings of the two inscriptions of 1563 and 1697 that Edouard Chavannes published in 1902 (see note 1). By "the Emperor T'ang," Mannerheim, or his informant, no doubt meant Tang era repairs, which the 1563 inscription mentions. That stone may have been recarved in the late nineteenth century (Wang Chang's record of the 711 stele dates to 1805, indicating that it was recarved earlier). The fact that the Tangut stele had been uncovered for less than a century when Bonin visited Liangzhou plus the miraculous qualities or *ling* believed to inhere in it may account for the protectiveness of its guardians.

Evidently the two towers that Mannerheim mentions were all that remained in 1908 of the lavish temple complexes described in the earlier inscriptions. When I visited the town in 1988, not even these monuments had survived; only the old bell tower (restored in the Ming) testifies to the former presence of the Dayun Temple. Curiously, Mannerheim does not mention the bell tower, but perhaps his two-day battle with the cold to photograph the Tangut stele blunted his attention to the surrounding attractions. From the bell tower one can now peer down into the courtyard of a neighboring grade school, where, according to local sources, the Qingying si used to be and where the scholar-official and antiquarian Zhang Shu unbricked the stele in 1804.

Zhang Shu (1781–1847), a native of Wuwei (Liangzhou) and author of a local gazetteer, describes his youthful discovery of the 1094 stele thus:

> This stele is within the wall of my [native town of] Wuwei. In the north corner of the Qingying Temple there was a stele column that

had been bricked up all around for a long time. Moreover, the older folks do not know what stele it is and only said that it cannot be opened because, if it is, then a hail storm disaster will surely occur. In the year Jiaqing *jiazi* [1804] on the pretext of illness I left Yuping, Guizhou, and returned home. Enjoying my leisure with friends, we went to look [at the stele] and instructed the [attendant] monk to break open its encasement. He refused. We pressed him and still he would not. At last we said that if there was some terrible disaster we would take responsibility for it and the monk-intendant would not be troubled. Finally he agreed. Thereupon we summoned a number of workers[85] to break open the brick covering its front side, and the stele appeared. It is about one *zhang* in height. More than an inch of dust had accumulated; we wiped it away and suddenly characters appeared and could all be recognized. Looking closer, however, we could not read a single character. The shape of the characters was square, not a bit different from today's seal script. The seal script heading has the six words "Tianyou min'an stele" [*sic*]. I said that the back side of the stele must certainly have the translation, and so ordered [the workers] to crack its back side, revealing its substance to be in fact a translation [of the Tangut text on the front]. . . . My discovery of this stele has now made it available to the world for the first time. Epigraphers now have another curious text [for their collections].[86]

We do not know when and why the stele was bricked up. It may have been rather late, for the 1622 inscription notes that there were two steles, of the Tang and the Song, that could be consulted ("Song" refers to the Xia stele of 1094).[87] The 1563 inscription quotes from the Han text of the 1094 inscription, but the authors of it and the 1622 text could have consulted a rubbing made before the stele was enclosed in bricks. Perhaps inhabitants of the temple covered up the stele during a "time of troubles" in Liangzhou, at the end of the Yuan or the Ming. Another intriguing question is, was the stele concealed to preserve its potency or to inhibit its effective action?

Zhang Shu also does not mention the Dayun Temple or the bell tower, but modern tourist guides to Liangzhou make it clear that the latter structure, originally built (they claim) in the fourth century (possibly at the same time as the temple) and later hung with a bell cast in the Tang, was intimately associated with the Dayun Temple and was in fact part of that temple.[88] Thus Qingying was an affiliated cloister adjacent to the bell tower (and Dayun Temple) that subsequently was transformed into a school, as happened to so many temples in the twentieth century. Probably the two towers that Mannerheim found in 1908 were all that remained of the Qingying and Dayun temples. We can further identify these two towers with some certainty.

The Qingying Temple can be traced back to the early Ming. The text of an inscription dated 1588 (Wanli 16) records that during the Yongle period (1403–1425), the emperor decreed that on the ruins of an old Beidou gong (Big Dipper Palace?) the Qingying Chan temple be built. Some earlier structure or structures had occupied the space adjoining the Dayun Temple; the predecessor of the Beidou gong may have been another Buddhist establishment active during the Xia period. The name Beidou gong most likely designates a Daoist establishment; whether it was built during the Yuan or had existed earlier under the Xia is unknown.

In the years after its founding, benefactors raised funds to repair the Qingying Temple. An especially generous donor contributed a three-pillared Heavenly King Hall, a bell tower, and a drum tower in 1583. This bell tower may have become associated with the Dayun Temple and survives today as the structure described above. In 1588 further additions and repairs were made; here the text first mentions a wooden stūpa *(guxian ta)* with monks' quarters encircling it on the left and the right.[89]

The gazetteer of 1775–1776 contains a list of Daoist and Buddhist temples in and around Liangzhou (Wuwei).[90] Among the dozens of mostly Buddhist establishments, in the northeast part of town one could find the Dayun and Qingying temples. Their entries state: "Dayun si, northeast corner, has a stūpa, built by Zhang Tianxi during the Jin [fourth century]" and "Qingying si, west of Dayun si, has a stūpa called Guxian *(you ta ming guxian)*; examining the Tripiṭaka and Song-Ming records, this was one built by King Aśoka during the time of Zhou King Jing." Two questions arise in connection with this datum for the Qingying si. First, the binomial *guxian* is not actually a name, as the above entry suggests, but rather a technical term that denotes one of the twelve musical pitches and here simply means wood.[91] The term occurs in the 1563, 1588, and 1672 texts, where I have translated it as "wooden stūpa." As for the issue of the stūpa's identification as an Aśokan reliquary, I will return to this point later.

The evidence adduced above affirms that the two towers seen by Mannerheim in 1908 but now no longer extant were the two stūpas of the Dayun and Qingying temples. The 1622 text observes that the Dayun Temple stūpa "with the Qingying Temple stūpa [forms] a twin peak piercing Heaven." Fifty years later the Qingying Temple inscription of 1672 tells us that "today this stūpa stands together with the Dayun Temple stūpa." Mannerheim describes the position of the 1094 stele as "at the foot of two very tall and similar pillar-like towers," which suggests that the two towers were not very far apart, hence that the Qingying and Dayun temples stood cheek by jowl in the northeast corner of Liangzhou. It is not clear if a wall originally separated the two temples and their stūpa towers.[92]

The Qingying Si: Stūpa Worship in the Qing

As we saw above, according to the inscription of 1588 (Wanli 16) the Qingying si originated in the Yongle period (1404–1425) as a Chan monastery, built on the site of the ruins of the Beidou gong (a Yuan structure?).[93] After nearly two hundred years, the Qingying si too needed refurbishing. A series of private donations from the 1560s on culminated in offical funding of a complete restoration effort. Yuan Hongde, the assistant administration commissioner (*canyi*, rank 4b) of the Shanxi Provincial Administration Commission (which embraced Gansu), composed the 1588 commemorative inscription. His superior, commissioner (*buzheng shi*, rank 2b) of the Shanxi Provincial Administration Zhang Sizhong, composed the seal script heading. The participation of these officials, acting in the name of the central government *(fengchi),* underscores again the apotropaic function of a Liangzhou temple in its sacred and imperial roles.

This text exudes a more confident and cosmopolitan tone than the later 1622 inscription to the Dayun Temple; it boasts that "Liangzhou is the 'collar and lapel' of the Western Regions, and foreign *(fan)* monks of all kinds appear in its midst." Without question these foreign monks included Tibetan clerics for whom Liangzhou was either a primary destination or a stopover on the way to and from northeast Tibet (Kokonor/Amdo), Mongolia, or the Chinese interior, principally, I would guess, Wutai shan and Beijing.

Yuan describes the various features of the newly restored monastic compound, from its guardian kings' hall and bell and drum towers inside the front gate, to the main hall, and behind it the two halls to Amitābha and Dizang (Kṣitigarbha). Here, on the central path, is a tablet reading "Fan wang gong" (Palace of Brahma), which leads right to the wooden stūpa *(guxian ta);* the meditation hall and monks' quarters surround it on the left and the right. Yuan then waxes eloquent: "[We] rejoice at its completion. [The restored temple] is a beautiful vista of imposing splendor, a wonderful monastery that strengthens border defenses, a strong fortress that armors Xiliang [Liangzhou or Wuwei]." The stūpa was a vital link in Liangzhou's defenses.

Yet Yuan Hongde was no devotee of the religion. For him, Buddhism is an elderly but slightly disreputable relative: an undeniable presence that must be indulged yet is flawed. He proceeds to unfold an analysis of Buddhism, which relates it functionally to the "error" of Mohism, as the first step for barbarians on the civilizing path to Confucianism (paraphrasing Mencius). In Yuan's eyes, it is fitting, therefore, that the monastery play its role as a guardian at (or outside) the portals of true civilization.

Almost a hundred years later, as the Manchus were consolidating their power over Inner Asia, an inscription of 1672 (Kangxi 11) begins with the assertion that the "Qingying si was originally called the Beidou Palace; the Beidou Palace has a wooden stūpa that may go back to the Jin, when Zhang Zhonghua (fl. ca. 347) gave up the land within his palace to build a temple and stūpa."[94] Mimicking the claim made much earlier (no later than 711) for the Gantong Stūpa of the Dayun si, this assertion, albeit prefaced with the tentative particle *gai*, implies that the Qingying stūpa may also be of Aśokan origin. Whereas the Gantong Stūpa presumably dated from Zhang Tianxi's reign (ca. 363–376), supporters of its new neighbor here claim an even earlier origin under the rule of Tianxi's predecessor Zhonghua.

One might suppose that the stūpa at the Dayun Temple was losing its charisma—and its patrons—to the temple next door. It is possible, however, that all along, or at least from the Xia period on, there were two temples and two stūpas side by side in the northeast corner of Liangzhou. Paired stūpas occur at other Xia sites, such as Baisikou in the Helan shan foothills.[95] Unfortunately, we must rely on relatively late sources for the particulars of the Dayun Temple's companion.

Qing officials sponsored the Qingying restoration project of 1672 and the erection of a commemorative stele. Sun Sike, regional commander (*zongbing guan* rank 2a) and assistant commissioner in chief (*dudu qianshi*, rank 2a), composed the text. Sun refers to the 1588 text, which, however, provides no support for the claim of Jin origin. He relates how funds were raised to repair first the temple halls and then the stūpa, which work he describes in detail. Particularly arresting are the two hundred "stūpa lamps" *(ta deng)*, hung or attached somehow to the outside body of the structure and which one can easily imagine acted as a frontier beacon.

Sun proceeds to reveal that he has studied the Buddhist scriptures and has learned that a stūpa is the whole body of the Tathāgata *(rulai quanshen)*, so that

> to see a stūpa is to see the Tathāgata. Therefore those who repair old stūpas are reborn in White Body Heaven *(baishen tian)*.[96] Their bodies are fresh and white, and enter the Coral Forest *(shanhu lin)*.[97] Those who sweep stūpas are reborn in Thought Scorching Heaven *(yizao tian)*; their bodies are clean and pure, like a bright mirror. Those who remove trees and grass from within the stūpa [grounds] are reborn in Light Voice Heaven *(guangyin tian)*,[98] [filled with] copius treasures and palaces, radiant light of dazzling brilliance, quantities incalculable. Those who offer flowers and incense to the stūpa are reborn in Tuṣita Heaven. All the pores of their skin exude sandalwood incense, and they are complete in the three insights, six supernatural powers, and the eight liberations.[99]

I have not been able to identify White Body Heaven or Thought Scorching Heaven; they may represent distortions of (and Daoist accretions to) the original Sanskrit terms.

Sun goes on to say that the sick, crippled, and blind will all be cured of their ailments (by the stūpa's powers?). For Sun, a military man, and the pious community of believers on whose behalf he wrote, the stūpa remained the focus of their devotions and provides peerless opportunities for merit making. The difference in attitude of Sun Sike and Yuan Hongde is striking.

The third and last inscription to the Qingying si recorded by Zhang Shu, dated 1711 (Kangxi 50), omits the 1672 claim to antiquity and acknowledges but does not develop the theme of the stūpa as the Buddha's body. Author Li Ruyin, a local scholar, praises the temple as one of the major sights of Liangzhou. He informs us that the northeast corner of the city sits in low-lying swampy ground that had to be built up to make a foundation for the construction of the stūpa. The stūpa was rebuilt in 1526; in 1709 an earthquake toppled its crown and smashed tiles and bricks (presumably the Dayun Temple would also have suffered in the earthquake and needed repair). Li undertook the restoration project on behalf of the local saṅgha, with the support of the populace, who contributed labor and supplies. This was clearly a community project, with no official agenda, even though the two other signatories at the end are ranking officials. Nor does Li, a modest product of the local school, voice any particular pretensions in this short text.

Our last remaining source for the Qingying Temple, the entry in the gazetteer of 1775 cited earlier, openly asserts the claim of Aśokan origin for the temple's tower: "Qingying si, west of Dayun si, has a stūpa called Guxian; examining the Tripitaka and Song-Ming records, this was one built by King Aśoka during the time of Zhou King Jing." What is significant here is not that the claim is spurious, which obviously it is, but that the authors needed or desired to advance such a claim. If the claim was made to bolster the prestige of the Qingying Temple, one wonders if it implicitly and deliberately poached upon the Dayun Temple. Could there be more than one Aśokan stūpa in a given location? The 1672 Qingying inscription reveals a particular form of stūpa cult, but how widespread or popular it was is difficult to say without further documentation or without a larger comparative context in which to assess these texts.

Conclusion

Merit making remains a constant thread throughout the history of these two temples. Usually the temple's or stūpa's merit is first catalogued, for it establishes the grounds for community support in the periodic project of restoring the structure or expanding it. Because the community frequently included the imperial state, given the overlapping of sacred and strategic imperial space at Liangzhou, often the larger concerns of the Chinese or Inner Asian state combined with local religious practices to shape the forms of piety expressed in these inscriptions.

Even in the absence of the imperial state, as in the tenth century, the geography of Liangzhou as a threshold between the sinitic and Central/Inner Asian realms guaranteed diversity of religious practice and practicioners, and highlighted the apotropaic functions of the Dayun Temple, guarding the northern approach to the town.[100] I have the impression that these protective functions lost their urgency as the Qing consolidated control over Inner Asia. At roughly the same time the Qingying si emerged as a companion and rival to the Dayun Temple, and early Qing inscriptions for these temples reveal more purely local religious concerns. Surely this situation changed again in the nineteenth century, but we have no further inscriptional evidence from that troubled era or later.

Under what circumstances and why stūpas in China were identified as Aśokan reliquaries deserves wider study. In the case of the Dayun tower, Aśokan identity raised the status and merit of the stūpa but also increased its performative responsibility to the community and the dynasty. The Tanguts explicitly credited the Gantong Stūpa with exemplary powers, repeated by the Ming scholar Shen Yong in the 1563 inscription. Later texts are less fulsome and explicit in their attributions, possibly because their authors no longer could read the 1094 inscription. The Dayun Temple, however, remained a source of protective power, a vital link in the defenses of Liangzhou, thanks to the pacifying strength of the dharma.

The rise of the Qingying Temple in the Ming and its quest for Aśokan ancestry, may be linked to the disappearance of the 1094 stele pillar. With the authoritative record of the tradition entombed in brick, perhaps only a dim memory remained and no one mounted a challenge to the relocation of the Aśokan stūpa to the Qingying temple nearby.

CHAPTER 5

Annotated Translation of the 1094 Stele Inscriptions

IN THE FIRST MONTH of 1094, according to its inscription, a stele was erected to celebrate the completion of state-sponsored repairs to the Gantong Stūpa of the Huguo Temple at Liangzhou.[1] Its origins as one of the 84,000 stūpas erected all over the world by Aśoka to house Buddha relics endowed it with numinous powers to produce resonant prodigies in response to natural and human events. These miraculous powers protected the Xia state on several occasions by repelling invaders or assuring victory on the battlefield. In gratitude, the court undertook to repair this precious national treasure after an earthquake in 1092 had weakened the structure. Repairs began in the middle of 1093, shortly after the Xia court had reestablished relations, briefly, with the Song court.[2] A great Buddhist celebration was held to commemorate the occasion; gifts were distributed to the temple community and rewards to all persons involved in the repair work. The names and titles of many persons connected to the event appear at the end of the text.

Under the Xia, Liangzhou was an important imperial cult site, a regional trading center with a thriving economic base in livestock (famous throughout the world, according to the Jin dynastic history) and irrigated agriculture, a military headquarters, seat of the superior prefecture *(fu)* of Xiliang, and an imperial retreat; in short, a city second in importance only to the capital at Xingzhou.[3] It had a mixed population of Tibetans, Chinese, and Tanguts (including other Inner and Central Asian elements), and a large Buddhist establishment. Judging by the history of the Dayun Temple discussed in the previous chapter, the Huguo Temple was situated in the northeast quarter of the city, the stūpa was located within the Huguo Temple complex, and the Shengrong Temple was located outside and north of the town. The previous chapter relates Zhang Shu's discovery of the stele pillar in 1804. Today the stele, designated as one of the nation's cultural treasures, is housed in the Wuwei Municipal Musuem.[4]

On one side of the stone appears the Tangut text of twenty-eight columns with sixty-five character spaces per column. On the other side the Han text occupies twenty-five extant columns (a twenty-sixth is perhaps effaced) with seventy character spaces per column. At the top the faces of both sides of the stele bear similar carved *apsarasas* (messengers from Heaven) with swirling scarves, flanking the seal script heading. Undoubtedly the Tanguts considered the Tangut face to be the "front." Chinese authors writing about the stele (see Appendix B), with a few exceptions, also denote the Tangut side of the stele as the front side and the Chinese as the reverse side. Damage around the edges of the stele has severely effaced the first two columns and the final column of the Han text, while the Tangut text is over 99 percent intact and readable.

After its 1804 discovery, the Chinese text of the 1094 inscription was first published in 1868.[5] Thirty years later the French sinologist Gabriel Devéria published a transcription of the Chinese text, a photograph of the Tangut inscription, and the first attempted translation of the Chinese into a Western language. Thirteen versions of the Chinese text and seven transcriptions of the Tangut text were published between 1898 and 1988. Discovery and study of the inscription marked the first step in the recovery of the Tangut language.

In the first volume of *Seika go no kenkyū* (1964), Nishida Tatsuo included a transcription of both Chinese and Tangut inscriptions (Appendix B, no. 16) but translated only the Tangut (into Japanese and English). Like Devéria (no. 6), Lu Zengxiang (no. 11), and Luo Zhenyu (no. 10), Nishida and later authors break the text into (numbered) lines, indicating the beginning and end of columns. I follow this format. As Nishida and other scholars have observed, the two texts differ markedly in style and content, so that clearly one is not a translation of the other; I will say more about this in the next chapter. Many flaws in earlier translations of the Tangut text resulted in part from an inadequate understanding of the Chinese text. My translation attempts to improve our understanding of both texts. I have not solved all the problems that arise in them, but I have been able to make significant improvements in my earlier published translation of the Chinese text,[6] as well as in Nishida's translation of the Tangut text.

Although several rubbings of the Chinese inscription exist, no photograph of it has ever been published, although photographs of the Tangut rubbing have been reprinted several times. I have examined rubbings of both sides of the stele in Beijing,[7] photographs of which are reproduced in Appendix A here, and compared them to all available reproductions of the document. Where the stele has been effaced and the reading is disputed, I have chosen the one that makes best sense to me, without trying to reconcile every discrepancy. Unless otherwise indicated, in transcribing the Chinese text I tend to follow Devéria, Lu Zengxiang, or Luo Fucheng (no. 12), and favor vulgar *(suzi)* over "correct" forms of characters. In most cases titles are translated according to Charles Hucker's *A Dictionary of Official Titles in Imperial China*. However desirable, I have not attached a transcription of the Tangut text, which would be of limited use to the reader and pose formidable typesetting or handwriting challenges. The interested reader should consult Shi Jinbo's transcription of both the Tangut and the Chinese in his *Xi Xia fojiao shilüe* (pp. 241–246), in conjunction with my annotations here, which indicate where I differ from Shi and from my 1988 transcription of the Chinese text.

My translation of the Tangut may at times sound awkward to the English ear; I try to stay as close as possible to the original grammatical structure and literal meaning. Since the latter and any extended or figurative connotations stemming from it are not always obvious, I do not try to smooth over uncertain passages, preferring to leave them in the raw, so to speak, and open to the reader's interpretation. In Chapter 6 I analyze the structure of the texts and their various subsections; here I will only point out that the Tangut text is largely in verse form.

In the following translation, I use brackets to enclose omitted, missing, or reconstructed passages; I use parentheses to enclose editorial comments or explanations. Ellipses indicate illegible text (normally at the end of columns).

Translation of the Tangut Text

(seal script heading:)
Imperially Decreed Stele Inscription of the Gantong Stūpa

T1 Stele Inscription to the Gantong Temple in Liangzhou of the Great State of White and High.[8]

T2 The explicator,[9] humane teacher,[10] director of the Calendar Board,[11] assistant director of the Saṅgha Office,[12] supervisor of the Shengrong [Temple],[13] superintendent[14] of education, trustworthy, Mingwang[15] Qi'e. The explicator, humane teacher, transmitter of edicts in the Inner Palace Council,[16] director of the Army Inspectorate,[17] superintendent[18] of military studies and munitions, and so forth,[19] scholar of excellent truth, Ge Zhang-ndindzio (?).[20]

T3 Although since high antiquity the nature of water is to not move, wind arises whipping up waves that swell and roll without cease. Although the root of the True Body[21] does not change, karmic effects spread and appear, and troubles oppress never to cease. The Tathāgata[22] transforms the deluded, and the beings of the Six Paths of Transmigration obtain a name. The Holy One harmonizes dust and dirt,

T4 in transmigration through the Three Realms[23] sentient beings obtain birth. To the world above of utmost peace, few are those who one by one make their way; to the hell below of intense suffering, by the tens of thousands they rush to throng. Cherishing compassion, extending compassion, not begrudging compassion, the myriad buddhas have appeared in the world to exhort and save the people. Without form, assuming form, forms innumerable, in the country of Magadha[24]

T5 on the Vajra throne [the Buddha] achieved supreme enlightenment. The Golden Mouth (i.e., Buddha) in one utterance expounded the correct doctrine. Enlightening all according to their capacities, overcoming greed and ignorance, [he] is the honored teacher. The Transformation Body[25] manifested virtue and subdued evil spirits. Extending everywhere throughout the universe *(dharmadhātu)*, tending and tempering the misguided, [he] is father and mother. As for causes [of buddhahood] of past, present, and future,[26] among the myriad accomplishments of the Six Pāramitās,[27] wisdom is the greatest. Understanding and meritorious practice [gives rise to] the sublime bodily signs;[28]

T6 in one lifetime the fruits of merit from many *kalpas* were all fulfilled. The abiding days of the Efficacious Honored one came to a close; transforming [he] entered into nirvāṇa. Yet the fortunes of common people have not ended; the true relics in reality have remained. This Liangzhou stūpa is among the 84,000 reliquaries built to house the relics that Aśoka distributed around the world,

T7 a storage place of [*xing*]²⁹ *yan* relics. Although it was a true stūpa, it was already in ruins. When Zhang Gui was Son of Heaven, upon its [site he] had a palace built. That was Liangzhou, named Wuwei Commandery. After receiving the throne, Zhang Gui's grandson Zhang Tianxi³⁰ then gave up the palace and, inviting skilled artisans, had a seven-storied stūpa built. After this³¹ [the precious stūpa or Liangzhou]

T8 became Tangut territory and was often repaired; blessings were sought, offerings were made, and auspicious signs appeared; [it] is the pillar and root of the state. From the time [it] was built up to today, the fifth year *jiaxu* of Tianyou min'an, 820 (*sic*)³² years' time has passed. Afterward, in the second year of Da'an [1075],³³ the base supports of the precious stūpa collapsed. The Shijing (Sagacious and Pure) Empress

T9 Dowager and the Zhenling cheng³⁴ (Precious Necropolis Wall) Emperor commissioned various supplies, directors, artisans and others [to repair it]. Just as repair work was about to commence, at night a great wind arose and atop the stūpa a divine lamp appeared. At daybreak [the stūpa] had naturally righted itself and resumed its former [shape]. Again, in the eighth year of Da'an [1081] the Eastern Han (i.e., the Song), spreading evil intent, issued forth a large army and

T10 surrounded. . . . At the time when the Qiang³⁵ troops reached Liangzhou, a black wind blew so heavy and dark that hands held together could not be seen. [Above the stūpa] a lamplight shone brightly, enveloping the stūpa, and because of it the two armies fled in defeat and so dared not look [upon it] as before. After this, the Desheng (Abundant Potency) Empress Dowager and the Renjing (Humane and Pure) Emperor received [rule over] the land.³⁶ Then, in Tian[an]

T11 liding second year (1086),³⁷ it was ordered at all times to burn incense and distribute vows [to the stūpa?] without cease. Campaigning again in Han territory, the Empress Dowager herself went out at the head of the cavalry.³⁸ Just then in the middle of the night a lamplight [above the stūpa] beamed out, twinkling as brightly as the noonday sun. Entering the Han battle formation, [our troops] inflicted a great defeat. Of the numerous prodigies that before and since

T12 have appeared, all as in this case are without compare. Lucky and unlucky prodigal omens being frequent and widespread, in the past [our] forebears reported [them], so as to make clear their distinctions. In thus possessing such mighty merit, this golden stūpa of Liangzhou has passed through many years, winds whipping and rain lashing, until its colors have faded. Last year[39] there was a great earthquake, and seeing its timbers destroyed and its pillars knocked askew,

T13 the Desheng Empress Dowager and the Renjing Emperor, above to requite the merit of the Four Graces,[40] below to follow the governing of the Three Realms,[41] acting in reliance on the Six Pāramitās and proceeding in accord with the the Four Profoundly Great Vows,[42] therefore commissioned directors to assemble the various artisans, and in the fourth year *guiyou* of Tianyou min'an, on the twelfth day of the sixth month (8 July 1093), the repair work commenced.

T14 Construction was completed in the first month of the following year, on the fifteenth day (2 February 1094). The wonderful stūpa's seven stories [recall] the seven elements of *bodhi*;[43] the four sides of the splendid sepulcher govern the four rivers.[44] The tile-covered wooden beams resemble flying birds; the golden crown and jade pillar stand tranquil and secure; the splendid beauty of the seven treasures[45] is brilliant; all the colors and adornments harmoniously stand out. The golden light encircling the *bodhi* glows

T15 luminously;[46] the bodhisattvas painted on the walls resound with life. A dark mist appears over the temple buildings; the seven-storied wonderful stūpa adores the iron image[47] [?]. Finely woven hanging pennants cluster in flowery bunches; the silver-white incense burners gleam brightly. The various dharma objects are all set in place; the sacrificial utensils are each and every one whole and complete. Distributed in permanent endowment on behalf of the Buddha,

T16 fifteen ounces of yellow gold, fifty ounces of silver, for inner and outer [clothing] sixty lengths of patterned fine silk, seventy pairs of mixed brocade banners of patterned fine silk, and a thousand strings of cash; in permanent endowment on behalf of the monks, four government tiller households,[48] a thousand strings of cash, and a thousand measures *(hu)* of grain. On the fifteenth day of that year, it was ordered that the director of the Secretariat,⁴⁹ Liang . . .⁵⁰

T17 Zhenie,⁵¹ and director of the Capital Security Office,⁵² Wo Qujie,⁵³ be commissioned to compose a laudatory ode. A great feast was held, a ritual site⁵⁴ for teaching and confessions was established, and sūtras were chanted.⁵⁵ Thirty-eight persons were ordained as monks, and the lives of fifty-four persons condemned to die have been spared. Incense, flowers, and bright lamps of all kinds have been provided, and there is no deficiency of food and clean water.

T18 Bequests to the junior and senior supervisors and to the various artisans were generously bestowed according to the rank of each. (Eulogy text begins in next column.)

T19 A five-hued auspicious cloud covers [the stūpa] at dawn and golden rays fly; the myriad buddhas of the Three Times⁵⁶ circle around at night and the holy lamp appears. In one *kalpa* all was completed; having obtained the way and the land of our forebears, [our] hearts rejoice. All seven stories inspected, [we] have people of blessing and wisdom come to this Buddha shrine. For the black-headed [ones] under Heaven, in both suffering and joy [this is] the place to seek blessings;

T20 for the red-faced⁵⁷ [ones] on earth, in both strength and defeat it is the pillar and root. [From] the eighteen hells guilty beings obtain release; [to] the forty-nine stories [in the heavenly palace] of the happy Maitreya [they] hasten in eagerness. In the dim obscurity of the Three Realms, the lamp of wisdom is raised and everything illumined; [for] sentient beings in the sea of desire, a bridge of discernment is built and all cross over.

T21 Reconstruction of the divine temple is completed; in grandness of merit nothing before compares. Repair of the precious stūpa is finished; in fullness of good causes its endowments are lofty. Human bodies have no substance and resemble bubbles in the tide or the plantain;⁵⁸ human destiny lacks constancy, like autumn dew or summer blossoms to the eye.⁵⁹ Especially marvelous in charity and renunciation, the Three-Wheel Body⁶⁰ exhaustively clarified the principle of emptiness.

T22 With unshakable resolve, not clinging to the two extremes⁶¹ [one may] achieve the other shore. [We] pray that the throne be strong and secure, imperishable as the eastern bamboo; that the luxuriant intelligence of the divine mind swell endlessly, like the silver crests on the golden sea; that benefits of numerous deeds [through] correct thought and correct strength reap abundant rewards; that by reckoning the fruits of karma and making offerings to the Buddha and the Law our prayers may be fulfilled.

T23 [May] the winds and rains come in due course, and the precious grains always ripen. [May] the borders be at peace and order, and the common people contented. The principles of the Law are deep and widespread; [though] the inherent faculty of mind be not great, skillful phrases transmit the truth, and wise people do not hesitate between virtuous and wicked conduct. [When those] before inscribe and set up a stone recording marvelous deeds—excellent names! excellent names!—later people, examining and bringing [it] to light, will forever transmit the story.

T24 The court official overseeing the duties of making stūpa renovations and commemoration,[62] director of the Fiscal Commission,[63] army supervisor of the Southern Court,[64] the *jianpin*[65] subject Mai Majie.[66] The court official overseeing the duties of making stūpa renovations and commemoration, director of the Auxiliary Palace Fiscal Commission,[67] supervisor[68] of the two groups [attached to] the Shengrong [Temple] and the Gantong Stūpa, the monk who understands (expounds) scriptures, the subject Yaonie Yong[quan].[69]

T25 Assistant overseer of stūpa repairs, recipient of directives[70] in the Auxiliary Palace Fiscal Commission, the sacrificial officer,[71] the subject Muyang Eyi.[72] Supervisor of both[73] Fan (Tibetan?)[74] and Han monks at the Gantong Stūpa, the scarlet-robed monk, the subject Wangna Zhengyu. Assistant overseer of stūpa repairs, director of monks[75] at the Chongsheng Temple, scarlet-robed monk, the subject Lingjie Chengpang.[76] Assistant overseer of artisans,

T26 director of Han monks at the Gantong Stūpa, the scarlet-robed monk Jiu Zhiqing.[77] Assistant overseer of artisans [engaged in] stūpa repairs, assistant director of Han monks at the Gantong Stūpa, the scarlet-robed monk Bai[78] Zhixuan. Overseer of tile artisans at the stūpa, master of monks[79] Zhang Fanyi.[80] Overseer of provisions for artisans Bai Ashan.[81]

T27 The writer, scholar of rhyme, *lingpi*[82] officer of Audience Ceremonies,[83] the subject Hun-Weiming Yu.[84] Writer of the Han text, composer [of documents] in Han and Khitan [languages], the subject Zhang Zhengsi.[85] Assistant overseer of painters,[86] the monk Xie Zhixing.[87] Assistant overseer of carpenters, the monk Jiu Zhi[bo?].[88] Overseer of scaffolding,[89] Liu Gouer,[90] Sun....[91]

T28 Fifth year of Tianyou min'an *jiaxu*, first month *jiaxu*, fifteenth day *wuzi*,[92] the commemoration concluded. Overseer of stone inscribing[93] Weiyi[94] Yiyai, [and stone carvers?] Ren Yuzi, Zuo Zhixin, Kang Gouming,[95] Zheng[96] Sandui, Sun Kedu,[97] Zuo Jiyi, Zuo Paner,[98] Zuo Aling, Wang Zhen,[99] Yin Sun[?]. Decor artisan[100] Guo Daonu; metalwork artisan Yang[101]...

Translation of the Han Text

(seal script heading:)
Stele Inscription Commemorating Restoration of the Gan[tong Stūpa] in the [Huguo] Temple at [Liang Prefecture]

H1 [twenty-seven empty character spaces]...causes and conditions of wisdom, if each is compared...in general have many similarities to the teaching of the Five Constants[102] (i.e., Confucianism). Its substance penetrates humans deeply, and causes the wise and foolish to submit wholeheartedly and turn to a faith weightier than the vast ocean's expanse...

H2 [twenty-one empty spaces] [King Aśoka] caused 84,000 precious stūpas to be erected to enshrine Buddha relics and requite the Buddha's manifold favors. Now the stūpa at Wuwei Commandery is one of this number. In the more than a thousand years from Zhou to Jin there was no record made of its rise and decay.[103] When Zhang Gui[104] assumed power...

H3 and ruled at Liang, [he built a palace on the former site.... (Seven graphs missing)][105] [During Zhang Tian]xi's reign[106] in the palace appeared numerous miraculous omens.[107] Tianxi marveled at these phenomena. At that time someone addressed Tianxi, saying, "Formerly King Aśoka enshrined relics of the Buddha and erected stūpas throughout the world. This palace rests on the old foundations of one of those stūpas." Tianxi thereupon foreswore his palace, turning it into [a temple].

Annotated Translation 127

H4 On the site he erected a stūpa, and to suit [the need he summoned engineers] who were like Ban Shu[108] in skill to come manage its work. Its design was subtle; its guiding principles were quite unusual. The materials were simple; the traces of axe and hatchet were very crude, so that it looked as if easy to match. Yet successive generations of skilled artisans, however they governed their hearts and exercised their minds, could never fathom its standards. The construction of this stūpa has endured to the present,

H5 over [seven hundred][109] twenty years. Moreover, it is now a hundred years since the state of Da Xia was founded, possessed all the western lands, and made Liang an attached commandery.[110] The resonant responses aroused by the stūpa cannot be exhaustively recorded. Nonetheless, those who are well informed and credible say that, when in the past there had been a tilting [of the tower], each time they had tried to straighten it up, by dusk there always arose a great wind and rain, and all around could be heard only the sound of axe and chisel. The next day, the tower was standing erect.

H6 [Occasions similar] to this occurred again. During the rule of the former sovereign,[111] the Western Qiang invaded our borders and encroached on the territory of Liang.[112] That evening likewise arose a great thunderstorm; in the inky darkness shone a wondrous light above [the stūpa]. Gazing upon it, the Qiang cowered at its wondrousness and withdrew. Recently, owing to a breach of peace with the Southern State (Song), once again the imperial carriage was yoked.[113] [Empress Liang] campaigned in person and commanded the royal subjects to make prostrations and humbly pray. Hence, that our heavenly soldiers won successive victories must be owing to the hidden protection of the [stūpa].

H7 The year before last (1092) in winter there was a great earthquake in Liang Prefecture,[114] in consequence of which the stūpa tilted again. Local officials submitted an urgent report giving an account of the event. An edict ordered that repairs be undertaken, but before the recruited craftsmen had gathered, [the stūpa] reverted and righted itself. Now the Two Sages[115] (Empress Liang and eleven-year-old Chongzong), having taken the reins of state and followed the Former Meritorious (first Empress Liang and Huizong), have made civil affairs radiant and military discipline awesome; [all affairs] within and without are greatly ordered. The sacrifices to Heaven and Earth are always dignified, always reverential; offerings in the ancestral temple accord with the season and the concern....[116]

H8 The teaching of the Buddha is what [we] especially esteem. From the nearby capital precincts all the way to distant frontier posts; in mountains, forests, streams, valleys, villages and settlements, [wherever may be found] the sites of Buddhist temples, if of a single pillar or piece of tile but a scrap remains, there are none that are not repaired. How much more so those famous sites manifesting grandeur, for are they not the imperishable [monuments] of past and present? Hence this stūpa has been singled out and honored for its enduring spirit responses. Consequently it was ordered to augment its embellishments. Thereupon...[117]

H9 was put in charge of the work. All sorts of craftsmen contributed their skills; plasterers, painters, [some] to lay mortar on it, [some] to fill in its ornamentation. Its furnishings were lacquered in red; gold and malachite interweaving, radiant as sun and moon, in its elegance it looked like new. How splendid! How imposing! None can describe it. Moreover Wuwei is the hub of traffic from all four directions; carts and horses pass each other daily by the thousands. Hence among the milling throngs there are none who are not moved to visit the temple, carry out some good works, [expressing reverence][118]

H10 and faith. Thus have our Two Sages given rise to the thought of enlightenment. Grandly they carry out Buddhist activities, promote limitless good effects, and guide the blind and the deaf, so that daily accrue abundant benefits. How sublime and majestic! Truly are they what are called great illuminators of the barque of compassion.[119] Wondrous indeed! Since the Buddha appeared in the world, many years have passed and his teachings have been widely disseminated. What various schools esteem is in each case different, yet of those who uphold it [the dharma], there are none who do not exalt and

H11 extol it. Even the cruel and benighted also believe with great reverence; how much more so those who habitually exercise their wisdom. Thus there are those who use the adornments of the seven treasures[120] to build stūpas and to build temples; there are those who use wood and stone, tile and brick, to build stūpas and to build temples. Casting molds, colorful paints, mud plaster, and sand are all used to build them.[121] Therefore Buddhist stūpas and temples fill the universe; yet spirit responses so luminous as [in this][122]

H12 extraordinary case have never before been heard of. Can it be that the Buddha's awesome power has been singularly generous here? Can it be that the divine efficacious protection has that which it favors? If not, then our [state of] Great Xia has a deep root of good fortune, which the true virtue and true responsiveness [to the Buddha-nature] of our Two Sages has achieved.[123] The work of restoration commenced in the sixth month of the *guiyou* year [27 June–25 July 1093] and lasted until the first month of the *jia xu* year [19 January–17 February 1094], when labor was declared to be completed. [That month]

H13 on the fifteenth day it was ordered by edict to celebrate. Thereupon the dharma drums were beaten, the pious ones[124] widely assembled, and conjointly a dharma service was held, broadly benefiting everyone and further feasting[125] the monks. At a great assembly, thirty-eight monks were ordained and special amnesty was granted to fifty-four persons condemned to execution. To signalize the mighty event, a special bequest was made of fifteen ounces of gold, fifty ounces of silver, [sixty][126] bolts of silk cloth for garments,

H14 seventy pairs of brocaded silk banners of various patterns, and one thousand strings of cash, to be used as permanent endowment *(changzhu)* on behalf of the Buddha. An additional bestowal was made of one thousand strings of cash, one thousand bushels of grain, and four government households[127] to provide permanent endowment *(changzhu)* for the Fan and Han monks so that those who burn incense at dawn and dusk will be provided therein and those who eat rice gruel twice a day (morning and noon) will be supplied therein. As for temple buildings, hallways, monks' quarters, and meditation cells, for all materials used to repair dilapidations . . .

H15 there is no expense not provided therein. Thus, in what is needed there is no deficiency, and good fortune likewise is without measure. Therewith an edict was issued on behalf of the emperor,[128] ordering this subject to relate the event in summary form. In obedience to the edict, not obtaining withdrawal [out of unworthiness for the task], he has taken up the brush, composed his thoughts, and respectfully written this eulogy. Its text reads:

H16 How lofty the stūpa, whose foundations were laid by Aśoka. By virtue of causation it has engendered boundless blessings, houses the Buddha relics, and is fully ample in dignity. In over a thousand years, there was no record of its ruin and restoration. When Western Liang established its regime, a king called Zhang Gui had a palace built right on its former site. When [Zhang] Tianxi succeeded,

H17 divine miracles numerously arose and its responses were made manifest, so the stūpa was restored and the palace dismantled. Since Great Xia founded a state and possessed all the territory of Liang, the stūpa's auspicious prodigies have been too numerous to count. It has been known to have tilted, but, with the divine assistance of wind and rain, it always righted itself, achieving something never before observed. When the former Sovereign ruled, the Qiang invaded the border of Liang.

H18 Likewise there was thunder and lightning, violently creating utter darkness. A lamp appeared shining brightly, a holy light illumining sageliness. The invading troops cowered at this wonder and stealthily withdrew in their tracks. When relations with the Southern Court (Song) were severed and the Sovereign's armies again campaigned, beforehand an imperial officer was ordered reverently to offer prayers and sacrifices. Our might thus uplifted, the news of our victories consequently became known. It must be that the hidden protection [of the stūpa]

H19 assists those possessing the Path *(dao)*. Moreover, two years ago in winter, in the cyclical year *renshen* (1092), there was an earthquake in Wuwei. The stūpa was again knocked askew, and its sublime eminence was disturbed. [The Two Sages] desired to levy one hundred thousand craftsmen, but with the dragon kings and heavenly beings supporting and upholding [the tower], what need was there to rely on human strength? The Two Sages, full of reverence, again decreed its repair. [With the summoning of] mortarers and painters, there was nothing needed that was not supplied.

H20 The five colors were brightened anew; gold and malachite added to its luster. The renewal of old things is what is called surpassing benefit. Our Empresses and our Emperors for generations have venerated the Light [of faith] and have earnestly upheld the Indian scriptures *(zhudian),* ever reverent, ever dignified. From sincerity does virtue accumulate within, and the surpassing fruit [of enlightenment] is manifested without. Our enlightened Monarch's subtle virtues [will assure] boundless longevity.

H21 [six spaces left blank] Erected on the fifteenth day *wuzi* of the first month *jiaxu shuo* of the fifth year *jiaxu* of Tianyou min'an [1 February 1094]. The calligrapher of the Fan (Tangut) stele eulogy, *lingpi*[129] officer for Audience Ceremonies,[130] Hun-Weiming Yu. The secretary for correspondence with North and South (Liao and Song), Zhang Zhengsi, did the calligraphy [of the Han text] and also the seal script headings. The stone artisans Weiyi Yiyai, Ren Yuzi, Kang Gou[ming].[131]

H22 The court official overseeing the duties of commemorating the temple,[132] director of the Secretariat,[133] holder of [the rank of] Complete Fulfillment,[134] Liang Xingzhenie.[135] The court official overseeing the duties of commemorating the temple, director of the Capital Security Office[136] and concurrently director of the Calendar Board[137] and the Army Board,[138] the *lüjing*[139] scarlet-robed monk Wo Qujie.[140] The court official overseeing the duties of commemorating the temple and supervising restoration, director of the Fiscal Commission,[141] army supervisor[142] of the Right Wing,[143] the *qiejie*[144] subject Mai Majie.[145] The court official overseeing the duties of commemorating the temple and supervising restoration,

H23 director of the Auxiliary Palace Fiscal Commission[146] and concurrently supervisor of monks both at the Shenrong Temple and the Gantong Stūpa, the *lüjing* scarlet-robed monk Yaonie Yongquan. Overseer[147] of provisions for supplying temple restoration, director of the Auxiliary Palace Fiscal Commission, the *couming*[148] subject Wu Modou.[149] Assistant overseer of temple and stūpa restoration, director of the Auxiliary Palace Fiscal Commission, the *liming*[150] subject Liu Quliyai.[151] Assistant overseer of temple and stūpa restoration, [director] of monks at the Chongsheng Temple,

H24 the scarlet-robed monk Lingjie Chengpang.[152] The supervisor of both Fan and Han monks at the Huguo Temple, Gantong

Stūpa, scarlet-robed monk Wangna Zhengyu.[153] Overseer of the various artisans engaged in temple restoration, director of Han monks at the Gantong Stūpa, the scarlet-robed monk Jiu Zhiqing.[154] Overseer of [artisans inscribing] the stone stele [commemorating] restoration of the temple,[155] assistant director of Han monks at the Gantong Stūpa, scarlet-robed monk Bai Zhixuan. [Overseer of artisans engaged in][156] tile work for repair of the temple and the stūpa,

H25 [[157]] [stūpa master Zhang Fanyi. Overseer of provisions for the artisans Bai Ashan. Assistant overseer of artisans in charge of colors (paints), the monk Xie Zhixing. Assistant overseer of carpenters, the monk Jiu Zhi[?]. Overseer of scaffoldings, the monk] Liu Gouer. Stone artisans: Zuo Zhixin, [Zheng] Sandui, Zuo [Aling], Wang Zhen, Sun Duer, Sun [Ke]du, Zuo [Ji]yi, Zuo Paner, Sun Rezi . . .

CHAPTER 6

Reading between the Lines: A Comparison and Analysis of the Tangut and Han Texts

BACK TO BACK on a stone slab, the 1094 inscriptions of Liangzhou capture the tensions in the fine balancing of protocol, pragmatic compromise, and political defiance at work in late-eleventh-century Xia. Between them unfolds a dialogue over the formulation of Tangut/Xia identity, at a time when competing claims of ethnicity, culture, rulership, gender, and statehood carried weighty political consequences. In this chapter I will discuss the structure and significance of the two texts translated in Chapter 5.[1]

Structure, Style, and Authorship

Both texts of the 1094 stele inscription treat basically the same topics in the same order, and the length of subsections is in most cases also the same. Yet in style and in the precise content of each topical subsection, the Tangut and Han texts diverge markedly. Without doubt they were composed independently true to the stylistic conventions of each language in compositions of this nature. The Tangut text is somewhat longer and often more detailed than the extant Han text. On the basis of their divergent datings of the earthquake of 1092 (T12, H7 and H19), moreover, I speculate that the Tangut text was composed earlier than the Han text (Chapter 5, note 39). We can outline the basic structure of the texts as follows:

A. Introduction
   1. T 1–2: Full title of inscription, followed in T2 by the introduction of two high-ranking officials as "explicators," who perhaps presided over the ceremonies or composed this portion of the text.
   2. H1: Effaced.

B. Discourse on Buddhism
- 1. T 3–6: A lengthy summary of the Buddha's origins and history in verse form.
- 2. H 1–2: A cursory description of Buddhism, parts effaced.

C. History of stūpa at Liangzhou (ca. six columns each)
- 1. T 6–12: Minor but significant variations from H.
- 2. H 2–6.

D. Recent damage suffered by the stūpa, the throne's patronage of Buddhism and repair of the stūpa, description of stūpa
- 1. T 12–15.
- 2. H 7–12: This section is longer than T, as it includes material covered elsewhere or not at all in T.

E. Ceremony and endowments to temple (three columns each)
- 1. End of T15 to top of T18: Lists endowments first, then describes the ceremony; does not introduce eulogy.
- 2. H 13–15: Describes ceremony first, then lists endowments, introduces eulogy.

F. Verse eulogy (five columns each).
- 1. T 19–23: Five paired couplets of four and seven characters each per column (4–7 4–7 4–7 4–7 4–7) until last column (4–4–4–4–4–4–4 8–7–4–7). Buddhist content, no repetition of previous lines, lengthy vow.
- 2. H 16–20: Thirteen four-character phrases per column, twelve in last column. Repeats, virtually verbatim, the history of stūpa and its repair recited in lines 2–7.

G. Date and list of names (five columns each)
- 1. T 24–28: Date appears at top of T28; names and titles can in most cases be matched with those in H. More names preserved.
- 2. H 21–25: Date appears at top of H21, followed by names and titles; last column badly effaced.

Perhaps the first striking difference lies in tone. The Tangut inscription overflows with allusive, metaphorical Buddhist language, largely absent in the Han version. Whereas the Tangut text elaborates Buddhist themes, the Han text gives a straightforward narrative account, stressing historical themes, employing clichés typical of Chinese historical prose, and inserting a little more local color.

The seemingly more "secular" tone of the Han inscription may reflect the literary preferences or experience of the author, or the models followed in composing the piece, or an effort to play to the loyalties of the longtime resident Han population of Liangzhou. An emphasis on local history as an essential component of the "national" identity and welfare might appeal more effectively to the likely audience of the Han text: ethnic Han and Chinese-reading patrons of the temple. The Tangut text expresses a devotion to Buddhism and to stūpa worship shared by a large segment of the Xia population and elites, and closely mirrors the empress dowager's personal piety. As we have seen, the cult of stūpa worship had extensive local roots and a long history, which the court appropriated to serve the political needs of the state and, more specifically at this time, the regency. Furthermore, the Aśokan ancestry imputed to this particular stūpa legitimated claims to a kind of superpotency by historicizing its links to the source of power, the historical Buddha himself. In both cases, official patronage of a popular Buddhist site would strengthen local loyalties to the central government.

Aside from its Buddhist content, the language of the Tangut text exhibits a rich lyrical quality deriving from a complex verse structure used extensively throughout the text. I have not tried to reconstruct the rhyme scheme. According to more expert opinion, Tangut verse form is characterized by initial rhyme and both grammatical and semantic parallelism.[2] The latter, at least, is so strongly pronounced as to be of great help to the translator, and I have sought to preserve it in my English rendition. T 3–4 provide good examples of this parallelism in my translation. Kychanov links this verse style to Central Asian traditions among Altaic and Tibetan speakers.[3] Numerous examples of this style can be found among the Tangut literary compositions in the Kozlov collection in St. Petersburg.

Who composed these texts? Unlike the other temple inscriptions examined in previous chapters, no compilers are identified as such. Both inscriptions tell us the name and official titles of the two persons who did the calligraphy *(shu)* for the Tangut and Han texts, respectively (H21 and T27). In the subsection preceding the verse eulogy *(ming)* that occurs about two-thirds of the way through each text, we learn that (1) In H15 an unnamed subject was ordered by imperial edict to compose the eulogy, and (2) in T 17–18 director of the Secretariat Liang (Xing)zhenie and director of the Capital Security Office Wo Qujie were commissioned to go (to Liangzhou, presumably) and to compose a laudatory verse for the fifteenth day of the first month, 1094. It seems unlikely that Liang and Wo personally wrote any part of the Tangut text; the commissioned verse or ode must refer to something to be delivered during the ceremonies at the temple.

The Tangut calligrapher named in T27/H21, Hun-Weiming Yu, was a rhyme scholar and *lingpi* officer in the Office for Audience Ceremonies *(gemen si)*. *Lingpi,* a Tangut title of uncertain meaning, seems to be concerned with document editing.[4] His double surname includes the imperial clan name, perhaps the result of marriage or special reward.[5] The Han calligrapher (T27/H21), Zhang Zhengsi (a Chinese), held the title of secretary for correspondence with Liao and Song (*gong xie nanbei zhangbiao,* or "skilled writer [for documents] between the Khitans and the Chinese"). Did these two have a hand in composing the respective texts of the inscriptions?

Who, moreover, were the two persons introduced as "explicators" in T2? What was their function here, and did mention of them appear in a now effaced portion at the beginning of the Han text? Both held high positions in the central government, one a director of the Calendar Board (a third-rank agency) and assistant director of the Saṅgha Office (a second-rank agency), the other in the Inner Palace Council (a second-rank agency) and director of the Army Inspectorate (a third-rank agency), placing them close to the empress and in her trust. Both also carry the designation of "humane teacher."[6] These two could very well be the authors of part of the Tangut text, which, beginning in the next line, instructs through the use of parables and metaphor (*yu,* the Chinese gloss for the Tangut term identifying their function, translated here as "explicator," *yuzhe*). They were officials, real or honorary Tanguts (judging by their names), at least lay Buddhists (Mingwang Qi'e is not titled a monk although he held clerical positions), scholars and teachers, employing language appropriate to the occasion to propagate basic Buddhist truths.

Since the Han text lacks a corresponding explication of Buddhist themes, mention of these two persons probably did not occur in any effaced portion of its first lines. This omission highlights the orientation of the Tangut text toward the inner, power-holding, and staunchly Buddhist elite of the Xia court.

This second line of the Tangut text, which constitutes its opening passage, poses the most difficulty of all in translation. In time I am sure that we will puzzle out the meanings of the two men's titles, my English renderings of which must now stand with question marks, implied if not actually inserted. I sense that they are of critical importance to understanding the text and the events it encodes, and I use the word "encode" deliberately. Tangut was an encoding script, its main purpose seemingly to conceal and protect.[7] Likewise, the two individuals introduced in this line stand in front like wrathful guardian deities, concealing and protecting the dharma and its upholders, here the empress dowager and her son.

The Buddhist Vision of State, the State Vision of Buddhism

Both texts convey a clear political message: This stūpa enshrines Buddha relics and radiates Buddha-power; imperial promotion of its cult protects the state and enhances the legitimacy of the throne. Enemies had better think twice before challenging that power. H12 makes the point emphatically: "Can it be that the Buddha's awesome power has been singularly generous here? Can it be that the divine efficacious protection has that which it favors? If not,[8] then our [state of] Great Xia has a deep root of good fortune, which the true virtue and true responsiveness [to the Buddha-nature] of our Two Sages has achieved." If the author of the Han text hoped to dissuade potential defectors or rebels, then the authors of the Tangut text paint the stūpa as the instrument of both national and personal salvation (T 19–20):

> For the black-headed [ones] under Heaven, in both suffering and joy [this is] the place to seek blessings; for the red-faced [ones] on earth, in both strength and defeat it is the pillar and root. [From] the eighteen hells guilty beings obtain release; [to] the forty-nine stories [in the heavenly palace] of the happy Maitreya [they] hasten in eagerness. In the dim obscurity of the Three Realms, the lamp of wisdom is raised and everything illumined; [for] sentient beings in the sea of desire, a bridge of discernment is built and all cross over.

The Tangut text also explicitly names the stūpa as the foundation of the state (T8): "[The precious stūpa] became Tangut territory and was often repaired; blessings were sought, offerings were made, and auspicious signs appeared; [it] is the pillar and root of the state."

Thus the functions of the stūpa are, in our analytical categories, simultaneously religious and political: protection and enlightenment leading to salvation of sovereign, subject, and the state defined by their relationship. Our texts furnish a clear illustration of this vision.

In more striking terms, the Tangut text affirms the Buddhist commitment of the dynasty. T13 informs us that the empress dowager and the emperor have acted in accordance with the "Six Pāramitās" and the "Four Profoundly Great Vows," that is, they have taken lay bodhisattva vows and are pursuing the fulfillment of those vows through public acts designed to instruct, uplift, and save sentient beings, as well as to enhance their own enlightenment and the accrual of merit from those deeds. H10 expresses the throne's commitment to Buddhism as the aspiration for enlightenment, which leads the "Two Sages" to perform numerous deeds of compassion. This aspiration for enlightenment is the starting point for the pursuit of bodhisattvahood. Both texts leave little room for doubting the throne's zeal or sincerity in embracing its goals, which implies or requires the politicization of its vision.

Like its Northern Liang and Northern Wei predecessors, Tangut Buddhism was a state religion in the ways identified and discussed by Chisui Satō for the Northern Wei.[9] Satō defines three aspects of a state-supported religion: (1) state control of the religious community through monastic officials and regulation of ordination; (2) development of the content of the religion, its doctrines (or practices, one supposes), to serve the state, to which it was indebted; and (3) the state's use of the religion to control the general population. Satō focuses on the second aspect in his analysis of Yungang statuary and finds that images of Śākyamuni and Maitreya dominate the expression of faith, from which he concludes that the caves express "a Buddhistically tinged view of the Emperor, a view that sought to make the series leading from the emperors of the past to the one of the present coincide with the one leading from Gautama to Maitreya."[10] Our inscriptions are not so informative as the Yungang caves and do not permit so substantive an analysis of the content of Tangut Buddhism. For that we must rely on twelfth- and early-thirteenth-century sources, which reflect the progressive influence of Tibetan missionary activity on Xia Buddhism, iconography, architecture, and in particular the state cult.[11]

The third aspect, the state use of Buddhism to control its subjects, tends to elicit blanket negative condemnations from modern scholars, especially those trained in a Marxist tradition. Chinese scholars, not surprisingly, are inclined to dismiss "Buddhism" as more oppressive and corrupting than "Confucianism," an assumption grounded more in cultural biases than in historical analysis. The evidence from the eleventh century is too scanty to allow a definitive judgment on the question of state control of the population. If by control we mean indoctrination in a set of values and loyalties (as opposed to, for example, mechanisms for collecting taxes), then without question the Xia state, like every state, pursued this program from the very beginning, in its dissemination of a writing system, establishment of schools, patronage of Buddhists (and Confucians), translation and printing of texts, and so forth. But who was the target of this indoctrination, and when? Who needed to be controlled the most, and when? The throne's concerns focused naturally on its officials, military officers, and tribal aristocrats, but more specifically on the question of defining and demarcating who belonged to or could enter the ranks of the elite. To the extent that Buddhism was the religion of the dynasty, it was also the religion of the elite, in the way that Confucianism can be considered the religion of the Chinese elite. We might then ask, did the throne or state view it as a means of shaping or controlling elite loyalties and values?

Perhaps a more important political and cultural function of Buddhism, for Xia rulers, was not so much its utility in controlling people, but rather its capacity to tolerate difference and promote community among people of diverse background, language, and livelihood. (The same could be said for Confucianism.) As a common set of elite values emerged gradually, its debt to Buddhism was at least the equal of its debt to Confucianism. In these inscriptions the throne speaks in the language of Buddhism to transcend particularity; it speaks in the language of politics and ethnicity to privilege particularity. As the passages quoted above reveal, in places the two overlap: the particularities of Tangut ethnicity and Xia statehood stand in a privileged relationship to the power of the Buddhist dharma and its receptacles (e.g., the stūpa).

The Rhetoric of Politics and Ethnicity

A close examination of some eleven points of divergence between the two texts for what they might reveal about the audience and the intent of each yields the following observations: First, the Tangut text uses what I call the language of political legitimacy far more frequently than the Han text. Second, the Han text smooths over or omits insulting references to the Song or culturally specific references to the Tanguts found in the Tangut text. Furthermore, the Tangut text omits culturally specific references to the Chinese found in the Han text.

1. First, compare the two headings: The top half of the seal script heading of the Han text is partially effaced, but it can be reliably reconstructed to read "Stele Inscription Commemorating Restoration of the Gan[tong Stūpa] in the [Huguo] Temple at [Liang Prefecture]." The intact Tangut text announces, "Imperially Decreed Stele Inscription of the Gantong Stūpa." Use of the term "imperially decreed" (Chin. *chi*) asserts the independence and legitimacy of the Tangut throne and government vis-à-vis Song and Liao, in official correspondence with whom the Tanguts were not allowed to use such language. Its regular use of the language of political legitimacy, as I have termed it, distinguishes the Tangut text from the Han.

2. T1 gives us the official Tangut name of the Xia state: the Great State of White and High (lit. *bai gao guo da;* in Chinese rendered Bai Gao Da [Xia] Guo), also absent from the Han text, perhaps effaced. Note that the Tangut version of the state's name does not include the word Xia, which occurs in Tangut texts composed only after the Mongolian conquest of 1227.[12]

3. In the brief discourse on Buddhism in the extant portion of H1, the text assures us that *prajña* or wisdom is compatible with Confucianism: "in general [it has] many similarities to the teaching of the Five Constants." The Tangut text contains no such nod toward Confucian categories. The composers of these two texts had their respective audiences in mind.

4. Relating the rebuilding of the stūpa under the fourth-century Former Liang regime (ca. 313–376), H 2–3 says: "When Zhang Gui assumed power and ruled at Liang..." whereas T7 reads: "When Zhang Gui was Son of Heaven (Chin. *tianzi*)...." In the eulogy of the Han text, H16 refers to Zhang Gui as *wang*, king or prince. In official Chinese historiography, Zhang Gui was an autonomous local ruler but a Jin subject, much as contemporary Song and later Chinese regarded the Tanguts. Would an assertion of imperial status for the Former Liang ruler have been unacceptable or offensive to the Xia Chinese (who would not be expected to read the Tangut text)? Its presence in the Tangut text promotes Xia legitimacy through inheritance of the upgraded legacy of Liangzhou's past.

The Northern Wei conquest of Liangzhou in 439 profoundly influenced the nature of Tuoba Wei Buddhism, adding essential ingredients of emperor-worship and a Maitreya cult to produce the Northern Wei equation of emperor and Buddha, so vividly expressed in the Datong cave-temple statuary.[13] Weiming Yuanhao, the first Tangut emperor, appropriated the Wei legacy by professing descent from the Wei rulers. His clan had adopted the Tuoba surname early in the Tang period. Clearly the Tangut monarchs sought to position themselves in a sacral-political genealogy, to which the Tangut text of this inscription also subscribes. Tangut Buddhism, however, differed from that of the Wei. Too much had changed in the interim.

5. T 6–8 omit the historical and cultural references of H 2–4: "In the more than a thousand years from Zhou to Jin . . ." (H2) and the engineers with the skill of Ban Shu (H4). Allusion to Ban Shu would have meant little or nothing to most Tangut readers but would have been immediately recognized by a literate Chinese (see Chapter 5, note 108 to H4).

6. H5, explaining Liangzhou's current status, notes that ". . . the state of Da Xia was founded, possessed all the western lands, and made Liang an attached commandery." T 7–8 bluntly summarizes, "After this [Liangzhou/the stūpa] became Tangut [Mi] territory," using the Tangut ethnonym Mi instead of the more ethnically neutral Da Xia. Mi definitely resonated with Tangut readers.

Here we may also ask, why do these texts pass over in silence the centuries intervening between Zhang Tianxi's construction of the stūpa and the Tangut conquest of Hexi? Why no mention of the earlier Tang inscription, from which it would appear that the Xia authors derived their account of the stūpa's origins? Perhaps the authors merely wished to get on with the story and not to dawdle over details inessential to the thrust of their message. Perhaps, too, they wished to suggest a direct connection between the earlier rulers of Liangzhou and their own overlords. In such a case one would expect some mention of the Tuoba Wei incorporation of Liangzhou into its empire, in the light of the Tangut founding emperor's claim of descent from the rulers of the Later Wei (see Chapter 2). If, in the absence of documentation, the authors were reluctant to fabricate their own, this was not the case for the Tang. We may conclude, therefore, that the authors of the 1094 texts were not particularly interested in the history of the stūpa, except insofar as it bore directly on their own concerns, the religious potency of the site and its role in the political legitimation of the Liang-Weiming regime.

7. T 9–10 attribute the Qiang (Kokonor Tibetan) invasion of Liangzhou to the "evil intent" of the "Eastern Han" (Song), who also sent a great army against Xia at this time (1081). This critical reference to the Song is absent in H6, which blandly refers to a "breach of peace with the Southern State." Note also the different directional modifiers used to denote the Song state; in Tangut texts

the Chinese are regularly "east" and downhill from the "high" Tanguts.[14] T10 forcefully describes the effect of the miraculous stūpa's numinous power: "because of it the two armies [Chinese and Tibetan] fled in defeat and so dared not look [upon it] as before." H6 leaves the impression that this fate befell only the Tibetans.

8. T 8–9, and T11 give Tangut reign era dates for three important events in Xia history, which the Han text relates in sequence with time words like "later" and "after the Two Sages assumed the reins of state." The Han text names only the reign era for the date of completion of temple repairs (Tianyou min'an). Reign era names constitute language of political legitimacy. In the tenth century, Chinese envoys from Shazhou to Khotan regularly used royal Khotanese era names in diplomatic correspondence, a protocol that acknowledged the prestige and political status of the Khotanese court in the region.[15] Either the Song unification of China rendered such practices problematic for Chinese living in close proximity to Song but under non-Han rule or other reasons explain why the Han text uses reign names less often than the Tangut text.

The three reign dates in question are Da'an 2 (1075), Da'an 8 (1081), and Tianan liding 2 (1086). Da'an was a reign name used by the Tanguts from 1074 to 1084, and then in 1085 the Khitans adopted and used it until 1095.[16] The fact that the Liao court was using the Da'an reign title at the time of this inscription must explain its absence from the Han text, for the reader will recall that Zhang Zhengsi, the calligrapher of the Han text, was a secretary for correspondence with Song and Liao, and would have been intimately familiar with all protocol requirements for Xia documents directed to those courts. This sensitivity strengthens the impression that the authors of these texts had a very wide audience in mind and that Khitans (or Liao Chinese) were included in the audience of the Han text.

Presumably, as vassals of Liao the Tanguts did not use their own reign titles in correspondence with the Khitans, following the practice between Xia and Song (strict parity was observed in Liao-Song protocol). Did the author of the Han text deliberately omit details that might offend a Chinese or a Khitan reader? Might there have been Khitan guests at the ceremony in Liangzhou? (By the treaty of 1044 Song envoys to Xia stopped at Yuzhou, north of the border, and never even got as far as the capital, much less farther, which helps explain the paucity of reliable Song information about Xia.[17] We have no evidence that Liao envoys were similarly restricted.)

The question of the reign date following Da'an, Tianan liding, is more complex. I speculate that the Tianan liding of the Tangut text is an error for Tianyi zhiping, and I have consigned the details of my argument to the long note appended here.[18]

As we might expect, the Tangut text's use of reign era names accompanies references to the empresses dowager Liang by formal titles, my next point.

9. T 8–9 and T13 mention the two empresses and the two emperors by Tangut titles posthumously bestowed (in the case of Huizong and the first Empress Dowager Liang) or used during their lifetimes (in the case of Chongzong and the second Empress Dowager Liang). The Han text refers to the throne more discreetly: "Two Sages" (regent and emperor), "former Sovereign," and so forth. In the Tangut text, the empress is always named first, followed by the emperor, as in the imperial prefaces to Buddhist sūtras of this era.[19] Even H20 boldly announces: "Our Empresses and our Emperors for generations have venerated the Light," but the Tangut text highlights the empress' preeminence and makes it clear that she, not merely the "throne," led troops against Song in 1087 (T11: "the Empress Dowager herself went out at the head of the cavalry"; H6 reads "campaigned in person," leaving the subject implicit).[20] The youth of the emperor left no doubt who was meant in either case, but the open assertions of the Tangut text might have been thought jarring to the Chinese audience of the Han text, numbers of whom must have strongly disapproved of her "usurpation" of imperial prerogative.[21]

But just how concerned were the empress and the author of the Han text to avoid alienating Chinese subjects? Were not the real contenders for power her Tangut peers in the military aristocracy, her own clan, and the Weiming nobility? They as well as the Saṅgha establishment were the intended audience for these assertions, not the Chinese. We ought to understand, then, that they would read the Tangut rather than (or in addition to) the Chinese text. Yet, the careful wording of the Han text means that someone took pains to cultivate a certain audience, convey a certain impression. The empress needed to legitimate her position before all influential groups in the Xia government and elite, not to mention the hostile Khitans; the Weiming, who helped her to eliminate her brother, needed to reassure their Chinese constituency, who probably figured among their staunchest supporters.

10. In H7, this reassurance took the form of proclaiming of the boy emperor Chongzong (r. 1086–1139) and his mother that the "Two Sages ... have made civil affairs radiant and military discipline

awesome.... The sacrifices to Heaven and Earth are always dignified, always reverential; offerings in the ancestral temple accord with the season and the concern." Missing in the Tangut text, this explicit reference to emphatically Chinese concerns might also be read as an assertion by the Han text of the language of political legitimacy, since these rituals were the proper functions of a Chinese Son of Heaven (although perhaps not unique to the Chinese monarch).[22] And, significantly, the ancestors in that ancestral temple were Weiming, not Liang.

11. T 19–20 of the verse eulogy also alludes to ancestors, but evoking the progenitors of the Tanguts in an emotive and exclusive way. Here, in the last couplet of column 19 and the first couplet of column 20, we find the numinous stūpa linked with the well-being of the Tanguts: "For the black-headed [ones] under Heaven, in both suffering and joy [this is] the place to seek blessings; for the red-faced [ones] on earth, in both strength and defeat it is the pillar and root." "Black-headed" and "red-faced" are familiar tropes for the Tanguts, found frequently in Tangut literature.[23] Chinese and Tibetans also used the epithet "black-headed," and Tibetans referred to themselves as "red-faced," too, but here the paired phrase belongs unmistakably to Tangut folklore. One entry (33.251) in the Tangut dictionary *Wenhai* identifies Mu/Mbu as the "father of the black-headed, the name of an ancestor"; another (10.241) names his son.[24]

T19 stresses the geographic as well as ethnic connection between the numinous stūpa and the Tanguts: "the myriad buddhas of the Three Times circle around at night and the holy lamp appears. In one *kalpa* all was completed; having obtained the way and the land of our forebears, [our] hearts rejoice." Here "the land of our forebears," obtained presumably in the conquests of the first three Tangut rulers (Li Jiqian, Li Deming, and Weiming Yuanhao), broadly signifies the Ordos and Gansu territories where émigré Tanguts (and other non-Han peoples) settled in massive numbers during the Tang. This appeal therefore works on several levels: ethnocultural, ancestral-familial, geographic, and religious.

The passages discussed above illustrate how the authors of the two texts tailored their rhetoric to suit their audiences. One could hypothesize that a Weiming sympathizer composed the Han text and a Liang proponent the Tangut text. The argumentation of the Tangut text is more didactic and polemical than the Han text, reflecting Empress Liang's piety and political needs. It is important to remember that her son, eleven-year-old Chongzong, also figured in her considerations (and possibly in the audience for the ceremonies conducted at the stūpa). He would have studied a copy of this text, absorbing both Buddhist lessons and family history, in a version designed to impress upon him the great merit of his mother's line in defending the throne of his father's line.

Names and Titles: Chancellery Practice in a Multiethnic Empire

The 1094 stele inscription can be analyzed as an official document of the Xia state and throne. Excluding the two shorter and earlier Buddhist inscriptions discussed in Chapters 2 and 3, for which no original steles or Tangut versions survive, it is the only such document extant for the eleventh century and thus invites comparison with data on Tangut administration from later and more abundant twelfth- and early-thirteenth-century sources. The danger of comparison lies in reading back later norms and practices into an earlier period. With that caution in mind, however, we can attempt a systematic examination and interpretation of the names and titles preserved in the texts.

Excluding those of the empress, the emperor, and historical figures, at best thirty-two names can be recovered from the Tangut text and twenty-six from the Han text. At least three of the officials named in the Tangut text have no Han equivalent: Mingwang Qi'e (T2), Ge Zhang-ndindzio (T2), and Muyang Eyi (T25), all Tanguts. Five or six more names have apparently been effaced in the Han text: Zhang Fanyi (T26), Xie Zhixing (T27), Jiu Zhi[bo?] (T27), Yin Sun[?] (T28), Guo Daonu (T28), and Yang[?] (T28). Two officials named in the Han text have no Tangut equivalent: Wu Modou (H23) and Liu Quliyai (H23). Likewise the Tangut version of Sun Rezi (H25) apparently has been effaced from T28 (or may be the partially visible name currently reconstructed as Yin).

Effaced or no longer readable names occur primarily in the list of miscellaneous artisans, supervisors, and stone carvers that fills the final columns of both inscriptions. Judging by their surnames, most were Chinese: Zhang, Bai, Xie, Jiu, Liu, Sun, Ren, Zuo, Kang, Zheng, Wang, Gao, Yang. The supervisor of stone carvers, Weiyi Yiyai, was probably Tangut. Moreover, the occurrence of four Zuos and three Suns indicates family specialization, probably registration with the government as hereditary artisan households.[25]

Trying to discern whether someone was Tangut (Dangxiang or other) or Chinese on the basis of family and personal name can be uncertain business. How and to what extent did names serve as ethnic markers in Xia, and what meanings did ethnicity carry at this time? Simple answers elude us. Tangut literary remains preserve numerous lists of clan or family names, divided with deceptive neatness into two categories, Tangut *(fan)* and Han; in dictionaries such as *Wenhai* such entries are simply denoted as "clan names" (i.e., Tangut names) and "Han names."[26] To cite one example, extant portions of the Tangut and Chinese versions of the Xia classified lexicon *Zazi* both contain name lists of varying lengths. The extant Chinese text opens with 138 Han names, grouped in pairs, followed by sixty pairs of Tangut names. In the Tangut text *Sancai zazi,* Tangut names come first, in all 244 pairs, followed by a short section containing forty-six personal names, then eighty-four Han surnames in forty-two pairs.[27]

It is commonly assumed that the Han names are all single surnames, assembled in pairs for literary or aesthetic reasons, whereas the Tangut names are, with a few exceptions, all double surnames. By and large this is the case, but it does not mean that someone with a Chinese surname, like Liu, was necessarily ethnic Han or that someone with a Fan surname was necessarily Tangut by origin (or Tibetan, Khitan, Uighur, Sogdian, or Turk). The Xiongnu state builders of the third to fifth centuries used the Liu surname,[28] and although by the tenth century these Lius had presumably intermarried into local Chinese communities, some of them may have intermarried with any of the numerous non-Chinese groups settled west and north of Shanxi during the Tang period. Not all Tanguts had double surnames; some, for reasons of family tradition or expediency, used or adopted single Chinese-style surnames, often abbreviating and sinicizing a native clan name, a practice well documented for the northern dynasties of earlier centuries.[29] I suspect that Wo Qujie and Mai Majie of our texts (discussed below) may illustrate this practice. Likewise, local Chinese undoubtedly adopted Tangut surnames, through marriage or imperial bestowal, for example, as happened under the Khitans and the Mongols.

We can only speculate on the principles governing the composition of Xia name lists, let alone how people actually read or used them. The Xia population and ruling elite included other ethnic groups, notably Tibetans and Uighurs, who are mentioned frequently in the Tiansheng code. Most likely their common surnames appear together with Tangut names in these lists under the rubric of Fan.[30] Although I indicate in my annotations to the translation (Chapter 5) when I have found a name from the 1094 inscriptions in these lists, these name lists by themselves tell us little about the cultural or ethnic identity of the name bearers. That identity can only be determined from context.

The assertion or assignment of ethnicity through such markers as names became, under the volatile circumstances of the eleventh century (and later), a voluntary, contingent, and political act, and was not a fixed biological or genealogical condition. Seemingly contradictory phenomena emerge, such as the ultranativist regent's clan of Liang, using a surname that was both Chinese and Tangut, and that must have been understood as such by the Tanguts. Indeed it is registered under both rubrics in Xia name lists. My usage of the terms "Chinese" ("Han") and "Tangut" ("Fan") therefore cannot be more precise than my subjects, and often by "Tangut" I mean any non-Han Inner Asian subject or agent of Xia. When the context requires or permits greater specificity, I supply it. Because the matter was clearly of concern to contemporary Xia writers and statesmen, I try to discern patterns in the usage of supposedly "Han" or "Fan" names and suggest what these patterns might mean.

Ethnicity was a highly charged category of denotation and connotation throughout this period. Xia Chinese played a visible and necessary part in government; Xia law and practice tended to promote ethnic equality and did not restrict intermarriage. Ethnic groupings of monks is a special case that needs to be analyzed in the broader context of the history of local monastic and administrative practices. Yet although the Tanguts did not impose sweeping legal discrimination of the Mongolian-Yuan kind,[31] they remained sensitive to the need to demarcate lines of privilege and access to power in order to protect their own position, and so legislated accordingly. For example, article 844 of the Tiansheng code requires Chinese officials in the Xia government to wear Chinese-style caps on duty, presumably to mark their ethnic status, a consideration in certain matters of protocol, as we shall see below.[32]

A careful examination of the individuals with official rank in the 1094 texts will elucidate Tangut strategies of accommodation and protection, and may explain, for example, why some names occur in one text but not in the other. We have already considered above the case of the two "explicators" named in T2, and will leave them aside for now. The next four officials named in the Tangut text and the first four in the Han text (excluding for now the two calligraphers Hun-Weiming Yu and Zhang Zhengsi) are identical and appear in the same order in both texts: Liang Xingzhenie (T 16–17, H22), Wo

Qujie (T17, H22), Mai Majie (T24, H22), and Yaonie Yongquan (T24, H23). All four occur together in H 22–23, at the beginning of the last section. The Tangut text splits them up, the first two appearing in lines 16–17, and the other two heading the list of names in the last section.

In the Han text the titles of all four are prefaced with the phrase *duda goudang*, which may be understood to mean "court officials overseeing the duties of. . . ." The duties referred to are specified in the phrase immediately preceding *duda goudang*; in the case of Liang and Wo it is *qing si* "commemorating the [restored] temple." T 16–17 omits this designation (*du'an toujian*, from Tangut) for Liang and Wo, and instead relate that these two were ordered to go (to Liangzhou) and compose a laudatory verse. Wo Qujie and Liang Xingzhenie, thus, fulfilled purely honorary roles as representatives of the central government sent to Liangzhou to participate in (or preside over, if the empress and the emperor did not do so personally) the ceremonies marking completion of repair.

Mai Majie and Yaonie Yongquan played a more active role, on the site supervising the repair project. In their case, *duda goudang* is modified by the prefix *qing si jian xiu*, "commemorating the [restored] temple and supervising restoration" in H22 (and its equivalent in T24), thus "court officials overseeing the duties of temple commemoration and restoration." Mai and Yaonie were probably already in Liangzhou, as their titles suggest, Mai as army supervisor of the Southern Court (Right Wing) and a director of the Fiscal Commission (rank 2), and Yaonie, a high-ranking monk, as superintendent of monks at the Shengrong Temple and the Gantong Stūpa and a director of the Auxiliary Palace Fiscal Commission (rank 4). Their postings to these fiscal agencies were probably special assignments received in connection with the temple repair project.

In regard to Liang Xingzhenie and Wo Qujie, H22 provides more information than T17; it reveals, for instance, that Wo too was a scarlet-robed monk and a director of the Calendar Board (rank 3) and the Army Board, as well as the Capital Security Office (rank 2). The Tiansheng code does not mention the Army Board (Chin. *tongjun si*) in articles describing the bureaucratic hierarchy, although the name does appear in Gule Maocai's late-twelfth-century glossary, so it was not clear if the post was merely an honorary one. That an ordained monk should serve in such high central government positions is a noteworthy phenomenon that was apparently not restricted to the regency era of Tangut politics, as numerous references in the Tiansheng code suggest.

The multiple directorships (executive officers) of many of these offices (recall that Mingwang Qi'e, T2, was also a director of the Calendar Board) looks like a variation on Song practice and raises the question of how this multiple staffing actually worked and to what extent it was used to achieve ethnic or other kinds of checks and balance. Presumably some directors were more powerful than others. Under the circumstances, considerations of protocol and precedence assumed the utmost importance for the Tanguts. The Tiansheng code provides several guidelines on the matter in article 704:

> If among people holding office a Tangut, Chinese, Tibetan, or Uighur serve together and occupy variously ranked posts or perform different functions, then precedence (lit. "seating") will be determined in accordance with the established rank of each. Exceptions: If [they] perform the same functions and their posts are equivalent, then rank shall not be considered and the Tangut should take precedence. If the rule is violated, those having rank will be fined one horse, and commoners will receive thirteen strokes of the rod.[33]

Article 705 elaborates a special instance:

> If an imperial relative and a Tangut hold the same post and perform the same functions, then in [determining] seniority in agencies of capital standing (?),[34] the imperial relative should take precedence. If two Tanguts occupy the same post, then in determining seniority and in handling documents, it should be [according to] difference in rank. If ranks are equal, then where there are civil and military ranks, civil rank should take precedence. If [they] have the same civil and military rank, then the person of greater age should be considered [senior].[35]

Wo Qujie and Mingwang Qi'e, one of the two "explicators" of T2, were both directors of the Calendar Board. The other ranked office given for each is also of the same level (rank 2); we do not know what honorary ranks they may have held. If both were Tanguts, as I suspect, then presumably one was older than the other and perhaps on that basis took precedence when they met (or sat) over duties concerned with the Calendar Board. If Wo was Chinese (and wore his Chinese cap to work), then Mingwang took precedence.

We may finally observe that of these four top officials at least three were Tanguts, all four if we include Wo Qujie (in Tangut Wo's personal name means "golden dog"; compare Mai Majie below). I have already reviewed the case for considering Liang Xingzhenie as a Tangut rather than a Chinese, despite the prevailing view among contemporary Chinese scholars that the Liang clan was of Chinese origin. The personal name of this director of the Secretariat was certainly not Chinese, and I would argue that even if the Liang name was originally Chinese, this holder of it was not. In any event, he was a member of the regent's clan and thus of the inner elite. If the Secretariat had multiple directors in the late eleventh century, as the mid-twelfth century law code prescribes, however, then this Liang's position was not necessarily all that powerful (unlike that of his recently deceased kinsman, the empress' brother Liang Qibu); he presumably shared this dignity with other Tanguts, though perhaps not with Weiming clansmen in 1094. Yet his superior rank of "Complete Fulfillment" *(shou juzu)* assured him ritual precedence and might have dictated that he and not some other chief officer of the Secretariat go to Liangzhou on this occasion. This would have suited the purposes of the empress Liang.

As for Mai Majie, the element *mai* is written with the same Tangut graph used for the element *ming* of Mingwang Qi'e's name; and the personal name Majie, "golden horse," was almost certainly a Tangut appellation. He was an army supervisor of the Right Wing, an important military post not likely to be entrusted to a Chinese in the late eleventh century.

None of the remaining officials were designated *duda goudang (du'an toujian);* they held positions in local or regional administrative units connected specifically with the repair project and the temples. Let us consider the next four officials named in the two inscriptions: Muyang Eyi (T25), Wu Modou (H23), Wangna Zhangyu (H24, T25), and Liu Quliyai (H23). Of interest here is the fact that Muyang Eyi is not mentioned in the Han text, whereas Wu Modou and Liu Quliyai are not mentioned in the Tangut text. Muyang, a Tangut, was a "recipient of edicts" *(chengzhi)* in the Auxiliary Palace Fiscal Commission and assistant supervisor of temple repairs. He was therefore subordinate to Wu Modou (a Chinese?), a director of the same agency and supervisor of temple repairs. Was there no room for both names? Did ethnic considerations decree that the Tangut text would include Muyang and the Han text Wu? And was Liu Quliyai also excluded from the Tangut text because, as assistant supervisor of temple repairs (like Muyang) but also a director of the Auxiliary Palace Fiscal Commission (like Wu), he too outranked Muyang? Was Liu a Chinese with a Tangutized personal name, or a hybrid Fan? In either case, his use of a clearly non-Chinese personal name presumably conveyed more than fashionable trends in naming.

Wangna Zhengyu, probably a Tangut, had nothing to do with the Auxiliary Palace Fiscal Commission; he was supervisor of Han and Fan monks at the Huguo Temple and the Gantong Stūpa, and the only one of these four who was a monk and whose name appears in both texts.

Including Yaonie Yongquan (in the first group of four), we have here three directors of the Auxiliary Palace Fiscal Commission, out of a possible four prescribed by the twelfth-century law code. This concentration was obviously dictated by the requirements of the project. Of these three, the highest in rank was a Tangut and a monk, Yaonie Yongquan.

In sum, of the eight officials discussed so far only one, Wu Modou, seems to have been Chinese, but even his personal name is suspect and looks Inner Asian.[36] The evidence bespeaks a systematic exclusion of Chinese from the top ranks of officials involved in the stūpa repair and celebration project. Whether or not this exclusion was typical of the government in general for this period is a question meriting further study.

The other persons named with titles were all monks associated with the temple complex or lay supervisors of various aspects of the repair project. More Chinese emerge in their ranks (in order of appearance):

1. Lingjie Chengpang (T25, H24), a Tangut scarlet-robed monk, assistant supervisor of stūpa repairs, and director of monks at the Chongsheng Temple;
2. Jiu Zhiqing (T26, H24), a Chinese scarlet-robed monk, (assistant?) supervisor of artisans, director of Han monks at the Gantong Stūpa;
3. Bai Zhixuan (T26), a Chinese or Tuyühun scarlet-robed monk, assistant supervisor of artisans, assistant director of Han monks at the Gantong Stūpa, and thus the immediate subordinate of Jiu Zhiqing.
4. Zhang Fanyi (T26), a Chinese, supervisor of tile artisans, master of monks (although not designated a monk, which he presumably was);
5. Bai Ashan (T26), a Tuyühun (judging by both parts of his

name),³⁷ supervisor of provisions for artisans, perhaps related to Bai Zhixuan, which would strengthen the case for regarding the latter as a Tuyühun with a monastic personal name;

6. Xie Zhixing (T27), a Chinese monk, assistant supervisor of painters;
7. Jiu Zhibo (T27), a Chinese monk, assistant supervisor of carpenters;
8. Liu Gouer (T27, H25), a Chinese (?) monk, supervisor of scaffoldings.

If most of these figures were Chinese, the Tangut Lingjie Chengpang took precedence in the listing and apparently in his posts.

Finally, there are the two calligraphers, Hun-Weiming Yu (T27, H21) and Zhang Zhengsi (T27, H21), in that order, a member (or affiliate) of the royal clan and a Chinese, respectively. As I speculated above, the compound surname of the first suggests a Tuyühun nobleman married to an imperial princess. Hun-Weiming was a Tangut literatus, scholar of rhyme (this datum is absent from H21), and a *lingpi* in the Office for Audience Ceremonies *(gemen si)*. According to Charles Hucker, the Office of Audience Ceremonies in Song and Jin times retained some of its former Tang function of collecting memorials, which may also have been the case in Xia.³⁸ The Tangut agency was fairly important (rank 2), and its protocol officers were instrumental in enforcing such provisions of the code as article 704 quoted above, as that article goes on to describe. In editing the text of the inscription, Hun-Weiming Yu would have verified that the involved officials were listed in the appropriate order of precedence (the two "explicators" of T2 being an exception).

Zhang Zhengsi composed letters and other documents in Chinese for diplomatic correspondence with the Song and Liao courts. Here, however, no title indicates to which office he was attached or what level of bureaucratic rank he enjoyed, leaving the impression that he was a humble Chinese scribe. Such clerks, of whom probably the overwhelming majority were Chinese, provided the mainstay of the government. For one thing, they were literate, which could not always be assumed of their superior officers.³⁹ For another, at least one or two clerks had to be on duty around the clock in all government offices, to keep tabs on state property and paperwork.⁴⁰ It is likely that Zhang Zhengsi plied his skills in the capital, attached to the Central Secretariat, given the nature of his duties.

Now that we have examined the names of persons, let us turn to the designations of titles of rank and office. Here an alternation between transliteration and translation of Tangut terms and Sino-Tangut calques from one language to the other becomes readily observable, but the principles governing the choice or decision about when to translate and when to transliterate are not so apparent. Both devices frequently occur together in one and the same document, for one and the same term. We do not yet clearly understand the Tangut system of titles and ranks, what they meant and conferred on the bearer, under what circumstances and how they were bestowed, how they related to each other systemically. The Tangut system was probably not much less complicated than the Song, and we have far less information about it.

The Han text follows chancellery conventions worked out for correspondence between Xia and Song (perhaps Liao too) when it gives a Chinese transliteration of Tangut government titles, many originally based on and translated from Chinese models. A good example is the rendering of Liang Xingzhenie's office in H22 as *mingsai zheng*, which transliterates the Tangut calque of *zhongshu zheng*, or director of the Central Secretariat. The Tangut graphs do not, however, directly translate the Chinese words *zhong* and *shu*; the first means something like "remonstrate," and the second means "clean."[41]

It would be analogous to the American government instructing Mexico that it must not use the titles "Department of State" or "Department of Defense" to refer to its own governmental agencies in official correspondence with the United States. Instead, the Mexicans are to employ the Spanish versions of those titles in diplomatic documents that are otherwise written in English. In effect this was the arrangement worked out for diplomatic correspondence with the Song court, whose representatives refused to acknowledge Xia letters or envoys using Chinese administrative nomenclature.[42] That this seemingly clumsy way of conforming to the demands of Song protocol makes familiar titles look exotic is probably a good thing and should prevent us from assuming that they in fact signified similar things. Surely the Tangut Secretariat worked differently from the Song agency bearing that name. But why should a document ostensibly generated for internal use resort to these devices? Before answering this question, let us examine systematically all the occurrences of this sort.

In the Chinese text of the inscription I have found twelve instances in which a Tangut phrase was transliterated. They are listed below, first the Chinese phonetic transcription of the Tangut, then the Chinese translation.

H21
   1. *dianji lingpi, gemen* [*lingpi*]

H22
   2. *mingsai zheng, zhongshu zheng*
   3. *huai wo le, shou juzu*
   4. *woze luo, huangcheng si*
   5. *dingzhi luo, da heng li yuan*
   6. *waimu luo, tongjun si*
   7. *lüjing, jingjie*
   8. *niezu, jianjun*
   9. *qiejie?*

H23
   10. *wugu, toujian*
   11. *couming?*
   12. *liming?*

Numbers 1, 2, 4, 5, 6, 8, and 10 designate government offices and/or official posts with known Chinese equivalents. Numbers 3, 9, 11, and 12 transliterate original Tangut titles or honorary ranks, only the first of which can be identified from other internal sources. The other three do not appear in the Tangut text of the inscription, in two cases because the bearer is not mentioned there. In the case of *qiejie*, the Tangut text gives what appears to be a different title for the bearer. But transcriptional practices were not consistent, and a great variety of Chinese graphs can be found transcribing the same Tangut words.

More interesting is number 7; *lüjing* transliterates a Tangut phrase or Buddhist title meaning "understands/expounds the scriptures." That no Chinese equivalent or translation was used suggests that *lüjing* was a fairly prestigious title of Tangut origin that would be recognizable to an ethnic Han or sinophone reader of this inscription.

In fact, I am tempted to conclude that all the transliterations appearing in the Han text were in common use and would be immediately understood by the educated hearer/reader. Otherwise the document becomes incomprehensible, as it would have struck a "foreign" Chinese not familiar with Xia vernacular, and that would have vitiated its rhetorical impact. Thus, in the process of meeting their own governing needs and in conforming to the requirements of intercourse with Song China, the Tanguts created a hybrid administrative idiom, traces of which can be found scattered throughout Song private letters and histories. Like yet another "encoding" script, in addition to their writing system itself, it protected Chinese from acknowledging their rival and concealed the rival's true identity. Presumably Song intelligence officers and protocol functionaries had a key to that idiom, but it has been lost.

Later, we find that the Tangut phrase for Secretariat may appear in translated form and transliterated, side by side. An instance of this usage appears in the memorial of presentation prefacing the Tiansheng code, which lists twenty-three people involved in compiling the code. The first two high-ranking officials held the obviously honorary post of *zhongshu ling,* here in a transliterated form. The third held the first of the six chief executive posts in the Secretariat, and in his title the ministry appears in its translated form.[43] Why the distinction in rendering "Secretariat"? Was it transliterated when denoting a purely honorary title and translated when the attached title denoted an actual executive position? It remains to collect more instances of this usage before we can explain its import.

What about transliterations of Chinese terms and names in the Tangut text? One might expect a large number, but surprisingly one finds relatively few. Leaving aside consideration of personal names, which pose special problems, we count transliterations of two place names (Liangzhou and Wuwei), one administrative loan word *(zheng),* and three Buddhist terms (*sheli,* [*sarīra,* "relic body"], Ayu [Aśoka, a personal name], and *boluomi* [*pāramitā,* "perfection"]). The only other transliteration occurs in T25 and T26, where a Tangut graph is used to spell the Chinese word *zhong,* in the meaning of a "group" or collectivity of monks. Why the Tanguts should prefer to borrow this particular Chinese word rather than using one of their own defies easy explanation. In fact, many Chinese loan words made their way into Tangut, though few appear in this text.

The incidence of transcription in these texts, therefore, documents the emergence of a hybrid administrative vocabulary that had become fairly well known. It also points to the numbers of Chinese loan words in common usage and to a flexible approach in rendering Buddhist terms through both transliteration and translation, which probably reflects the predominantly Chinese originals from which Buddhist translations were made at this time (it would be interesting to compare translations made from Chinese and Tibetan).

The foregoing analysis suggests that over several generations Xia rulers and their partners constructed an administrative apparatus that achieved a high degree of articulation in response to the needs of the state. Although the governing system owed much to its Chinese models, it was unique in many of its particulars, reflecting its Inner Asian sources and its solutions, some more successful than others, to the need to accommodate an ethnically and linguistically diverse population of mixed livelihoods and ecological adaptations. It will be the task of another study to exploit the Tiansheng code in an attempt to reconstruct that system in at least its normative structures and processes. Moreover, Tangut rulers, like the Chinese emperor Sui Wendi, found in Buddhism the most effective and widely shared cultural language for bridging some of those differences. To accomplish that bridging, they had to construct myths, elaborate a state cult, and regulate the Saṅgha, for we can be sure that Buddhist practice and belief varied widely among the people whom they ruled.

CHAPTER 7

Conclusion

IN LATE-ELEVENTH-CENTURY XIA, faith in the Buddha, his word, and the divine powers of protection adhering in relics and the structures housing them had become one of the underpinnings of the Weiming dynasty and the state it founded. The throne strove to establish a particular, even unique, relationship between itself and the potency of the Buddha, whose protective and salvific powers it could then channel on behalf of the state and the Tangut people. The welfare of the state and its subjects, then, depended on the cultivation of that imperial relationship (pursuit of the bodhisattva ideal) and the creation of institutions for its manifestation and dissemination. The state, the privileged elites, the Saṅgha, the Huguo Temple and its lay supporters, the Kāśyapa Rulai Temple and its adherents, the inhabitants of Liangzhou or Ganzhou created and participated in institutions that served to define the self-understanding and status of individuals or groups as members of the community.

Surrounded by hostile and powerful neighbors who challenged or tried to constrain their state-building activities, Tangut rulers not surprisingly showed a special interest in the apotropaic qualities of Buddhism. All the factions struggling to shape the state-building process seemed to share this interest, according to the evidence at our disposal. We have no reason to suppose that at any time the Weiming and their allies were less committed to Buddhism than their rivals, the Yeli, the Mocang, and the Liang. The Weiming struggle to keep and solidify power over the throne and the military, however, inclined them, whenever possible, to adapt the institutions of the centralized Chinese monarchy. These measures met stiff resistance throughout the eleventh century.

In our inscriptions, as in their lifetimes, the empresses Liang took on the role of defending the Tangut Xia against the Chinese Song as well as against their own male relatives. They challenged the conventions for "women" in the same way and for reasons similar to those for which earlier Weiming emperors (Jingzong, Yizong) challenged the conventions for "barbarians" and strove for parity with Song. But whereas the later Weiming strategy was to seek parity or a compromise (symbolized by Han rites), the Liang empresses rejected compromise. Instead, they used the military and the Saṅgha to resist internal as well as external domination and to assert another vision of the Tangut state (symbolized by Tangut rites), which many Tanguts must have shared with them. The Tangut text expresses the second empress Liang's challenge and vision; the Han text partially softens the message for a largely Han audience.

What happened in twelfth-century Xia with the apparent demise of the maternal regent's power? Weiming Renxiao came to the throne in 1139 at age sixteen, an adult for all practical purposes. Born after the last wars with Song had been fought, he was the first Xia ruler not to come of age on the battlefield. Xia stayed more or less out of the fighting between the Jurchens and the Chinese and did not challenge the Jurchens militarily along their own borders. If the throne's commitment to Buddhism wavered following the purges that accompanied the Weiming restoration of 1099, it revived under Renzong (r. 1139–1193). His mother, Lady Cao, was perhaps a daughter of the Cao family that had ruled Shazou in the late tenth and early eleventh centuries, and almost certainly was a devout Buddhist.

In the dramatically altered political landscape of the mid–twelfth century, Song China was no longer a threat to Xia, permitting a post facto "reconciliation." The Jurchen conquests also brought new waves of Han and Khitan immigrants to Xia, feeding the cultural renaissance of the twelfth century but also introducing new sources of political instability. A surrendered Chinese military officer, Ren Dejing, rose to become a powerful minister and nearly succeeded in carving out an independent state from the southeast provinces around Lingwu. Ren Dejing, however, is not presented in the Song dynastic history as a spokesman for Confucian cultural values; to the contrary, he reportedly opposed the educational and bureaucratic reforms of Renzong on "Mohist" grounds.

At the same time, Tibetan influence in Hexi and at the Tangut court was growing. From these currents emerged a particular blend of Tibetan Buddhism and Confucian ethical statecraft, which left its mark on the ruling vision and ideological foundations of the Tangut monarchy in its mature form.

The "voices" that I have tried to elicit from Xia sources do not speak in unison, nor are they "pure" and unambiguous. In the final analysis, they remain untransparent and untranslatable. We cannot reconstruct them as some kind of "authentic" native alternative to the prevailing Chinese Confucian repertoire. But we also cannot read them as a corrupted (i.e., sinified) parody of some pristine, now lost Tangut original. The very act of making and legitimating a state was transformative; it created something new.

Analysis of the 1094 inscriptions and other eleventh-century materials suggests a number of critical moments, or defining characteristics, in the evolution of Tangut statehood. In particular, ethnic pluralism emerges as a prominent fact of life and became institutionalized in various provisions of the twelfth-century law code. The categories "Han" and "Fan" were both literary conceits and political strategies for marking off a new "field" and defining its borders as distinct from "China," "Khitan," "Tibet." The viability of the new "field" depended on sustaining a balance between "Han" and "Fan." Fan, as we also saw, at one level denoted "Tangut," the ruling element that negotiated the balance and legitimated the "field." At another level, Fan included a mixed array of Inner Asians, who along with "Han" and "Tangut" stood in particular relationships with each other that expressed that balance and its legitimating fulcrum.

A tension always existed between the inherently exclusive claims of ethnicity and genealogy, and the ambitions of Tangut rulers, whose legitimating myths were both exclusive (we the Mi people) and inclusive (we are recognized leaders of the Fan). The inclusion of Han people and cultural elements was at first a geopolitical imperative; it did not redirect the focus of legitimating appeals, for which Fan remained the primary subject. The question of how Xia Chinese viewed themselves under these circumstances, how they formulated their identities, has so far not been posed or examined. Yet it would seem to be of critical importance in understanding the success of Tangut legitimation. To what extent, in fact, did the balance between "Han" and "Fan" involve a meshing of the two? And, if meshing occurred, at what level of the social hierarchy and with what consequences? How would our conventional notions of what it meant to be "Chinese" be modified by the experiences of Xia Chinese?

Buddhism, one might suppose, provided Xia rulers with a means of appeal that crossed ethnic, genealogical, and class lines to embrace all segments of the population. Everyone participated in the popular rituals of the religion, and yet we should beware of assuming that ideological uniformity and social control resulted from imperial patronage of Buddhists. For one thing, the privileging of the Saṅgha gave it the power to mediate state control. For another, the existence of communities of monks organized along principles of ethnic segregation alerts us to the fact that monks, like everyone else in Xia and like monks anywhere in the world, were first of all members of local social and political communities. The concern with ethnic boundaries was not a function of royal patronage of Buddhism, but rather a pervasive feature of Tangut society.

The Tiansheng code indicates that ethnic and genealogical claims played a fundamental role in the structure and functioning of the administrative apparatus of state, a situation no doubt even truer of the eleventh than of the twelfth century. For the earlier period these claims and the continual struggles with Song imposed constraints on the inclusivity of legitimating appeals that Tangut rulers or elites could make. Xia was not setting itself up to rule "all under Heaven." In this respect it was closer to Liao than to Jin, despite the Khitan success in presiding over "all under Heaven" with the Song, and remained so throughout the twelfth century as well.

Appendices

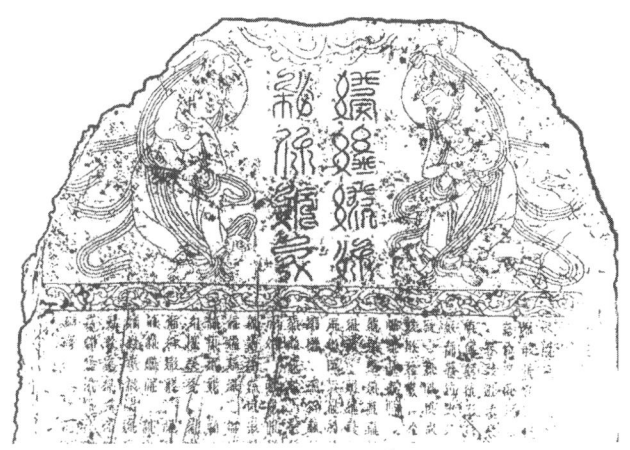

APPENDIX A
Photoreproductions of Rubbings of the 1094 Gantong Stūpa Stele Inscriptions

8th

Photoreproduction of the Tangut text of the 1094 stele inscription. Seal script heading and first eight character spaces of all twenty-eight columns.

1094 Tangut text, with the ninth and twenty-third character spaces indicated.

1094 Tangut text, with the twenty-second and fortieth character spaces indicated.

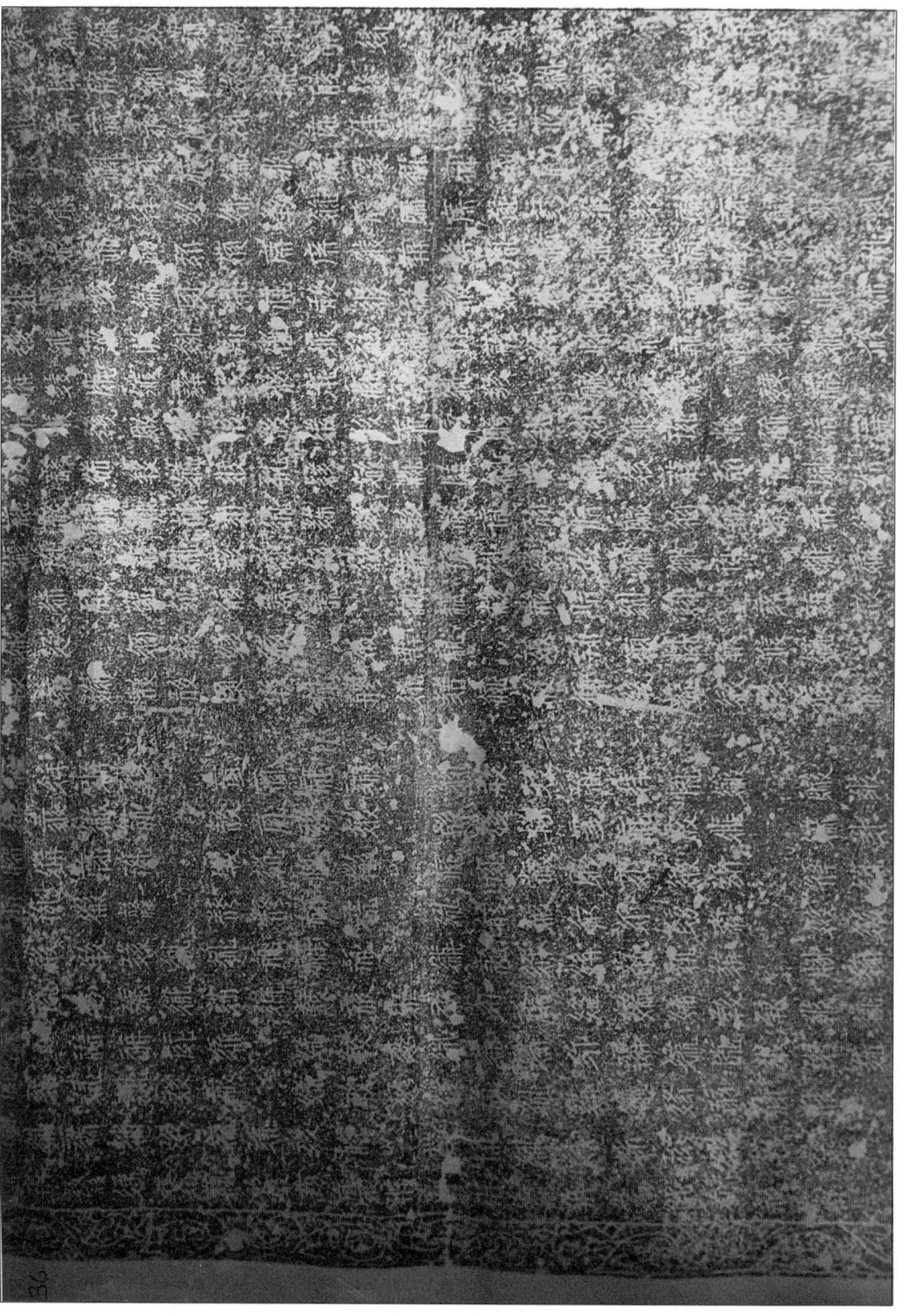

1094 Tangut text, with the thirty-sixth and fifty-third character spaces indicated.

1094 Tangut text, to the bottom of the rubbing (sixty-fifth character spaces no longer legible).

Photoreproduction of the Han text of the 1094 stele inscription. Seal script heading (here mostly effaced) and first section.

1094 Han text, second section.

1094 Han text, third section.

1094 Han text, fourth section.

1094 Han text, to the bottom of the rubbing.

APPENDIX B
Chronology of Sources Recording or Discussing the Inscriptions on the Gantong Stūpa Stele

The works discussed here are not listed in the bibliography unless also cited in the notes. Available bibliographical data are supplied here for works not cited elsewhere. Works that appear in the bibliography are marked with an asterisk.

1. Chu Shangling 初尚齡 (?).
Jijin suojian lu 吉金所見錄, published ten years before Zhang Shu's account, in 1827 (Daoguang 7), Guxiang shu she zang edition. *Juan* 13:9 cites the comments of Liu Qingyuan 劉青園 (Shilu 師陸). Devéria mistakenly attributed this work to Liu Qingyuan. The relevant passage that Devéria translates from *Jijin suojian lu* diverges from the text that I consulted in the Harvard-Yenching Library and translate as follows:

> Liu Qingyuan says: Local people at Liangzhou have excavated a number of jars of old coins. Among them, [those dated] Kaiyuan (713–741) are most numerous. All the various coins of Northern Song, Liao, and the Xi Xia reign periods Yuande, Tiansheng, Qianyou, Tianqing, Huangjian, and Guangding are also quite numerous. And of this kind of Fan (Tangut) character coin there are also several items. I joined the investigation and found over a thousand coins. In addition, at the Dayun Temple in Liangzhou I found an old stele. On its front side were just these [Tangut] characters. The seal script on the reverse side of the stele could be deciphered to read "erected in Tianyou min'an fifth year." Thus one can know that this cash is written in Xi Xia Fan script.

One need not read Liu's statement as a claim to having discovered the stele; he evidently came upon it after Zhang Shu had it uncovered (see below). This passage, however, was a possible source for Yan Kejun's remarks (no. 3 below).

2. Zhang Shu, 1781–1847. Native of Wuwei.
**Yangsu tang wenji*, published in 1837 (Daoguang 17). *Juan* 19:18b–20a describes his discovery of the stele in 1804; this passage was

173

later reprinted in *Gansu xin tongzhi* 92:30ab (see no. 9), and in *Longyou jinshi lu* 4:56ab by Zhang Wei (see no. 14), who puzzled over Zhang Shu's erroneous attempt to decipher the Tangut heading. He does not record the stele texts. Zhang Shu's note is quoted above in Chapter 4.

3. Yan Kejun, 1762–1843.

* *Tieqiao jinshi ba*, 4 *juan*, probably published between 1827 and 1837 (the editions I examined have no prefaces). *Juan* 4:18ab credits Liu Qingyuan with discovery of the stele. Yan's comments are reprinted by Luo Fucheng (p. 178; no. 12 below). Yan's entry is titled "Jieqing Temple Gantong Stūpa stele, Tianyou min'an fifth year first month." It begins:

> This stele is located at the Dayun Temple in Liangzhou. It was erected in the fifth year of the Tianyou min'an reign era of the Xi Xia [emperor] Chongzong. The names of the compilers have been effaced. Zhang Zhengsi did the calligraphy as well as the seal script headings. Collectors of bronze and stone inscriptions have not yet recorded this item; it was first discovered by *xiaolian* 孝廉 Liu Shilu (Qingyuan) [*sic*]. Both sides of the stele are engraved with characters. On the front side the Xi Xia script cannot be read. Comparing it with the regular (i.e., Chinese) writing on the reverse side, there is some discrepancy in the number of lines and words per line, so it is also hard to match [word for word].

4. Wu Rongguang 吳榮光, 1773–1843.

Comments attributed to Wu are cited by Lu Yaoyu, Lu Zengxiang, and Zhang Wei (nos. 5, 11, and 14) from a work called *Yunqing guan jinshi ji* 筠清館金石記, which I was unable to locate. It may be a different or an earlier draft of the *Yunqing guan jinwen* 金文, published in 1840 (Daoguang 22, per Hummel, *Eminent Chinese of the Ch'ing Period*, 873), which contains no mention of the stele. The biography of Wu by Fang Chao-ying (Hummel, 873) remarks that a catalogue of Wu's collection of bronzes and stone inscriptions, under the title *Yunqing guan jinshi wenzi mu* 金石文字目, exists only in a manuscript.

5. Lu Yaoyu 陸耀遹, 1771–1836.

Jinshi xubian 金石續編, 21 *juan*, preface dated 1868 by Lu Zengxiang (his son? see no. 11 below). *Juan* 20:1b–5a records the Chinese text, for the first time, along with the comments of Wu Rongguang and Lu Zengxiang (20:4b–5a):

> After Xi Xia Li Jiqian's grandson Yuanhao set up a state, in three generations the throne passed to Qianshun. Qianshun was enthroned in Song Yuanyou 2 [*sic*], a *dingmao* year. [In that year Xia] changed the reign era to Tianyi zhiping. Again, three years later in the *gengwu* year, the reign era was changed to Tianyou min'an. This stele was erected in Tianyou min'an 5, a *jiaxu* year, in the first month; which actually was the ninth year of Song Yuanyou and therefore the eighth year of Qianshun's reign. In the fourth month of that year Song changed the reign era to

Shaosheng. On the reverse (*sic*) side of the stele is the Fan text, which cannot be read. According to the names listed at the end of the above recorded Han character stele, where it says "writer of the Fan stele . . . *dianji ling* . . . Hun-Weiming Yu," we know that the above stele preserves their national script. (*Yunqing guan jinshi ji*)

According to a supplemental entry in the catalogue of the original work titled *Yunqing guan jinshi ji*, the epitaph to the Buddha-relic stūpa of the Dayun Temple is precisely this stele. (Lu Zengxiang *zhi* 志)

Wu Rongguang's chronology of reign eras typifies the confusion adhering to narratives of this half-decade of Xia history.

6. G. Devéria, ? fl. 1897.

*"Stèle Si-Hia de Leang-tcheou," *Journal asiatique*, n.s., 11 (1898): 53–74; an almost identical version also appeared in *Mémoires présentés par divers savants à l'Académie des inscriptions et belles-lettres*, ser. 1, no. 11 (1901): 147–175. Transcription and translation of Chinese text, photograph of rubbing of Tangut text. In 1896 Devéria obtained rubbings of both texts through the French Consul in Beijing, M. Gerard, but for some reason did not publish a photograph of the Chinese rubbing. Later he presented the rubbings to the Institut de France. (An inquiry to that institution in 1987 revealed only that the rubbings are no longer there.) His transcription adheres to the format of the inscription, reproducing the original columns. The French translation is a pioneering effort.

7. Wang Renjun 王仁俊, 1866–1913.

Xi Xia wenzhui 西夏文綴, 2 *juan*, preface dated 1904–1905; published as a supplement to his *Liao wen cui* 遼文萃 (19??). Wang's text is identical to Lu Yaoyu's (no. 5), although he corrects some of the vulgar forms found in Lu's text. He gives as his source a rubbing of the stele (the same as Lu's?), but locates it in Lanzhou.

8. Ye Changchi 葉昌熾, 1849–1917.

Yushi 語石, 10 *juan*, published in 1909. *Juan* 1:27 (in the Guoxue jiben congshu edition reprinted by the Shanghai Commercial Press in 1936) discusses the Gantong stele, without recording the text:

Throughout the Song period, with Liao and Jin, South and North shared borders. Apart from this there were yet the Zhao family scions (i.e., the Tangut royal family), who occupied Lingwu and established reign eras. . . . As for their stone engravings, there was only the Gantong Stūpa stele, erected in the fifth year of Tianyou min'an. It is located in present-day Wuwei district of Liang prefecture. The local people call it the Fan character stele because one side of it is written in Xi Xia script.

9. *Gansu xin tongzhi* 甘肅新通志, comp. An Weixun 安維峻 and Sheng Yun 升允, published in 1909. *Juan* 92:30ab records only Zhang Shu's account of his discovery but no text.

10. Luo Zhenyu 羅振玉, 1866–1940.

Xichui shike lu 西陲石刻錄, 1 *juan*, Xue chuang congke edition, privately published in 1914. Records both texts, being the first to transcribe the Tangut. Luo notes (34a):

> [The stele] is one *zhang* high, three feet (*chi*) four inches (*cun*) in breadth. All four edges are severely defaced. Twenty-six columns are preserved, and each column retains seventy characters. The heading is written in seal script: [blank] [blank] *zhong xiu* 重修 [blank] [blank] *si gan* 寺感 [blank] [blank] *bei ming* 碑銘, three columns of twelve characters. The reverse (*sic*) side of the stele is quite complete. It is three feet nine inches in breadth and contains the Xi Xia text. [The stele] is in Gansu, Wuwei.

It is puzzling how a stele can be wider on one face than on the other, unless what Luo refers to here is the space occupied by the text (there are three more lines of Tangut text).

11. Lu Zengxiang 陸增祥, 1816–1882.

Baqiongshi jinshi buzheng 八瓊室金石補正, 130 *juan*; posthumously published in 1925 (according to the prefaces), Xigulou edition. *Juan* 122:14a–16a records the Chinese text and comments by Wu Rongguang (except for the last sentence translated above). Lu Zengxiang's text is fuller than Lu Yaoyu's and corrects a number of the latter's mistranscriptions. It is prefaced with these remarks:

> Including the heading [the stele] is seven feet seven inches high, two feet eight inches wide, has twenty-five columns with seventy characters per column. The diameter of the characters is 0.8 (inches?). The Chinese seal script heading consists of three columns of twelve characters: [blank] [blank] *zhong xiu* [blank] [blank] *si gan* [blank] [blank] *bei ming*. . . . [The stele] is in Gansu, Wuwei.

These statistics, and Lu's text, differ sufficiently from Luo Zhenyu's to make it difficult to determine if Lu's editors consulted Luo's work, published ten years earlier. Hummel (at the end of the biography of Wang Chang by Fang Chao-ying) gives Lu Zengxiang's dates as 1833–1889 (*Eminent Chinese of the Ch'ing*, 807).

12. Luo Fucheng 羅福成, 19?–?, son of Luo Zhenyu.

Luo reproduced both texts plus Yan Kejun's comments in *Xi Xia wen zhuanhao* (compiled in 1930, published in 1932), 151–178. In amending previous texts, Luo Fucheng appears to have consulted Devéria. His prefatory comments read:

> The stele is eight feet four inches high and three feet in breadth. All four edges are severely defaced. I count twenty-six columns and seventy characters in each column. The heading is written in seal script. Its text says: Liangzhou Newly Restored Huguo Temple Gantong Stūpa Stele Inscription, in three columns and twelve characters, of which today there

Chronology of Sources   177

remain only six characters. The first column is severely obliterated, so today there remain only twenty-five columns.
Luo, alas, accidentally omits twenty-one characters of text on p. 159.

13. Luo Fuyi, 1905–1981, son of Luo Zhenyu.
Xi Xia wencun, 1 *juan* plus a supplement, privately published in 1935. Luo Zhenyu's Han text (no. 10) without notes.

14. Zhang Wei, 1891–19?.
Longyou jinshi lu; preface dated 1936; published in Gansu in 1943. *Juan* 4:52b–61a records both texts and the edited comments of Zhang Shu, Wu Rongguang, Lu Zengxiang (as appended to Lu Yaoyu's text), Luo Zhenyu, and Ye Changchi, along with his own remarks. Zhang's transcription of the Chinese text often varies from Devéria's or Luo Fucheng's, to whose work he apparently did not have access. Zhang's commentary (57ab) is very long, and I offer only the following excerpt:

> The heading of this stele is Liangzhou Newly Restored Huguo Temple Gantong Stūpa Stele Inscription. Tianyou min'an was the reign name at the time when the stele was erected; to take it as the name of the stele is, of course, not impossible, but the stele heading does not actually have these six characters in seal script. It is puzzling how Zhang Shu could have so erred. The draft of the [*Gansu*] *Xin tongzhi* accordingly says that the stele erected at that time was named after the reign title. This is extremely problematic and consequently further compounds the error (there follows a lengthy discussion of the stele and Xia history).

Zhang Wei perhaps did not realize that Zhang Shu's mistaken reconstruction of the inscription title was based on his attempt to guess the meaning of the Tangut seal script heading.

15. Luo Fuyi (see no. 13 above).
In *Wenwu* 文物 4, no. 5 (1961): 71–72, Luo Fuyi reprinted an uncorrected copy of Luo Fucheng's 1932 text (no. 12), mistakenly dated the stele to 1095, and reversed the statistics concerning the number of columns and characters per column in the two texts.

16. Nishida Tatsuo.
Seika go no kenkyū (1964), 1:157–176, discusses and transcribes both Chinese and Tangut inscriptions, but translates only the Tangut. On p. 158, Nishida notes that he used rubbings found in the collection of Professor Naitō Konan, the great Japanese sinologist of the early twentieth century, in the archives of Kyoto University's Jinbun kagaku kenkyū so.

17. Han Yincheng.
Dangxiang yu Xi Xia ziliao huibian (1983), 1:139–146. Transcription of Chinese text. Han consulted a rubbing in the Beijing Municipal Library and the texts of Lu Yaoyu, Luo Zhenyu, and Zhang Wei (nos. 5, 10, and

14), reproducing in full the latter's commentaries. Han also provides the first punctuated Chinese text.

18. Chen Bingying.
Xi Xia wenwu yanjiu (1985): Han text, 107–110; translation of Tangut text (into Chinese), 110–113; Tangut text, 165–175.

19. Shi Jinbo.
Xi Xia fojiao shilüe (1988): Tangut text, 241–246; translation of Tangut text (into Chinese), 247–250. The best available transcription of the Tangut text.

20. Ruth W. Dunnell.
*"The 1094 Sino-Tangut Gantong Stūpa Stele Inscription of Wuwei," in *Languages and History in East Asia, Festschrift for Tatsuo Nishida on the Occasion of His 60th Birthday* (1988), transcription and translation of Han text (into English), 193–207.

Abbreviations Used in the Notes

Buddiiskie sochineniia   E. I. Kychanov, *Tangutskie rukopisy i ksilografy,* vol. 2: *Buddiiskie sochineniia*
Cihai   Shu Xincheng et al., comps., *Cihai*
Ding   Ding Fubao, *Foxue da cidian*
JS   Tuotuo et al., comps., *Jinshi*
Kodeks   E. I. Kychanov, *Izmenennyi i zanovo utverzhdennyi kodeks*
Kychanov   Gromkovskaia, L. L., and E. I. Kychanov, *Nikolai Alexandrovich Nevskii*
LS   Tuotuo et al., comps., *Liaoshi*
Nishida Catalogue   Catalogue of Xia canonical texts in *Seika mon kegonkyō, The Hsi-Hsia Avatamsaka Sūtra* 3:13–59
Nishida 1964   Nishida Tatsuo, *Seika go no kenkyū*
Shi 1988   Shi Jinbo, *Xi Xia fojiao shilüe*
SHY   Xu Song, *Song huiyao jigao*
SS   Tuotuo et al., comps., *Song shi*
T   Takakusu Junjirō and Kaikyoku Watanabe, eds., *Taishō shinshū daizōkyō*
Tō   Hakuju Ui et al., eds., *A Complete Catalogue of the Tibetan Buddhist Canons*
Tongyin   Li Fanwen, *Tongyin yanjiu*
TRK   Z. I. Gorbacheva and E. I. Kychanov, *Tangutskie rukopisi i ksilografy*
Wenhai   Shi Jinbo, Bai Bin, and Huang Zhenhua, *Wenhai yanjiu*
XCB   Li Tao, *Xu zizhi tongjian changbian*
XXJ   Dai Xizhang, *Xi Xia ji*
XXSS   Wu Guangcheng, *Xi Xia shushi*

Notes

1. INTRODUCTION

1 This is Ksenia B. Kepping's translation of the Tangut; see "The Name of the Tangut Empire," *T'oung Pao* vol. 80, pt. 4–5 (1994): 357–376.

2 For an overview, see Dunnell, "Hsi Hsia," in *The Cambridge History of China,* volume 6: *Alien Regimes and Border States,* ed. Herbert Franke and Denis Twitchett (Cambridge: Cambridge University Press, 1994), 154–214.

3 Peter K. Kozlov, a Russian officer on a reconnaissance mission to the Sino-Mongolian frontier in 1908–1910, uncovered a library and numerous paintings and statues in the sand-buried ruins of Khara-khoto, formerly the Tangut frontier outpost of Edzina, and conveyed its contents back to St. Petersburg. A preliminary catalogue of the Tangut manuscripts and blockprints in the Khara-khoto collection was published in 1963: Z. I. Gorbacheva and E. I. Kychanov, *Tangutskie rukopisi i ksilografy* (Moscow, 1963; hereafter TRK). A second volume of TRK, devoted to the huge Buddhist portion of the archive, has been prepared by Kychanov and will be forthcoming (hereafter *Buddiiskie sochineniia*). The Chinese documents were catalogued and described in L. N. Men'shikov, *Opisanie kitaiskoi chasti kollektsii iz Khara-khoto (fond P. K. Kozlova)* (Moscow, 1984). The art treasures housed in the Hermitage can now be studied in the beautiful catalogue *Lost Empire of the Silk Road: Buddhist Art from Khara Khoto (X–XIIIth century),* ed. Mikhail Piotrovsky (Milan: Electa and Thyssen-Bornemisza Foundation, 1993). The exhibition at Lugano, Switzerland, 25 June to 31 October 1993, was the first time these artifacts had traveled en masse outside of St. Petersburg. The excellent catalogue essays introduce the reader to the Kozlov expedition, Xia history, and preliminary interpretations of Xia iconography.

4 Eric Grinstead (see bibliography for one example), working in England and Denmark, has made invaluable contributions to the enterprise. A good

introduction to the history of the field is Nie Hongyin, "Tangutology during the Past Decades," *Monumenta Serica* 41 (1993): 329–347.

5 Stanley Weinstein makes a similar argument regarding the rise of the Tiantai, Faxiang, and Huayan Buddhist schools in the Tang: "That each of these schools came to the forefront among the Buddhist elite at the time that it did was attributable not so much to the momentum of its own inner doctrinal development as to the close connection that existed between the de facto founder of the school and the imperial family." See "Imperial Patronage in T'ang Buddhism," in *Perspectives on the T'ang*, ed. Arthur Wright and Denis Twitchett (New Haven: Yale, 1973), 305.

6 Dunnell, "The Hsia Origins of the Yüan Institution of Imperial Preceptor," *Asia Major* 5, no. 1 (1992): 85–111, and Elliot Sperling, "Lama to the King of Hsia," *The Journal of the Tibet Society* 7 (1987): 31–50, address the role of Tangut Buddhism in Inner Asian political and cultural history of the twelfth and thirteenth centuries.

7 Art historian Rob Linrothe and I are engaged in a long-term cooperative study of Tangut Buddhist cults and iconography of the later Xia period. See his forthcoming article in *Marg*, "Renzong and the Patronage of Tangut Buddhist Art: The Stūpa and the Ushnīshavijayā Cult."

8 I will say more about the law code below. A brief English description by E. I. Kychanov, its translator, is "Monuments of Tangut Legislation (12–13th centuries)," in *Études Tibétaines*, Actes du XXIXe congrès international des Orientalistes, July 1973 (Paris: Asiathèque, 1976), 29–42. For the published Russian translation with facsimile of text, see Kychanov, *Izmenennyi i zanovo utverzhdennyi kodeks deviza tsarstvovaniia nebesnoe protsvetanie (1149–1169)* (Moscow, 1987–1989; hereafter *Kodeks*).

9 An abundance of material in Song sources on Kokonor makes this an ideal dissertation topic. See, for example, the multivolume anthologies of Tang and Liu, 1896; Liu and Tang, 1989; and Chen and Chen, 1990.

10 A stimulating recent contribution to world-system theory is Barry K. Gills and Andre Gunder Frank, "The Cumulation of Accumulation: Theses and Research Agenda for 5000 Years of World System History," *Dialectical Anthropology* 15 (1990): 19–42.

11 Representative recent works include Sechin Jagchid and Van Jay Symons, *Peace, War, and Trade along the Great Wall* (Bloomington: Indiana University Press, 1989); Thomas J. Barfield, *The Perilous Frontier: Nomadic Empires and China* (Cambridge, Mass.: Basil Blackwell, 1989); and Arthur Waldron, *The Great Wall of China* (Cambridge: Cambridge University Press, 1990).

12 For an overview of the non-Chinese dynasties of the tenth through thirteenth centuries, see Franke and Twitchett, eds., *The Cambridge History of China*, volume 6.

13 *Peace, War, and Trade along the Great Wall*, 14. Jagchid is not referring to economic power here, either.

14 John A. Lynn, "Clio in Arms: The Role of the Military Variable in Shaping History," *The Journal of Military History* 55 (Jan. 1991): 83–95. I thank Paul Forage at the University of Michigan for bringing this article to my attention.

15 "Clio in Arms," 84.

16 *Coercion, Capital, and the European States, A.D. 990–1990* (Basil Blackwell, 1990), as discussed in Lynn, "Clio in Arms," 85.

17 See, for example, Paul C. Forage, "The Sino-Tangut War of 1081–1085," *Journal of Asian History* 25, no. 1 (1991): 1–28.

18 David Kaiser, *Politics and War: European Conflict from Phillip II to Hitler* (Harvard University Press, 1990), as reviewed in Lynn, "Clio in Arms," 87.

19 David Ralston, *Importing the European Army: The Introduction of European Military Techniques and Institutions into the Extra-European World, 1600–1914* (University of Chicago Press, 1990), as reviewed in Lynn, "Clio in Arms," 92. Whether or not nationalism was also a Western import remains debatable, at least for Japan.

20 Rey Chow, "Where Have All the Natives Gone?" in her *Writing Diaspora: Tactics of Intervention in Contemporary Cultural Studies* (Bloomington: Indiana University Press, 1993), 30–36.

21 Jonathan Spence has proposed another understanding of "modern" in the preface of his *The Search for Modern China* (New York: Norton, 1990): "I understand a 'modern' nation to be one that is both integrated and receptive, fairly sure of its own identity yet able to join others on equal terms in the quest for new markets, new technologies, new ideas. If it is used in this open sense, we should have no difficulty in seeing 'modern' as a concept that shifts with the times as human life unfolds" (xx). Spence does not see China as ever having achieved, since 1600 or to the end of this century, a convincing state of the modernity he defines above, hence the ongoing "search" for "modern" China. (China may have achieved "modernity" at times before 1600, however.)

22 Gills and Frank, "Cumulation," 36.

23 It is important to distinguish a China-centered perspective from a sinocentric one. The former seeks to approach and study China without the assumption that the West is the norm and everything else a pale imitation of it or deviation from it. To be China-centered is to seek out and analyze Chinese perspectives, norms, and assumptions. I would like to think of my own approach as, in reversible order of importance depending on one's interest: Tangut-centered, China-centered, Asian-centered, and world-centered. This may also describe the hierarchy of systems of accumulation in which the Tangut state participated, in world-system theory.

24 Pamela Kyle Crossley, "The Rulerships of China," *The American Historical Review* 97, no. 5 (Dec. 1992): 1472.

25 Christopher Beckwith has dismissed the "Sino-Tibetan" theory, com-

menting that "contemporary political-racial considerations (rather than linguistic ones) seem to be keeping Tibetan bound to Chinese" (*The Tibetan Empire in Central Asia: A History of the Struggle for Great Power among Tibetans, Turks, Arabs, and Chinese during the Early Middle Ages* [Princeton, N.J.: Princeton University Press, 1987], 4, n. 2). Nonlinguists who study both Chinese and Tibetan may indeed wonder how any two languages could be more different.

26 K. B. Kepping, "Elements of Ergativity and Nominativity in Tangut," in *Ergativity, Towards a Theory of Grammatical Relations,* ed. Frans Plank (London and New York: Academic Press, 1979), 263.

27 "The Rulerships of China," 1474. The emphasis is mine.

28 Dunnell 1983; Friedland 1969; Okazaki 1972.

29 Dunnell 1983, chap 2.

30 This view is affirmed by Paul Forage in his study, "The Sino-Tangut War of 1081–1085."

31 An important beginning is Ksenia Kepping's linguistic reconstruction of Tangut kinship terminology in her article "Tangut (Xixia) Degrees of Mourning," *Linguistics of the Tibeto-Burman Area* 14, no. 2 (fall 1991): 1–63.

32 On the importance of understanding early Japanese marriage customs and their relationship to the structure and distribution of power, see William H. McCullough, "Japanese Marriage Institutions in the Heian Period," *Harvard Journal of Asiatic Studies* 27 (1967): 103–167.

33 Mikiso Hane, *Premodern Japan* (Boulder, Colo.: Westview Press, 1991), 59, n. 1.

34 Priscilla Ching Chung, *Palace Women in the Northern Sung, 960–1126* (Leiden: E. J. Brill, 1981), 3, 69.

35 My summary here relies on Chung, *Palace Women,* chapter 1. Chung quotes a report that the mother of the first two emperors purportedly advised Taizu not to allow his juvenile son to succeed, for he might fall victim to the same kind of coup that gave Taizu the Later Zhou throne. Interestingly, popular opinion, according to Chung, held that Taizong had murdered his brother and usurped the throne (4). Taizong then forced his brother's son to commit suicide and named his own son as heir apparent. That son went insane, and Taizong was eventually succeeded by his third son.

36 Chung, 70–72. Chung describes Empress Dowager Liu as "undoubtedly the most ambitious and aggressive of the Northern Sung regents." She succeeded in banishing officials opposed to her continued rule as Renzong's regent and punished her critics, performed the ceremonial plowing and ancestral rituals in the temple to the imperial ancestors, "made final decisions on state polices and on the delegation of power, and functioned much like the organizing-type emperors described by James T. C. Liu."

37 Holmgren, "Imperial Marriage in the Native Chinese and Non-Han

State, Han to Ming," in *Marriage and Inequality in Chinese Society*, ed. Rubie S. Watson and Patricia Buckley Ebrey (Berkeley and Los Angeles: University of California Press, 1991), 58–96. See bibliography for her other articles.

38 J. Holmgren, "Observations on Marriage and Inheritance Practices in Early Mongol and Yüan Society, with Particular Reference to the Levirate," *Journal of Asian History* 20, no. 2 (1986): 162.

39 See Kenneth Ch'en, *Buddhism in China: An Historical Survey* (Princeton, N.J.: Princeton University Press, 1964), 425–426.

40 Arthur Wright, *Buddhism in Chinese History* (Stanford, Calif.: Stanford University Press, 1959), 70. See also his "The Formation of Sui Ideology, 581–604," in *Chinese Thought and Institutions,* ed. John K. Fairbank (Chicago: University of Chicago Press, 1957), 71–104.

41 Wechsler, *Offerings of Jade and Silk* (New Haven and London: Yale University Press, 1985), 72.

42 Weinstein, *Buddhism under the T'ang* (Cambridge: Cambridge University Press, 1987), 53.

43 *Buddhism under the T'ang*, 54–55.

44 See Michel Strickmann's review of *Political Propanganda and Ideology in China at the End of the Seventh Century* in *The Eastern Buddhist*, n.s., 10, no. 1 (May 1977): 159. Pañcavarṣika refers to the "great quinquennial festival" of giving; see John S. Strong's discussion in *The Legend of King Aśoka: A Study and Translation of the Aśokāvadāna* (Princeton, N.J.: Princeton University Press, 1983), 91–96.

45 Farquhar, "Emperor as Bodhisattva in the Governance of the Ch'ing Empire," *Harvard Journal of Asiatic Studies* 38, no. 1 (1978): 5–34. Farquhar evidently did not see Forte's study before his article went to press, for he does not mention Wu Zhao.

46 Herbert Franke does this for the Yuan period in *From Tribal Chieftain to Universal Emperor and God: Legitimation of the Yüan Dynasty* (Munich: Verlad der Bayerischen Akademie der Wissenschaften, 1978). Dunnell, "The Hsia Origins of the Yüan Institution of Imperial Preceptor," attempts to fill in another piece of the puzzle.

47 Ainslee T. Embree, ed., *Sources of Indian Tradition,* vol. 1, rev. ed. (New York: Columbia University Press, 1988), 133–138, for a passage from *Dīgha Nikāya* on kingship and the Divine Wheel. I am grateful to Jan Nattier for this reference.

48 Chisui Satō, "The Character of Yün-kang Buddhism: A Look at the Emergence of a State-Supported Religion in China under the Northern Wei," *The Memoirs of the Toyo Bunko* 36 (1978): 79.

49 Farquhar, "Emperor as Bodhisattva," 10–11; Ch'en, *Buddhism in China,* 124–126; Wright, "The Formation of Sui Ideology."

50 *Political Propaganda and Ideology,* 150–153.

51 "The Formation of Sui Ideology," 83.

52 Weinstein, *Buddhism under the T'ang*, 54. In "Notes on T'ang Culture, III," *Monumenta Serica* 30 (1972–1973): 100–103, Edward H. Schafer relates that Xuanzong ordered monumental images of himself, the Buddha, and the highest Daoist divinity to adorn all the Kaiyuan monasteries and Daoist temples in the land (101). I thank Rob Linrothe for this and other references to Xuanzong's self-projections.

53 Ch'en, *Buddhism in China*, 434–435; on Maitreya, see the conference volume edited by Alan Sponberg and Helen Hardacre, *Maitreya, the Future Buddha* (Cambridge University Press, 1988), especially the essays by Joseph Kitagawa, Jan Nattier, and Daniel Overmyer.

54 Raoul Birnbaum, *Studies on the Mysteries of Mañjuśrī* (Society for the Study of Chinese Religions Monograph 2, 1983), 25–38, for a summary of Amoghavajra's (705–774) efforts to establish a national cult to Mañjuśrī on Wutai shan. One important function of the cult was to protect the Tang state (31, passim).

55 Birnbaum, *Studies on the Mysteries of Mañjuśrī*, 9.

56 Birnbaum, 37.

57 Raffaello Orlando, "A Study of Chinese Documents Concerning the Life of the Tantric Buddhist Patriarch Amoghavajra (A.D. 705–774)" (Ph.D. dissertation, Princeton University, 1981), 32. I thank Rob Linrothe for bringing this passage to my attention.

58 "Emperor as Bodhisattva," 15.

59 Crossley, "The Rulerships of China," 1482; Farquhar, "Emperor as Bodhisattva," 16, on Ming emperor Yongle's designation of his late parents as reincarnations of Mañjuśrī and Tārā, the female protector-deity of Tibet (according to Tibetan sources); Yuan emperors from Qubilai were also identified as reincarnated bodhisattvas (14–15), but of Qing emperors only Qianlong had his bodhisattva identity "publicly" displayed, the famous portrait reproduced in Farquhar's article being only one of at least six, according to Robert N. Linrothe (personal communication, 24 December 1993).

60 Farquhar, "Emperor as Bodhisattva," 19–20, refers to a letter sent by the Dalai Lama and the Panchen Lama to Qing Taizong in 1640, addressing him as "Mañjuśrī–Great Emperor." Further, during his visit to Beijing in 1653, the Dalai Lama presented the Shunzhi emperor with a gold plate inscribed "God of the Sky, Mañjughoṣa-Emperor and Great Being."

61 Crossley analyzes this development for Qing emperors in "Rulerships of China," 1482–1483.

62 Shi Jinbo, *Xi Xia fojiao shilüe* (Yinchuan, 1988), 106, expresses the idea of a Buddhist decline in Gansu after the An Lushan rebellion. I remain skeptical, since he provides no supporting evidence or argument, but the rise of Islamic powers in India and Central Asia (the Kharakhanids) certainly made the Buddhist Xia state a welcome haven for Central Asian and Indian Buddhists. Shi's monograph was reissued by the Commercial Press in Taipei in 1992, with a new preface by the author dated to September 1991. So far

I have seen only this preface, not the new edition, and all my references are to the 1988 edition.

63 *From Tribal Chieftain to Universal Emperor and God,* 52.

64 A study of this link should begin with Liu Xinru's *Ancient India and Ancient China: Trade and Religious Exchanges* A.D. *1–600* (Delhi: Oxford University Press, 1988).

65 Shi, *Xi Xia wenhua* (Changchun, 1986), 118–119; Kychanov, "Gosudarstvo i buddizm v Si Sia (982–1227)," in *Buddizm i gosudarstvo na dal'nem vostoke* (Moscow, 1987), 130–145.

66 Tuotuo et al. comps., *Song shi* (rpt. Taipei: Dingwen shuju, 1978) 486: 14027 (hereafter SS).

67 Elizabeth Endicott-West, "Hereditary Privilege in the Yüan Dynasty," in *Niguča Bičig, an Anniversary Volume in Honor of Francis Woodman Cleaves,* ed. Joseph Fletcher et al. (*Journal of Turkish Studies* 9 [1985]), 20.

68 Nie Hongyin translates a line from a 1224 Tangut document from Khara-khoto as "this Ndźiwuwa went through the official career and imperial examination when he was young" ("Tangutology during the Past Decades," 333). Kychanov's original Russian translation, published in 1971, was critiqued in 1978 by Huang Zhenhua, but neither the original text nor Huang Zhenhua's literal Chinese rendering *(zi ren yong you zi ru guan xue dao shang suo jing),* which Huang rearranges into Chinese syntax as *zi (you) Renyong zi shao chu shen xue tu* ("this Renyong, from youth having embarked on the path of study"), justifies Nie's reference to "imperial examination." See Huang Zhenhua, "Ping Sulian jin sanshi nian di Xi Xia xue yan jiu," *Shehui kexue zhanxian* 2 (1978): 319.

69 "Gosudarstvo i buddizm v Si Sia," 130.

70 Liu Xinru, "Buddhist Institutions in the Lower Yangtze during the Sung Dynasty," *Bulletin of Sung-Yuan Studies* 21 (1989): 31–51.

71 "Gosudarstvo i buddizm v Si Sia," 142–143.

72 Catherine Bell, *Ritual Theory, Ritual Practice* (Oxford: Oxford University Press, 1992), 191–192.

73 Dunnell, "The Hsia Origins of the Yüan Institution of Imperial Preceptor," 104–105.

74 Howard Wechsler, *Offerings of Jade and Silk,* chap. 12.

75 Recent studies include Tao Jing-shen, *Two Sons of Heaven: Studies in Sung-Liao Relations* (Tucson: University of Arizona Press, 1988), and Morris Rossabi, ed., *China among Equals: The Middle Kingdom and Its Neighbors, 10th–14th Centuries* (Berkeley and Los Angeles: University of California Press, 1983).

76 A thorough discussion of legitimation in Chinese history and of the Jin debate is Hok-lam Chan, *Legitimation in Imperial China: Discussions under the Jurchen-Chin Dynasty (1115–1234)* (Seattle: University of Washington Press, 1984).

77 Tuotuo et al., comps., *Jin shi* (rpt. Beijing: Zhonghua shuju, 1975) 9: 218 (hereafter JS).

2. BUDDHISM AND MONARCHY IN THE EARLY TANGUT STATE

1 Throughout this book I refer to the first emperor as Yuanhao, as he is best known, or as Jingzong, his temple name. The surnames Tuoba, Li, and Zhao were all bestowed upon the Tangut royal clan at various stages in its history, but seldom did its members themselves use the name Zhao (the Song imperial surname). The native clan name of Weiming was adopted under Yuanhao. Distant branches of the clan retained or assumed the surname Li to distinguish themselves from the main branch. Disinheritance probably occurred, among other ways, when a family dropped out of the hierarchy of mourning relationships to the emperor. See Ksenia B. Kepping, "Tangut (Xi Xia) Degrees of Mourning"; and Kychanov, *Kodeks* 2:37–38.

2 Shi, *Fojiao shilüe*, 25 (hereafter Shi 1988).

3 Shi 1988, 16–23; and Shi, *Xi Xia wenhua*, 60–63.

4 See Kychanov, *Kodeks* 1:364; 4:166, 177–178 (translation), 541–542 (text). A popular practice of animal sacrifice is discussed by Kychanov in "Ob odnom obriade religii bon sokhranivshemsia v buddiiskikh ritualakh tangutov," *Kratkie soobshcheniia instituta etnografii ANSSSR* 35 (1960): 86–90.

5 One source for this discussion is the Chinese version of Nakamura Hajime, *Zhongguo fojiao fazhan shi,* trans. Yu Wanju (Taipei: Tianhua chuban shiye banfen youxian gongsi, 1984), 1:399–416. See also Jan Yün-hua, "Buddhist Relations between India and Sung China," parts 1 and 2, *History of Religions* 6, no. 1 (Aug. 1966): 24–42, and 6, no. 2 (Nov. 1966): 135–168.

6 SS 490:14103–14106; Xu Song, ed., *Song huiyao jigao* (rpt. Beiping, 1936; Taipei, 1975) (hereafter SHY), 197, *fanyi* 4:85–90 (pp. 7742–7744); *dao shi* 2:5–9 (pp. 7877–7879). A late source is Yu Qian, comp., *Xin xu gaoseng zhuan siji* (1923; rpt. Taipei, 1967), 1. See also Jan Yün-hua, "Buddhist Relations between India and Sung China."

7 Hereafter Yu Qian, *Xin zhuan*. This early-twentieth-century work must be used with care, for it perpetuates some of the errors addressed by Jan Yün-hua in his study. It contains some intriguing information not found in other sources available to me and provides a convenient summary of popular hagiography.

8 "Buddhist Relations between India and Sung China," part 1, 141–142.

9 See Lewis Lancaster's note on the mistaken identity of Fatian and Faxian in his *The Korean Buddhist Canon, a Descriptive Catalogue* (Berkeley and Los Angeles: University of California Press, 1979), 395–396; and Jan Yün-hua's earlier discussion, "Buddhist Relations," pt. 1, 35.

10 Yu Qian, *Xin zhuan* 1:1a–2b; SHY 200, *dao shi* 2:5b (p. 7877).

11 According to Zhipan's *Fozu tongji* 43:398a (T. 2035, cited in Jan, "Buddhist Relations" pt. 2, 147), this took place in 980. Empress Wu reportedly initiated the practice of bestowing purple robes on monks as a

high honor, after the Chinese practice of presenting high officials with a gold seal attached to a purple cord (Weinstein, *Buddhism under the T'ang,* 192, n. 21, citing Can Ning, *Da Song sengshi lüe,* T. 2126, 248c–249a).

12 Yu Qian, *Xin zhuan* 1:2b–3b; see also the entries for Shihu and Fatian in Mochizuki Shinkō, *Bukkyō daijiten,* 6th ed. (Tokyo: Sekai seikei kankō kyōkai, 1972), 2920c and 4631a, respectively; and Zhipan, *Fozu tongji* 43:398a. Zhipan dates these events all to ca. 980.

13 E. I. Kychanov, "Pravovoe polozhenie Buddiiskikh obshchin v tangutskom gosudarstve," in *Buddizm, gosudarstvo i obshchestvo v stranakh tsentral'noi i vostochnoi Azii v srednie veka,* ed. G. M. Bongard-Levin et al. (Moscow, 1982), 49–50. Regarding the work *Zuisheng foding tuoloni jing* (T. 974a [383c–384b], "The Most Excellent [All-conquering] Buddhoṣṇīṣa-dhāraṇi Sūtra"), see Lancaster, *The Korean Buddhist Canon,* 374–375 (K1091); Ono Gemmyō *Bussho kaisetsu daijiten* (Tokyo, A31–1936), 4:32a.

14 SHY 200, *dao shi* 2:6b (p. 7877), and Jan, *Buddhist Relations,* pt. 1, 31.

15 Yu Qian, *Xin zhuan* 1:3a has Xianping 1, but its dates are not reliable and it has conflated Faxian with Fatian. See Zuxiu, *Longxing fojiao biannian tonglun* (compiled 1164), 29 (p. 355), in the *Xu zangjing* (Shanghai: Hanfenlou rpt., 1923), IIB–iii/2–4. Appended to this work are four prefaces to Buddhist works written by Song emperors, two for the same monk, Tianxizai/Faxian. Lancaster's *The Korean Buddhist Canon,* 420–421, lists several works attributed to Song Taizong.

16 Yu Qian, *Xin zhuan* 1:4b–6a.

17 *Xin zhuang* 1:4b–6a; Jue'an (Ming dynasty), *Shishi jigu lüe* 4 (T. 2037–4), 866c; and Jan, "Buddhist Relations," pt. 2, 143.

18 See the passages cited by Jan from 1030 and 1041, regarding complaints by Fahu and Weijing (pt. 2, 143 and n. 97).

19 Bowring, "Brief Note: Buddhist Translations in the Northern Sung," *Asia Major,* 3rd ser., vol. 5, pt. 2 (1992), 79–93.

20 Huang Chi-chiang, "Imperial Rulership and Buddhism in the Early Northern Sung," in *Imperial Rulership and Cultural Change in Traditional China,* ed. Frederick P. Brandauer and Chun-chieh Huang (Seattle and London: University of Washington Press, 1994), 161, 165.

21 Faure, *The Rhetoric of Immediacy: A Cultural Critique of Chan/Zen Buddhism* (Princeton, N.J.: Princeton University Press, 1991), 137. In note 21 Faure notes that the tooth of the Buddha played an important role in the legitimation of the Liang, Chen, and Sui dynasties.

22 Jan, "Buddhist Relations," pt. 2, 144–159.

23 Kirkland, "A World in Balance: Holistic Synthesis in the *T'ai-p'ing kuang-chi,*" *Journal of Sung-Yuan Studies* 23 (1993): 43–70.

24 *Xin zhuan* 1:6b. Yu conflates Fa Jixiang and Zhi Jixiang into one person; Zhipan, *Fazu tongji,* 412c reports that Zhi Jixiang reached the Song court in 1053 (Jan, "Buddhist Relations," pt. 2, 159).

25 T. 1188 (814c–820a). For this title see also Wang Renjun, *Xi Xia yiwen zhi* (1904–1905); Yu Qian, *Xin zhuan* 1:7a. The Sanskrit text has been translated in Ronald M. Davidson, "The *Litany of Names of Mañjuśrī*," in *Tantric and Taoist Studies in Honour of R. A. Stein*, vol. 1, ed. Michel Strickmann (Brussels: Institut Belge des Hautes Études Chinoises, 1981), 1–69.

26 See Kychanov, 49–50; "Pravovoe polozhenie," Kychanov, "Tibetans and Tibetan Culture in the Tangut State of Hsi Hsia (982–1227)," in *Proceedings of the Csoma de Körös Memorial Symposium (1976)*, ed. Louis Ligeti (Budapest, 1978), 208.

27 Yu Qian, *Xin zhuan* 1:7ab. This datum does not invite confidence.

28 *Xin zhuang* 1:7b. Mochizuki, *Bukkyō daijiten*, 4069c, gives the 1046 date and says nothing about his being a Xi Xia monk.

29 See Lancaster, *The Korean Buddhist Canon*, 474–476.

30 Yu Qian, *Xin zhuan* 1:3b–4b.

31 The Unshakable Buddha, Akṣobhya, is one of the five Wisdom Buddhas of the Yoga tantras, and in the more prominent Buddha family centered on Vairocana, Akṣobhya occupies the East. The other prominent family of the five Buddha families that evolved in India, the Vajra family, features Akṣobhya at the center. According to David Snellgrove, the Tathāgatha family centered on Vairocana Buddha (Śākyamuni) includes tantras more closely related to traditional Mahāyāna teachings and so was accepted in China and Japan. The Vajra family, in contrast, features tantras popular mainly in Tibet, such as the *Hevajra Tantra* and *Kālacakra Tantra*, whose central deities (Hevajra, and so forth) are wrathful manifestations of Akṣobhya. Snellgrove, *Indo-Tibetan Buddhism: Indian Buddhists and Their Tibetan Successors* (Boston: Shambhala, 1987), 1, 189–211. For specific attributes of Akṣobhya, see Mochizuki, *Bukkyō daijiten*, 23c–24a.

32 This fivefold scheme derives from the Tantric arrangement of Five Buddha Families, which in one important Yoga tantra, the "Symposium of Truth," appear as Sarvatathāgata (All Buddhas), presided over by Śākyamuni (Vairocana); Tathāgata (Buddha) family; Vajra family; Lotus family; Gem (Ratnasambhava) family. The latter four families are led by bodhisattvas and presided over by Vairocana, who manifests himself in the four directions as Akṣobhya (East), Ratnasambhava (South), Amitābha (West), and Amoghasiddhi (North) (Snellgrove, *Indo-Tibetan Buddhism*, 197). The fivefold scheme of our text lists what became a standard five families, adding to the above four a "karma" family, which evidently refers to the Action Family of Amoghasiddhi, separated out from the Gem family of Ratnasambhava and led by the bodhisattva Viśvakarma ("Universal Action") (Snellgrove, 242). Snellgrove views the emergence of the Yoga tantras as constituting a distinctive Vajrayāna practice, different from Mahāyāna tantras and consecration practice (240–243).

33 I.e., the Vajra family, with Akṣobhya Buddha at its center.

34 T. 326; "The Text of the Penitential Offering to the Thirty-five Buddhas' Names" *(Sanshiwu foming li chan wen)*, a popular confessional text (Ono, 4:83d).

35 Listed in Ding Fubao, *Foxua da cidian* (rpt. Beijing, 1984), 1048 (Mochizuki, *Bukkyō daijiten*, 2289b–c), the ten vows appear at the end of the last chapter in the forty-chapter version of the *Avatamsaka Sūtra* (called the *Gaṇḍavyūha Sūtra*, T. 293). See Thomas Cleary's translation of the *Gaṇḍavyūha, Entry into the Realm of Reality* (Boston and Shaftesbury: Shambhala, 1989), 387–394. A version incorporating sixty-two vows to "live the Life of Samantabhadra" from the *Gaṇḍavyūha Sūtra* is translated in W. T. de Bary, ed., *The Buddhist Tradition in India, China and Japan* (New York: Vintage, 1972), 172–178.

36 These figures add up to 98, not 108. An apocryphal tale?

37 This must refer to T. 1318, *Yuqie jiyao jiu a'nan tuoluoni yankou guiyi jing,* translated by Amoghavajra, a disciple of Vajrabodhi. Stephen Teiser cites Japanese sources regarding this and related liturgical texts, in *The Ghost Festival in Medieval China* (Princeton: Princeton University Press, 1988), 107–108, nn. 114, 115. A translation of this text by Charles Orzech will be included in the forthcoming anthology *Religions of China: In Practice,* ed. Donald S. Lopez, Jr. (Princeton University Press).

38 SHY 200, *dao shi* 1:8b.

39 I thank Timothy Barrett for this discovery (personal communication, 22 November 1993). See the *Zhonghua da zang jing, di er ji* (Taipei, 1968), 47: 30134, *Yuqie jiyao yankou shishi yi.*

40 The newspaper *Guangming ribao* reported the discovery on 22 September 1991; *Zhongguo wenwu bao* published a more detailed report on the front page of its 29 December 1991 issue. *Beijing Review* gave a brief summary in its 16–22 December 1991 issue. The temple was dynamited by local farmers seeking treasure. A cache of Tangut sūtras was found, some titles evidently translated from Tibetan. The Yinchuan cultural authorities sent photographs of several title pages to Shi Jinbo for identification, and I examined them in his presence in August 1992.

41 Zang Lihe et al., comps., *Zhongguo gujin diming da zidian,* 3rd edition (Taipei: Commercial Press, 1972), 1122, quoting from *Longshu yu wen* by Wang Shizhen (an early Qing work). See also Gu Zuyu, *Dushi fangyu jiyao,* Letian renwen congshu edition (Taipei, 1973), 72:3085.

42 Huang Qinglan, *Chaomu kesong baihua jieshi,* 3rd ed. (Taipei: Fojiao chuban she, 1982), *xia,* 12–13. I thank Miriam Levering for this valuable reference.

43 Victor Mair, among others, has speculated on links between Dunhuang and Sichuan in the Tang period, in his *Tun-huang Popular Narratives* (Cambridge: Cambridge University Press, 1983), 25.

44 Wu Guangcheng, *Xi Xia shushi,* preface dated 1826 (rpt. Taipei: Guangwen shuju, 1968), 12:4b (hereafter XXSS).

45 SS 490:14106; Li Tao, *Xu zizhi tongjian changbian* (xinding edition; rpt. Taipei, 1974), 118:2a (hereafter XCB).

46 For example, Shi 1988, 29, 335.

47 Karl A. Wittfogel and Feng Chia-sheng, *History of Chinese Society, Liao (907–1125)* (Philadelphia: The American Philosophical Society, 1949), 291–309.

48 Ibid., 304 n. 34.

49 Tuotuo et al. comps., *Liao shi* (rpt. Beijing, 1974), 22:267 (hereafter LS). *Fan jue jing* does not appear to be the title of a text.

50 E. I. Kychanov, *Buddiiskie sochineniia* "Introduction," p. 30.

51 That status quo may have included internal use of a title akin to emperor for Li Deming; SS 485:13989 records that in 1012–1013 (Song, Xiangfu 5) Li Deming bestowed a posthumous imperial title on his father, which Yuanhao later supplemented. Scholars have variously interpreted this entry, either suggesting that Li Deming also probably called himself emperor in secret, or that the *Song shi* dating is wrong and Yuanhao later bestowed all the imperial titles on both his father and his grandfather.

52 SS 485:13989 notes that Deming's mother was Yeli shi, and gives her title. XCB 65:11b records a Song court conversation about Deming's many mothers. Most likely "mother" refers to one of Li Jiqian's wives. This Wang was of a prominent Tangut clan whose name occurs repeatedly in the sources for the eleventh century. This clan name is not found among those recorded for the Dangxiang of the Tang through early Song periods, prompting speculation that it may be of Tibetan provenance or that the Dangxiang clans recorded in Chinese sources represent only one constituency in the emerging Tangut elite.

53 *Song shi* 485:13990. The wording of the text suggests that Tanguts were not allowed to accompany the offerings to Wutai shan. Perhaps this was related to the fact that in 1007 an envoy of the Uighur qan at Ganzhou, a Buddhist nun, received permission to visit Wutai shan (SS 490:14115). At that time the Ganzhou Uighurs were bitter enemies of the Tanguts, and so the Song court nurtured the relationship with them. In 1072 the Kokonor Tibetan leader Muzheng sent two Indian monks to the Song court who in the following year were escorted to Wutai shan, at their request (SHY 197, *fan yi* 4:90 [p. 7744]).

54 XCB 121:1a.

55 The name of the capital changed several times; by the early twelfth century it had assumed the name of Zhongxing. Under Yuanhao its name was changed from Xingzhou to Xingqing. See Ruth Dunnell, "Naming the Tangut Capital: Xingqing, Zhongxing and Related Matters," *Bulletin of Sung-Yuan Studies* 21 (1989): 52–66.

56 Shi 1988, 118, 123. Not all scholars have acknowledged the references in Tangut sūtras to a "Northern Wutai Mountain" as denoting a complex separate from the famous site in Shanxi. If indeed the latter is what

these references point to, we must conclude that monks registered at temples in Jin territory traveled freely to Xia monasteries and the Tangut court. Evidence supporting the creation of a Wutai shan in the Helan Mountains comes from a parallel example in sixth-century Silla. See Lewis R. Lancaster and C. S. Yu, eds., *Introduction of Buddhism to Korea: New Cultural Patterns* (Berkeley, Calif.: Asian Humanities Press, 1989), 21.

57 Dunhuang Research Institute, *Dunhuang Mogao ku gongyang ren tiji* (Beijing: Wenwu chuban she, 1986), 168. Cave 444 also has inscriptions recording offerings made by Khotanese heirs apparent.

58 Zhiguang and Huizhen, comps., *Mizhou yuanyin wangsheng ji* (1200), T. 1956, 1007. For a description of the original Xia text of this title (in Chinese, not in Tangut), see Men'shikov, *Opisanie kitaiskoi chasti kollektsii iz Khara-khoto,* 241–242, no. 197. For a Tangut gloss for this occurrence (in Chinese) of the title of *tidian* (superintendent), see the Tiansheng code, chapter 10, article 690, which prescribes staffing for the government's Buddhist bureaucracy: "for the *chujia gongde si* (Office of Merit and Virtue for Those Who Leave the Home), six *yan guo chu* (superintendents) and six recipients of edicts" (*Kodeks* 3:115, 421–422). For a fuller discussion of the Tangut phrase that is rendered in Chinese as *yan guo chu,* and translated as "superintendent" *(tidian),* see Chapter 5, note 14.

59 Disagreement exists over when the Tanguts actually incorporated Shazhou (Dunhuang). Most Song sources date the conquest to 1036, but the Uighurs of Shazhou evidently remained autonomous and continued sending tribute missions to Song, Liao, and even Jin; the first Xia date found at Dunhuang is 1070 (Tiansi lisheng guoqing 2). This has led many scholars to speculate that Xia did not actually incorporate Shazhou until later in the eleventh century. Chen Bingying argues that the Tanguts did conquer the region in 1036, but only extended "loose rein" control over it, which gave it leeway in the conduct of trade and diplomatic relations. See his review of the problem and sources, "Xi Xia yu Dunhuang," *Song Liao Jin Yuan shi* 5 (1991): 55–67 (or in *Xibei minzu yanjiu* 1 [1991]: 78–90). An established Japanese view is Nakajima Satoshi, "Seika jidai no Sashu," in *Tonkō no rekishi* (Tokyo: Daitō shuppansha, 1980), 357–361.

60 See my treatment of Hexi and Qingtang in "Hsi Hsia," 172–176.

61 SS 485:13993; Zeng Gong, *Longping ji,* Songshi ziliao cuibian ed. (rpt. Taipei: Wenhai chuban she, 1967), 20:5a. In Song texts, Fan usually refers to "Tibetan," whereas the Tanguts, when writing in Chinese, used the word Fan to translate their own ethnonym. An extended discussion on the term Fan follows in Chapter 6.

62 XCB 109:15a.

63 XCB 115:18a.

64 XCB 156:2ab. "Jiwaiji" is a Qing orthographic revision of a name or title that I have not yet identified.

65 See Dunnell, "Hsi Hsia," 181–189.

66 The principles governing the formation of Tangut graphs differed markedly from Chinese. See the studies by Hwang-cherng Gong, "Chinese Elements in the Tangut Script," *The Bulletin of the Institute of History and Philology* 53, pt. 1 (Taiwan, 1982): 167–187; "Xi Xia wenzi yansheng guocheng di chongjian," *Bulletin of the Institute of China Border Area Studies* 15 (Oct. 1984): 63–80; "Xi Xia wen di yifu yu shengfu jiqi yansheng guocheng," *The Bulletin of the Institute of History and Philology* 56, pt. 4 (Taiwan, 1985): 719–758. For theories about the invention of the Tangut script, see Shi Jinbo, *Xi Xia wenhua*, 11–15.

67 E. I. Kychanov, "Xian gei Xi Xia wenzi chuangzao zhe di songshi," in *Zhongguo minzu shi yanjiu*, ed. Bai Bin et al. (Beijing, 1989), 144–155. SS 486:14025 records that in 1162 the Xia court honored the inventor of the Tangut script, Yeli Renrong, as Prince of Broad Grace (Guanghui wang).

68 Shi 1988, 27.

69 See Niu Dasheng, " 'Jiajing Ningxia xin zhi' zhong di liangbian Xi Xia yiwen," *Ningxia daxue xuebao* 4 (1980): 44–49. The inscription can be found in Hu Ruli, comp., and Guan Lu, ed., *Jiajing Ningxia xinzhi* (rpt. Yinchuan: Ningxia renmin chuban she, 1982), 153–154; Zhang Jincheng (fl. 1776), comp., and Yang Huanyu (*jinshi* 1771), ed., *Ningxia fuzhi* (rpt. Taipei: Changwen chuban she, 1968), 19:22a–3a; and Luo Fuyi, *Xi Xia wencun* (n.p., 1935), 13b–14b. It is possible that some scholars have connected this presentation of relics by an Indian monk with Yuanhao's alleged detention of Indian monks in 1036 (see nn. 44–46 above and text). Wu Guangcheng seems to have been unaware of this inscription. If there was a Tangut version of the inscription, it has not survived, not surprisingly.

70 I translate all Chinese-style official titles according to Charles O. Hucker, *A Dictionary of Official Titles in Imperial China* (Stanford: Stanford University Press, 1985). Zhang Zhi was evidently a Chinese member of the inner ruling circle; high military appointments were normally reserved for Tanguts (see Dunnell, "Tanguts and the Tangut State"). Yang (name missing) may not have been Chinese, given the Tanguts' disposition toward dual staffing to maintain an ethnic balance.

71 An abbreviation of the full title Yuanhao assumed; see below.

72 *Han zu* here refers to the founders of the Han dynasty.

73 This relic burial resembles some of the Tang finds from the Famen si at Xi'an. See Roderick Whitfield, "Esoteric Buddhist Elements in the Famensi Reliquary Deposit," *Asiatische Studien* 44, no. 2 (1990): 247–258, illus.

74 Strong, *The Legend of King Aśoka*, 306 and chap. 2.

75 XCB 122:10b–11a.

76 SS 485:13995. For a discussion of Qing accession rituals and the role of "assuming the imperial position" therein, see Evelyn Rawski, "Music and Rulership in Qing Accession Rituals during the Seventeenth and Eighteenth Centuries," paper presented on 17 March 1993 to the Faculty Seminar of

the Center for Chinese Studies, University of Michigan. This paper represents part of Rawski's research for a forthcoming book on the social history of the Qing imperial family.

77 This is the XCB 123:2b version; SS 485:13995 has a different opening: "Your servant's ancestors originally were the descendants of emperors. When the fortunes of Eastern Jin ended, [they] laid the initial foundations of the Later Wei." Although XCB is closer to the event and less polished, it omits many passages included in SS.

78 The bracketed portion is absent from XCB, and I wonder if it was a later interpolation, possibly by the Yuan editors of *Song shi*.

79 XCB abbreviates this section: "The soldiers and people repeatedly petitioned to establish a state. Thereupon, receiving investment, [I] assumed the imperial position *(ji huangdi wei)*."

80 This section is entirely omitted from XCB.

81 XCB omits "in your profound wisdom and perfection, whose benevolence extends to all things."

82 This section is also absent in XCB, which seems to have severely abbreviated the end of the letter.

83 SS 485:13995–13996 and XCB 123:2a.

84 S. A. M. Adshead, *Central Asia in World History* (New York: St. Martin's Press, 1993), 50.

85 XCB 123:2b–3a.

86 XCB 125:11ab.

87 Similar arguments were advanced by ninth-century Tang officials to justify Tang refusal to harbor a defeated Uighur *qaghan:* "Moreover, foreigners and Chinese [occupy] different lands. What could they have in common?... How could we dare to disregard the natural boundaries [established by] Heaven and Earth?" See Michael R. Drompp, "Centrifugal Forces in the Inner Asian 'Heartland': History *versus* Geography," *Journal of Asian History* 23, no. 2 (1989): 141.

88 One version of Fan's letter is recorded in XCB 130:6a–1a; another is found in Fan's collected works, *Fan wenzheng gong ji* (Sibu congkan jibu ed., Shanghai: Commercial Press, 1929), 9:6b–10b. The discrepancies between the two versions are interesting. Were certain portions edited out of the latter to defend Fan's name against charges of improper communication with the enemy? I cite the fuller XCB text. See also Tang Kaijian, "Xi Xia shi zhaji," in *Zhongguo minzu shi yanjiu* 2, ed. Bai Bin et al. (Beijing: Zhongyang minzu xueyuan chuban, 1989), 196–197.

89 Wittfogel and Feng, *Liao*, 85.

90 On this point, see Tang Kaijian, "Xi Xia shi zhaji," 196–197.

91 Dunnell, "Tanguts and the Tangut State," 130. For the exact calculations, see Huang Qingyun, "Guanyu Bei Song yu Xi Xia heyue zhong yin zhuan cha di shuliang wenti," *Zhongxue lishi jiaoxue* 9 (1957): 19–20.

92 Dunnell, "Hsi Hsia," 189–190. Sima Guang's account of the deaths

of the Yeli brothers shows that the much-touted Song subversion played little if any meaningful role in the Yeli affair. See his *Sushui jiwen,* in *Congshu jicheng jian bian,* vol. 131 (Taipei: Shangwu yinshu guan, 1966), 9:9a–9b; 10:5b, 9a; 11:11b–12a. Likewise, Li Tao casts doubt on the subversion theory in XCB 168:8a.

93 XCB 162:1a–1b; Mocang is transcribed Micang here.

94 XCB 162:1a–2a; Dunnell, "Tanguts and the Tangut State," 133–136.

95 Shi 1988, 117–126.

96 T. 262; Nishida Tatsuo, Catalogue of Xia canonical texts in *Seika mon kegonkyō, The Hsi-Hsia Avatamsaka Sūtra,* vol. 3, 229. The text of the preface is reproduced in *Xi Xia wen zhuanhao,* a special issue of the *Bulletin of the National Library of Peiping* 4, no. 3 (Jan. 1932): 191–193; and in Shi 1988, 234–236. Shi dates the preface to 1049–1069. Author Wang Puxin refers to the empress and infant emperor taking the reins of power immediately following a discussion of sūtras translated under "the previous court." If "previous court" means Yuanhao, then he refers to the Mocang empress and Liangzuo, that is, he composed this preface before her death in 1056. Or, if "previous court" means Weiming Liangzuo, then he refers to the first Liang empress and Liangzuo's young son, who became the emperor Huizong in 1068.

97 This derivation was suggested by Professor Jack Dull, University of Washington, in May 1991.

98 Li Fanwen (Bu Ping), "Xi Xia huangdi chenghao kao," *Ningxia shehui kexue* 1981:70–82. The Chinese translation *fengjiao,* if we understand the Tangut graphs semantically, refer to an ancient method of weather forecasting; perhaps Yuanhao excelled in divination, a topic of great interest to the Tanguts. We do not yet fully understand the import of these "wall" or tomb titles.

99 See Nishida Tatsuo, *Seika mon kegonkyō, The Hsi-Hsia Avatamsaka Sūtra,* vol. 2 (Kyoto: Kyoto University Faculty of Letters, 1976), appendix, 5–7, for his transcription of the preface to "Da Bai Gao Guo xin yi sanzang sheng jiao xu" in the Stockholm Folksmuseum collection of Sven Hedin. He dates it to the Yuan; the preface is probably a mid-twelfth- or early-thirteenth-century composition (see Shi 1988, 283–285).

100 T. 446, Nishida catalogue, 160; Shi 1988, 316–324. Nomura Hiroshi, "Seikago yaku kei shi kenkyū—Seikago bunken ("nusugi") yori mita Ri Gen-ko no yaku sei jigyo ni tsuite," *Bukkyō shi gaku kenkyū* 19, pt. 2 (1977): 71–120. The text can be found in Eric Grinstead, ed., *The Tangut Tripitaka,* Sata-Pitaka Series 86 (New Delhi, 1973), vol. 4, 906c–907. This text is in the Beijing Municipal Library but not in the Kozlov collection. It may be apocryphal, for I have identified no original Sanskrit title for it. According to Ding, *Foxue da cidian* 1189c and 143a, it comprises the first chapter of the *Sanqie sanqian foming jing* ("Sūtra on the Three Thousand Buddha Names of the Three Kalpas"; T. 446, 364a, gives the title *Sanqie*

sanqian fo yuan qi), the other two chapters being the separate titles of *Xianzai xian qie qian foming jing* ("Sūtra on the Thousand Buddha Names of the Present Bhadra Kalpa") and *Weilai xingsu qie qian foming jing* ("Sūtra on the Thousand Names of the Future Constellation Kalpa").

101 See Dunnell, "The Hsia Origins of the Yüan Institution of Imperial Preceptor," 85–111.

102 XXSS 18:8b–9a.

103 Nishida Tatsuo doubts their contribution. See his *Seika mon kegonkyō*, vol. 1, 6 and n. 9. E. I. Kychanov also questions suppositions that Uighur Buddhists or Buddhist texts played a discrete or significant role in the evolution of Tangut Buddhism (*Buddiiskie Sochinenie,* 27–29).

104 Miao Quansun (1844–1919), *Liao wencun* (rpt. Taipei: Chengwen chuban she, 1967), 6:3b–4. I am grateful to Sam Grupper for this reference.

105 Denis Twitchett, "The Khitan and the Liao Dynasty," in *The Cambridge History of China, volume 6,* 114–116; J. Holmgren, "Marriage, Kinship and Succession under the Ch'i-tan Rulers of the Liao Dynasty," *T'oung Pao* 72, nos. 1–3 (1986): 44–91.

106 Wittfogel and Feng, *Liao,* 303; LS 68:1064–1065, 18:221.

107 LS 19:228, 238; 68:1066–1070.

108 Miao Quansun, *Liao wencun* 6:3a; unpublished translation and study by Sam Grupper (1991), presented at the 1991 meeting of the Association for Asian Studies in New Orleans. In Grupper's interpretation, Xingzong used Buddhism to help resolve or manage his internal crisis of authority; furthermore, Liao Buddhism "played a prominent role in the more militant aspects of the projection of Qitan/Liao power in Northeastern and Inner Asia," 21.

109 LS 19:231; 115:1526.

110 Wu Fengyun, "Xi Xia lingyuan ji qi jianzhu tedian," *Ningxia wenwu* 1 (1986): 26–31; republished virtually unchanged in Shi Jinbo, Bai Bin, and Wu Fengyun, eds., *Xi Xia wenwu* (Beijing: Wenwu chuban she, 1988), 1–8.

111 Dunnell, "The Fall of the Xia Empire: Sino-Steppe Relations in the Late 12th–Early 13th Centuries," in *Rulers from the Steppe: State Formation on the Eurasian Periphery,* ed. Gary Seaman and Daniel Marks (Los Angeles: University of Southern California Ethnographics Press, 1991), 178–179.

3. BUDDHISM UNDER THE REGENCIES (1049–1099)

1 Shi 1988, 59–63.

2 Paul Smith's chapter on the reign of Shenzong (1068–1085) in the forthcoming *Cambridge History of China,* vol. 5: *The Sung,* argues that Chinese policy makers perceived Liangzuo's military activities of the middle 1060s as a threat to vital Song security interests but could not formulate an effective policy to deal with Xia. Nineteen-year-old Song Shenzong came to the throne determined to go on the offensive (like Han Wudi).

3 See Wang's biography in SS 328:10579 and accounts of his activities in Chen Bangzhan, *Song shi jishi benmo* (Beijing: Zhonghua shuju, 1977), 41, and in Peng Baichuan (12th c.), *Taiping zhiji tonglei,* Shiyuan congshu edition (Taipei: Chengwen chuban she, 1966), 14, 15.

4 Jennifer Holmgren's analysis of the Liao situation is very suggestive for the Xia case. See her "Marriage, Kinship and Succession."

5 The disaggregation (but not dispersal or disappearance) of central authority in the face of the Song onslaught could, in fact, be seen as a positive advantage: "Protracted campaigns against people without any central authority, living in small and mobile settlements, are very costly, if not logistically impossible." Quoted from R. Brian Ferguson and Neil L. Whitehead, "The Violent Edge of Empire," in *War in the Tribal Zone,* ed. Ferguson and Whitehead (Santa Fe: School of American Research Press, 1992), 19.

6 LS 115:1527; XCB 168:4b. The Khitans aimed to avenge humiliations endured in a punitive war against Yuanhao in 1044–1045 over the status of some Dangxiang vassals along their common border in Shanxi (LS 19:230–232).

7 The text is recorded in Hu Ruli, *Jiajing Ningxia xin zhi* 2:153; see also Niu Dasheng, " 'Jiajing Ningxia xin zhi' zhong di liangbian Xi Xia yiwen," *Ningxia daxue xuebao* 4 (1980): 44–48. Niu argues (p. 45) that because Wu Guangcheng's *Xi Xia shushi* (19:11a) records that in the tenth month of 1055 the Chengtian Temple was erected (or opened, *qi*), the 1050 date of this inscription and the phrase following the date, *jian ta zhi chen,* must refer to the day on which construction was begun, not completed. Niu observes that it would take five or six years to build a temple. This neat resolution of discrepancies between the two versions may be entertained, although I remain uneasy about the unnamed sources of Wu's version and his failure to cite the stele inscription itself. Why have a stele carved before the temple was built? And are we meant to read the description of the temple's foundations, steps, and relics coffin in the future tense?

8 The Buddha's incarnation and deeds as Śākyamuni.

9 There appear to be two missing graphs at the beginning of this phrase, which continues with six graphs, *mo shi dun dao cheng(deng) tu.* One scholar wants to read this passage as the two names Kumoluoshi (Kumārajīva) and Fotudeng, a plausible solution but one I am not persuaded fits the context, since the Buddha seems to be the agent of the activities being related. See Niu Dasheng, " 'Jiajing Ningxia xin zhi'," 44.

10 Or should *suiji* begin the second phrase, thus: "In accord with inherent capabilities, [the Buddha] manifested great compassion and saved living beings."

11 *sanling:* heaven, earth, and humans. Shu Xincheng et al., comps., *Cihai* (rpt. Hong Kong: Zhonghua Shuju, 1947), 18.

12 *Jiajing Ningxia xin zhi* 2:153. I take the first *sheng* (Sages) to refer to

Li Deming and Yuanhao, and the second *sheng* (Sage) to refer to reigning emperor.

13 There were, however, many Tanguts who were not literate, even among the ranks of the elite (see Chapter 6).

14 *Rhetoric of Immediacy,* 137.

15 XCB 179:7b and SHY 42, *li* 60:40b. Tangut envoys evidently earlier requested another Tripiṭaka; see Dai Xizhang, *Xi Xia ji* (*Zhonghua wenshi congshu* edition [Taipei, 1968]), 12:10a (hereafter XXJ); and Wang Jingru, *Xi Xia yanjiu,* vol. 1 (Beiping, 1933), 2, 12, where he cites *Xi Xia changbian,* meaning XCB. XCB 179 does not record the Tangut request that Wang cites, as far as I can discern.

16 Hu Ruli, comp., *Ningxia xin zhi,* Hongzhi 14 [1501] ed. (rpt. Taipei: Chengwen chuban she, 1968), 7:336. See below and note 31 for the Song edict preserved by Ouyang Xiu.

17 Recently Chen Bingying has revisited the issue of when the Tanguts conquered Shazhou and what kind of control they exerted over it. See Chapter 2, n. 58. On the Uighur-sponsored regime at Shazhou of the Shazhou Beiting qaghan, or Shazhou *zhenguo,* see SHY 198, *fan yi* 5:3b. At least until the early twelfth century, groups of Uighurs evidently remained autonomous under Tangut suzerainty and engaged in relations with other states (JS 3:56, 58; Elizabeth Pinks, *Die Uiguren von Kan-chou in der frühen Sung-zeit* [Wiesbaden: Otto Harrassowitz, 1968]).

18 Pinks, *Die Uiguren von Kan-chou,* 75 and passim; SS 490:14115.

19 For example, see Liu Yuquan, "Guanyu Shazhou Huihu dongku di huafen," *Dunhuang yanjiu* 2 (1988): 2–4.

20 Pinks, *Die Uiguren,* 106–115 passim; SS 490:14114–14118; SHY 197, *fan yi* 4:1–11.

21 Zeng Gong, *Longping ji* 20:10a, SS 492:14163.

22 XCB 184:15b, 185:4b–5a.

23 Wang Cheng (d. ca. 1200), *Dongdu shilüe* (rpt. Taibei: Wenhai chuban she, 1967), 128:1a.

24 An early discussion is in Berthold Laufer, "Loan Words in Tibetan," in *Sino-Tibetan Studies,* vol. 2 (rpt. New Delhi, 1987), 656–667. See also Gerard Clauson, *An Etymological Dictionary of Pre-Thirteenth-Century Turkish* (Oxford: Clarendon Press, 1972), 321, where Clauson notes that its earliest meaning was that of "religious teacher." Victor Mair has elaborated the etymology of *boshi/bakshi* in his "Perso-Turkic *Bakshi* = Mandarin *Po-shih:* Learned Doctor," in *Journal of Turkish Studies,* Richard Nelson Frye Festschrift 1, vol. 16 (1992): 117–127. I thank Professor Mair for bringing his article to my attention.

25 Hilda Ecsedy, "Old Turkic Titles of Chinese Origin," *Acta Orientalia Hungarica* 18 (1965): 90.

26 Dunnell, "Hsi Hsia," 189, n. 69.

27 XCB 184:15b.

28 I read Yuanhao's moves against the Yeli as an attempt to stem the influence of that powerful Tangut clan, in which, it must be admitted, he was successful. They do not appear in later sources, nor is their clan name registered in the names lists discussed in Chapter 6.

29 XCB 185:4b–5a.

30 XXSS 19:13a.

31 XXJ 12:18b–19a, quotes the edict from *Ouyang wenzhong ji* (see Shi 1988, 61, n. 1); see also *Song dazhao lingji*, 911, misleadingly dated Jiayou 3, which prints Jiayou 7 for Jiayou 4 in the second occurrence of the date in the edict. The edict appears in "Nei zhi ji," 5:645, in *Ouyang Xiu quanji* (rpt. Taipei: Shijie shuju, 1961), and is dated the twelfth month, presumably of Jiayou 2, since the entries follow chronological order, and the one after is dated to the first month of Jiayou 3.

32 One of these allies may have been Wang Puxin, a highly decorated official holding an appointment to the Bureau of Military Affairs, who wrote the preface to the new Tangut translation of the "Lotus Sūtra" (Shi 1988, 234–236) quoted in Chapter 2.

33 SS 485:14001.

34 Shen Kuo, *Mengxi bitan jiaozheng*, ed. Hu Daojing (rpt. Taipei, 1965), 25/3:452. See also Paul Forage, "Science, Technology, and War in Song China: Reflections in the *Brush Talks from the Dream Creek* by Shen Kuo (1031–1095)," Ph.D. dissertation, University of Toronto, 1991.

35 See Gabriella Molè, *The T'u-yü-hun from the Northern Wei to the Time of the Five Dynasties* (Rome, 1970), 52, 58, 105–106, 109.

36 An interesting example is suggested by Shi Jinbo, who argues that a preface to one of the manuscript editions of the Tangut rhyme dictionary *Wuyin qieyun* in the St. Petersburg archive was written by the Xia emperor, probably Yuanhao or his successor, Yizong. In this preface the author uses the phrase (translated into Chinese) *yi zhen gongde li*, "by the power of My meritorious attainments," *gongde* being a Buddhist technical term denoting virtuous deeds or qualities. See "Xi Xia wen wenxian xintan," in *Xi Xia wenwu*, ed. Shi Jinbo, Bai Bin, and Wu Fengyun (Beijing: Wenwu chuban she, 1988), 46.

37 *Song dazhao lingji*, 912, 917. See also Shi 1988, 61–63. The 1062 date is a reasonable guess derived from its placement in *Song dazhao lingji*.

38 XCB 188:2b–3a. Gusiluo died in 1065 and was succeeded by Dongzhan (SS 492:14162).

39 SHY 199, *fan yi* 6:4b.

40 LS 56:908; Wittfogel and Feng, *Liao*, 227–228.

41 XXJ 13:5a–6a, 9a; *Song dazhao lingji*, 911–912. What kind of artisans is not specified.

42 XCB 198:12a. According to the 1062 decree, Song promised to deliver the Buddhist canon in Jiayou 11, four years later. Renzong died in 1063, and Jiayou changed to Zhiping. It is not clear why Song needed four

years to print and deliver a Tripiṭaka, nor have I found corroboration that the Buddhist books were delivered at the specified time.

43 For example, *Jiajing Ningxia xin zhi* 3:236, mentions the Anqing si in Mingsha prefecture southwest of Ningxia (formerly the Tangut capital of Zhongxing), noting that it contained a stūpa and was reportedly built during Liangzuo's reign.

44 LS 22:267.

45 XXJ 14:1a; XCB, *shi bu* 2:24b; Shen Kuo, *Mengxi bitan*, 25/3:452. Tangut armies had been attacking Song border posts the last three years of Yizong's reign, leading to the Song seizure of Suizhou (Suide) in 1067. Yizong very likely lost his life taking revenge for the loss of Suizhou.

46 SS 14:271; *Song dazhao lingji*, 917.

47 XCB 320:7ab, reported under the fourth month of Yuanfeng 4 (1081). XXSS 24:13b dates Huizong's switch to Han rites to the first month of 1080, but on what basis is not revealed.

48 XCB 312:7ab alone among accounts of these events relates that Huizong planned to eliminate Liang Yimai (Liang xianggong) and his *shumu*, both of whom tried to dissuade him from restoring Han rites. *Shumu* denotes the wife of the father's younger brother, so it presumably refers to the wife or wives of Huizong's Weiming uncle(s). The text implies that they were either widows or acted independently of their possibly exiled Weiming husbands, and they may have been of the Liang or allied clans.

49 SS 350:11073, in the biography of Zhang Shouyue. This is a rare, almost unique reference to Daoists in eleventh-century Xia, but it should come as no surprise to find Daoists, with their well-developed apotropaic repertoire, active in the Tangut lands. The twelfth-century Xia law code defines the administrative structure of the Daoist "church," reflecting its subordinate status to the Buddhist Saṅgha (*Kodeks* 3:109, 410–411 [article 675]; Shi 1988, 150).

50 SS 486:14009. A notable detail revealed in these transactions is that the price for one set of the Kaibao canon remained stable at around seventy Tangut horses; in 1035 Jingzong "paid" fifty mounts in "tribute" for a canon, and in 1073 the Song court generously returned the Tanguts' seventy horses. The three surviving Song edicts of 1058, 1062, and 1073 quote from the Xia request, indicating that the Tanguts understood the customary value of the canon to be seventy tribute horses, which they duly presented.

51 Kuan Ren, ed., *Fojiao shouce* (Beijing: Zhongguo wenshi chuban she, 1991), 188–189.

52 *Song dazhao lingji*, 917; quoted in XXJ 15:11b–12a.

53 XCB 244:11b–12a.

54 Wang Jingru, "Xin jian Xi Xia wen shike he Dunhuang Anxi dongku Xia Han wen tiji kaoshi," in *Wang Guowei xueshu yanjiu lunji*, ed. Wu Ze (Shanghai: Huadong shifan daxue, 1983), 1:233–234, Shi 1988, 304–305.

55 Shi 1988, 65–70; p. 46 above.

56 Shi 1988, 234–238.

57 Shi 1988, 64–73. For examples, see Zhou Shujia's catalogue of Tangut sūtras in the Beijing Library in *Xi Xia wen zhuanhao,* 324, and that volume's frontispiece photograph no. 3 of the text of the *Cibei daochang chan fa* (see below); and Nishida Tatsuo, *The Hsi-Hsia Avatamsaka Sūtra,* vol. 2 (Kyoto, 1976), 7–10. In the introduction to his catalogue *Buddiiskie sochineniia,* 30–32, Kychanov also lists all those texts in the Khara-khoto collection with colophons indicating that they were translated under the two Liang empresses. This enumeration, eleven for the first Empress Liang and four for the second, obviously includes only a small number of the total texts translated at that time.

58 T. 1909, composed under the Liang dynasty (502–519), apparently an apocryphal work. See Nishida catalogue, no. 162; *Buddiiskie sochineniia,* nos. 307–315.

59 This refers, presumably, to a talented monk-translator.

60 I have amended Shi's translation in places (Shi 1988, 239–240), and I thank Ksenia B. Kepping for helping to interpret the first two lines. Shi has eliminated the first two lines preceding the text of the preface, which give the titles and names of the empress and emperor. For a photograph of the preface, see *Xi Xia wenzhuan hao,* frontispiece photograph no. 3, and no. 92 in Zhou Shujia's catalogue in the same volume, 323–324.

61 T. 447, translator unknown, Liang dynasty (502–557), companion to the "Sūtra on the Thousand Buddha Names of the Past Ornamented Kalpa" cited in Chapter 2. Shi 1988, 76–77; Shi, " 'Xi Xia yijing tu' jie," *Wenxian* 1 (1979): 215–229; a better reproduction of the blockprint is in Shi Jinbo et al., eds., *Xi Xia wenwu,* no. 371. It is interesting that such an illustration would accompany this particular text.

62 Shi proposes that the surname Bai may be an Uighur ethnic marker (1988: 149) but does not adduce any supporting evidence. In Chapter 6 I suggest that Bai may be a Tuyühun surname. It is possible that Tuyühun elements were absorbed into the Uighur confederation, accounting for the surname Hun (abbreviated from Tuyühun?) in the chapter on the Uighurs in the Tang history (Ouyang Xiu and Song Qi, *Xin Tang shu* [rpt. Beijing: Zhonghua shuju, 1975], 217 *shang,* p. 6114), but I have not found Bai there as a Uighur name. Hun also appears as a "Tangut" surname in the 1094 inscription, in the compound name Hun-Weiming. Chapter 6 discusses at length the significance of names as ethnic markers.

63 Shi 1988, 316–324; see n. 99, Chapter 2.

64 T. 665; Nishida catalogue, no. 87; *Buddiiskie sochineniia,* nos. 166–180. Shi 1988:74; Shi Jinbo, "Xi Xia wen 'Jin guangming zuisheng wang jing' xuba kao," *Shijie zongjiao yanjiu* 3 (1983): 45–53.

65 The full form of the title appears in the preface to the *Cibei daochang chanfa,* reproduced in *Xi Xia wen zhuanhao,* frontispiece photograph no. 3. *Da ming,* "great enlightenment," has various Buddhist associations; *da ming*

also appears in the title of the tenth-century Khotanese king Li Shengtian; see Zhang Wei, *Longyou jinshi lu* (Gansu, 1943), 3 ("Song shang"), 5a.

66 On the "four great vows" *(si hongyuan),* Mochizuki (1755–1756) elaborates variations; the most common include: (1) to save all those who have not been saved, (2) to liberate all those who have not been liberated, (3) to calm all those who are agitated, and (4) to help all those who have not achieved nirvāṇa to achieve nirvāṇa. Another version of the four vows differs most in the third vow: (1) to save all sentient beings, (2) to cut off the inexhaustible perturbations, (3) to study the inexhaustible dharma methods, and (4) to obtain the inexhaustible Buddha fruit (Ding Fubao, *Foxue da cidian,* 380). A bodhisattva of the first stage also makes "ten great vows" (Paul Williams, *Mahāyāna Buddhism: The Doctrinal Foundations* [London and New York: Routledge, 1989], 206–207).

67 Shi, " 'Xi Xia yijing tu' jie," 219. It is possible that one or more bearers of these names was a Uighur; Cao was a prominent clan in the Dunhuang/Shazhou area, which in the late tenth and early eleventh centuries ruled Shazhou, in close association with the Ganzhou Uighurs and the Khotanese.

68 Shi 1988:136.

69 E. I. Kychanov, "From the History of the Tangut Translation of the Buddhist Canon," in *Tibetan and Buddhist Studies Commemorating the 200th Anniversary of Alexander Csoma de Körös,* ed. Louis Ligeti (Budapest, 1984), 381; *Buddiiskie socheneniia,* no. 108, inv. no. 4773; Nishida catalogue, no. 207; T. 366. The catalogue of the Khara-khoto archive in St. Petersburg compiled by Gorbacheva and Kychanov, *Tangutskie rukopisi i ksilografy* (TRK), no. 147, gives it the Sanskrit title *Buddha-bhāṣita Amitāyus-sūtra.*

70 T. 475; Nishida catalogue, no. 114; *Buddiiskie sochineniia,* no. 161, inv. 119; Grinstead, *Tangut Tripitaka* 9:2034. I transcribed the postscript in St. Petersburg from inv. no. 2311, which differs slightly from the version in Grinstead. The second monk, whose name I have not yet identified, copied the text.

71 See n. 58 above.

72 T. 166; Nishida catalogue, no. 205; translated by Faxian of the Northern Song (Ono Gemmyō, *Bussho kaisetsu daijiten* 2:76b). This text is preserved in the Sven Hedin collection of the Stockholm Folkensmuseum; see Nishida, *Seika mon kegonkyo* 2, appendix, 3, 7. On the apocryphal and political associations of this sūtra, see E. Zürcher, " 'Prince Moonlight': Messianism and Eschatology in Early Medieval Chinese Buddhism," *T'oung Pao* 68, nos. 1–3 (1982): 1–75.

73 T. 1114; translated by Fatian (late eleventh century). Also preserved in Stockholm; see Nishida, *Seika mon kegonkyo* 2, appendix, 8–9. Bhṛkuṭī appears with Tārā as companions of Avalokiteśvara in early Esoteric Buddhist sculpture; see Robert N. Linrothe, "Compassionate Malevolence:

Wrathful Deities in Esoteric Buddhist Art" (Ph.D. dissertation, University of Chicago, 1992), 195–196.

74 *Li ji* is the Chinese gloss for the second highest honorary rank in the Tangut "Table of Ranks" (inv. no. 5921; see Li Fanwen, "Xi Xia guanjie fenghao biao kaoshi," *Shehui kexue zhanxian* 3 (1991): 75; Shi Jinbo, "Xi Xia wen 'guanjie fenghao biao' kaoshi," in *Zhongguo minzu gu wenzi yanjiu,* ed. Zhongguo minzu gu wenzi yanjiu hui (Tianjin, 1991), 247, 262).

75 Chapter 5, T17: "A great feast was held, a ritual site for teaching and confessions was established, and sūtras were recited." This sentence might also be construed to read: "A great feast was held, the *(Cibei) daochang chanfa* was distributed, and canonical texts were recited." Either way it appears that the ceremonies at the temple included a confession ritual.

76 Ono *Bussho kaisetsu daijiten* 4:318c–319b.

77 Ono, 4:318d–319b; T. 1909, 1:922.

78 It appears that she had not been married to Huizong until after the events of 1081, hence the extreme youth of his successor. XCB 312:7ab notes that Huizong's plotting to kill Liang Yimai and his *shumu* in 1081 was reported to Liang Yimai, who resorted to the classic ruse of inviting the emperor to a banquet. After heavy drinking, Yimai's men attacked the emperor and his guests in the back garden, allegedly slaying his wife and killing or wounding nearly a hundred guests. Huizong escaped. His wife here presumably was not a Liang. Huizong's subsequent incarceration may have been to protect him from further harm, while also providing an opportunity for marrying him to a Liang woman. We cannot trust all the details of this story, but they raise some interesting questions. Who was the *shumu* acting in concert with Liang Yimai? What was the source of this story? A border dispatch containing the deposition of a Tangut defector or captured officer? Who was the wife of Huizong allegedly killed in this incident? Why was Huizong not married already to a Liang? In any case, the late marriage explains why Weiming Qianshun was only three when he came to the throne in 1086. Rumors had it that Weiming clansmen objected to Qianshun's succession, since it promised only to perpetuate Liang dominance under Liang Qibu. Some said that Qianshun was not a legitimate royal scion.

79 XXJ 19:16a.

80 XCB 454:4b (1091/1).

81 XXJ 19:22b–25b, 20:1b–2a.

82 XCB 467:5a, 468:7b–8a.

83 XCB 471:2a reports one Song military commissioner writing to court that "[Xia] should be taken and destroyed."

84 XCB 476:10b, 482:9a, under 1093.

85 XCB 478:2a–3a.

86 XCB 467:8a.

87 XCB 467:2ab, 469:11ab, 407:20b.

88 XXSS 29:15a–16a; Wu cites "Xin lu" *(xin shilu?)* as his authority for

dating the assassination of Liang Qibu to 1094/10. This source is not extant or known to me.

89 Shi Jinbo glosses *huai wo le* as *shou juzu* (to receive the complete precepts), the same graphs used in the technical term *juzu jie*, completed precepts. The gloss on this highest of state honors in the "Table of Ranks" does not clarify the relationship between the holder of the rank and the status of his Buddhist practice. See Li Fanwen, "Xi Xia guanjie fenghao biao kaoshi," 171–179; Shi Jinbo, "Xi Xia wen 'guanjie fenghao biao' kaoshi," 245–266. Refer also to the note to H22 in Chapter 5.

90 *Mengqi bitan* 25/4:453.

91 XXJ 20:19ab; *Song dazhao lingji*, 921. The resumption of these exchanges would only have occurred if the Tanguts fulfilled the condition set out in the last line of the Song edict of 1093/4: to submit an oath letter *(shibiao)*; "then afterwards regular tribute and yearly gifts can [resume] according to the old precedents." Since the Tanguts presented tribute at the following New Year celebration, we can assume that such an oath letter was submitted.

92 TRK 342, inv. 812 in the Kozlov archives (examined January 1994). *Buddiiskie sochineniia*, no. 193 (but inv. no. 812 is not listed under no. 193 or no. 194). See also Kychanov, "From the History of the Tangut Translation of the Buddhist Canon," 381–382. Here Kychanov theorizes that this edition was "connected with the palace revolution, which resulted in the collapse of the power of the representative figures of the Liang House, who aimed to usurp the Tangut throne," referring to Liang Qibu. Equally likely, the commissioning of this translation and printing was connected with imperial activities celebrating the restored Liangzhou stūpa. The Tangut edition probably corresponds to T. 363 (*Dacheng wuliangshou jing*, 3 *juan*, translated by Faxian in 991, under the northern Song), and was probably translated from Tō. 49 in the Tibetan canon, *'Phags-pa' od-dpag-med-kyi bkod-pa zhes-bya-ba theg-pa chen-po'i mdo* (see Hakuju Ui et al., eds., *A Complete Catalogue of the Tibetan Buddhist Canons [Bkan-hgyur and Bstan-hgyur]* [Sendai, Japan: Tōhoku Imperial University and Saito Gratitude Foundation, 1934]). This in turn was translated in the ninth century by Jinamitra, Dānaśīla, and Yes-shes sde from the Sanskrit *(Ārya-amitā-bhavyūha-nāma-Mahāyāna-sūtra)*, and is also commonly called the "Larger Sukhāvatī-vyūha." See *The Nyingma Edition of the sDe-dge bKa'-'gyur/bsTan'-gyur, Research Catalogue and Bibliography* (Oakland, Calif.: Dharma Press, 1982), 1:204–208 (compare this to text no. 115, pp. 303–307). Nishida catalogue, no. 37, suggests that the Tangut text corresponds to T. 936 and Tō. 361, but those two texts appear to be too short to be the same or to be the source of the Tangut text.

93 Fang Guangchang, *Fojiao dianji baiwen*, in Zongjiao wenhua congshu (The Religious Culture Series), ed. Wang Zhiyuan (Beijing: Jinri Zhongguo chuban she, 1989), 59–60; Ono, 10:427.

94 SS 485:14017.
95 SS 486:14018.
96 According to Wu Guangcheng's account, the empress dowager herself sent a reproachful note to the Liao emperor. Displeased, he let it be known that Liao would raise troops to help the Tanguts, but he never lifted a finger and further, so the story goes, took revenge by poisoning her (XXSS 30:12ab, 31:1ab).
97 LS 115:1528, 25:302–304, 26:307–311.
98 XCB 506:6b.
99 XCB 507:8b–11a.
100 Dunnell, "Hsi Hsia," 195–196, and sources cited; XCB 516:20b records that Song officers captured and publicly executed four Qingtang agents sent to obtain Xia assistance.
101 SHY 199, *fan yi* 6:33b–34a.
102 Dongzhan died in 1086 (SS 492:14165); SHY 199, *fan yi* 6:38ab.
103 SS 492:14165.
104 XCB *shibu*, 23:13a; in SS 492:14163, *panci* is glossed as *gongxian*. See also James R. Hamilton, *Les Ouigours à l'Époque des Cinq Dynasties d'après les documents chinois* (Paris: Presses Universitaires de France, 1955), 117, 125, for its usage in tenth-century Dunhuang letters to the Ganzhou qaghan. XCB 444:2a offers *pancha*.
105 SS 328:10583, under the notice on Wang Hou, son of Wang Shao.
106 *Qingtang lu* is preserved in Tao Zongyi *Shuofu* 35:11b–13a (Huafen lou edition; rpt. Taipei: Commercial Press, 1972). XCB 516:20a also confirms Li Yuan as its author, but he has eluded biographers, and there is some disagreement over whether the original work had one, two, or three *juan*. See Dunnell, "Tanguts and the Tangut State," 152–153, n. 96, for details. The extant text has one *juan*.
107 The text has thirty *(san shi)*, but thirty tiers seems unprecedented for a stūpa, and the usual thirteen is more likely.
108 *Lifa* is an awkward expression in the context; according to the late Professor James T. C. Liu, *li* may be a corruption of another graph meaning "to violate," an interpretation supported by what follows.
109 See Dunnell, "Tanguts and the Tangut State," 147–154; Li Yuan, *Qingtang lu*, in Tao Zongyi, *Shuofu* 35; Maeda Masana, *Kasai no rekishi chiri gakuteki kenkyū* (Tokyo, 1964), 622 and passim; Iwasaki Tsutomu, "Songdai Hexi zangzu yu fojiao," *Xibei shidi* 1 (1992): 110–124 (original Japanese published in *Tōyōshi kenkyū* 46:1 [June 1987]: 107–142; and an English version, "The Tibetan Tribes of Ho-hsi and Buddhism during the Northern Sung Period," appeared in *Acta Asiatica* 64 [Tokyo, 1993]: 17–37).
110 Dohi Yoshiyazu, "Ki i gun (Tō kōki godai Sōsho) jidai," in *Tonkō no rekishi*, ed. Enoki Kazuo, 261–262 (Tokyo: Daitō shuppansha, 1980).
111 LS 26:308.

112 Later sources do, however, hint at a lapse of patronage or at least a decline of imperially sponsored dharma. For example, in a short piece written by a Tangut emperor called "Preface to the Tripiṭaka of Saintly Teachings Newly Translated by the Great State of White and High," dating probably to Renxiao's reign or later, the author notes that after Yuanhao's reign, "the dharma did not flourish, sagely deeds did not accumulate, merit was not complete, people . . . did not cultivate the pure path and loved those who regularly committed the ten evils" (Shi 1988, 283–285). It remains to identify the precise time and political context of this imperial document, before we can use it as "evidence" of eleventh- or early-twelfth-century activities, but it is not the only reference in later Tangut sources to a "time of troubles" for Buddhists at court. The language may recall the rhetoric of *mofa,* or "end of the Law," but without doubt it refers to real political events in Xia. For a discussion of *mofa,* see Jan Nattier, *Once Upon a Future Time: Studies in a Buddhist Prophecy of Decline* (Berkeley, Calif.: Asian Humanities Press, 1991).

113 See note 70 above; Kychanov, "Gosudarstvo i Buddizm v Si Sia (982–1227)," 135.

114 XXSS 31:16b–17a.

115 According to the pamphlet handed out to this tourist in the spring of 1988, "The Giant Buddha Temple in Zhangye" *(Zhangye Dafo si).* For centuries travelers through the Gansu corridor have remarked upon this landmark. Paul Pelliot provides further details in *Notes on Marco Polo,* vol. 1 (Paris: Imprimerie Nationale, 1959), 152.

116 Zhong Gengqi, comp., *Ganzhou fuzhi,* Qianlong 44 [1779] woodblock ed. (rpt. Taipei: Chengwen chuban she, 1976), 5:19a, 11:65b–66a, 13:26b–28b, 806–826, 25b–28b.

117 A Xia *dhāraṇī* text in the Taishō Tripiṭaka has a preface dated to 1200 that names the monk-compilers, one of whom hailed from the Xiusheng Temple of Lion Peak (Shizi feng) at Ganquan (see T. 1956, *Mizhou yuanyin wangsheng ji,* 1007).

118 Here Kāśyapa refers to the sixth of the seven ancient buddhas of the time preceding Śākyamuni, rather than to the famous disciple of Śākyamuni, of whom it is prophesied that when Maitreya descends to earth, he will emerge from hiding to proffer the new Buddha Śākyamuni's robe and bowl. This legend seems to borrow elements from that well-known prophecy.

119 I.e., in the present world.

120 In Mahāyāna scripture, aspirants on the bodhisattva path progress through ten stages (Skt. *bhumi;* Chin. *shidi*), of which the eighth stage is that of *acalā* or *budong,* unperturbedness or unshakable repose (Ding, 113). Paul Williams describes all ten stages in *Mahāyāna Buddhism,* 204–214.

121 Zhong Gengqi, *Ganzhou fuzhi* 13:27b.

122 The reference to Kāśyapa and Tuṣita Heaven led me first to interpret

this as a legend about Mahākāśyapa, a chief disciple of Śākyamuni, and Maitreya. See note 118 above.

123 Durt, "The Meaning of Archaeology in Ancient Buddhism: Notes on the Stūpas of Aśoka and the Worship of the 'Buddhas of the Past' According to Three Stories in the *Samguk Yusa,*" in *Buddhism and Science: Commemorative Volume, 80th Anniversary* (Seoul: Dongguk University, 1987), 11 (1233). I thank Rob Linrothe for drawing my attention to this article. Durt also points to a text in the Chinese canon, T. 1462 (*Samantapāsādikā,* composed by the fifth-century Pali scholar Buddhagosa), containing similar legends, to which the Tanguts may also have had access. The Tibetan text, *Li yul lung-bstan-pa,* was translated and published by R. E. Emmerick, *Tibetan Texts Concerning Khotan,* London Oriental Series 19 (London, 1967).

124 "The Meaning of Archaeology in Ancient Buddhism," 2 (1224).

125 Zhong Gengqi, *Ganzhou fuzhi* 5:19a.

126 On the situation in Gansu in the early Ming, see Henry Serruys, "The Mongols of Kansu during the Ming," *Mélanges chinois et bouddhiques* 10 (1952–1955): 215–346, esp. the introduction.

127 The cult of relics pervaded Chinese society as well; even Chan Buddhists of the Song were obsessed with relics; see T. Griffith Foulk and Robert H. Sharf, "On the Ritual Use of Ch'an Portraiture in Medieval China," *Cahiers d'Extrême Asie* 7 (1993): 149–219. On Maitreya worship in early (fourth to fifth century) Liangzhou, see Chisui Satō, "The Character of Yünkang Buddhism," 49 passim. Satō speculates that the statue of Maitreya at Yungang represented the reigning Northern Wei emperor.

128 Jin Bohong, *In the Footsteps of Marco Polo* (Beijing: New World Press, 1989), 106–107.

129 *In the Footsteps of Marco Polo,* 107.

130 In "Xi Xia houji zhidu kaoshu" (*Ningxia shehui kexue* 2 [1993]: 94), Gu Jichen remarks that the Liang regime maintained Tangut independence of both Song and Liao, and that Qianshun's recovery of power (what I call the Weiming Restoration) was accomplished at the price of renewed dependence on Liao. Although in other respects Gu Jichen's treatment of empressorial power lacks depth and rigor, this point is important and deserves a more prominent position in his analysis.

4. A HISTORY OF THE DAYUN (HUGUO) TEMPLE AT LIANGZHOU

1 For the 711 text, see Wang Chang (1725–1806), *Jinshi cuibian,* Shike shiliao xin bian ed. (Taibei: Xinwenfeng shuban, 1982), 69:28b–31b. For the 1094 inscription, see Ruth W. Dunnell, "The 1094 Sino-Tangut Gantong Stūpa Stele Inscription of Wuwei: Introduction, Translation of Chinese Text, and Source Study," in *Languages and History in East Asia: Festschrift for Tatsuo Nishida on the Occasion of His 60th Birthday,* ed. Akihiro Satō (Kyoto, 1988); and Appendix B. The rubbings and French translations of the 1563 and 1697 texts come from E. Chavannes, "Dix inscriptions chinoises

de l'Asie centrale, d'après les estampages de M. Ch.-E. Bonin," *Memoires présentés par divers savants à l'Académie des Inscriptions et Belles-lettres,* ser. 1, vol. 11, no. 2 (1902): 193–295 (also published as a separate extract in 1902, 103 pp.). Zhang Wei (1891–19??) published an incomplete text of the 1622 text (taken from an unpublished work called *Wuwei xianzhi gao*) in his *Longyou jinshi lu,* preface dated 1936, 9:11a–12a.

2 These texts were recorded by Zhang Shu (d. 1847), in *Liangzhou fuzhi beikao* (Wuwei: Wuwei shi shi zhi bianzuan weiyuan hui bangongshi jiao yin, 1986), vol. 3, *yiwen,* 11:853–855, 878–882. This gazetteer existed in manuscript form and did not circulate widely up to its publication in 1986.

3 See the comments of Zhang Wei, in *Longyou jinshi lu* 2:19ab. Zhang was scandalized by the mistakes in the reengraving.

4 Liu erred here, for Zhang came to power only in 363 in the first year of the Xingning era (363–365). See Sima Guang (eleventh century), *Xin jiao zizhi tongjian zhu* (rpt. Taipei: Shijie shuju, 1977), 101:3193.

5 Weinstein, *Buddhism under the T'ang,* 42, summarizes the event.

6 Although *lan* by itself reads better as "balustrade" (as suggested by Herbert Franke), the context of the entire phrase, which stands in unambiguous symmetry with the preceding reference to sweeping pines, seems to require a botanical interpretation.

7 In Chinese architecture, a *jian* is normally the space between two pillars (a standardized span). Here I assume that the supports defining the four sides of the stūpa are connected by the wooden outer walls containing the doors and windows mentioned in this passage. Thus *jian* here means face, side, or bay (as it is often translated).

8 Denis Twitchett, "Hsüan-tsung (reign 712–756)," in *The Cambridge History of China,* volume 3: *Sui and T'ang China, 589–906,* ed. D. Twitchett (London and New York: Cambridge University Press, 1979), 366–367; Sima Guang, *Zizhi tongjian* 217:6660–6661.

9 Weinstein, *Buddhism under the T'ang,* 54: "It should be noted that many of the Buddhist K'ai-yüan monasteries were created by simply redesignating the Ta-Yün monasteries established half a century earlier by Empress Wu."

10 Chou Yi-liang, "Tantrism in China," *Harvard Journal of Asiatic Studies* 8, nos. 3–4 (March 1945): 285; Raffaello Orlando, "A Study of Chinese Documents Concerning the Life of the Tantric Buddhist Patriarch Amoghavajra," 133–144, 161, 165.

11 Quoted from the translation of T. 2056, by Orlando, "Amoghavajra," 144 (165 for another description of the same event); see also Chou Yi-liang, "Tantrism in China," 293–294 and n. 46, which explains that Geshu Han was of Turkic origin and his family had some special ties with Central Asian Buddhism, for his father, Geshu Daoyuan, a Tang officer in the Anxi Protectorate, was designated in 710 by Ruizong to escort the remains of Śikṣānanda back to Khotan. Empress Wu had invited the Khotanese monk

Śikṣānanda to come to China in 695 to retranslate the *Huayan jing (Avataṃsaka Sūtra)*; see Weinstein, *Buddhism under the T'ang*, 45. On Geshu Han's victories over the Tibetan armies and his role in the An Lushan rebellion, see Denis Twitchett, *The Cambridge History of China*, volume 3, 426, 432–433, 448, 457, 459–460, 562–563; Liu Xu et al., comps., *Jiu Tang shu* (Beijing: Zhonghua shuju, 1987), 104: 3211.

12 SHY 195, *fang yu* 21:14b.

13 SHY 195, *fang yu* 21:15b–16a. Youlonghu = Zhebu Youlongbu or Yulongbu of SS 492:14154.

14 In contemporary Chinese scholarship, this name is read Boluozhi, which reading I adopted in *The Cambridge History of China*, volume 6, rather than Fanluozhi (or Panluozhi). Edwin Pulleyblank, in *Lexicon of Reconstructed Pronunciation in Early Middle Chinese, Late Middle Chinese, and Early Mandarin* (Vancouver: UBC Press, 1991), 19–20, avers that there is no evidence for reconstructing a reading of "bo" for the graph *fan*, despite efforts of Chinese scholars to construct a reading of, for example, Tufan (Tibet) as Tubo, to approximate more closely the native Tibetan reading of the country's name (Bod). Victor Mair, however, has adduced considerable evidence to support the reading "bo." See his "*Tufan* and *Tulufan*: The Origins of the Old Chinese Names for Tibet and Turfan," *Central and Inner Asian Studies* 4 (1990): 14–70. See also Mair's review of Pulleyblank's *Lexicon* in *Sino-Platonic Papers* 31 (1991): 37–39, and Pulleyblank's response to it in *Sino-Platonic Papers* 35 (1992): 32–37.

15 SHY 195, *fang yu* 21:19a, 21b.

16 SS 492:14157.

17 Iwasaki Tsutomu, reads this as two temples in "Songdai Hexi zangzu yu fojiao," *Xibei shidi* 1 (1992): 111.

18 See n. 23 below. For the legend of King Aśoka and the 84,000 stūpas, see Strong, *The Legend of King Aśoka*, 219–221.

19 Existing studies include Akira Hirakawa, "The Rise of Mahāyāna Buddhism and Its Relationship to the Worship of Stūpas," *Memoirs of the Research Department of the Toyo Bunko* 22 (Tokyo, 1963): 57–106; and André Bareau, "La construction et le culte des stūpa d'après les *Vinayapiṭaka*," *Bulletin de l'École Française d'Extrême-Orient* 50, no. 2 (1962): 229–274, in addition to the works cited below. For a response to Hirakawa's ideas, see Gregory Schopen, "The Phrase 'sa pṛthivīpradeśaś caityabhūto bhavet' in the *Vajracchedikā*: Notes on the Cult of the Book in Mahāyāna," *Indo-Iranian Journal* 17 (1975): 147–181. Hirakawa argues for the lay origins of Mahāyāna and Schopen for a monastic, text-centered genesis. Paul Williams reviews the issue in *Mahāyāna Buddhism*, 20–26.

20 Gustav Roth, "Symbolism of the Buddhist Stūpa," in *The Stūpa: Its Religious, Historical and Architectural Significance*, ed. Anna Livera Dallapiccola et al. (Wiesbaden: Franz Steiner Verlag, 1980), 183–187; Hirakawa, "The Rise of Mahāyāna Buddhism," 91–94. Regarding the contro-

versy over whether or not monks were allowed to build reliquaries and worship the Buddha's relics, see Gregory Schopen, "Monks and the Relic Cult in the *Mahāparinibbānasutta:* An Old Misunderstanding in Regard to Monastic Buddhism," in *From Benares to Beijing: Essays on Buddhism and Chinese Religions in Honour of Prof. Jan Yün-hua,* ed. Koichi Shinohara and G. Schopen (Oakville, Ontario: Mosaic Press, 1991), 187–201. Schopen takes issue with Hirakawa and says that monks were not prohibited from so doing.

21 T. 2042; translated by An Faqin at Loyang in A.D. 306.

22 Strong, *Legend of King Aśoka,* 219–221.

23 E. Zürcher sketches the search for Aśoka's relics in the fourth century in *The Buddhist Conquest of China* (Leiden: E. J. Brill, 1972), 1:277–280. An interesting study of this phenomenon in a Korean context is Hubert Durt, "The Meaning of Archaeology in Ancient Buddhism: Notes on the Stūpas of Aśoka," 1223–1241.

24 Ch'en, *Buddhism in China,* 201–202. On stūpa building as a merit-making activity, see Louis Ligeti, "Le mérite d'ériger un *stūpa* et l'histoire de l'éléphant d'or," in *Proceedings of the Csoma de Körös Memorial Symposium* (Budapest, 1978), 223–284.

25 Hirakawa, "The Rise of Mahāyāna Buddhism," 85–91.

26 Gustav Roth, "Symbolism of the Stūpa," 185.

27 Lothar Ledderose, "Chinese Prototypes of the Pagoda," in *The Stūpa: Its Religious, Historical and Architectural Significance,* ed. Anna Libera Dallapiccola, 241–242.

28 Yang Hsüan-chih, *A Record of Buddhist Monasteries in Lo-yang,* trans. Yi-t'ung Wang (Princeton University Press, 1984), 15–16.

29 Wang Jingru, "Xin jian Xi Xia wen shike he Dunhuang Anxi dongku Xi Xia Han wen tiji kaoshi," 233–234.

30 E. I. Kychanov, "Pravovoe polozhenie Buddiiskikh obshchin v tangutskom gosudarstve," 42–43 (this article forms chapter 10 of Kychanov's introductory volume on the Tiansheng Code: *Kodeks* 1:401–421); see also Kychanov, "Buddhism and State in Hsi Hsia from Juridical Aspect," *Acta Orientalia Hungarica* 34, nos. 1–3 (1980): 105–111. Kychanov does not provide the original Tangut text and translates the name as "Help to the State," not "Protect the State," but there is little doubt that he means the Huguo si.

31 SS 485:13995.

32 T. 245/246; Mochizuki, 4105c. An apocryphal text believed to have been composed in fifth-century China and retranslated by Amoghavajra. Still useful is M. W. de Visser, *Ancient Buddhism in Japan: Sūtras and Ceremonies in Use in the Seventh and Eighth Centuries A.D. and Their History in Later Times,* vol. 1 (Paris: Librairie Orientaliste Paul Geuthner, 1928). I have adapted Raoul Birnbaum's translation of the title (see his *Studies on the Mysteries of Mañjuśrī,* 31). More recently Charles Orzech has written about

this sūtra; see his "Puns on the Humane King: Analogy and Application in an East Asian Apocryphon," *Journal of the American Oriental Society* 109, no. 1 (Jan.–March 1989): 17–24; and his forthcoming translation of an excerpt of the text in *Religions of China in Practice,* ed. Donald S. Lopez, Jr. (Princeton University Press). Orzech translates the title as "The *Prajñāpāramitā Sūtra* For Humane Kings Who Wish to Protect Their States" and argues vehemently against translating *ren* as "benevolent."

33 Weinstein, *Buddhism under the T'ang,* 78.

34 C. I. Beckwith points out the temple's longer name in "The Revolt of 755 in Tibet," in *Contributions on Tibetan Language, History and Culture,* ed. Ernst Steinkellner and Helmut Tauscher (Vienna: Arbeitskreis für Tibetische und Buddhistische Studien Universität Wien, 1983), 12. Beckwith substitutes Huguo for Zhenguo, but the source he cites, E. O. Reischauer, trans., *Ennin's Diary* (New York: Ronald Press, 1955), 252, n. 944, has "Pao-mo-chen-kuo." *Baomo,* however, is a grammatically awkward and unlikely phrase, as *bao,* to protect, usually takes as its complement the thing that it protects. *Mo,* therefore, may be a corruption of the graph for Tang, the dynasty: "protect the Tang and defend the nation" fits nicely (thanks to Herbert Franke for suggesting this solution).

35 Birnbaum, *Studies on the Mysteries of Mañjuśrī,* 31.

36 Perhaps for similar reasons Qubilai had a Huguo renwang si ("Monastery of the Humane King Who Protects the State") built at the Yuan capital, Dadu. See Zhi Pan, *Fozu tongji* 49:434a, 437b, for the reestablishment of the temple in 1346. There was also a Huguo si at Shazhou in the late Tang (Maeda Masana, *Kasai no rekishi chiri gakuteki kenkyū,* 300 and n. 48).

37 XCB 121:1a.

38 The relationship between the supervisor *(tiju)* of a temple and the supervisor of a group or groups of monks at that temple is not clear. The official named in T2, supervisor of the Shengrong Temple, was clearly a central government official and a layman. His office presumably encompassed and outranked that of Yao'nie, also a court official. See Chapter 5, note to T2.

39 In the Song system, *seng zheng* were appointed by the central government to supervise monastic registration, ordination, and so forth, at the prefectural level or to supervise particular well-known and powerful public monasteries, such as the monastic complexes at Wutai shan or Tiantai shan (Xie Zhongguang and Bai Wengu, *Zhongguo sengguan zhidu shi* [Xining: Qinghai renmin chuban she, 1990], 171–173).

40 See the note to T25 in Chapter 5 regarding Wangna Zhengyu.

41 Possibly related, in religious affiliation if not genealogically, to Bai Zhiguang, the Anquan State Preceptor (see Chapters 3 and 6).

42 Sun Xiushen and Dang Shoushan, " 'Liangzhou Yushan shifo ruixiang yinyuan ji' kaoshi," *Dunhuang yanjiu* 3 (1983): 102–107.

43 Zhang Siwen, "Gansu sheng Yongchang xian Houda si (Shengrong si) liu ti wenzi shike," *Xibei minzu yanjiu* 2 (1989): 210.

44 Sun and Dang, " 'Liangzhou Yushan,' " 103, 105, citing Daoxuan's chronicle *Xu gaoseng zhuan* (T. 2060) for corroborating literary evidence. I have not located the relevant passage in Daoxuan's chronicle, but rather in T. 2064 (*Shenseng zhuan* 3), 965bc. Sun and Dang say that when the temple was built in Zhou, it was named Ruixiang ("Auspicious Image") si, but this name does not occur in the extant portion of the "Record." It does appear in *Shenseng zhuan*, a Ming work commissioned and prefaced by the Yongle emperor.

45 Sun and Dang, " 'Liangzhou Yushan,' " 105.

46 Zhang Siwen, "Gansu sheng," 210, does not offer an explanation.

47 The reference to the Dayun si comes one line after a mention of Tang emperor Zhongzong (line 15), whose brief reign spanned the first two months of 684.

48 According to Sun and Dang, " 'Liangzhou Yushan,' " the stele was originally erected inside the Dayun grounds (107), at the Gantong Lower Temple, based on references in line 24 (103), which they reconstruct as follows (roughly translated): " . . . first stopped at this site. Afterward this place was changed to the Baima si. At the time that Yuwen destroyed the dharma (574), its land . . . of the lay dwellers many were uneasy. Consequently again bestowed [on it the name] of Gantong [Xia] si. At that time the Five Liang. . . ." Sun and Dang read this line as referring to the Dayun si in Liangzhou, which, then, was called Gantong Lower Temple before it was renamed the Dayun Temple under Empress Wu. It is not clear to me what the antecedents of this fragment are, but Sun and Dang's reading suggests that around the time that the Yushan temple received the name Gantong si from the Sui emperor, the (later) Dayun Temple in Liangzhou received the name Gantong Lower Temple—lower, perhaps, in relation to the temple to its north at Yushan. Further, before that the Liangzhou temple apparently went by the name of Baima si (White Horse Temple), another name not recorded in the 1094 or any other inscription examined here.

49 Zhang Siwen describes the stūpa, which he was unable to enter and climb up during a visit in 1985 because the door was locked ("Gansu sheng," 211)!

50 A general discussion of ethnic groups in Xia is Shi Jinbo, "Xi Xia jingnei minzu kao," in *Qingzhu Wang Zhonghan xiansheng bashi shou chen xueshu lun wenji* (Liaoning: Liaoning daxue chuban she, 1993), 407–417.

51 Shi Jinbo, Bai Bin, and Huang Zhenhua, *Wenhai yanjiu* no. 33.141; *Kodeks* 3:159, 514–515.

52 Kychanov, "Pravovoe polozhenie Buddiiskikh obshchin," 48 and passim.

53 For example, the 1195 commemorative publications of Empress Luo (Shi 1988, 273–274), or Renzong's issue (undated) of two texts in Fan and Han editions of 15,000 (p. 270), or Renzong's 1184 birthday issue of Fan and Han editions of 51,000 (p. 262).

54 Shi 1988, 267.

55 Kychanov, "Pravovoe polozhenie," 30–31.

56 Kychanov, "Pravovoe polozhenie," 49–50; I am preparing a study of this subject.

57 On ethnic communities in Shazhou in an earlier period, see, L. I. Čuguevskii, "Touen-Houang du VIIIe au Xe siècle," in *Nouvelles contributions aux études de Touen-houang*, vol. 2, ed. Michel Soymié (Geneva: Librairie Droz, 1981), 1–56; and Maeda, *Kasai no rekishi chiri gakuteki kenkyū*, 277–317. In Ningxia, the seat of the Ming garrison *(wei)* at the site of the former capital of Xia, separate Prefectural Buddhist Registries governed Han and Fan (Tibetan) monks. See Hu Ruli, *Jiajing Ningxia xin zhi* 1:62, reference to *Han seng gangsi* and *Fan seng gangsi*.

58 The "hundred thousand craftsmen" of H19 should not be taken literally.

59 The fifteenth of the first month was the Lantern Festival, which marked the end of the New Year cycle in China. Jacques Gernet gives a lively account of the lantern festival using Song sources in his *Daily Life in China on the Eve of the Mongol Invasion, 1250–1276* (1959; Stanford, Calif.: Stanford University Press, 1962), 188–190. For an eighteenth-century description of this festival in Tibet, see R. A. Stein, *Tibetan Civilization* (1962; Stanford: Stanford University Press, 1972), 215.

60 XCB 479:12a; XXJ 20:19ab; *Song dazhao lingji*, 921. See Chapter 3, n. 91.

61 *Kodeks* 3:114, 420.

62 The "Lotus Sūtra" was probably translated into Tangut under the first empress dowager Liang, judging from the extant preface, although Shi argues for an earlier date (*Fojiao shilüe*, 75). See Chapter 2, n. 96.

63 Quoted from the translation by Leon Hurvitz, *Scripture of the Lotus Blossom of the Fine Dharma (The Lotus Sutra)* (New York: Columbia University Press, 1976), 184.

64 William E. Soothill and Lewis Hodous, *Dictionary of Chinese Buddhist Terms* (rpt. Taipei: Ch'eng Wen, 1975), 14; Mochizuki *Bukkyō daijiten* 2:1889–1890. Jeffrey Hopkins, in *Meditation on Emptiness* (London: Wisdom Publications, 1983), 206, renders the seven qualities as "seven branches of enlightenment—mindfulness, discrimination of phenomena, effort, joy, pliancy, meditative stabilization, and equanimity." See also Chapter 5, T14 and note 43. For other cosmological and planetary associations of the number seven, see Adrian Snodgrass, *The Symbolism of the Stūpa* (Delhi: Motilal, 1992), 236–244.

65 Soothill and Hodous, 177, 243; Ding, 387. See Chapter 5, n. 44.

66 Mochizuki 2:1920. Soothill and Hodous name the seven kingly treasures as the *cakravartin*'s wheel (gold, silver, or iron, depending on the monarch's qualifications), elephants, swift steeds, pearls, able ministers of the treasury, jewels of women, and loyal generals (11–12). Strong lists them

thus: wheel, elephant, horse, woman, gem, treasurer, and minister (*The Legend of Aśoka*, 46 and n. 21). Liu Xinru discusses the origins of the "seven treasures" in *Ancient India and Ancient China*, 92–102.

67 R. A. Stein comments on "red-faced" and "black-headed" (also an epithet of the Chinese people) in "Mi-ñag et Si-hia: Géographie historique et légendes ancestrales," *Bulletin de l'École Française d'Extrême-Orient* 44, no. 1 (1947–1950): 229, n. 2.

68 Nishida Tatsuo, "Seika go 'Tzukizuki rakushi' no kenkyū," *Kyōto daigaku bungakubu kenkyū kiyō* 25 (Showa 61 [1987]): 24; a Tangut composition titled "Song to the Newly Renovated [Academy of] Great Learning" mentions a beautifully adorned seven-tiered "tower."

69 Chavannes, "Dix inscriptions chinoises de l'Asie centrale, d'après les estampages de M. Ch.-E. Bonin," 233–241 (41–49).

70 This should probably be Zhizheng (1341–1368), as the 1622 inscription and the 1588 Qingying si inscription both affirm that this quarter of Liangzhou suffered destruction in fighting at the end of the Yuan.

71 I do not have any further information about the matter, and since the gazetteer had not yet been published, presumably Zhiman has left no trail in the Japanese record, and this inscription is the main source for his life.

72 See Frederick Mote and Denis Twitchett, eds., *The Cambridge History of China*, volume 7: *The Ming* (Cambridge University Press, 1988), chapter 5.

73 Evidence that Ming frontier officials made just that analogy comes from the chapter on the Tatars (Mongols) in the Ming dynastic history. Zhang Tingyu, comp., *Ming shi* (Beijing: Zhonghua shuju, 1974), 327:8489, quotes a border officer referring to the precedent of the rebellious "Xi Xia faction" *(Xi Xia dang)* in a memorial to court.

74 *The Cambridge History*, vol. 7, 477.

75 Zhang Wei (1891–?) copied this text from a draft manuscript of a Wuwei gazetteer *(Wuwei xianzhi gao)* and appended a postscript saying that this stele was erected at the Dayun Temple in the Eastern Town (of the Five Liang; i.e., in the eastern quarter or suburb) in the second year of Tianqi (1622). Earlier in the nineteenth century Zhang Shu copied the text into his gazetteer, *Liangzhou fuzhi beikao (yiwen,* 10:859–862). If Zhang Wei was a descendant of Zhang Shu, as I have wondered, he should have owned a copy of Shu's manuscript. The *Wuwei xianzhi gao* that Zhang Wei consulted may be the same or similar to the work I examined in Beijing (see n. 81 below).

76 Da Yun was a celebrated general, whose biography in *Ming shi* relates that he was a native of Liangzhou from a hereditary military family and earned his reputation in service along the Qinghai-Gansu frontier (239:6223–6225). At least once he defended Liangzhou from Mongol raiders (see also *Ming shi* 327:8489, 330:8548).

77 On Ming cultic practices in connection with the Dark Emperor, see Gary Seaman, *Journey to the North: An Ethnohistorical Analysis and Anno-*

tated Translation of the Chinese Folk Novel Pei-yu Chi (Berkeley and Los Angeles: University of California Press, 1987), esp. Introduction. Owing to the Qing taboo on the graph *xuan*, which was part of Kangxi's first name, Zhang Shu's text (860) has Yuan di; Zhang Wei's text has Xuan di.

78 I suspect that the text is corrupted here; furthermore, the punctuation in the 1986 edition of *Liangzhou fuzhi beikao* often seems wrong to me.

79 Bonin reported seeing the date 1697 on the reverse side of the stone ("Dix inscriptions chinoises," 241 [6]), as discussed below.

80 On the Yulanpen or ghost festival, see Teiser, *The Ghost Festival in Medieval China*.

81 Zhang Zhijun, Zhang Qimei, et al., comps., *Wuliang kaozhi liu de ji quanji*, preface dated Qianlong 40 (1775–1776), 1, *Wuwei xian zhi*, 30a, *si miao*. I consulted the edition in the Beijing Normal University Library and thank Nie Hongyin for assisting my work there.

82 *Liangzhou fuzhi beikao*, 2, *gu ji*, 1:607.

83 C. G. Mannerheim, *Across Asia From West to East in 1906–1908*, 2 vols. (Oosterhout, The Netherlands: Anthropological Publications, 1969), 1:489–491.

84 Chavannes, "Dix inscriptions chinoises," 193 (1). M. G. Devéria had access to the rubbing(s) secured through the auspices of the French ambassador in 1896, and he first published his findings in "Stèle Si-Hia de Leang-Tcheou," *Journal asiatique*, 9th ser., 11 (1898): 53–74.

85 From Zhang's account in his *Liangzhou fuzhi beikao*, 2, *gu ji*, 1:608, we learn that there happened to be workers there engaged in some other labor.

86 Zhang Shu, *Yangsu tang wenji* (Donghua shuju kanben, published in 1837 [Daoguang 17]), 19:18b–20a. See Appendix B for a discussion of Zhang's attempt to read the Tangut seal script.

87 Zhang Shu, *Liangzhou fuzhi beikao*, 3, *yiwen*, 10:859.

88 On the ancient bell, see also Zhang Wei, *Longyou jinshi lu*, 2:71b. Zhang only says that the bell is not later than the Five Dynasties era (tenth century).

89 Zhang Shu, *Liangzhou fuzhi beikao*, 3, *yiwen*, 10:853–854.

90 Zhang Zhijun et al., *Wuliang kaozhi liu de ji quanji*, 1, *Wuwei xian zhi*, 30a, *si guan*.

91 Chavannes, "Dix inscriptions chinoises," 237 (45), n. 2. Chavannes notes that the 1563 text substitutes *guxian ta* for the equivalent expression in the 711 text, *mu futu*. That the 1563 inscription copies text from both the 711 and 1094 texts supports the gloss offered by Chavannes.

92 Yan Kejun (1762–1843), *Tieqiao jinshi ba* (rpt. Taipei: Yiwen yinshu guan, 1966), 4:18ab (see Appendix B), records the discovery of the 1094 stele, mistakenly crediting it to Liu Qingyuan, under an entry titled "Jieqing Temple Gantong Stūpa stele, Tianyou min'an fifth year first month." He goes on to write that the "stele is located at the Dayun Temple in Liang-

zhou." It is unclear to which temple the name Jieqing refers; it may be an error for or variant of Qingying.

93 Zhang Shu, *Liangzhou fuzhi beikao*, 3, *yiwen*, 10:853–855.

94 *Liangzhou fuzhi beikao*, 3, *yiwen*, 11:878. For Zhang Zhonghua, see Sima Guang, *Xin jiao zizhi tongjian zhu* 97:3079.

95 On Baisikou, see Ningxia Huizu zizhiqu wenwu guanli weiyuanhui bangongshi, "Ningxia Helanxian Baisikou shuangta kance weixiu jianbao," *Wenwu* 8 (1991): 14–26.

96 So far I have been unable to identify this heaven; there is a *baishen guanyin* (White Body/Robed Guanyin), implying a possible connection with Amitābha's Pure Land. Rob Linrothe has suggested that this notion may be of Daoist origin.

97 *Shanhu* (coral, *pravāda*) is one of the seven treasures. I have not identified the Coral Forest.

98 Soothill and Hodous, 202: Ābhāsvara, "the heaven of utmost light and purity, i.e the third of the second dhyāna heavens, in which inhabitants converse by light instead of words" Ding: 502–503, 1390: The realm of form has four meditation heavens, of which this is the second (or the third in the second series; sometimes all three of the second meditation heavens are called Light Voice). At the time of great fires, the first meditation heaven and the realm of form will be destroyed, and all beings will flock to this heaven to await the rebuilding of the world. If a great flood or wind destroys the world, this second heaven will also be destroyed (502–503, 1390). A description of Light Voice Heaven as the Second Concentration (of four) in the Form Realm can be found in Leah Zahler and Jeffrey Hopkins, eds. and trans., *Meditative States in Tibetan Buddhism* (London: Wisdom Publications, 1983), chap. 2, "Cyclic Existence," 42.

99 Zhang Shu, *Liangzhou fuzhi beikao*, 3, *yiwen*, 11:880. The three insights are (1) *suming ming*, awareness of one's past lives; (2) *tianyan ming*, awareness of future lives, i.e., of the cycle of birth and death that produces all sentient beings; and (3) *loujin ming*, the awareness of present sufferings, which leads to the destruction of afflictions *(kleśas)* (Soothill and Hodous, 66; Ding, 154).

The six supernatural powers are *abhijñā* or *ṣaḍabhijñā*; the third insight above is also the sixth supernatural power (Soothill and Hodous, 138; Ding, 326). The Eight liberations define the stages of increased awareness through meditation, culminating in final extinction of sensation and thought (Soothill and Hodous, 39–40; Ding, 68). In chapter 8 of the "Lotus Sūtra," the Buddha gives a prophecy of future buddhahood to a disciple and describes his buddha-world: "Its multitude of voice-hearers shall be such that no count or numeration, no measure or calculation, may know it, all of them having gained to perfection the six penetrations, the three clarities, and the eight deliverances" (Hurvitz, *Scripture of the Lotus Blossom*, p. 159).

100 Normally the main entrance to the monastic compound *(shan men)* faced south, but there are exceptions, and it would be interesting if this temple's main gate faced north.

5. ANNOTATED TRANSLATION OF THE 1094 STELE INSCRIPTIONS

1 Some scholars, including Luo Zhenyu (1914), Luo Fucheng (1932), Luo Fuyi (1961), and Nishida Tatsuo (1964) (see Appendix B), read the second character in the name of the stūpa as *ying*, rather than *tong*. All the other text editions, however, give *tong*, which likewise occurs in lines 22–23 of the Han text. The Tangut text also requires *tong*. *Gantong*, "spiritual resonance," is a term encountered frequently in medieval Chinese Buddhist literature from the mid–seventh century onward. Raoul Birnbaum addressed this topic at the 1985 annual meeting of the American Oriental Society in Ann Arbor, Michigan, in the specific context of Mount Wutai. He observed that Tang and early Song authors sometimes use the terms *gantong* and *ganying* interchangeably, with no discernible difference in function or meaning.

2 See Chapter 3, n. 91.

3 See Tuotuo et al. comps., *Jin shi* (Beijing: Zhonghua shuin, 1975), 134:2876; E. I. Kychanov, "Tangutskie istochniki o gosudarstvenno-apparate Si Sya," 183, 210; or *Kodeks* 3:109–111 (translation), 410–414 (text), for chapter 10 of the twelfth-century Tangut law code, which contains a classified list of government departments. The name Liangzhou does not occur in the list, but Xiliangfu is listed as one of three superior prefectures (Dunnell, "Naming the Tangut Capital," 60–61).

4 See *Wenwu* 4, no. 5 (1961): 15.

5 Appendix B contains a chronology of sources (arranged by date of publication) recording or discussing the inscriptions, to which the following discussion refers. The 1868 publication is number 5 in Appendix B.

6 Compare Dunnell, "The 1094 Sino-Tangut Gantong Stūpa Stele" (1988).

7 I thank Shi Jinbo for making the rubbings available for my inspection.

8 Ksenia Kepping has argued from grammatical considerations for translating *bai gao guo da* (in Tangut word order) in this fashion. See her analysis in "The Name of the Tangut Empire."

9 Kychanov translates this phrase as "poiasniaiushchii v stikhakh" or "explaining in verse" (Kychanov, 137). It seems to identify a function peculiar to the occasion that the two individuals served, namely, the teaching of Buddhist lessons by the use of parables. Unless otherwise specified, all further references to Kychanov followed by page number indicate his translation of the Tangut text in L. L. Gromkovakaia and E. I. Kychanov, *Nikolai Alexsandrovich Nevskii* (Moscow, 1978).

10 The Tangut word order yields the Chinese translation *shi ren*, a noun followed by its modifier, as Tangut grammar dictates, hence "humane

teacher." In the "Table of Ranks" and the Tiansheng code, the title *ren shi* appears, the same Tangut graphs but in the reverse order, requiring a reading like "teacher of humanity." It is not clear if these two titles were actually the same. See Shi Jinbo "Xi Xia wen 'guanjie fenghao biao' kaoshi," 245–261 (the continuation of the table that appears on p. 261 is upside down and incomplete); Li Fanwen, "Xi Xia guanjie fenghao biao kaoshi," 74, 76 (the order of items in Li's Tangut table on p. 74 is in error; the section containing titles of the Secretariat and the Military Commission appears at the bottom right and should be moved to the second place at the top of the right column); *Kodeks* 3:202, 601, also 113–114, 418 (page numbers denote translation and original text, respectively).

11 Glossed in Gule Maocai (twelfth c.) *Fan Han heshi zhangzhong zhu,* ed. Huang Zhenhua, Nie Hongyin, and Shi Jinbo (Yinchuan, 1989), 28a, as *da heng li yuan; Kodeks* 3:110, 411. A third-rank office. See note 137 to H22 below for a fuller discussion. There Wo Qujie is also named a director of this agency. The Tiansheng code prescribes four directors for this agency (*Kodeks* 3:115, 422).

12 *Gongde si:* a second-class office. The twelfth-century law code prescribes, in lieu of director *(zheng),* six state preceptors *(guo shi)* for the two branches of the *gongde si* and four assistants or deputies (to the state preceptors) for the *zhujia gongde si*. On twelfth-century sources for the Saṅgha Office, see Dunnell, "Politics, Religion, and Ethnicity in Eleventh Century Xia: The Construction of Tangut Identity in the 1094 Wuwei Stele Inscription," *Central and Inner Asian Studies* 7 (1992): 61–114; *Kodeks* 3:115, 421. The system described in the code and the one we have here differ in several respects.

13 The Tangut term translated as "supervisor" is glossed *tiju* in Chinese (H23). T24 introduces another supervisor of the Shengrong Temple and Gantong Stūpa, Yaonie Yongquan. The post was a central government appointment and, given the rank of this holder, points to the high status of the Shengrong Temple. In the glossary to his translation of the Tiansheng code, Kychanov lists the two graphs glossed *tiju* here with the nominalizing suffix, and translates the phrase as *revizor* (inspector), but I have not yet found them in the code in reference to a temple or Saṅgha office. Instead, one finds what appears to be a Tangut transcription of Chinese *tiju,* two entirely different graphs, occurring in close proximity with two other graphs that can be glossed in Chinese as *sheng chun* (holy and pure) and that refer to monks or monk communities. The four graphs occur together (*sheng chun* [*ti*] [*ju*]) in chapter 10, article 675 (*Kodeks* 3:110, 412), which lists government agencies (including places) in five ranked classes. They comprise the last entry in the third or middle class, and thus constitute an administrative unit. Kychanov reads the graph I translate as "pure" to be a transliteration *(yang/yong)* and the four graphs together as *sheng yang di ju,* which he provisionally translates as "department for the provision of ritual meals." In chapter 11,

article 776 (pp. 158, 512), *sheng chun* modifies the monastic context in which *tiju* are to be appointed, one director and one deputy. Kychanov's translation may require revision, but the exact meaning of the graphs is not yet clear to me. Wu Fengyun provides the Chinese gloss *ju sheng ying di* and speculates that it denoted an office to oversee the imperial tombs ("Xia Xia lingyuan ji qi jiangong tedian," *Ningxia Wenwu* 1 [1986], 28).

14 The Tangut term (Chin. *yan guo chu*) occurs often in the Tangut code, where Kychanov (*Kodeks* 4:646 in the glossary) translates it as "consultant" (e.g., 3:123–124, 444, art. 702, referring to "consultants" to military commanders and vice-commanders). While working in the Kozlov archives in St. Petersburg in 1994, Shi Jinbo found a corresponding Chinese gloss to this expression: *tidian*, "superintendent" (personal letter from Nie Hongyin, 13 November 1994). Hucker notes that a *tidian* is "comparable to and sometimes interchangeable with *t'i-chü*" (p. 497, no. 6475). That does not appear to be the case in Tangut. Another Tangut phrase renders *tiju* (see above, note 13; T24 and T25), and presumably represented something distinct from this Tangut phrase glossed *tidian*. The Tiansheng code prescribes six superintendents *(yan guo chu)* for the government agency overseeing the monastic community (*chujia gongde si*; see Chapter 2, note 57.) The full phrase here (in Chinese translation) is *cai xue yan guo chu*; my English translation "superintendent of education" is provisional.

15 Nevskii has registered this name in his dictionary, but does not cite the source (*Tangutskaia filologiia* [Moscow, 1960], 1:195) or give a reading. The first graph occurs in another name in T24, rendered *mai* in the corresponding name in H22. In *Wenhai* 44.212, it has a *fanqie* reading of "ming."

16 This office is listed tenth in the second-class category of government offices described in article 675, chapter 10, of the Tangut law code (*Kodeks* 3:109, 410). Article 690 assigns six "recipients of edicts" to this office (pp. 115, 420). Glossed by Gule Maocai, *Fan Han heshi zhangzhong zhu*, 28a, as *neisu*.

17 The graph I translate as "army" is unclear. Shi translates it as *quan* and the office as *quanzhu si*, which I have not found attested elsewhere. The office of Army Inspectorate (Chin. *junjian si* or *jianjun si* in Chin. word order) is listed in the third class of government offices described in article 675 of chapter 10 of the Tangut law code as "border and interior army inspectorates." They are named individually in article 690 of chapter 10 (*Kodeks* 3:110, 116, 411, 425–426).

18 *Yan guo chu* or *tidian*; see note 14 above.

19 The meaning of the phrase is not clear but almost certainly has to do with military functions. Graphs 49 and 50 occur elsewhere in the code in a phrase that Kychanov translates as "serving in the depot for military supplies" (see the glossary at the back of volume 4 of *Kodeks*, p. 672; I have not yet located the phrase in question).

20 The reading "Ge" (Shi's "Shuang" follows *Wenhai* 42.161) is based on *Tongyin* 25A12, where it is glossed as a clan name and given the phonetic reading "ge." The other three elements in the name are carved small to fit into the following space. "Zhang" is a registered Chinese phonetic gloss on the graph, which means *tong* (youth). The two other small graphs in the personal name are now too fuzzy to reconstruct with certainty, but one possibility, *Tongyin* 14A24 (ndin) and 38A36 (dzio?), produces the Chinese semantic gloss of *lingyou* (efficacious support). The Tangut *Sancai zazi* (transcription of ms. in the St. Petersburg archive, in the possession of Shi Jinbo) registers Geling (Wenhai reading) as a Fan surname (no. 116).

21 Chin. *zhenshen*; Skt. *dharmakāya*. In some schemes the Buddha has two bodies, in others three, of which the True Body is the original, pure, and omniscient form, coexistent with the Buddha-truth (Mochizuki, 2042).

22 The Tangut renders Chin. *rushi*; here understood as *rulai*, the Tathāgata, "Thus-come-one," or Buddha.

23 The three realms *(sanjie)* are the realm of desire *(yu)*, the realm of form *(si)*, and the formless realm *(wusi)* (Soothill and Hodous, 70). For a description of the three realms, see Zahler and Hopkins, *Meditative States in Tibetan Buddhism*, chap. 2.

24 The region of north-central India where early Buddhism flourished, corresponding largely to today's Bihar.

25 Skt. *nirmāṇakāya*. In the three bodies scheme *(trikāya)*, the transformation or reward body *(hua/ying shen)* is the third of the Buddha bodies, the one that appears before sentient beings (Soothill and Hodous, 142; Mochizuki, 2042).

26 Recalling the common expression "buddhas of the past, present, and future," the "causes" probably refer to the realization of buddhahood in the past, present, and future, the "causes" being valid for all times. (I thank Dan Stevenson for this explanation; personal communication, 17 September 1993).

27 The six perfections *(pāramitās)* are (1) perfection of giving *(dāna)*, (2) perfection of morality *(śīla)*, (3) perfection of patience *(kṣānti)*, (4) perfection of vigor *(vīrya)*, (5) perfection of meditation *(dhyāna)*, and (6) perfection of wisdom *(prajñā)* (Soothill and Hodous, 134; Ding, 323, 771–772).

28 The reconstruction of this last graph of the column is supplied by Luo Fucheng and remains uncertain. The proposed graph appears to be mistranscribed by Luo, Nishida, Shi, and Chen; the proper form is *Tongyin* 49A43. Abandoning strict parallelism, we can read the binomial (Chin. *jiexing*) as referring to "meritorious practice" and "wisdom" (or understanding), the two foundations of buddhahood, which produce the wonderful physical and spiritual bodies of the Buddha (Dan Stevenson, personal communication, 17 September 1993).

29 This represents the last character of line 6, according to Nishida's transcription (*Seika go no kenkyū*, 164); it is no longer visible and the mean-

ing remains obscure. Nishida translates: "the relic of the Aśoka-eye." (All further references to Nishida 1964 followed by page number indicate vol. 1 of *Seika go no kenkyū*).

30 Zhang Tianxi began to rule Liangzhou in 363; see Chapter 4, note 4.

31 A better translation would be "later," since the temporal shift is in centuries. The two Tangut graphs, however, literally mean "this after." In Chapter 6 I ponder some possible reasons why the text here passes over these centuries in silence.

32 The year 1094 minus 720 (not 820) is 374, the middle of Zhang Tianxi's reign; the numeral "8" in the text must be a mistake for "7." See note to H5.

33 See my discussion in the next chapter about the Da'an reign period, which I date from 1074 to 1084.

34 Imperial designations with the element (Chin.) *cheng* (wall) in them are posthumous titles, part of a series of "wall" titles conferred on many Tangut emperors the precise significance of which is not yet fully understood. The Zhenling cheng emperor was Huizong (Weiming Bingchang, r. 1068–1086).

35 At Song prompting, the Qingtang Tibetans also sent armies against Xia during the Yuanfeng campaign (XCB 313:10a; SS 486:14010; 492: 14164–14165), although it does not appear that they accomplished much.

36 The second Liang empress dowager and Chongzong (Weiming Qianshun, r. 1086–1139), referred to here by honorary titles rather than posthumous titles.

37 This reign date seems to be wrong and should be Tianyi zhiping 2, 1087, for the new emperor came to the throne in 1086, at which time the reign date was changed from Tianan liding 2 to Tianyi zhiping 1. Grammatically, the passage indicates a time after Chongzong's enthronement. For a fuller discussion of the problem, see Chapter 6.

38 For an autumn attack on the Song border post at Zhenrongjun in 1087 led by the empress dowager, see XCB 405:5ab.

39 The earthquake occurred late in 1092. H7 says "the year before last" *(qiannian)*, and H19 gives the cyclical date for 1092. "Last year" makes sense if we imagine that the writer or writers composed the Tangut text of the inscription at the end of 1093, which is possible if the date of formal completion of construction and celebration, the fifteenth day of the first month of the following year (i.e., 1094), was known for certain in advance. Since the stele pillar was erected on that day (per H21), and since carving the pillar would require some time, it seems likely that the texts were composed in advance and that the author(s) of this one simply did not "predate" this reference. Possibly the Tangut text was composed and carved first, since its complex script would require more time than the Han text to be transferred to stone.

40 The four graces *(si'en)* commonly comprise (1) the grace of father and

mother, (2) the grace of sentient beings, (3) the grace of a king, and (4) the grace of the three jewels, i.e., Buddha, dharma, and saṅgha (Ding, 391). Mochizuki lists another set first: (1) the grace of mother, (2) the grace of father, (3) the grace of the Tathāgatha, and (4) the grace of a dharma teacher's preaching (*Bukkyō daijiten*, 1725).

41 The Tangut phrase renders Chin. *xia sanyou zhi yuan* and thus forms a paired couplet with the preceding phrase, *shang si'en gong hui*. Thus I take *yuan* as a verb, meaning to take as condition, to reason, to lay hold of (Soothill and Hodous, 440). The *sanyou* are the same as the *sanjie*, three realms, i.e., desire, form, and formlessness (see note 23).

42 See Chapter 3, note 66.

43 Chin. *qideng jue*, Skt. *saptabodhyaṅgāni*; the seven characteristics of *bodhi* or enlightened mind: (1) *nian (smṛti)*, mindfulness, (2) *zefa (dharma-pravicaya)*, discrimination of phenomena, (3) *jingjin (vīrya)*, effort, (4) *xi (prīti)*, joy, (5) *qing'an (praśrabdi)*, lightness of body and mind, (6) *ding (samādhi)*, concentration, and (7) *she (upekṣā)*, equanimity (see Chapter 4, note 64).

44 I follow Shi in translating the Tangut graph as "river" *(he)*. If one read this as the "four currents" *(siliu)*, it would refer to the illusions of seeing, desire, existence, and ignorance (Soothill and Hodous, 178; Ding, 391). The reading "four rivers" *(sihe)* yields a more interesting interpretation based on a semimythical geography. Mochizuki does not gloss this term. Soothill and Hodous briefly define the four rivers as the Ganges, Sindhu (Indus), Vākṣu (Oxus), and Śītā (Tārīm), reputed to arise out of a lake, Anavatapta, in Tibet (177, 380). Ding (p. 387) provides more detail, citing the *Xiyu ji*. In Jambudvīpa, the southern of the four great continents of Indian mythical geography, there is a "Cold Lake" (Anavatapta), out of which the four rivers arise. The Ganges flows east out of the lake into the southeastern sea; the Indus flows south out of the lake into the southwestern sea; the Oxus flows west out of the lake into the northwestern sea; and the Śītā flows north out of the lake into the northeastern sea and is said to be the source of China's rivers.

45 Gold, silver, lapis lazuli, crystal, agate, rubies or red pearls, and carnelian (Mochizuki 2:1920). See Chapter 4, note 66. "Seven Treasures" recalls the opening to chapter 11 of the "Lotus Sūtra," "Apparition of the Jeweled Stūpa:"

> At that time, there appeared before the Buddha a seven-jeweled stūpa, five hundred yojanas in height and two hundred and fifty yojanas in breadth, welling up out of the earth and resting in mid-air, set about with sundry precious objects.... Jeweled rosaries trailed from it, and ten thousand millions of jeweled bells were suspended from its top.... Its banners were made of the seven jewels, to wit, gold, silver, vaidūrya, giant clam shell, coral, pearl, and carnelian; and its height

extended to the palaces of the four god kings. (Hurvitz, *Scripture of the Lotus Blossom of the Fine Dharma*, 183)

46 The first two graphs of this phrase may be glossed in Chinese as *jue rao; bodhi* (enlightenment), encircle (surround). The golden light apparently emanates from this *bodhi,* which dwells within the stūpa and may manifest itself as the gilded metal disk atop the stūpa, which "glows luminously."

47 The two words translated as "iron image" (lit. "iron man") are very indistinct in the inscription. Could they refer to a statue of the Buddha in the icon hall opposite the stūpa?

48 H14 gives *guanzuo sihu;* the Tangut graphs literally render "four households till arrow," which Kychanov (139) renders "four families of farmers and [masters in the production of] arrows" and Nishida (1964: 169), "four farm houses." This phrase evidently denotes households in various occupational categories (here, farming and fletching) attached to the government and subject to assignment by it (though it is not clear what degree of legal authority or ownership the government has relinquished here to the temple). *Changzhu* (households or persons attached to monasteries and temples) are mentioned frequently in the Tiansheng code. See Chapter 6 for further comment.

49 See note 133 below. The highest-ranking agency of the Xia government, for which the Tiansheng code prescribes six chief executives and six "transmitters of directives" (*Kodeks* 3:114, 419). The graph for "director" (Chin. *zheng*) used here is not the same as that used in the code to mean "chief executive" (lit. "great") for the Secretariat and the Military Commission. But for other agencies of the government, the code does use this graph to mean "chief executive" or "director." If the two terms are not synonymous here, we might suppose that a separate "director" *(zheng* or *ling)* was appointed above the named "chief executives," as a purely honorary posting. Otherwise, we do not know how many other directors may have served along with Liang Xingzhenie in the late eleventh century. For a phonetic transcription of *zhongshu ling* (director of the Secretariat), see the memorial of presentation prefacing the Tiansheng code (*Kodeks* 2:10, 246), where the first two individuals named are both *zhongshu ling*. In the title of the third named person (not a *ling*), *zhongshu* appears as the Tangut calque of that title, not a phonetic transliteration. Chapter 6 discusses transliteration and translation.

50 The last two graphs are now illegible.

51 See H22 for Liang Xing [hang?] zhenie.

52 Lit. "Palace Provisioning Office;" see Gule Maocai, *Fan Han heshi zhangzhong zhu*, 28a, for the gloss *huangcheng si*. Ranked eight of seventeen agencies in the second class, for which the Tiansheng code prescribes four directors and four *chengzhi* (*Kodeks* 3:109, 115, 410, 421).

53 See H22. There Wo Qujie has several other official titles and is also

identified as a "*lüjing* recipient of the scarlet [robe] monk." The first two graphs turn out to be a Chinese transcription of two Tangut graphs meaning "understands the scriptures," a clerical title. These two graphs occur in T24 as part of the clerical designation of Yaonie Yongquan. Wo's name, Qujie, in Tangut means "dog gold," i.e., Golden Dog. Words denoting animals occur frequently in Tangut names. Wo was probably a Tangut, despite his single surname (it is registered in the lists of Fan, but not in the lists of Han surnames in both versions of the Xia classified lexicon, *Zazi* [see note 69 below]).

54 Originally I understood the phrase (in Chin.) *fa shuo zui chan daochang* as a title of a sūtra, thus: "the *Cibei daochang chanfa* was distributed." But I no longer think that this text was distributed at the ceremony, so I have amended the translation, rendering *daochang* as ritual site, i.e., any sacred space for religious activities (following Griffith Foulk as cited by Peter Gregory in *Tsung-mi and the Sinification of Buddhism* [Princeton, N.J.: Princeton University Press, 1991], 42).

55 A parallel passage occurs in a Xia imperial preface (in Chinese) to an 1189 edition of the "Sūtra on the Visualization of Maitreya Bodhisattva's Rebirth in Tuṣita Heaven" (*Guan Mile pusa shang sheng doushuaitian jing,* T. 452; Nishida catalogue, no. 6; *Buddiiskie sochineniia,* nos. 149–158):

> ... to come to the Great People-Saving Temple (Dadumin si) and hold a great dharma assembly seeking rebirth in the inner palace of Tuṣita [before] Maitreya; to make great offerings on an altar of burning *kleśa*s; to make a great distribution of food and conjointly to recall the Buddha and chant mantras; to read Tibetan, Tangut and Chinese sūtras and Mahāyāna texts; to preach the dharma and conduct a Mahāyāna repentance; to distribute one hundred thousand rolls of the "Sūtra on the Visualization of Maitreya Bodhisattva's Rebirth in Tuṣita Heaven" in Tangut and Chinese and fifty thousand rolls each in Chinese of the "Diamond Sūtra" *(Jingang jing),* "The Sūtra on the Vow of Samantabhadra" *(Puxian xing yuan jing),* and "The Avalokiteśvara Sūtra" *(Guanyin jing);* to feed monks, liberate creatures, rescue the poor, release the imprisoned, in all seven days and nights of various dharma activities.

Examination of the photograph of this portion of the original text in Men'shikov, *Opisanie kitaiskoi chasti kollektsii iz Khara-Khoto* (p. 501) reveals errors in the transcription by Shi 1988 and in the version published by Edouard Chavannes in his review article "A. I. Ivanov: *Stranitsa iz istorij Si-sia* (Une page de l'histoire du Si-hia; Bulletin de l'Academie impériale des sciences de Saint-Pétersbourg, 1911, p. 831–836)" in *T'oung Pao,* ser. 11, no. 12 (1911): 441–446.

56 *Sanshi,* past, present, and future (compare line 5).

57 "Black-headed" and "red-faced" are two common epithets by which

Tangut writers referred to themselves, the Tangut people, most frequently in verse. Scholars, especially Nishida Tatsuo (for example, in "Seika go 'Tsukizuki rakushi' no kenkyū," 74), have speculated on the referents of these epithets, suggesting each designates a specific segment or group in the population. These epithets function mainly, it seems, as poetic tropes for "us." However, see the unpublished study by Ksenia B. Kepping, "The 'Blackheaded' and 'Red-faced' in the Tangut Texts."

58 The metaphor comes from the *Vimalakīrti nirdeśa-sūtra* (*Weimoji suo shuo jing*, T. 475:539), and illustrates the unreality of dependent or conditioned phenomena, like the body, with ten comparisons, to foam *(jumo)*, bubbles *(pao)*, flame *(yan)*, plantain *(bajiao)*, illusion *(huan)*, dream *(meng)*, shadow *(ying)*, echo *(xiang)*, cloud *(fuyun)*, and lightning *(dian)*. This passage is quoted in Ding, 689 (Soothill and Hodous, 249). For the corresponding passage in the Tangut translation of this sūtra, see Grinstead, *The Tangut Tripiṭaka* 9:2036. The origins of the metaphor in Indian philosophy are elaborated in Donald S. Lopez, *A Study of Svātantrika* (Ithaca, N.Y.: Snow Lion Publications, 1987), chap. 3.

59 I have not yet identified the source of this metaphor.

60 Shi 1988, 250, glosses this as the three wheels of the Buddha: body, mouth, and mind. However, it may also invoke an Esoteric Buddhist doctrine associated with Vairocana that specifies three "wheel bodies" of this buddha. Thus, the Buddha's original body is called the "self-nature wheel body" *(zixing lunshen)*; the body in its bodhisattva aspect is the "true law wheel body" *(zhengfa lunshen)*; and the body in its wrathful guardian deity *(mingwang*, "bright king") aspect is the "instruction wheel body" *(jiaoling lunshen)* (Ding, 1014; see also Mikkyō Jiten Hensankai, comp., *Mikkyō daijiten* [Kyoto, 1969–1970], 844). The latter two wheels are associated with the "Five Great-Power Bodhisattvas" of the *Renwang jing*, who together with the Five Buddhas form the "Shapes of the Three Wheels" *(sanlun shen)*, in the phraseology of de Visser, *Ancient Buddhism in Japan*, vol. 1, 142–158. See also T. 994 (*Renwang huguo banruo boluomiduo jing tuoluoni niansong yigui*), 514-515.

61 The two extremes or sets of antitheses are variously defined: (1) that things exist and that things do not exist *(you wu)*; (2) permanence (immortality) and impermanence (annihilation) *(chang duan)*; and (3) karmic accumulation and karmic extinction *(zengyi, sunmie)*. See Soothill and Hodous, 30–31; Ding, 47.

62 *A liwu u kha* (Chin. *du'an toujian*). For my explanation of this phrase and its Chinese equivalent, *duda goudang*, see the corresponding note to H22 (n. 132) and Chapter 6.

63 Gule Maocai, 28a, provides the gloss *sansi*. See also *Kodeks* 3:109, 114, 410, 420. Ranked fourth in the second class, it has a prescribed staff of four directors *(zheng)* and eight "recipients of edicts" *(chengzhi)*.

64 Chin. *nanyuan junjian*. For a preliminary discussion of the four direc-

tional courts, see Dunnell, "Naming the Tangut Capital." H22 names Mai Majie as army supervisor of the Right Wing *(youxiang niezu)*, giving a Chinese transcription *(niezu)* of the Tangut title of army supervisor (Chin. *jianjun*). See note 142. Mention of the four courts occurs throughout the law code; chapter 10, article 675, refers several times to the northern, southern, and western courts (*Kodeks* 3:110, 412). The data provided here suggest that the Right Wing of the Tangut military (which normally supervised six of the twelve regular army inspectorates) was headquartered at the Southern Court in Liangzhou. The bureaucratic rank of this post (if it was so ranked) is not known.

65 A Tangut rank *(pie tin)*, which Shi translates *jianpin* and which does not correspond to the rank, apparently transcribed from Tangut, that precedes Mai Majie's name in H22. In the "Table of Ranks," document no. 4170, the entry Shi translates as *jianchen* is glossed by four smaller graphs explaining that it is equivalent to the second class. Document no. 5921 lists seven grades of rank, the first three containing only two entries each (see Shi, "Xi Xia wen 'guanjie fenghao biao' kaoshi," pp. 266, 262). If *jianpin* belongs to this category, then it appears to have been a relatively high rank.

66 *Mbei rie kei*. The first graph (Chin. *mo, ming, mai*) is the same as the first graph in Mingwang Qi'e's name. Mingwang is registered as a double surname in the Tangut *Zazi*. The second graph may be *rei* (*Tongyin* 47B47), which means "horse," or *mbaw* (*Tongyin* 8A48), which transliterates the sound "ma" in names and terms (*ma* can mean "horse" in Chinese). The difference between the two is one small stroke in the upper left corner, which is smudged in the rubbing. Either way, Mai's personal name, Majie, evidently means "golden horse," as the third graph, *kei* (*Tongyin* 27B76), means metal, gold, and appears to be the "Tangut" reading of Chinese character *jin*.

67 Chin. *xinggong sansi zheng;* the law code lists an Auxiliary Palace Board *(xinggong yuan)* and a Southern Court Auxiliary Palace Fiscal Commission *(nanyuan xinggong sansi)* (*Kodeks* 3:110, 412), both of the fourth rank. The latter appears to be a branch office of the central Fiscal Commission attached to the Southern Court (at Liangzhou), the principal site of imperial soujourns outside the capital.

68 The Tangut term is glossed *tiju* in Chinese (H23). See note 13 on the occurrence of this title in T2.

69 H23 calls Yaonie Yongquan a *"lüjing* recipient of the scarlet [robe] monk" *(lüjing cifei seng)*. As explained earlier (see note 53 on Wo Qujie in line 17), *lüjing* transcribes the two Tangut graphs found here meaning "understands/expounds the scriptures." Yaonie may be the same surname as Yaonü, listed in the Chinese edition of the Xia lexicon *Zazi* (Shi Jinbo, "Xi Xia Han wen ben 'Za zi' chutan," in *Zhongguo minzu shi yanjiu,* ed. Bai Bin et al. [Beijing: Zhongyang minzu xueyuan, 1989], 178); it is registered in the Tangut edition of *Zazi, Sancai zazi* (I consulted an unpublished version in

Shi Jinbo's possession, transcribed from the original housed in St. Petersburg. See Bibliography.). The last graph in this line of the Tangut text is illegible.

70 The Tangut term is glossed *chengzhi* in Gule Maocai, 28b. Chapter 10, article 690, of the Tiansheng code prescribes four *chengzhi* for the office of the Southern Court Auxiliary Palace Fiscal Commission (*Kodeks* 3:116, 427).

71 The Tangut term is *tu mie,* translated as *jiguan* ("sacrificial officer") by Shi (1988, 249) but not found in the "Table of Ranks" (see Shi, "Xi Xia wen 'guanjie fenghao biao' kaoshi"). See note 149 below.

72 This individual is not mentioned in H.

73 Chin. *erzhong*, in which Chinese *zhong* (group, mass) is transliterated into Tangut.

74 The Tangut word is usually glossed *zang*, meaning Tibetan. H24 gives *fan,* which when juxtaposed with Han, as it is there, usually means Tangut. However, the corresponding Tangut term here is not one that Tanguts used to refer to themselves, as far as we know. Therefore if we understand Fan in this passage to refer to Tibetans, not Tanguts, it means that the inscription does not specifically designate a director of Tangut monks.

75 The Tangut graphs translate as *sengjian,* which may represent an abbreviation of *seng toujian* ("overseer of monks"), found in the Tiansheng code, chapter 11, article 775 (*Kodeks* 3:157, 511). In the corresponding entry of H 23–24, the graph *zheng* occurs at the end of column 23 but is no longer legible; however, since H24 gives the same office for Jiu Zhiqing (ditto T26) as *seng zheng*, I have translated "director of monks," rather than "overseer of monks."

76 Lingjie is registered in the list of Tangut surnames in *Sancai zazi,* no. 23. See also H23–24.

77 H24 designates Jiu Zhiqing as supervisor, not assistant supervisor, of artisans, although the graph *ren*, which precedes the graph *jian* ("supervisor"), could be a mistake for *xiao* ("small," thus "assistant"). But perhaps T26 has erred, for the next individual it names is also an assistant supervisor of artisans as well as assistant director of Han monks, making him Jiu Zhiqing's subordinate. One might expect that Jiu should therefore be a supervisor, not assistant supervisor, of artisans. In T26, the graph for "assistant" occurs in the second character space.

78 The name has been effaced in H24, while the job title awkwardly renders "supervisor of [artisans inscribing] the stone stele [commemorating] restoration of the temple" *(xiu tasi jian shibei)*. On Bai as a Tuyühun surname, see Molè, *The T'u-yü-hun,* 206–207, n. 539, and Chapter 6.

79 Chin. *sengzhu;* see the Tiansheng code, chapter 11, article 775 (*Kodeks* 3:157, 511).

80 See H25.

81 Asha (Ashan) was a Tibetan designation for the royal Tuyühun. Géza

Uray, "The Annals of the 'A-Ža Principality: The Problems of Chronology and Genre of the Stein Document, Tun-huang, vol. 69, fol. 84," in *Proceedings of the Csoma de Körös Memorial Symposium (1976)*, ed. Louis Ligeti (Budapest: Akadémiai Kiadó, 1978), 541–578. One could reasonably suppose these Bais to be of Tuyühun ancestry.

82 *Lingpi* (*ru phie* in Sofronov's reconstruction) is a Tangut office or title, transliterated (as is the name of the office), not translated, in H21: "The calligrapher of the Fan stele eulogy, *lingpi* in the Office of Audience Ceremonies, Hun-Weiming Yu." See Men'shikov, *Opisanlie*, 147, 206, 506, for a Chinese transcription of *lianpi*, evidently the same title, in sūtra colophons dated 1210: "Zhongsheng Puhua Temple *lianpi* Zhang Gai and deputy *(fushi)* śramana Li Zhibao, respectfully distribute; Xitian Zhiyuan engraved [the blocks]; Suo Zhishen did the calligraphy." This example gives the impression that the *fushi* is an assistant to the *lianpi,* since no other antecedent to the former appears in the colophon. *Lingpi* is not prescribed for the Office of Audience Ceremonies in the Tiansheng code, nor do the graphs appear in Kychanov's glossary in volume four of *Kodeks*.

83 The Tangut graphs are glossed *gemen* in Gule Maocai, 28b. Ranked twelfth in the second class of offices listed in the Tiansheng code, chapter 10, article 675 (*Kodeks* 3:109, 411); article 690 states that the agency should be staffed with four officials called (Chin.) *dao zhi* or announcers (115, 421).

84 See H21. In this compound surname, the Tangut character for *ming* in the royal surname, Weiming, has been mistranscribed by Nishida and his predecessors. The element Hun suggests Tuyühun ancestry and is registered in the list of Fan (Tangut) surnames in the Chinese text of *Zazi* (Shi "Xi Xia Han wen ben 'Za zi' chutan," 178).

85 See H21.

86 Lit. "artisans of red and white."

87 Effaced in H25. Sīn is a phonetic reading of the Tangut character, here a surname, for which Kepping has identified the Chinese gloss of *xie*. See K. B. Kepping, *Les kategorii: utrachennaia kitaiskaia leishu v tanguts kom perevode* (Moscow, 1983), 138.

88 Effaced in H25.

89 Lit. "silk net," network, binding; by extension perhaps scaffolding of bamboo tied together with silken cords.

90 Partially effaced but still readable in H25. The two graphs I translate "Gouer" occupy one graph space and are virtually illegible. Shi (1988, 249) translates (Liu) Xingzhen; my reading yields Tangut graphs *Tongyin* 25A16, *khwI*, meaning "dog" (Chin. *gou*), and *Tongyin* 52B14 (*Wenhai* 77.162), meaning "son, child" (Chin. *zi*) or "clan name" (Chin. *shi*), thus equivalent to Chinese *er* (child) and nicely matching H25 Liu Gouer.

91 Previous reconstructions of these last two names are Kychanov (1978, 142): Liu Huai and [?] Sun; Nishida (1964, 176): Liu [?], Sun; and Shi (1988, 249): Liu Xingzhen, Sun ??

92 Following Liao practice, the Xia cyclic day was one day ahead of the Song cyclic day, hence *wuzi* rather than *dinghai*. Since the first day of the Song calendrical year *(shuo)* of 1094 was *guiyou,* the corresponding Tangut day was *jiaxu*.

93 Clearly the names that follow do not designate overseers, but the artisans who carved the stone inscription, as listed at the end of H21 and H25. Probably the first-mentioned individual here and in H21, Weiyi Yiyai, supervised the the other carvers.

94 The same Tangut graph (Wenhai 50.271) apparently used to render Wei in this double surname also renders *yong* in Yaonie Yongquan's name (end of T24). In the case of Weiyi Yiyai, the graph is obscure and I first read it as Wenhai 22.232, *na*. In Yaonie Yongquan's name it is quite clear and there can be no mistake. Following Shi Jinbo's lead, I have altered the reading of the former from *na* to *wei* to match the corresponding spelling of the name in the Han text. It is not unusual for one Tangut graph to have several different transcriptional values.

95 Khon Ta-mie most likely corresponds to H21 Kang Gou[ming]. My reading differs from Shi 1988, 250.

96 Shi (1988, 250) has "Kang San [?]." My reading of the fortieth graph in this column yields *Tongyin* 38A13, which is attested in Kepping, *Les kategorii*, 137, as a transcription for the Chinese names Zheng and Cheng. Zheng (Sandui) is still readable in H25.

97 Shi's "Wanqian" ("ten thousand, thousand") translates my "Kedu."

98 Shi (1988, 250) reads the name as (Zuo) Dangxing. My reading yields the Tangut graphs *Tongyin* 7A53 (*Wenhai* 30.261), with the attested Chinese gloss of Pan (Kepping, *Les kategorii*, 118, 541) and *Tongyin* 52B14 (*Wenhai* 77.162), the same graph translated "er" in the name Liu Gouer in line 27 (see note 90). "Paner" matches the Chinese graphs still legible in H25.

99 Shi has run together the two names Wang Zhen and Yin Sun? as Yang Zhengyin, but clearly at least four (probably five) graphs and two names are indicated. The graph Shi translates as Yang may also render the Chinese surname Wang (Kepping, *Les kategorii,* 107, 109, 138). The graph that Shi reads Zheng may also render the Chinese *zhen* (Kepping, 119). My preference for Wang Zhen matches the half legible occurrence of this name in H25.

100 Lit. "beautiful/adornment artisan."

101 This Yang could also be read Wang.

102 In Han formulations, the "way of the five constants" *(wuchang zhi dao)* comprises *ren*, humaneness; *yi,* appropriateness; *li,* ritual propriety; *zhi,* wisdom; and *xin,* truthfulness (*Cihai, ziji* 67).

103 From Aśoka's death, dated by modern historians to 232 B.C., to the Jin (A.D. 265–316) and Eastern Jin (317–420) scarcely adds up to one thousand years, so this figure may reflect the custom of pushing back the Bud-

dha's birthday to predate that claimed for Lao Zi by hostile Daoists. According to E. Zürcher, in the sixth century Chinese Buddhists adopted the twenty-fourth year of King Zhao as the Buddha's birthday, corresponding either to 1029 or to 958 B.C. (per the *Bamboo Annals*). See his " 'Prince Moonlight,' " 19.

104 Founder of the Former Liang regime, ca. 313–376. Liang, originally a Jin province, remained loyal to Jin under the autonomous, hereditary rule of Zhang Gui (254–314), a Jin military officer appointed to govern the region, and his descendants. Michael C. Rogers, *The Chronicle of Fu Chien, A Case of Exemplar History* (Berkeley and Los Angeles: University of California Press, 1968), 9–13.

105 Partially reconstructed from line 16 by Luo Fucheng.

106 Zhang Tianxi ruled from 363 to 376, at which time Fu Qian annexed Liang (Sima Guang, *Xin jiao zizhi tongjian zhu, juan* 101 passim).

107 Among the omens reported for Zhang Tianxi's reign were earthquakes, a common phenomenon in this region, and the sprouting of hair by Buddhist statues made of metal, equally widespread (Zhang Shu, *Liangzhou fuzhi beikao* 2, *xiangyi guji*, 1:585).

108 "Ban Shu" refers to a famed Chunqiu carpenter of the ancient state of Lu, Gong Shu Ban, also called Lu Ban (*Cihai, ziji* 154, *wuji* 12). In T7 (graphs 52–53), Kychanov (138 [misnumbered as 142]) and Nishida (1964, 164) both misread the two Tangut words (Ba Lu per Nishida) as a Tangut artisan's name. Ban Shu was the tutelary god of artisans (F. W. Mote, personal communication, 15 May 1982). The Tangut phrase should be glossed *jiqiao*, "skilled."

109 The figure 800 (at the end of line 4) was supplied by Luo Fucheng from T8, but the arithmetic demands 700 (1094 minus 720 is 374, the middle of Zhang Tianxi's reign). Perhaps the Tangut numeral eight has been mistakenly substituted for seven, which it resembles. If the Tanguts were counting from the middle of Zhang Gui's reign, 274 would still be too early.

110 Liangzhou came under permanent Tangut control only in 1031 or 1032. T 7–8: "... when Liangzhou was possessed by the Mi [Mi-nyag, or Tanguts] ..."

111 *Xianhou* can also be understood as "former dowager." For a contemporary Song usage of *xianhou* to refer to the Xuanren empress dowager Gao, mother of Song Shenzong, after her death in 1093, see SS 328:10567, in the biography of An Dao.

112 T 9–10: in Da'an 8 (1081), the Han country in the east (Song) sent a large army against Xia, while a Tibetan army attacked Liangzhou. See SS 486:14010–14011, for the concerted invasion of Xia in the late fall or early winter of 1081.

113 Given that Chongzong came to the throne in 1086 at age three, there can be no doubt that this refers to the war carriage of the second Liang empress dowager (d. 1099). T 10–11 refers to Tianan liding 2 (1086) and

describes the stūpa's response. The campaign in question almost certainly took place in 1087, in the autumn attack on Zhenrongjun led by the empress (XCB 405:5ab).

114 SS 67:1485, *wu xing zhi,* Yuanyou 7 (1092), seventh month, records earthquakes in Lanzhou, Zhenrongjun, and Yongxingjun (southern Gansu and western Shanxi); and in the tenth month in Huanzhou, just southeast of Liang Prefecture.

115 *Ersheng:* for a parallel usage in a contemporary Song source, referring to the Xuanren empress dowager Gao and her son Zhezong, see XCB 445:13a. For a discussion of its Tang usage and its Tibetan and Turkic equivalents, see R. Stein, " 'Saint et Devin,' un titre tibétain et chinois des rois tibétains," *Journal asiatique* 269, nos. 1–2 (1981): 231–275. In a Tibetan document from Dunhuang, the 'A-zha (Tuyühun) ruler and his mother are named in the phrase *yum-sras,* "the majestic mother and son" (G. Uray, "The Annals of the 'A-Ža Principality," 553).

116 At the end of the column Devéria supplies the two graphs *zhi yu.*

117 Devéria reconstructs the last two graphs of the line as *zhong jiang,* "the many artisans." Nishida (1964, 167) leaves them blank; he reads two characters (badly obscured) in a corresponding passage of T13 as naming an official of the stūpa.

118 Devéria and Luo Fucheng supply *wu bu,* but the 1563 inscription quotes this passage with the words *er jing.*

119 Barque of compassion: the ferry in which the compassionate bodhisattva transports sentient beings beyond *samsāra* to salvation or paradise (Soothill and Hodous, 400; Ding, 1164). The "thought of enlightenment" *(bodhicitta),* referred to in the previous sentence, is a prerequisite to embarking on the bodhisattva path. This passage strongly suggests that the empress dowager and the emperor have embraced the bodhisattva career.

120 See note 45 to T14.

121 Compare the passage from chapter 2 of the "Lotus Sūtra":

When the Buddhas have passed into extinction,
Persons who make offerings to their śarīra
Shall erect myriads of millions of kinds of stūpas,
[Using] gold and silver and *sphātika* [crystal],
Giant clam shell and agate,
Gems of carnelian *(mei kuei)* and vaidūrya . . .
Or there are those who erect stone mausoleums
of *candana* [sandalwood] and aloeswood,
of hovenia and other timbers,
of brick, tile, clay, and the like.
Or there are those who in open fields,
Heaping up earth, make Buddha-shrines . . .

Leon Hurvitz, *Scripture of the Lotus Blossom of the Fine Dharma,* 38.

122 Devéria and Luo Fucheng supply *ci zhi,* as does the 1563 inscription.

123 This passage seems to argue that the Xia state's good fortune results not from the Buddha's partiality, but rather from the virtue and Buddha-nature of its rulers, a fine but critical distinction, I think.

124 Erich Zürcher glosses *you yuan* as those "destined to be saved" in " 'Prince Moonlight,' " 39.

125 Nie Hongyin glosses "to feed," proposing the graph as a vulgar form of *fan* (see Glossary). See *Kangxi zidian* (rpt. Beijing, 1958), 1417.

126 These last two graphs in the column are reconstructed from T17.

127 T16: "four households till arrow"; see note 48.

128 For this meaning of *zhaoci,* see Morohashi 10:35379.21.

129 See note 82 to T27.

130 *Dianji* transcribes the Tangut calque of *gemen;* see Gule Maocai, 28b, where the Tangut is transcribed *dingzhi* and glossed *gemen.* Both *dianji* and *dingzhi* occur in Gule as transcriptions for these Tangut characters (Hwang-cherng Gong, in a letter of 2 August 1986, brought this to my attention).

131 See T28.

132 *Duda goudang* occurs four times in the Chinese text; the last two instances are matched in T24 by a *liwu u kha. A liwu* is glossed by Gule Maocai, 28b, as *du'an; u kha,* rendered *jian* in the Chinese text in the meaning of "overseer," can be glossed *toujian.* The phrase *duda goudang* occurs in the Xia Sino-Tibetan 1176 Heishui stele inscription of Gansu, line 13 of the Chinese text; Wang Yao gives the corresponding Tibetan phrase the Chinese gloss of *jiaqian zongguan* (lit. "general administrator in the imperial presence") ("Xi Xia Heishui qiao bei kaobu," *Zhongyang minzu xueyuan xuebao* 1 [1978]: 61). My translation conveys the meaning of a central government official with special supervisory duties in this project. The Tangut phrase a *liwu (du'an)* also designates a regular post in administrative bureaus, the third in command after the chief executives and "recipients of edicts," and is translated by Kychanov as "desk head" (see, for example, *Kodeks* 3, art. 692, pp. 118, 431). Thus the phrase *du'an toujian* also literally means "desk head and overseer." That meaning does not seem appropriate in this context, and the Chinese and Tibetan expressions support the translation offered here. See also the discussion by Li Fanwen in *Xi Xia lingmu chutu canbei cuibian* (Beijing: Wenwu chuban she, 1984), 28.

133 *Mingsai* transcribes the Tangut calque of *zhongshu* (Gule Maocai, 27b; *Kodeks* 3:109, 410), the highest-ranked government department. The Tiansheng code prescribes six directors of the Secretariat, each designated by a special name and probably internally ranked (114, 419). Many, but not all, Tangut official titles are transcribed rather than translated in the Han text (see the discussion in Chapter 6 and note 49 to T16).

134 According to Kychanov in "Tangutskie istochniki o gosudanstven-no-apparate Si Sya," 187 (4b), 213 (4b): *huai wo le* transcribes a high Tan-

gut honorary rank, which Kychanov gives the Chinese gloss *shou quanbei* (Gule Maocai, 20a, glosses the two Tangut graphs *wo le as quanbei*). Shi's gloss, *ci juzu,* evokes the Buddhist term *juzu jie,* denoting fulfillment of the precepts for monkhood ("Xi Xia wen 'guanjie fenghao biao' kaoshi," 246, 262). Li Fanwen translates the title *shou quanzu* ("Xi Xia guanjie fenghao biao kaoshi," 73, 75). After heir apparent, this is the highest honorary rank in the table, equivalent to that of "great king" *(da guowang)*.

135 Devéria and Lu Zengxiang indicate that the graphs *xing zhe nie* occupy two character spaces; from the rubbing it appears that the two characters *xing zhe* occupy one space.

136 *Woze luo:* Gule Maocai, 28a, glosses *huangcheng si; Kodeks* 3:109, 115, 410, 421, an office of the second class with four directors and four *chengzhi*.

137 Gule Maocai, 28a, gives the phonetic gloss *dingchi luo,* an equivalent transcription of the *dingzhi luo* of our text. In his transcription of Gule's text, Nishida (1964, 214) gives the Chinese gloss *dianli si* ("Ministry of Rites"), which is a fabrication of possible semantic glosses for these two Tangut graphs, but all authentic editions of Gule's text gloss it *da heng li yuan* (lit. "great constant calendar agency"). Kychanov originally rendered this office from the Tangut law code as "agency governing the calendar" ("Tangutskie istochniki o gosudarstvenno-appanate Si Sya," 183, no. 20, 210, no. 20), but in his integral translation of the law code (*Kodeks* 3:110, 411), he translates it "agency [governing] ceremonials," without explaining the change. Shi Jinbo also opines that *dian li si* is an acceptable translation of the Tangut, but he understands its purpose as astronomical and calendrical, which is obscured in Nishida's and Kychanov's translations (Shi, *Xi Xia wenhua,* 172–173). Given the similarity of the Tangut graphs denoting this agency and the Office for Audience Ceremonies *(dingzhi/dianji luo,* Chin. *gemen si)*, this conflation is not surprising. Yet the two were different; see Chapter 6 for a discussion. Recall that in T2 Mingwang Qi'e is also named a director of the Calendar Board, for which the Tiansheng code prescribes four directors (see note 11 to T2).

138 Gule Maocai, 28a: *emo luo* matches our *waimu luo,* glossed *tongjun si;* this agency does not appear in chapter 10 of the law code or in the index appended to volume 4 of the code. It was no doubt immediately subordinate to the Military Commission *(shumi yuan),* the highest organ of government along with the Central Secretariat.

139 A transcription of two Tangut graphs meaning "understands/expounds the scriptures" (see note 53 above).

140 In T17 the same individual is designated only as director of the Capital Security Office.

141 See T24, note 63.

142 *Niezu* transcribes a Tangut title glossed *jianjun* in Gule Maocai, 28b.

143 In T24 Right Wing *(youxiang)* is replaced by Southern Court *(nanyuan)*; see note 64. Its bureaucratic rank is not given in the code.

144 *Qiejie*, an unidentified Tangut rank or title. T24 gives Mai Majie the title of *pie tin*, translated into Chinese as *jianpin* (see note 65).

145 Chinese *ma* (here a rare form) translates the Tangut *rie*, meaning "horse," *jie* transliterates the Tangut word meaning "gold." See note 66 to T24.

146 *Xinggong sansi:* see note 67 to T24.

147 "Overseer" translates *wugu*, a Chinese spelling of the Tangut *u kha*, normally rendered in this text as *jian*, and generally in Chinese as *toujian*.

148 *Couming* transcribes a Tangut title with no apparent analogue in the Tangut text, which does not mention Wu Modou. See the following note.

149 T25 names a different person, Muyang Eyi, who is assistant supervisor *(toujian xiao)* of temple repairs and *chengzhi* ("recipient of edicts," a deputy director, according to Kychanov) of the Auxiliary Palace Fiscal Commission, with a title, *tu mie*, translated by Nishida (1964, 174) as *zaiji guan*, by Shi (1988, 249) as *jiguan*, and by Kychanov (1978, 141) as the official who "addresses the deities with requests." Might this be Wu Modou's junior colleague?

150 *Liming* transcribes another Tangut title absent from T.

151 The three characters *qu li yai* occupy two spaces. This name also is not mentioned in the Tangut text.

152 The Chinese graph for *pang* given here is a local variant glossed *mang* in *Kangxi zidian,* 161, and in Xing Jun, *Longkan shoujing* (rpt. Beijing: Zhonghua shuju, 1985), 2:48a, but should be read *pang* here (see glossary under *pang/mang*). In T25, the corresponding Tangut character is transcribed in Gule Maocai, 9a, 12b, with the Chinese character *pang*$_2$ (see *Xiandai Hanyu cidian,* 766). In Kepping, "Elements of Ergativity," 197, 572, this Tangut word transcribes the Chinese name Pang (Juan) (I thank Nie Hongyin for bringing this to my attention).

153 In the rubbing, the three characters *na zheng yu* occupy two spaces and are written smaller than the character Wang. The name appears in T25, where all four characters are the same size, each occupying one space, and where I have read Wangna as a double surname. Na might also be read No (Mathews, no. 4604, pp. 645–646), and is here written with a variant graph.

154 The parallel passage of T26 denotes Jiu Zhiqing as assistant supervisor. See note 77.

155 T26: "Assistant overseer of artisans [engaged in] stūpa repairs." The Chinese text is extremely elliptical. If my translation is correct, the artisans referred to may be those named in H21: Weiyi Yiyai et al., who appear in T28 as the senior stone carvers.

156 Reconstructed from T26.

157 Devéria's text resumes in the thirty-eighth character space down the twenty-fifth column; Han Yincheng (Appendix B, no. 17, 146, note 19)

states that forty-one characters are missing before "Liu" This column has irregular spacing and more than seventy characters, listing mostly names, many carved small and crowded together. My tentative reconstruction down to Liu Gouer of the first thirty-seven characters draws on T 26–27.

6. Reading between the Lines: A Comparison and Analysis of the Tangut and Han Texts

1 Mark Elliot has attempted a similar analysis of an early Qing polyglot temple inscription in his "Turning a Phrase: Translation in the Early Qing through a Temple Inscription of 1645," in *Aetas Manjurica,* vol. 3, ed. Martin Gimm, Giovanni Stary, and Michael Weiers (Wiesbaden: Otto Harrassowitz, 1992), 12–41.

2 E. I. Kychanov, " 'Krupinki zolota na ladoni'—posobie dlia izucheniia tangutskovo pis'mennosti," in *Zhanry i stili literatur Kitaia i Korei,* ed. B. B. Vakhtin and I. S. Lisevich (Moscow, 1969), 221–222, n. 35.

3 E. I. Kychanov, *Vnov' sobrannye dragotsennye parnye izrecheniia* (Moscow, 1974), 30–45. See also James E. Bosson, *A Treasury of Aphoristic Jewels: The Subhāṣitaratnanidhi of Sa Skya Paṇḍita in Tibetan and Mongolian* (Bloomington: Indiana University Press, 1969), 6, 14 *passim.*

4 See note 82 in Chapter 5.

5 I speculate that the first element of his name, Hun, marks him as the scion of an old Tuyühun family who married an imperial princess.

6 See Chapter 5, note 10.

7 Nishida Tatsuo has suggested that the invention of the Tangut script may have been an attempt to create a standard language, unifying the diverse dialects spoken by the various Mi and Mi-nyag peoples (and, I would add, all the other Inner Asians); see Nishida's review of Kychanov's *Ocherk istorii tangutskogo gosudarstva,* in *Tōyōshi kenkyū* 28, nos. 2–3 (1969): 124. The view I have expressed here does not exclude this and other possibilities.

8 I.e., the Buddha is impartial and universal; therefore our particular fortune must be attributed to the virtues of our rulers.

9 Chisui Satō, "The Character of Yün-kang Buddhism," esp. 39–40. I own a copy of, but have not yet read, the recent book by James O. Caswell, *Written & Unwritten: A New History of the Buddhist Caves at Yungang* (Vancouver: University of British Columbia Press, 1988), so I cannot draw upon its insights for this study.

10 Satō, "The Character of Yün-kang Buddhism," 79.

11 Dunnell, "The Hsia Origins of the Yüan Institution of Imperial Preceptor."

12 Men'shikov, 498, illus. 22, reproduces a page of an 1184 Xia sūtra text in Chinese with the name "Bai Gao Da Xia Guo." See also Kepping, "The Name of the Tangut Empire."

13 Satō, "The Character of Yün-kang Buddhism," 38–83.

14 Kychanov, "Tibetans and Tibetan Culture in the Tangut State of Hsi Hsia (982–1227)," 211, where Kychanov cites Rolf Stein for the Tibetan notion that west denotes "upper" *(stod)* and east "lower" *(smad)*. See Stein, *Tibetan Civilization* (Stanford, 1972), 43–44.

15 Zhang Guangda and Rong Xinjiang, "Les noms du royaume de Khotan," in *Contributions aux études de Touen-Houang*, vol. 3, ed. Michel Soymié (Paris: École Française d'Extrême-Orient, 1984), 43.

16 This fact clinches the dates for Xia use of the Da'an reign title, which hitherto have varied by one or two years in the calculations of different scholars. We know that there were eleven Da'an years, because the St. Petersburg Tangut archive contains a sūtra fragment dated to Da'an 11 (see Chapter 3, note 69.) Da'an began no earlier than 1074, because the Kharakhoto archive contains a Xia preface in Chinese to the *Dabanruo boluomiduo jing* dated to the fifth year of Tianci lisheng guoqing, a *guichou* year, which was 1073 (see Men'shikov, p. 487, illus. 11). These considerations allow us to accept the statement in SS 486:14009, that in 1075 (Song Xining 8) a Tangut communiqué dated Da'an 2 reached a Song border office. Finally, Xia and Liao would not use the same reign title at the same time.

17 See SS 485:13999 for the terms of the 1044 treaty.

18 Huizong's death in 1086 resulted in a succession crisis; senior Weiming clan members reportedly opposed the enthronement of his three-year-old son, Qianshun (Chongzong), seeing him as an instrument of continued Liang control. In some Song sources he was even rumored not to have been a Weiming (Wu Guangcheng, XXSS 27:14b, citing Wang Cheng, *Dongdu shilüe*, in the biagraphary of An Dao). According to *Song shi* 486:14015, Tianan liding was used for only one year and its successor, Tianyi zhiping, for four years. Wu Guangcheng ends Da'an in 1085, starts Tianan liding in 1086, and asserts that in the eighth month of 1086 the reign date was changed to Tianyi zhiping (27:15b). Dai Xizhang also ends Da'an in 1085, makes 1086 Tianan liding 1 and 1087 Tianyi zhiping 1, but contradicts himself by stating that Qianshun was enthroned in Tianan liding 2 (XXJ 19:1a–2b). According to my calculations, Da'an ended in 1084, Tianan liding began in 1085, and if Qianshun was enthroned in Tianan liding 2, that should be 1086, not 1087. But T 10–11 states: "After this, the Desheng Empress Dowager and the Renjing Emperor received [rule over] the land. Then, in the Tian[an] liding second year, it was ordered at all times to burn incense and distribute vows without cease. Campaigning again in Han territory, the empress dowager herself went out at the head of the cavalry." This passage appears to say that Tianan liding 2 came after the enthronement of the new emperor and was the year in which the second Liang empress dowager led troops against Song. This could only be the case if Tianan liding is understood as a mistake for Tianyi zhiping.

Wu Guangcheng (28:5a) records the report of the empress dowager's participation in a Xia attack on Zhenrongjun in 1087 (reported in XCB 405:

5ab), which in Wu's dating is Tianyi zhiping 2. (Wu had no knowledge of the 1094 stele inscription.) Ordinarily one is reluctant to challenge the accuracy of an epigraphical source, but in this case the slip can be readily imagined: The two reign titles, Tianan liding and Tianyi zhiping, each comprise four graphs, each beginning with the same graph. The first two graphs of the reign title appear at the bottom of column 10 and the last two at the top of column 11. In fact, the last graph of column 10 has been effaced and is no longer legible. Its reconstruction as the Tangut equivalent of *an* for Tianan seems problematic to me, in part because it is neither the graph for *an* used in Da'an nor that used in Tianyou min'an. A reign title split between two columns offers a good opportunity for error by the carvers.

Wu Guangcheng's dating of the two reign titles fits the known facts best. If Tianyi zhiping had four years, it must have been adopted in 1086, because Tianyou min'an was definitely adopted in 1090, given the indisputable dating of the stele. If it was adopted in the middle of 1086, after Huizong's death and Chongzong's accession, Tianan liding might be recorded for only one year (1085), as *Song shi* states. The reign date of T11 should be the second year, if not of Tianan liding, then only of Tianyi zhiping.

Li Fanwen also discusses Tianan liding 2 in *Xi Xia lingmu chutu canbei cuibian,* 36, but his chart on page 37 shows Da'an ending in 1085 instead of 1084.

19 See frontispiece photograph no. 3, "Hexi zi Cibei daochang chan," *juan* 9, in *Xi Xia wen zhuanhao*, a special issue of *Bulletin of the National Library of Peiping* 4, no. 3 (May–June 1930; Jan. 1932).

20 See XCB 405:5ab.

21 Interesting to note, of sixteen honorific spaces left empty in H, four precede references to the throne, four precede references to imperial edicts, one precedes the name Great Xia, and seven precede mention of the Buddha. In T, all eleven honorific spaces precede mention of the throne: six the empress, and five the emperor. The apparent absence of honorific spaces before mention of the Buddha in T may be explained by this text's particular use of spacing to separate couplets in the verse portions that treat Buddhist matters.

22 The same argument could be made for H15's use of the locution *zhaoci,* an edict "issued on behalf of the emperor," likewise absent from T.

23 Kychanov, *Vnov' sobrannye dragotsennye parnye izrecheniia,* 46–47; Kychanov, "Gimn sviashchennym predkam tangutov," in *Pis'mennye pamiatniki vostoka, 1968* (Moscow, 1970), 223, n. 3, 226; R. A. Stein, "Mi-ñag et Si-hia: Géographie historique et légendes ancestrales," 229 and n. 2. For an analysis of the significance of these tropes and their specific referents and pattern of occurrence, see Kepping, "The 'Black-headed' and 'Red-faced' in Tangut Texts."

24 *Wenhai,* 149, 195, 407, 444.

25 On Xia hereditary occupational households, see Kychanov, "Tangut-

skii gvon," *Pis'mennye pamiatniki i problemy istorii i kul'tury narodov vostoka,* proceedings of the thirteenth annual scholarly session of the Leningrad branch of the Institute of Oriental Studies (Moscow, 1977), 1:35–39. A standard study of the Yuan practice is Ch'ü Ch'ing-yuan, "Government Artisans of the Yüan Dynasty," in *Chinese Social History: Translations of Selected Studies,* ed. E-tu Zen Sun and John DeFrancis (Washington, D.C.: n.p., 1956).

26 For a discussion of the issue, see Shi Jinbo, *Xi Xia wenhua,* 183–188.

27 Shi Jinbo, "Xi Xia Han wen ben 'Zazi' chutan," 170–171, 178–179. In the Chinese edition of the name list, the Fan surname section opens with the two names Weiming and Mocang. The occurrence of Mocang right after Weiming, the royal name, and the absence of the name Yeli suggest that the Mocang clan survived the downfall of its leader and retained its influence, although this is not especially evident in sources for the Liang regency period. Yet on the basis of other internal evidence, we cannot now date *Zazi* earlier than the mid–twelfth century.

28 Peter A. Boodberg, *Selected Works of Peter A. Boodberg,* comp. Alvin P. Cohen (Berkeley and Los Angeles: University of California Press, 1979), e.g., 47–73, annotated translations of biographies of several Xiongnu princes, including Helian Bobo (P'o-p'o, in Boodberg's reconstruction and in Pulleyblank's *Lexicon*), son of Liu Weichen and founder of the Ordos state of Da Xia in 407 (66–73), the inspiration for the Chinese name of the Tangut state.

29 Boodberg, "The Language of the T'o-pa Wei," *Harvard Journal of Asiatic Studies* 1 (1936), 167–185; rpt. in *Selected Works of Peter A. Boodberg,* 221–239, esp. 229.

30 Shi Jinbo quite correctly argues that the Tangut "Fan" incorporated many tribal or ethnic elements over the centuries, which are reflected in the name lists. Thus the argument about whether the royal clan was of Dangxiang Qiang or Xianbei descent is meaningless. See "Xi Xia jingnei minzu kao," 407–417.

31 The Yuan government did not, however, ban intermarriage. See Elizabeth Endicott-West, *Mongolian Rule in China* (Cambridge, Mass.: Harvard Council on East Asian Studies, 1987), 123.

32 *Kodeks* 3:194, 586.

33 *Kodeks* 3:124–125, 445. I have translated from the Tangut text, consulting Kychanov's Russian translation. The rest of the article describes the function of inspectors of the Office of Audience Ceremonies in enforcing protocol.

34 "Of capital standing" tentatively renders five Tangut graphs that Kychanov seems to omit from his translation.

35 *Kodeks* 3:125, 446. Presumably instances of identical birthdays did not arise (how did Tanguts calculate age?).

36 Cf. the name of the Xiongnu *shanyu* (equivalent of *qan*) Modu (com-

monly rendered Maodun or Modun); see David B. Honey, *The Rise of the Medieval Hsiung-nü: The Biography of Liu-Yüan*, Papers on Inner Asia, no. 15 (Bloomington: Indiana University Research Institute for Inner Asian Studies, 1990), 16, 38. XCB 358:7a registers a Weiming Moduo as head of a diplomatic mission to the Song court in 1085.

37 See note to T26 in Chapter 5.

38 *A Dictionary of Official Titles in Imperial China*, 279, no. 3180; see also SS 119:3936–3937.

39 In his introduction to the Tiansheng code, Kychanov observes that "to the chief executive of an agency belonged the highest power. If he was illiterate, then under him the role of the "transmitter of edicts" [i.e., 'recipient of edicts' or *chengzhi*] grew. In general in the daily work of an agency these or other matters were often decided precisely by the 'transmitter of edicts,' and only when he was not present would the agency chief do it himself" (*Kodeks* 1:331). Kychanov's footnote to the last sentence quoted above refers to the early-thirteenth-century "New Laws" (unpublished), suggesting that a trend toward the increasing powers of seconds-in-command at the expense of the nominal head of an agency may have been a later development. The multiple staffing of chief executives would tend to encourage such a tendency, however, especially if the highest posts were awarded to illiterate or semiliterate nobles as a means of rewarding the aristocracy. Certain articles of the Tiansheng code specify literacy as a qualification for advancement or assignment to particular offices, especially those of clerks and other lower-ranking staff members (1:333, 340).

40 Article 1439 of the Tiansheng code (*Kodeks* 4:213–214, 615–616).

41 See *Tongyin* 8B47 and 31B27, respectively; *Wenhai* 43.122 for the second graph (it does not record the first).

42 The locus classicus is in the biography of Pang Ji, who replaced Fan Zhongyan at Yanzhou and played a key role in negotiations with Yuanhao in the 1040s (SS 311:10200). After several military defeats, Song Renzong decided to negotiate and so directed Pang Ji to receive a Tangut envoy from Yuanhao, bearing a letter from Yuanhao's military chief, Yeli Wangrong:

> The envoy referred to Wangrong as *taiwei* (a lofty honorary title). Ji said, "*Taiwei* and *sangong* (Three Dukes) are not titles obtained by officers of subordinate states. If [the court] allows Wangrong to use it, then [we] will not achieve in making Yuanhao our servant *(chen)*. Now in their letter they call themselves '*ning ling*' or '*mo ning ling*,' which are all [names for] their government posts and do no harm to propriety." The court concurred.

Thereafter the Tanguts disguised all their titles by transliterating them. It remains to determine what exactly each transliteration represents: an honorary or noble rank, an official or titular rank, or a duty assignment (to use the terminology devised to describe the different kinds of Song titles). Some of these were native in origin, others modeled on the Chinese system. See the studies by Li Wei, "Xi Xia fanguan chuyi," in his *Xi Xia shi yanjiu* (Yinchuan: Ningxia renmin chuban she, 1989), 64–74; and Bai Bin, "Lun Xi Xia shichen di 'fan hao' wenti," in *Zhongguo minzu shi yanjiu* (Beijing: Zhongguo shehui kexue yuan minzu yanjiu suo chuban, 1987), 454–473.

43 *Kodeks* 2:10, 246; Shi Jinbo et al., "Xi Xia wen 'Tiansheng xinlü' jinlü biao kaoshi," in *Xi Xia wen shi conglun,* ed. Ningxia wenwu guanli weiyuan hui and Ningxia wenhua ting wenwu chu (Yinchuan: Ningxia renmin chuban she, 1992), 96–111.

A Select Glossary of Chinese Names and Terms

This glossary is arranged alphabetically by Chinese syllable. For example, Faxian comes before Fan. Only the titles of Xia emperors and their reign eras are listed here.

Alashan 阿拉善
Aligu 阿里骨
a shan pie 阿閃搊
a shu 阿叔
An Dao 安燾
Anqing si 安慶寺
Anquan guoshi 安全國師
Anxi 安西
An Zhongjing 安忠敬
Ayu 阿育
Ayuwang Temple 阿育王寺

Badaling Stūpa 八大靈塔
Basimu 拔思母
Bati 跋提
Bai Ashan 白阿山
Bai cheng 白城
Bai Faxin 白法信
Bai Gao Da [Xia] Guo
　　白高大[夏]國
bailan 白蘭
Baima si 白馬寺
baiqi 拜期
baishen tian 白身天
Baisikou 拜寺口
Baixi Qitejile 拜錫齊特濟勒

Bai Zhiguang 白智光
Bai Zhixuan 白至宜
Ban Shu 班輸
Bao'an 保安
Baobaoxi Jiduoji 寶保細吃多已
Baojue Temple 寶覺寺
Baomo zhengguo jin'ge si
　　保魔鎮國金閣寺
baosheng 寶生
Baoyi 寶義
Beidou gong 北斗宮
Beique 北却
Bijuzhi pusa yibaiba ming jing
　　毘俱胝菩薩一百八名經
boluomi 波羅密
Boluozhi 潘羅支
boshi 博士
bu 部
budong 不動
Budong Jingang 不動金剛
buluozi 部落子
buzheng shi 布政使

cai xue yan guo chu 才學言過處
canyi 參議
Cao 曹

Cao Guangzhi 曹廣智
Cao shi 曹氏
Chandu 釁都
chang duan 常斷
changzhu 常住
chen 臣
Chengde guozhu shengfu
  zhengmin daming
  成德國主盛福正民大明
Chengtian si 承天寺
chengzhi 承旨
chi 敕
Chicheng 赤成
Chong E 種諤
Chongsheng si 崇聖寺
Chongzong 崇宗
chujia gongde si 出家功德司
chujia tidian 出家提點
Chuanfa yuan 傳法院
Cibei daochang chanfa
  慈悲道場懺法
Cifu yuan gui 冊府元龜
ci juzu 賜俱足
cishen 祠神
ci zhi 茲之
couming 湊銘

Da'an 大安
Da Bai Gao Guo xinyi sanzang
  shengjiao xu
  大白高國新譯三藏聖教序
Dabanruo boluomiduo jing
  大般若波羅密多經
Dacheng (sheng) wuliangshou jing
  大乘(聖)無量壽經
Dade 大德
Dadu 大都
Dadumin si 大度民寺
Dafo si 大佛寺
da guowang 大國王
da heng li yuan 大恒曆院
daming huangdi 大明皇帝
Daqing 大慶
Da Xia 大夏

Da Yun 達雲
Dayun si 大雲寺
Dangchang 宕昌
Dangxiang [Qiang] 黨項[羌]
Dangxing 黨興
daochang 道場
Daoxuan 道宣
Daoyuan 道環
dao zhi 到知
*decheng guozhu [zhiguang]
  fusheng minzheng [shouyi]
  mingda huangdi Weiming*
  德成國主[智光]福盛民正[壽益]
  明大皇帝嵬名
Dejing 德靖
Desheng 德盛
dishi 帝師
dianji 典集
dianji ling [pi] 典集冷[批]
dianli si 典禮司
ding 定
dingchi luo 頂赤囉
dingji 頂疾
Dingnan jun 定難軍
dingzhi luo 頂直囉
Dongzhan 董氊
du'an toujian 都案頭監
duda goudang 都大勾當
dudu qianshi 都督僉事
dujie sanzang anquan guoshi
  瘦解三藏安全國師
duyi gouguan zuozhe
  都譯勾管作者
Dunhuang 敦煌

emo luo 遏暮囉
Etepeng 鄂特彭
er jing 而敬
ersheng 二聖
erzhong 二眾

Faguo 法果
Fahu 法護
Fa Jixiang 法吉祥

A Select Glossary

Fajin 法進
Fajing 法淨
Famen si 法門寺
fa shuo zui chan daochang
    法説罪懺道場
Fatian 法天
Faxian 法賢
Fan 番
fan 飰
fan jue jing 梵覺經
Fan seng gangsi 番僧綱司
Fan wang gong 梵王宮
Fan Zhongyan 范仲淹
fengchi 奉敕
Fengjiao cheng 風角城
Fengtian xiandao yaowu xuanwen
    shenmou ruizhi zhiyi quxie
    dunmu yigong
    奉天顯道耀武宣文神謀叡智制
    義去邪惇睦懿恭
fo 佛
Foshuo Amituo jing
    佛説阿彌陀經
Foshuo yueguang pusa jing
    佛説月光菩薩經
Fotudeng 佛圖澄
Fusheng chengdao 福聖承道
fushi 副使
futu 浮圖
Fuyan [Circuit] 鄜延 [路]
Fuzhou 鄜州

gai 蓋
Ganling Mountains 甘浚山
ganlu 甘露
Ganlu dashi 甘露大師
Ganquan 甘泉
Gantong daochang 感通道場
Gantong ta 感通塔
ganying 感應
Ganzhou 甘州
Gaochang 高昌
Gao shi 高氏
Gaotai Temple 高臺寺

gemen 閤門
Geshu Han 哥舒翰
Geshu Daoyuan 哥舒道元
gongde si 功德司
Gonghua 拱化
Gong Shu Ban 公輸班
Gongsu zhangxian huanghou
    恭肅章憲皇后
gongxian 貢獻
gong xie nanbei zhangbiao
    供寫南北章表
gou 狗
Gusiluo 唃廝囉
guxian ta 姑洗塔
Guzang 妓臧
Guazhou 瓜州
Guan Mile pusa shang sheng
    doushuaitian jing
    觀彌勒菩薩上生兜率天經
Guanyin jing 觀音經
guanzuo sihu 官作四戶
Guangding 光定
Guanghui wang 廣惠王
Guangsheng 光聖
guangyin tian 光音天
Guangyun 廣運
Guo Daonu 郭道奴
Guoqu zhuangyan qie qian
    foming jing
    過去莊嚴劫千佛名經
guoshi 國師
guo zhi su 國之俗

Haishen 海深
Han 漢
Han seng gangsi 漢僧綱司
Han zu 漢祖
Hao 昊
he 河
Hedong Circuit 河東路
Helan shan 賀蘭山
Helian Bobo 赫連勃勃
Hexi 河西
Heishui 黑水

Hongkai 洪鎧
Honglu si 鴻臚寺
Hongren si 宏仁寺
Hongyuan [si] 洪元[寺]
Hongzang si 宏藏寺
Houda si 後大寺
Hu cheng shengde zhiyi
　護城聖德至懿
Huguo renwang si 護國仁王寺
Huguo Temple 護國寺
Hualou 花樓
hua (ying) shen 化(應)身
Huayan jing 華嚴經
huai wo le 嚷挨黎
Huanqing 環慶
Huanzhou 環州
Huanzong 桓宗
huangcheng si 皇城司
Huangjian 皇建
Huang River 湟水
Huici dun'ai huanghou
　惠慈敦愛皇后
huixing 彗星
Huizhen 彗貞
Huizong 惠宗
Hun-Weiming Yu 渾嵬名遇

jiguan 祭官
ji huangdi wei 即皇帝位
jiqiao 技巧
Jiwaiji Fazheng 吉外吉法正
jiaqian zongguan 駕前總管
jiaxiang 家相
Jiaxing 嘉興
Jiayike 嘉伊克
jian 間
jianchen 諫臣
jianjun (si) 監軍(司)
jianpin 諫品
jian ta zhi chen 建塔之晨
Jiaohe 交河
jiaoling lunshen 教令輪身
jiedu shi 節度使
Jieqing Temple 皆慶寺

Jietan Cloister 戒壇院
jiexing 解行
Jie Zhixing 解智行
jin 金
Jin'ai 金哀
Jingang jing 金剛經
jingang shangshi 金剛上師
Jin'ge si 金閣寺
Jin guangming zuisheng wang jing
　金光明最勝王經
Jinshan 金山
jinshi 進士
jinwei 禁圍
Jinzongchi 金總持
Jing (Zhou King) 敬
jingjie 經解
jingjin 精進
Jingmu 敬穆
Jingshan 徑山
jingyuan 經院
Jingzong 景宗
Jiuquan 酒泉
Jiu Zhi [bo] 酒智[波]
Jiu Zhiqing 酒智清
ju sheng ying di 居聖埕地
juzu jie 具足戒
jue rao 覺繞
jun 郡

Kaibao 開寶
Kaiyuan si 開元寺
Kaiyun 開運
kamo 羯磨
Kang Gou[ming] 康狗[名]
Kangjing 康靖
Kāśyapa Rulai si 迦葉如來寺
Kumoluoshi 鳩摩羅什

Lanzhou 蘭州
Lebu 勒布
li 禮
Li 李
Li Awen 李阿溫
Li Deming 李德明

lifa 麗法
Li Jiqian 李繼遷
Lijing cheng 歷精城
liming 栗銘
Li Qing 李清
Li Ruyin 李如蔭
Li Shengtian 李聖天
Li Shougui 李守貴
Li Yuan 李遠
Li Yuanhao 李元昊
Li Zhibao 李智寶
lianhua 蓮華
lianpi 連批
Liang 梁
Lianghuang baochan 梁皇寶懺
Liang Qibu 梁乞逋
Liang shi 梁氏
Liang Xingzhenie 梁行者乜
Liang Yimai 梁乙埋
Liang Zhihui 梁智慧
Liangzhou 涼州
ling (director) 令
ling (efficacious) 靈
Lingjie Chengpang 令介成龐
ling (yan) ming 令(嚴)明
lingpi 冷批
lingtai 陵臺
lingyou 靈佑
Lingzhou 靈州
Liu Gouer 劉狗兒
Liu Quliyai 劉屈栗崖
Liu shi 劉氏
Liu Weichen 劉衛辰
Liu Xingzhen 劉行真
Liu Xiu 劉秀
Longcan 隴挼
Longshu yu wen 隴蜀餘聞
Longxing fojiao biannian tonglong 隆興弗教編年通論
Longyou 隴右
loujin ming 漏盡明
Lu Ban 魯班
Lubu 魯布

Lu Guangzu 魯光祖
Luohan Cloister 羅漢院
Luo shi 羅氏
lüjing 律晶
lüjing cifei seng 律晶賜緋僧

Mai Majie 埋薦皆
Mengshan 蒙山
Mizhou yuanyin wangsheng ji 密呪圓因往生集
Mianbi cheng 面壁城
Miaochuan 邈川
Miaofa lianhua jing 妙法蓮華經
ming 銘
Ming cheng 明城
mingsai 銘賽
mingwang 明王
Mingwang Qi'e 明旺契訛
Mocang dashi 沒藏大師
Mocang Epang 沒藏訛龐
Mocang shi 沒藏氏
mofa 末法
Mogao 莫高
mo ning ling 沒寧令
mo shi dun dao cheng (deng) tu 磨什鈍道澄圖
mu 牧
mu futu 木浮圖
Muyang Eyi 木楊訛移
Muzheng 木征

Nanping wang 南平王
nanyuan junjian 南院軍監
nanyuan xinggong sansi 南院行宮三司
neisu 內宿
Nisimen 你斯悶
nian 念
niezu 孽祖
ning ling 寧令
Nushe Eji 弩涉俄疾

panci (pancha) 般次(般擦)
pang/mang 厖

*pang*² 疮
Pang Ji 龐籍
Pang Juan 龐涓
Puxian xing yuan jing
  普賢行願經

qideng juezhi 七等覺支
Qi guo zhongwu wang
  齊國忠武王
Qiandao 乾道
Qianding 乾定
qian nian 前年
Qianyou 乾祐
qian zhi fu pa 簽帙複帕
Qiang 羌
Qiao shi 喬氏
qiejie 乞介
Qinfeng Circuit 秦鳳路
qing'an 輕安
Qingliang si 清涼寺
Qingping junwang 清平郡王
qing si 慶寺
qing si jian xiu 慶寺監修
Qingtang 青唐
Qingtang lu 青康錄
Qingyijiemou 青宜結牟
Qingying si 慶應寺
que 闕
Quye River 屈野河
quanzhu si 勸主司

ren (H24) 人
ren (humaneness) 仁
Ren Dejing 任得敬
Renduo 仁多
Renjing 人淨
Renqing 人慶
ren shi 仁師
*Renwang huguo banruo boluo-
  miduo jing*
  仁王護國般若波羅密多經
*Renwang huguo banruo boluo-
  miduo jing tuoluoni niansong
  yigui*

仁王護國般若波羅密多經陀羅
  尼念誦儀軌
Ren Yuzi 任遇子
Renzong 仁宗
Richeng 日稱
rulai quanshen 女來全身
rushi 如實
Ruixiang si 瑞像寺

Saimen 塞門
san gong 三公
sanjie 三界
sanling 三靈
sanlun shen 三輪身
Sanqie sanqian foming jing
  三劫三千佛名經
sanshi 三世
Sanshiwu foming li chan wen
  三十五佛名禮懺文
sansi 三司
seng dao 僧道
sengjian 僧監
seng toujian 僧頭監
sengzheng 僧正
sengzhu 僧主
Shazhou 沙州
Shazhou Beiting qaghan
  沙州北亭可汗
Shazhou zhenguo 沙州鎮國
shanhu lin 珊瑚林
shan men 山門
shanyu 單于
Shanzhou 鄯州
Shangqing 上青
shang si'en gong hui 上四恩功迴
she 捨
sheli 舍利
*shengong shenglu dejiao minzhi
  renjing huangdi*
  神功勝祿德教民治仁淨皇帝
Shenwu 神武
Shen Yong 沈庸
Shenzong 神宗
sheng chun 聖純

A Select Glossary

Shengde 聖德
Shengrong si 聖容寺
Shengwen 聖文
Shengwen yingwu chongren zhixiao
　聖文英武崇仁至孝
shi 氏
shibiao 誓表
Shi Budong 釋不動
shidi 十地
shi ren 師仁
Shizi feng 師子峯
Shihu 施護
Shijing 識淨
Shizu shiwen benwu xingfa jianli renxiao
　世祖始文本武興法建禮仁孝
Shoudeng 受登
shou juzu 受俱足
shou quanbei 受全備
shou quanzu 受全足
shu 書
shumi yuan 樞密院
shumu 叔母
Shuncheng yixiao huanghou
　順成懿孝皇后
shuo 朔
Shuofang jun 朔方軍
si 色
Siduodu 廝鐸督
si'en 四恩
Sigong 思恭
si guan 寺觀
si hongyuan 四弘願
siliu 四流
Sima Guang 司馬光
Sima Yi 司馬逸
Sineng 思能
Su Che 蘇轍
suming ming 宿命明
suzi 俗字
Suide 綏德
suiji 隨機
Suizhou 綏州

Sun 孫
Sun Duer 孫都兒
Sun Kedu 孫尅都
sunmie 損滅
Sun Rezi 孫惹子
Sun Sike 孫思克
Suo Zhishen 索智深

ta deng 塔燈
Taiping Xingguo si 太平興國寺
taiwei 太尉
Taizong 太宗
Taizu 太祖
Tang Yao 唐堯
Tao River 洮水
tidian 提點
tiju 提擧
Tian 田
Tianan liding 天安禮定
Tianci an 天賜庵
Tianci lisheng guoqing
　天賜禮盛國慶
tian dawang 天大王
Tiandu shan 天都山
Tianli dazhi zhixiao guangjing xuande jinzhong yongping
　天力大治智孝廣淨宣德盡忠永平
tianming 天命
Tianqing 天慶
Tiansheng 天盛
tiansheng quanneng fanlu [sheng you] fashi [bei he] guozheng huang taihou Liang shi
　天生全能番祿[聖祐]法式[悲和]國正皇太后梁氏
Tianshou lifa yanzuo
　天授禮法延祚
Tianxizai 天息災
tianyan ming 天眼明
Tianyi zhiping 天儀治平
Tianyou chuisheng 天祐垂聖
Tianyou min'an 天祐民安
tianzi 天子

tong 童
Tong Guan 童貫
tongjun si 統軍司
toujian 頭監
toujian xiao 頭監小
Tsongkha 宗哥
Tufan 吐蕃
Tuoba 拓拔

waimu luo 外母囉
wang 王
Wang Anshi 王安石
Wang Dan 王瞻
Wang Hou 王厚
Wang Puxin 旺普信
Wang Shao 王韶
Wang shi 罔氏
Wang Shizhen 王士禎
Wang Zhen 王真
Wangna Zhengyu 王㸰征遇
Weide Zhuang 威德幢
Weijing 惟淨
Weilai xingsu qie qian foming jing 未來星宿劫千佛名經
Weimi 嵬咩
Weimi Liegui 威密烈圭
Weiming Anquan 嵬名安全
Weiming Bingchang 嵬名秉常
Weiming Chunyou 嵬名純佑
Weiming Dewang 嵬名德旺
Weiming Liangzuo 嵬名諒祚
Weiming Moduo 嵬名謨鐸
Weiming Nangxiao 嵬名曩霄
Weiming Qianshun 嵬名乾順
Weiming Renxiao 嵬名仁孝
Weiming Shan 嵬名山
Weiming Xian 嵬名晛
Weiming Yanzong 嵬名彥宗
Weiming Zunxu 嵬名遵頊
Weimoji suo shuo jing 維摩詰所說經
Weimu shi 衛慕氏
Wei shi 嵬師
Weiyaini 嵬崖妳

Weiyi Yiyai 韋移移崖
weizhu 偽主
Wenhai 文海
Wenzhu [suo shuo] zuisheng mingyi jing 文殊[所說]最勝名義經
Wofo si (Dafo si) 臥佛寺(大佛寺)
Wopu Lingji 臥普令濟
Wo Qujie 臥屈皆
woze luo 臥(斡)則囉
Woziluo 斡(幹)資羅
wu bu 無不
wuchang zhi dao 五常之道
wugu 吳箇
wuhui 五悔
Wulahai 兀剌海
Wu Liang 五涼
Wulie 武烈
Wu Modou 吳沒兜
wusi 無色
Wutai shan 五臺山
Wuwei 武威
Wuwei xianzhi (gao) 武威縣志(稿)
Wuyin qieyun 五音切韵
wuzu 烏珠, 吾祖, 兀卒

xi 喜
Xi Fan 西番
Xihe Circuit 熙河路
Xiliang[fu] 西涼[府]
Xining 西寧
Xiping wang 西平王
Xitian Zhiyuan 西天智圓
Xi Xia 西夏
Xi Xia dang 西夏黨
Xiyu 西玉
Xiyu ji 西域記
Xia guo wang 夏國王
xia sanyou zhi yuan 下三有治緣
Xiazheng 瞎征
Xiazhou 夏州
Xianbei 鮮卑

A Select Glossary

Xiandao 顯道
xianhou 先后
xianhou zhi chao 先後之朝
Xianzai xian qie qian foming jing
  現在賢劫千佛名經
Xianzong 獻宗
xianggong 相公
Xiangzong 襄宗
xiao da wang 小大王
Xie Zhixing 謝智行
xin 信
xinggong sansi zheng 行宮三司正
xinggong yuan 行宮院
Xingqingfu 興慶府
xingshe 行捨
[xing] yan [杏]眼
Xingzhou 興州
xiu tasi jian shibei 修塔寺監石碑
Xiusheng si 誘生寺
Xu gaoseng zhuan 續高僧傳
Xuanren Empress Dowager Gao
  宣仁太后高氏
Xuan[wu] di 玄[武]帝

Yan'anfu 延安府
Yandan guoshi 燕丹國師
yan guo chu 言過處
Yansi ningguo 延嗣寧國
Yanzhou 延州
Yang 楊
Yang Bo 楊播
Yang shi 楊氏
Yang Zhengyin 楊正寅
Yaonie Yongquan 藥兜永詮
Yaonü 藥女
Yeli Renrong 野利仁榮
Yeli shi 野利氏
Yeli Wangrong 野利旺榮
Yeli Yuqi (Yuege)
  野利遇乞(約噶)
yi 義
Yi Gate 儀門
yiwen 藝文
yizao tian 意燥天

Yijing yuan 譯經院
yi zhen gongde li 以朕功德力
Yizong 毅宗
Yinchuan 銀川
Yin sun [?] 寅孫
Yingtian 應天
Yingwen 英文
Yingyun fatian shenzhi rensheng
  zhidao guangde xiaoguang
  應運法天神智仁聖至道廣德孝光
Yingzong 英宗
Yongan 永安
Yongchang 永昌
Yongle 永樂
Yongning 雍寧
Yongxingjun 永興軍
you jianyi dafu 右諫議大夫
Youlongbo (Zhebu Yulongbo)
  游龍鉢(折逋喻龍波)
you puye jian zhongshu shilang
  pingzhang shi
  右僕射兼中書侍郎平章事
you ta ming guxian
  有塔名姑洗
you wu 有無
youxiang niezu 右廂孽祖
you yuan 有緣
yu 欲
Yulan foshe 盂蘭佛社
Yulin 榆林
Yumi 於彌
Yuqie jiyao jiu a'nan tuoluoni
  yankou guiyi jing
  瑜伽集要救阿難陀羅尼焰口軌
  儀經
Yuqie jiyao yankou shishi yi
  瑜伽集要餤口族食儀
yuzhe 喻者
Yuande 元德
Yuan di 元帝
Yuan Hongde 袁宏德

zaiji guan 宰祭官
zang 藏

zaojing fang 造經房
zefa 擇法
zengyi 增益
Zhang Anshi 張安世
Zhang Fanyi 張梵嚟
Zhang Gai 張蓋
Zhang Gui 張軌
Zhang Shouyue 張守約
Zhang Sizhong 張思忠
Zhang Tianxi 張天錫
Zhangxian qinci huanghou
    章獻欽慈皇后
Zhangye 張掖
Zhang Zhengsi 張政思
Zhang Zhi 張陟
Zhang Zhonghua 張重華
Zhao 趙
zhaoci 詔辭
Zhaojian 昭簡
Zhaojian wenmu huanghou
    昭簡文穆皇后
Zhao Wanbi 趙完璧
Zhaoying 昭英
zhen 朕
Zhenguan 貞觀
zhenguo 鎮國
Zhenling cheng 珍陵城
Zhenrongjun 鎮戎軍
zhenshen 貞身
Zhenwu 貞武
zheng 正
Zhengde 正德
zhengfa lunshen 正法輪身
Zheng Sandui 奠三鎚
zhengtong 正統
zhi 智
Zhiguang 智光

Zhi Jixiang 智吉祥
Zhiman 志滿
*zhisheng luguang minzhi liji
    desheng huang taihou*
    智勝祿廣民治禮集德盛皇太后
zhi yu 至於
zhong 眾
zhongjiang 眾匠
Zhongsheng Puhua Temple
    眾聖普化寺
zhongshu 中書
zhongtu 中土
Zhongxingfu 中興府
zhu (pearls) 珠
zhu (ruler) 主
Zhu cheng 珠城
zhudian 竺典
zhujia gongde si 住家功德司
zhuanlun 轉輪
zi 子
*zi (you) Renyong zi shao chu shen
    xue tu*
    茲(有)仁勇自少出身學途
*zi ren yong you zi ru guan xue
    dao shang suo jing*
    茲仁勇幼自儒官學道上所經
zixing lunshen 自性輪身
zongbing (guan) 總兵(官)
Zong River 宗河
Zuxiu 祖琇
Zuisheng foding tuoluoni jing
    最勝佛頂陀羅尼經
Zuo Aling 左阿令
Zuo Jiyi 左計移
Zuo Paner 左伴兒
Zuo Zhixin 左支信

Bibliography

Adshead, S. A. M. *Central Asia in World History*. New York: St. Martin's Press, 1993.

Bai Bin 白濱. "Lun Xi Xia shichen di 'fan hao' wenti" 論西夏使臣的"蕃號"問題. In *Zhongguo minzu shi yanjiu* 中國民族史研究, 454–473. Beijing: Zhongguo shehui kexue yuan minzu yanjiu suo chuban, 1987.

Bareau, André. "La construction et le culte des stūpa d'après les Vinayapiṭaka." *Bulletin de l'École Française d'Extrême-Orient* 50, no. 2 (1962): 229–274.

Beckwith, Christopher I. "The Revolt of 755 in Tibet." In *Contributions on Tibetan Language, History and Culture*, ed. Ernst Steinkellner and Helmut Tauscher, 1–16. Proceedings of the Csoma de Körös Symposium, 1981. Vienna: Arbeitskreis für Tibetische und Buddhistische Studien Universität Wien, 1983.

———. *The Tibetan Empire in Central Asia: A History of the Struggle for Great Power among Tibetans, Turks, Arabs, and Chinese during the Early Middle Ages*. Princeton, N.J.: Princeton University Press, 1987.

Bell, Catherine. *Ritual Theory, Ritual Practice*. Oxford: Oxford University Press, 1992.

Birnbaum, Raoul. *Studies on the Mysteries of Mañjuśrī*. Society for the Study of Chinese Religions Monograph 2, 1983.

Boodberg, Peter. *Selected Works of Peter A. Boodberg*. Compiled by Alvin P. Cohen. Berkeley and Los Angeles: University of California Press, 1979.

Bosson, James E. *A Treasury of Aphoristic Jewels: The Subhāṣita ratnanidhi of Sa Skya Paṇḍita in Tibetan and Mongolian*. Bloomington: Indiana University Press, 1969.

Bowring, Richard. "Brief Note: Buddhist Translations in the Northern Sung." *Asia Major*, 3rd ser., vol. 5, pt. 2 (1992), 79–93.

Chan, Hok-lam. *Legitimation in Imperial China: Discussions under the Jurchen-Chin Dynasty (1115–1234)*. Seattle: University of Washington Press, 1984.

Chavannes, Edouard. "A. I. Ivanov: *Stranitsa iz istorij Si-sia* (Une page de l'histoire du Si-hia; Bulletin de l'Académie impériale des sciences de Saint-Pétersbourg, 1911, p. 831–836)." *T'oung Pao*, ser. 11, no. 12 (1911): 441–446.

———. "Dix inscriptions chinoises de l'Asie centrale, d'après les estampages de M. Ch.-E. Bonin." *Memoires présentés par divers savants à l'Académie des Inscriptions et Belles-lettres*, ser. 1, vol. 11, no. 2 (1902): 193–295; also published as a separate extract in 1902, 103 pp.

Chen Bangzhan 陳邦瞻 (fl. 1598). *Song shi jishi benmo* 宋史紀事本末. Reprint. Beijing: Zhonghua shuju, 1977.

Chen Bingying 陳炳應. "Chongxiu Huguo si Gantong ta bei (Xi Xia wen) 重修攎國寺感通塔碑(西夏文)." In *Xi Xia shilun wenji* 西夏史論文集, ed. Bai Bin. Yinchuan: Ningxia renmin chuban she, 1984.

———. *Xi Xia wenwu yanjiu* 西夏文物研究. Yinchuan: Ningxia renmin chuban she, 1985.

———. "Xi Xia yu Dunhuang 西夏與敦煌." *Xibei minzu yanjiu* 西北民族研究 1 (1991): 78–90.

Ch'en, Kenneth. *Buddhism in China: An Historical Survey*. Princeton, N.J.: Princeton University Press, 1964.

Chen Naiwen 陳乃文 and Chen Xiezhang 陳燮章, comps. *Zangzu biannian shiliao ji* 藏族編年史料集. Part 2, 2 vols. Beijing: Minzu chuban she, 1990.

Chou Yi–liang. "Tantrism in China." *Harvard Journal of Asiatic Studies* 8, nos. 3–4 (March 1945): 241–332.

Chow, Rey. *Writing Diaspora: Tactics of Intervention in Contemporary Cultural Studies*. Bloomington: Indiana University Press, 1993.

Ch'ü, Ch'ing-yuan. "Government Artisans of the Yüan Dynasty." In *Chinese Social History: Translations of Selected Studies*. Ed. E-tu Zen Sun and John DeFrancis. Washington, D.C.: n.p., 1956.

Chung, Priscilla Ching. *Palace Women in the Northern Sung, 960–1126*. Leiden: E. J. Brill, 1981.

Clauson, Gerard. *An Etymological Dictionary of Pre-Thirteenth-Century Turkish*. Oxford: Clarendon Press, 1972.

Cleary, Thomas. *Entry into the Realm of Reality*. Boston and Shaftesbury: Shambhala, 1989.

Crossley, Pamela Kyle. "The Rulerships of China." *The American Historical Review* 97, no. 5 (Dec. 1992): 1468–1483.

Čuguevskii, L. I. "Touen-Houang du VIIIe au Xe siècle." In *Nouvelles contributions aux études de Touen-houang*, ed. Michel Soymié, vol. 2. Geneva: Librairie Droz, 1981.

Dai Xizhang 戴錫章. *Xi Xia ji* 西夏記. 1924. Reprinted in vol. 4 of *Zhonghua wenshi congshu*, ed. Wang Youli. Taipei: Huawen shuju, 1968.

Davidson, Ronald M. "The *Litany of Names of Mañjuśrī*." In *Tantric and Taoist Studies in Honour of R. A. Stein*, ed. Michel Strickmann, vol. 1, 1–69. Brussels: Institut Belge des Hautes Études Chinoises, 1981.
de Bary, W. T., ed. *The Buddhist Tradition in India, China and Japan*. New York: Vintage, 1972.
Devéria, G. "Stèle Si-Hia de Leang-Tcheou." *Journal asiatique*, 9th ser., 11 (1898): 53–74.
Ding Fubao 丁福保. *Foxue da cidian* 佛學大辭典. 1922. Reprint. Beijing: Wenwu chuban she, 1984.
Dohi Yoshikazu 土肥義和. "Ki i gun (Tō kōki・godai Sōsho) jidai" 歸義軍 (唐後期・五代宋出)時代. In *Tonkō no rekishi* 敦煌の歷史, *Kōza Tonkō* 講座敦煌 2, ed. Enoki Kazuo 榎一雄, 233–296. Tokyo: Datō shuppansha, 1980.
Drompp, Michael R. "Centrifugal Forces in the Inner Asian 'Heartland': History *versus* Geography." *Journal of Asian History* 23, no. 2 (1989): 134–168.
Dunhuang Research Institute. *Dunhuang Mogao ku gongyang ren tiji* 敦煌莫高窟供養人題記. Beijing: Wenwu chuban she, 1986.
Dunnell, Ruth W. "The Fall of the Xia Empire: Sino-Steppe Relations in the Late 12th–Early 13th Centuries." In *Rulers from the Steppe: State Formation on the Eurasian Periphery*, ed. Gary Seaman and Daniel Marks, 158–185. Los Angeles: University of Southern California Ethnographics Press, 1991.
———."The Hsia Origins of the Yüan Institution of Imperial Preceptor." *Asia Major 5*, no. 1 (1992): 85–111.
———."Hsi Hsia." In *The Cambridge History of China*, volume 6: *Alien Regimes and Border States*, ed. Herbert Franke and Denis Twitchett. Cambridge: Cambridge University Press, 1994.
———."Naming the Tangut Capital: Xingqing, Zhongxing and Related Matters." *Bulletin of Sung Yuan Studies* 21 (1989): 52–66.
———."Politics, Religion, and Ethnicity in Eleventh Century Xia: The Construction of Tangut Identity in the 1094 Wuwei Stele Inscription." *Central and Inner Asian Studies* 7 (1992): 61–114.
———."Tanguts and the Tangut State of Ta Hsia." Ph.D. dissertation, Princeton University, 1983.
———."The 1094 Sino-Tangut Gantong Stūpa Stele Inscription of Wuwei: Introduction, Translation of Chinese Text, and Source Study." In *Languages and History in East Asia: Festschrift for Tatsuo Nishida on the Occasion of his 60th Birthday*, ed. Akihiro Satō, 187–215. Kyoto: Shokado, 1988.
———."Who Are the Tanguts? Remarks on Tangut Ethnogenesis and the Ethnonym Tangut." *Journal of Asian History* 18, no. 1 (1984): 78–89.
Durt, Hubert. "The Meaning of Archaeology in Ancient Buddhism: Notes

on the Stūpas of Aśoka and the Worship of the 'Buddhas of the Past' According to Three Stories in the *Samguk Yusa*." In *Buddhism and Science: Commemorative Volume, 80th Anniversary*. Seoul: Dongguk University, 1987.

Ecsedy, Hilda. "Old Turkic Titles of Chinese Origin." *Acta Orientalia Hungarica* 18 (1965): 83–91.

Elliot, Mark. "Turning a Phrase: Translation in the Early Qing through a Temple Inscription of 1645." In *Aetas Manjurica*, vol. 3, ed. Martin Gimm, Giovanni Stary, and Michael Weiers, 12–41. Wiesbaden: Otto Harrassowitz, 1992.

Embree, Ainslee T., ed. *Sources of Indian Tradition*. Vol. 1. Rev. ed. New York: Columbia University Press, 1988.

Emmerick, R. E. *Tibetan Texts Concerning Khotan*. London Oriental Series 19. London: Oxford University Press, 1967.

Endicott-West, Elizabeth. "Hereditary Privilege in the Yüan Dynasty." In *Niguča Bičig, an Anniversary Volume in Honor of Francis Woodman Cleaves*, ed. Joseph Fletcher et al. *Journal of Turkish Studies* 9 (1985): 15–20.

———. *Mongolian Rule in China*. Cambridge, Mass.: Harvard Council on East Asian Studies, 1987.

Fan Zhongyan 范仲淹 (989–1052). *Fan wenzheng gong ji* 范文正公集. Sibu congkan jibu edition. Shanghai: Commercial Press, 1929.

Fang Guangchang 方廣錩. *Fojiao dianji baiwen* 佛教典籍百問. In Zongjiao wenhua congshu (The Religious Culture Series), ed. Wang Zhiyuan. Beijing: Jinri Zhongguo chuban she, 1989.

Farquhar, David M. "Emperor as Bodhisattva in the Governance of the Ch'ing Empire." *Harvard Journal of Asiatic Studies* 38, no. 1 (1978): 5–34.

Faure, Bernard. *The Rhetoric of Immediacy: A Cultural Critique of Chan/Zen Buddhism*. Princeton, N.J.: Princeton University Press, 1991.

Ferguson, R. Brian, and Neil L. Whitehead, eds. *War in the Tribal Zone*. Santa Fe: School of American Research Press, 1992.

Forage, Paul C. "Science, Technology, and War in Song China: Reflections in the *Brush Talks from the Dream Creek* by Shen Kuo (1031–1095)." Ph.D. dissertation, University of Toronto, 1991.

———. "The Sino-Tangut War of 1081–1085." *Journal of Asian History* 25, no. 1 (1991): 1–28.

Forte, Antonino. *Political Propaganda and Ideology in China at the End of the Seventh Century*. Napoli: Istituto Universitario Orientale, 1976.

Foulk, T. Griffith, and Robert H. Sharf. "On the Ritual Use of Ch'an Portraiture in Medieval China." *Cahiers d'Extrême Asie* 7 (1993): 149–219.

Franke, Herbert. *From Tribal Chieftain to Universal Emperor and God: The Legitimation of the Yüan Dynasty*. Munich: Verlag der Bayerischen Akademie der Wissenschaften, 1978.

Franke, Herbert, and Dennis Twitchett, eds. *The Cambridge History of China*. Vol. 6, *Alien Regimes and Border States, 907–1368*. Cambridge: Cambridge University Press, 1994.

Friedland, Paul. "A Reconstruction of Early Tangut History." Ph.D. dissertation, University of Washington, 1969.

Gernet, Jacques. *Daily Life in China on the Eve of the Mongol Invasion, 1250–1276*. Translated by H. M. Wright. Stanford, Calif.: Stanford University Press, 1962. Originally published as *La vie quotidienne en Chine à la veille de l'invasion mongole, 1250–1276* (Paris: Hachette, 1959).

Gills, Barry K., and Andre Gunder Frank. "The Cumulation of Accumulation: Theses and Research Agenda for 5000 Years of World System History." *Dialectical Anthropology* 15 (1990): 19–42.

Gong Hwang-cherng 龔煌城. "Xi Xia wen di yifu yu shengfu jiqi yansheng guocheng" 西夏文的意符與聲符及其衍生過程. *The Bulletin of the Institute of History and Philology* 56, pt. 4 (Taiwan, 1985): 719–758.

———. "Xi Xia wenzi yansheng guocheng di chongjian" 西夏文字衍生過程的重建. *Bulletin of the Institute of China Border Area Studies* 15 (Oct. 1984): 63–80.

———. "Chinese Elements in the Tangut Script." *The Bulletin of the Institute of History and Philology* 53, pt. 1 (Taiwan, 1982): 167–187.

Gorbacheva, Z. I., and E. I. Kychanov. *Tangutskie rukopisi i ksilografy*. Moscow: Izdatel'stvo vostochnoi literatury, 1963.

Gregory, Peter. *Tsung-mi and the Sinification of Buddhism*. Princeton, N.J.: Princeton University Press, 1991.

Grinstead, Eric, ed. *The Tangut Tripitaka*. 9 vols. Sata-Pitaka Series, vols. 83–91. New Delhi, 1973.

Gromkovskaia, L. L., and E. I. Kychanov. *Nikolai Aleksandrovich Nevskii*. Moscow: Nauka, 1978.

Grupper, Samuel M. "Qitan Cakravartin Monarchy and Its Qara-Qitai and Mongol Legacies." Draft manuscript. 1991.

Gu Jichen 顧吉辰. "Xi Xia houji zhidu kaoshu" 西夏后妃制度考述. *Ningxia shehui kexue* 寧夏社會科會 2 (1993): 70–75, 94.

Gu Zuyu 顧祖禹 (fl. 1660). *Dushi fangyu jiyao* 讀史方輿紀要. Letian renwen congshu edition. Reprint. Taipei: Letian chuban she, 1973.

Gule Maocai 骨勒茂才 (12th c.). *Fan Han heshi zhangzhong zhu* 番漢合時掌中珠. Ed. Huang Zhenhua 黃振華, Nie Hongyin 聶鴻音, and Shi Jinbo 史金波. Yinchuan: Ningxia renmin chuban she, 1989. See also the editions published in Nishida Tatsuo, *Seika go no kenkyū*

1:189–223 ("The Timely Pearl in the Palm"), and in Luc Kwanten, *The Timely Pearl*.
Hamilton, James R. *Les Ouigours à l'Époque des Cinq Dynasties d'après les documents chinois*. Paris: Presses Universitaires de France, 1955.
Han Yincheng 韓蔭晟. *Dangxiang yu Xi Xia ziliao huibian* 黨項與西夏資料滙編. Vol. 1. Yinchuan: Ningxia renmin chuban she, 1983.
Hane, Mikiso. *Premodern Japan*. Boulder, Colo.: Westview Press, 1991.
Hirakawa, Akira. "The Rise of Mahāyāna Buddhism and Its Relationship to the Worship of Stūpas." *Memoirs of the Research Department of the Toyo Bunko* 22 (Tokyo, 1963): 57–106.
Holmgren, Jennifer. "Imperial Marriage in the Native Chinese and Non-Han State, Han to Ming." In *Marriage and Inequality in Chinese Society*, ed. Rubie S. Watson and Patricia Buckley Ebrey, 58–96. Berkeley and Los Angeles: University of California Press, 1991.
———. "Marriage, Kinship and Succession under the Ch'i-tan Rulers of the Liao Dynasty." *T'oung Pao* 72, nos. 1–3 (1986): 44–91.
———. "Observations on Marriage and Inheritance Practices in Early Mongol and Yüan Society, with Particular Reference to the Levirate." *Journal of Asian History* 20, no. 2 (1986): 127–192.
Honey, David B. *The Rise of the Medieval Hsiung-nü: The Biography of Liu-Yüan*. Papers on Inner Asia, no. 15. Bloomington: Indiana University Research Institute for Inner Asian Studies, 1990.
Hopkins, Jeffrey. *Meditation on Emptiness*. London: Wisdom Publications, 1983.
Hu Ruli 胡汝礪, comp. *Ningxia xin zhi* 寧夏新志. Hongzhi 14 [1501] edition. Reprint. Taipei: Chengwen chuban she, 1968.
Hu Ruli, comp., and Guan Lu 管律, ed. *Jiajing Ningxia xin zhi* 嘉靖寧夏新志. Jiajing 19 [1540] edition. Reprint. Yinchuan: Ningxia renmin chuban she, 1982.
Huang Chi-chiang. "Imperial Rulership and Buddhism in the Early Northern Sung." In *Imperial Rulership and Cultural Change in Traditional China*, ed. Frederick P. Brandauer and Chun-chieh Huang. Seattle and London: University of Washington Press, 1994.
Huang Qinglan 黃慶瀾. *Chaomu kesong baihua jieshi* 朝暮課誦白話解釋. 3rd edition. Taipei: Fojiao chuban she, 1982.
Huang Qingyun 黃慶雲. "Guanyu Bei Song yu Xi Xia heyue zhong yin zhuan cha di shuliang wenti" 關於北宋與西夏和約中銀絹茶的數量問題. *Zhongxue lishi jiaoxue* 中學歷史教學 9 (1957): 19–20.
Huang Yuji 黃虞稷 (1629–1691). *Liao Jin Yuan yiwen zhi* 遼金元藝文志. Reprint. Taipei: Shijie shuju, 1963.
Huang Zhenhua 黃振華. "Ping Sulian jin sanshi nian di Xi Xia xue yanjiu" 評蘇聯近三十年的西夏學研究. *Shehui kexue zhanxian* 社會科學戰線 2 (1978): 311–323.
Hucker, Charles O. *A Dictionary of Official Titles in Imperial China*. Stanford: Stanford University Press, 1985.

Hummel, Arthur W., comp. *Eminent Chinese of the Ch'ing Period*. 2 vols. Washington, D.C.: Government Printing Office, 1943–1944.

Hurvitz, Leon, trans. *Scripture of the Lotus Blossom of the Fine Dharma (The Lotus Sutra)*. New York: Columbia University Press, 1976.

Iwasaki Tsutomu 岩崎力. "Sōdai kasai Chibetto zoku to bukkyō" 宋代河西チベット族と佛教. *Tōyōshi kenkyū* 東洋史研究 46, no. 1 (June 1987): 107–142. (A Chinese translation was published as "Songdai Hexi zangzu yu fojiao" 宋代河西藏族與佛教. *Xibei shidi* 西北史地 1 [1992]: 110–124; and an English version, "The Tibetan Tribes of Ho-hsi and Buddhism during the Northern Sung Period," appeared in *Acta Asiatica* 64 [Tokyo, 1993]: 17–37).

Jagchid, Sechin, and Van Jay Symons. *Peace, War, and Trade along the Great Wall*. Bloomington: Indiana University Press, 1989.

Jan Yün-hua. "Buddhist Relations between India and Sung China." *History of Religions* 6, no. 1 (August 1966): 24–42; 6, no. 2 (Nov. 1966): 135–168.

Jue'an 覺岸 (late Yuan). *Shishi jigu lüe* 釋氏稽古略. In T. 2037–4.

Kangxi zidian 康熙字典. Reprint. Beijing: Zhonghua shuju, 1958.

Kepping, K. B. "The 'Black-headed' and 'Red-faced' in Tangut Texts." Manuscript of forthcoming work.

———. "Elements of Ergativity and Nominativity in Tangut." In *Ergativity, Towards a Theory of Grammatical Relations*, ed. Frans Plank, 263–277. London and New York: Academic Press, 1979.

———. *Les kategorii: utrachennaia kitaiskaia leishu v tangutskom perevode*. Moscow: Nauka, 1983.

———. "The Name of the Tangut Empire." *T'oung Pao* vol. 80, pt. 4–5 (1994): 357–376.

———. "Tangut (Xixia) Degrees of Mourning." Trans. Ruth Dunnell. *Linguistics of the Tibeto-Burman Area* 14, no. 2 (fall 1991): 1–63.

Kirkland, Russell. "A World in Balance: Holistic Synthesis in the *T'ai-p'ing kuang-chi*." *Journal of Sung-Yuan Studies* 23 (1993): 43–70.

Kuan Ren 寬忍, ed. *Fojiao shouce* 佛教手冊. Beijing: Zhongguo wenshi chuban she, 1991.

Kwanten, Luc. *The Timely Pearl: A 12th Century Tangut Chinese Glossary*. Indiana University Uralic and Altaic Series, vol. 142. Bloomington: Research Institute for Inner Asian Studies, 1982.

Kychanov, Ergenii Ivanovich. "Buddhism and State in Hsi Hsia from Juridical Aspect." *Acta Orientalia Hungarica* 34, nos. 1–3 (1980): 105–111.

———. "From the History of the Tangut Translation of the Buddhist Canon." In *Tibetan and Buddhist Studies Commemorating the 200th Anniversary of the Birth of Alexander Csoma de Körös*, ed. Louis Ligeti, 1:377–387. Budapest: Akadémiai Kiadó, 1984.

———. "Gimn sviashchennym predkam tangutov." In *Pis'mennye pamiatniki vostoka, 1968*, 217–231. Moscow: Nauka, 1970.

———."Gosudarstvo i buddizm v Si Sia." In *Buddizm i gosudarstvo na dal'nem vostoke*, ed. L. P. Deliusin, 130–145. Moscow: Nauka, 1987.

———. *Izmenennyi i zanovo utverzhdennyi kodeks deviza tsarstvovaniia nebesnoe protsvetanie (1149–1169)*. 4 vols. Moscow: Nauka, 1987–1989.

———. "'Krupinki zolota na ladoni'—posobie dlia izucheniia tangutskovo pis'mennosti." In *Zhanry i stili literatur Kitaia i Korei*, ed. B. B. Vakhtin and I. S. Lisevich, 213–222. Moscow: Nauka, 1969.

———. "Monuments of Tangut Legislation (12–13th Centuries)." In *Études Tibétaines*, Actes due XXIXe congrès international des Orientalistes, July 1973, 29–42. Paris: Asiathèque, 1976.

———. "Ob odnom obriade religii bon sokhranivshemsia v buddiiskikh ritualakh tangutov." *Kratkie soobshcheniia instituta etnografii ANSSSR* 35 (1960): 86–90.

———. "Pravovoe polozhenie Buddiiskikh obshchin v tangutskom gosudarstve." In *Buddizm, gosudarstvo i obshchestvo v stranakh tsentral'noi i vostochnoi Azii v srednie veka*, ed. G. M. Bongard-Levin et al., 28–62. Moscow: Nauka, 1982.

———. "Tangutskie istochniki o gosudarstvenno-apparate Si Sya." *Kratkie soobshcheniye instituta narodov Azii* 69 (1965): 180–196, 210–218.

———. *Tangutskie rukopisi i ksilografy*. Vol. 2: *Buddiiskie sochineniia*. Manuscript of forthcoming work.

———. "Tangutskii gvon." *Pis'mennye pamiatniki i problemy istorii i kul'tury narodov vostoka* 1:35–39. Proceedings of the 13th annual scholarly session of the Leningrad branch of the Institute of Oriental Studies. Moscow, 1977.

———. "Tibetans and Tibetan Culture in the Tangut State of Hsi Hsia (982–1227)." In *Proceedings of the Csoma de Körös Memorial Symposium (1976)*, ed. Louis Ligeti, 205–211. Bibliotheca Orientalis Hungarica, vol. 23. Budapest: Akadémiai Kiadó, 1978.

———. *Vnov' sobrannye dragotsennye parnye izrecheniia*. Moscow: Nauka, 1974.

———. "Xian gei Xi Xia wenzi chuangzao zhe di songshi" 獻給西夏文字創造者的頌詩. In *Zhongguo minzu shi yanjiu* 中國民族史研究, ed. Bai Bin et al., 144–155. Beijing: Zhongyang minzu xueyuan chuban she, 1989.

Lancaster, Lewis R. *The Korean Buddhist Canon, a Descriptive Catalogue*. Berkeley and Los Angeles: University of California Press, 1979.

Lancaster, Lewis R., and C. S. Yu, eds. *Introduction of Buddhism to Korea: New Cultural Patterns*. Berkeley: Asian Humanities Press, 1989.

Laufer, Berthold. "Loan Words in Tibetan." In *Sino-Tibetan Studies* 2:483–632. New Delhi: Rakesh Goel, 1987.

Ledderose, Lothar. "Chinese Prototypes of the Pagoda." In *The Stūpa: Its Religious, Historical and Architectural Significance*, ed. Anna Libera Dallapiccola, 238–247. Beiträge zur Südasienforschung Südasien-Institut Universität Heidelberg 55. Wiesbaden: Franz Steiner Verlag, 1980.

Li Fanwen 李范文. *Tongyin yanjiu* 同音研究. Yinchuan: Ningxia renmin chuban she, 1986.

———. "Xi Xia guanjie fenghao biao kaoshi" 西夏官階封號表考釋. *Shehui kexue zhanxian* 社會科學戰綫 3 (1991): 171–179.

———. (Bu Ping 卜平). "Xi Xia huangdi chenghao kao" 西夏皇帝稱號考. *Ningxia shehui kexue* 寧夏社會科學 (1981): 70–82. Reprint in Li Fanwen, *Xi Xia yanjiu lunji* 西夏研究論集, 76–99. Yinchuan: Ningxia renmin chuban she, 1983.

Li Fanwen, comp. *Xi Xia lingmu chutu canbei cuibian* 西夏陵墓出土殘碑粹編. Beijing: Wenwu chuban she, 1984.

Li Tao 李燾 (1115–1184). *Xu zizhi tongjian changbian* 續資治通鑑長編. *Xinding* edition, 1961; reprint Taipei: Shijie shuju, 1974.

Li Wei 李蔚. "Xi Xia fanguan chuyi" 西夏蕃官芻議. In his *Xi Xia shi yanjiu* 西夏史研究, 64–74. Yinchuan: Ningxia renmin chuban she, 1989.

Li Yuan 李遠. *Qingtang lu* 清塘錄. In *Shuofu* 説郛 35:11b–13a, comp. Tao Zongyi 陶宗儀. Huafen lou edition. Facsim. repro. Taipei: Commercial Press, 1972.

Ligeti, Louis. "Le mérite d'ériger un *stūpa* et l'histoire de l'éléphant d'or." In *Proceedings of the Csoma de Körös Memorial Symposium*, ed. Louis Ligeti, 223–284. Bibliotheca Orientalis Hungarica, vol. 23. Budapest: Akadémiai Kiadó, 1978.

Linrothe, Robert N. "Compassionate Malevolence: Wrathful Deities in Esoteric Buddhist Art." Ph.D. dissertation, University of Chicago, 1992.

———. "Renzong and the Patronage of Tangut Buddhist Art: The Stūpa and the Ushnīshavijayā Cult." Manuscript of forthcoming work.

Liu Jianli 劉建麗 and Tang Kaijian 湯開建, comps. *Songdai Tufan shiliao ji* 宋代吐蕃史料集. Vol. 2. Chengdu: Sichuan minzu chuban she, 1989.

Liu Xinru. *Ancient India and Ancient China: Trade and Religious Exchanges, A.D. 1–600*. Delhi: Oxford University Press, 1988.

———. "Buddhist Institutions in the Lower Yangtze during the Sung Dynasty." *Bulletin of Sung-Yuan Studies* 21 (1989): 31–51.

Liu Xu 劉昫 et al., comps. *Jiu Tang shu* 舊唐書. Beijing: Zhonghua shuju, 1987.

Liu Yuquan 劉玉權. "Guanyu Shazhou Huihu dongku di huafen" 關於沙州回鶻洞窟的劃分. *Dunhuang yanjiu* 敦煌研究 2 (1988): 2–4.

Lopez, Donald S., Jr. *Religions of China in Practice*. Princeton, N.J.: Princeton University Press, 1996.

———. *A Study of Svātantrika*. Ithaca, N.Y.: Snow Lion Publications, 1987.
Luo Fuyi 羅福頤. *Xi Xia wencun* 西夏文存. N.p., 1935.
Lynn, John A. "Clio in Arms: The Role of the Military Variable in Shaping History." *The Journal of Military History* 55 (Jan. 1991): 83–95.
Macdonell, Arthur A. *A Sanskrit Grammar for Students*, 3rd ed. 1927. Reprint. Oxford: Oxford University Press, 1987.
Maeda Masana 前田正名. *Kasai no rekishi chiri gakuteki kenkyū* 河西の歷史地理學的研究. Tokyo: Yoshikawa Kōbunkan, 1964.
Mair, Victor. "Perso-Turkic *Bakshi* = Mandarin *Po-shih*: Learned Doctor." In *Journal of Turkish Studies*, Richard Nelson Frye Festschrift I, vol. 16 (1992): 117–127.
———. Review of "Lexicon of Reconstructed Pronunciation in Early Middle Chinese, Late Middle Chinese, and Early Mandarin" by Edwin G. Pulleyblank. *Sino-Platonic Papers* 31 (October 1991): 37–39.
———. "*Tufan and Tulufan*: The Origins of the Old Chinese Names for Tibet and Turfan." *Central and Inner Asian Studies* 4 (1990): 14–70.
———. *Tun-huang Popular Narratives*. Cambridge Studies in Chinese History, Literature and Institutions. Cambridge: Cambridge University Press, 1983.
Mannerheim, C. G. *Across Asia from West to East in 1906–1908*. 2 vols. Osterhout, The Netherlands: Anthropological Publications, 1969.
Mathews, R. H. *Mathews' Chinese-English Dictionary*. Revised American ed. Taipei: Maling chuban she, 1972.
McCullough, William H. "Japanese Marriage Institutions in the Heian Period." *Harvard Journal of Asiatic Studies* 27 (1967): 103–167.
Men'shikov, Lev Nicolaevich. *Opisanie kitaiskoi chasti kollektsii iz Khara-Khoto (fond P. K. Kozlova)*. Moscow: Nauka, 1984.
Miao Quansun 繆荃孫 (1844–1919). *Liao wencun* 遼文存. 1896. Reprint. Taipei: Chengwen chuban she, 1967.
Mikkyō Jiten Hensankai 密教辭典編纂會, comp. *Mikkyō daijiten* 密教大辭典. 6 vols. Kyoto: Hōzōkan, 1969–1970.
Mochizuki Shinkō 望月信亨, ed. *Bukkyō daijiten* 佛教大辭典. 7 vols. 6th edition. Tokyo: Sekai seikei kankō kyōkai, 1972.
Molè, Gabriella. *The T'u-yü-hun from the Northern Wei to the Time of the Five Dynasties*. Rome: Istituto Italiano per il Medio ed Estremo Oriente, 1970.
Morohashi Tetsuji 諸橋轍次, comp. *Dai kanwa jiten* 大漢和辭典. 13 vols. Tokyo: Taishūkan shoten, 1955–1960.
Mote, Frederick, and Denis Twitchett, eds. *The Cambridge History of China*, volume 7: *The Ming*. Cambridge: Cambridge University Press, 1988.
Nakajima Satoshi 中嶋敏. "Seika jidai no Sashū" 西夏時代の沙州. In

Tonkō no rekishi 敦煌の歴史, *Kōza Tonkō* 講座敦煌 2, ed. Enoki Kazuo 榎一雄, 357–361. Tokyo: Daitō shuppansha, 1980.

Nakamura Hajime 中村元. *Zhongguo fojiao fazhan shi* 中國佛教發展史. 3 vols. Translated by Yu Wanju 余萬居. Taipei: Tianhua chuban shiye banfen youxian gongsi, 1984.

Nattier, Jan. *Once Upon a Future Time: Studies in a Buddhist Prophecy of Decline.* Berkeley: Asian Humanities Press, 1991.

Nevskii, N.A. *Tangutskaia filologiia.* 2 vols. Moscow: Izdat, Vostochnoi Literatury, 1960.

Nie, Hongyin. "Tangutology during the Past Decades." *Monumenta Serica* 41 (1993): 329–347.

Ningxia Huizu zizhiqu wenwu guanli weiyuanhui bangongshi 寧夏回族自治區文物管理委員會辦公室. "Ningxia Helanxian Baisikou shuangta kance weixiu jianbao" 寧夏賀縣拜寺口双塔勘測維修簡報. *Wenwu* 文物 8 (1991): 14–26.

Nishida Tatsuo. Review of E. I. Kychanov, *Ocherk istorii tangutskogo gosudarstva.* *Tōyōshi kenkyū* 東洋史研究 28, nos. 2–3 (1969): 120–126.

Nishida Tatsuo 西田龍雄. *Seika go no kenkyū* 西夏語の研究. Vol. 1. Kyoto: Zayūhō kankōkai, 1964.

———. "Seika go 'Tsukizuki rakushi' no kenkyū" 西夏語「月々樂詩」の研究. *Kyōto daigaku bungakubu kenkyū kiyō* 京都大學文學部研究紀要 25 (Showa 61 [1987]): 1–116.

———. *Seika mon kegonkyō* 西夏文華嚴經, *The Hsi-Hsia Avatamsaka Sūtra.* 3 vols. Kyoto: Kyoto University Faculty of Letters, 1975–1977.

Niu Dasheng 牛達生. "'Jiajing Ningxia xin zhi' zhong di liangbian Xi Xia yiwen" "嘉靖寧夏新志" 中的兩篇西夏佚文. *Ningxia daxue xuebao* 寧夏大學學報 4 (1980): 44–49.

Nomura Hiroshi 野村博. "Seikago yaku kei shi kenkyū (I)—Seikago bunken ('nusugi') yori mita Ri Gen-ko no yaku sei jigyō ni tsuite" 西夏語譯經史研究 (I) — 西夏語文獻 ('盜聞') よりみた李元昊の譯經事業について. *Bukkyō shi gaku kenkyū* 佛教史學研究 19, no. 2 (1977): 71–120.

The Nyingma Edition of the sDe-dge bKa'-'gyur/bsTan'-gyur, Research Catalogue and Bibliography. 8 vols. Oakland, Calif.: Dharma Press, 1982.

Okazaki Seirō 岡崎精郎. *Tangūto kodai shi kenkyū* タングート古代史研究. Kyoto: Kyōto daigaku tōyōshi kenkyū kai, 1972.

Ono Gemmyō 小野玄妙. *Bussho kaisetsu daijiten* 佛書解説大辭典. 12 vols. Tokyo: Daitō shuppansha, 1931–1936.

Orlando, Raffaello. "A Study of Chinese Documents Concerning the Life of the Tantric Buddhist Patriarch Amoghavajra (A.D. 705–774)." Ph.D. dissertation, Princeton University, 1981.

Orzech, Charles. "Puns on the Humane King: Analogy and Application in an East Asian Apocryphon." *Journal of the American Oriental Society* 109, no. 1 (Jan.–March 1989): 17–24.

Ouyang Xiu 歐陽修 (1017–1072). *Ouyang Xiu quanji* 歐陽修全集. Reprinted in Zhongguo xueshu mingzhu wenxue ming zhu, 3rd ser., ed. Yang Jialuo. 2 vols. Taipei: Shijie shuju, 1961.

Ouyang Xiu and Song Qi 宋祁 (998–1061). *Xin Tang shu* 新唐書. Bona edition; reprint Beijing: Zhonghua shuju, 1975.

Pelliot, Paul. *Notes on Marco Polo.* Vol. 1. Paris: Inprimerie Nationale, 1959.

Peng Baichuan 彭百川 (fl. 1113). *Taiping zhiji tonglei* 太平治蹟統類. Reprinted in vol. 10 of Shiyuan congshu, ed. Zhang Junheng. Taipei: Chengwen chuban she, 1966.

Pinks, Elizabeth. *Die Uiguren von Kan-chou in der frühen Sung-zeit.* Wiesbaden: Otto Harrassowitz, 1968.

Piotrovsky, Mikhail, ed. *Lost Empire of the Silk Road: Buddhist Art from Khara Khoto (X–XIIIth century).* Milan: Electa and Thyssen-Bornemisza Foundation, 1993.

Pulleyblank, Edwin G. *Lexicon of Reconstructed Pronunciation in Early Middle Chinese, Late Middle Chinese, and Early Mandarin.* Vancouver: UBC Press, 1991.

———. Response to Victor Mair's Review of *Lexicon of Reconstructed Pronunciation.* Sino-Platonic Papers 35 (November 1992): 32–37.

Rawski, Evelyn S. "Music and Rulership in Qing Accession Rituals during the Seventeenth and Eighteenth Centuries." Paper presented at the Faculty Seminar of the Center for Chinese Studies, University of Michigan, 17 March 1993.

Rhie, Marylin M., and Robert A. F. Thurman. *Wisdom and Compassion: The Sacred Art of Tibet.* New York: Asian Art Museum of San Francisco and Tibet House of New York, with Harry N. Abrams, Inc., 1991.

Rogers, Michael C. *The Chronicle of Fu Chien: A Case of Exemplar History.* Berkeley and Los Angeles: University of California Press, 1968.

Rossabi, Morris, ed. *China among Equals: The Middle Kingdom and Its Neighbors, 10th–14th Centuries.* Berkeley and Los Angeles: University of California Press, 1983.

Roth, Gustav. "Symbolism of the Buddhist Stūpa." In *The Stūpa: Its Religious, Historical and Architectural Significance*, ed. Anna Livera Dallapiccola, 183–209. Beiträge zur Südasienforschung Südasien-Institut Universität Heidelberg 55. Wiesbaden: Franz Steiner Verlag, 1980.

Sancai zazi 三才雜字. Tangut edition of the classified word list *Zazi* (see Shi Jinbo, "Xi Xia Han wen ben 'Zazi' chutan"); transcription of ms. in the St. Petersburg archive (TRK 23 inv. 2535b), in the possession of Shi Jinbo.

Satō, Chisui. "The Character of Yün-kang Buddhism: A Look at the Emergence of a State-Supported Religion in China under the Northern Wei." *The Memoirs of the Toyo Bunko* 36 (1978): 38–83.

Edward H. Schafer. "Notes on T'ang Culture, III." *Monumenta Serica* 30 (1972–1973): 100–103.

Schopen, Gregory. "Monks and the Relic Cult in the *Mahāparinibbānasutta*: An Old Misunderstanding in Regard to Monastic Buddhism." In *From Benares to Beijing: Essays on Buddhism and Chinese Religions in Honour of Prof. Jan Yün-hua*, ed. Koichi Shinohara and Gregory Schopen, 187–201. Oakville, Ont.: Mosaic Press, 1991.

——. "The Phrase 'sa prthivīpradeśaś caityabhūto bhavet' in the *Vajracchedikā*: Notes on the Cult of the Book in Mahāyāna." *Indo-Iranian Journal* 17 (1975): 147–181.

Seaman, Gary. *Journey to the North: An Ethnohistorical Analysis and Annotated Translation of the Chinese Folk Novel* Pei-yu Chi. Berkeley and Los Angeles: University of California Press, 1987.

Serruys, Henry. "The Mongols of Kansu during the Ming." *Mélanges chinois et bouddhiques* 10 (1952–1955): 215–346.

Shen Kuo 沈括 (1031?–1095). *Mengqi bitan jiaozheng* 夢溪筆談校證. Ed. Hu Daojing 胡道靜. Beijing, 1957. Reprint. Taipei: Shijie shuju, 1965.

Shenseng zhuan 神僧傳. T. 2064. Ming, prefaced by Yongle emperor.

Shi Jinbo 史金波. "Liangzhou Ganying ta bei Xi Xia wen jiaoyi buzheng" 涼州感應塔碑西夏文校譯補正. *Xibei shidi* 西北史地 2 (1984): 47–51.

——. *Xi Xia fojiao shilüe* 西夏佛教史略. Yinchuan: Ningxia renmin chuban she, 1988.

——. "Xi Xia Han wen ben 'Zazi' chutan" 西夏漢文木"雜字"初探. In *Zhongguo minzu shi yanjiu* 中國民族史研究 2, ed. Bai Bin et al., 167–185. Beijing: Zhongyang minzu xueyuan chuban, 1989.

——. "Xi Xia jingnei minzu kao" 西夏境內民族考. In *Qingzhu Wang Zhonghan xiansheng bashi shou chen xueshu lun wenji* 慶祝王鍾翰先生八十壽辰學術論文集, 407–417. Liaoning: Liaoning daxue chuban she, 1993.

——. "Xi Xia wen 'guanjie fenghao biao' kaoshi" 西夏文"官階封號表"考釋. In *Zhongguo minzu gu wenzi yanjiu* 中國民族古文字研究, ed. Zhongguo minzu gu wenzi yanjiu hui, 245–266. Tianjin: Tianjin guji chuban she, 1991.

——. *Xi Xia wenhua* 西夏文化. Changchun: Jilin jiaoyu chuban she, 1987.

——. "Xi Xia wen 'Jin guangming zuisheng wang jing' xuba kao" 西夏文"金光明最勝王經"序跋考. *Shijie zongjiao yanjiu* 世界宗教研究 3 (1983): 45–53.

———. "'Xi Xia yijing tu' jie" "西夏譯經圖"解. *Wenxian* 文獻 1 (1979): 215–229.

Shi Jinbo, Bai Bin 白濱, and Huang Zhenhua 黃振華. *Wenhai yanjiu* 文海研究. Beijing: Zhongguo shehui kexue chuban she, 1983.

Shi Jinbo, Bai Bin, and Wu Fengyun 吳峰云, eds. *Xi Xia wenwu* 西夏文物. Beijing: Wenwu chuban she, 1988.

Shi Jinbo, Huang Zhenhua, and Nie Hongyin, eds. *Xi Xia Tiansheng lüling* 西夏天盛律令. Volume 5 in the series on Chinese law, *Zhongguo zhenxi falü dianji jicheng* 中國珍稀法律典籍集成, ed. Liu Hainian and Yang Yifan (Beijing: Kexue chuban she, 1994).

Shi Jinbo et al. "Xi Xia wen 'Tiansheng xinlü' jinlü biao kaoshi" 西夏文"天盛新律"進律表考釋. In *Xi Xia wen shi luncong* 西夏文史論叢, ed. Ningxia wenwu guanli weiyuan hui and Ningxia wenhua ting wenwu chu, 96–111. Yinchuan: Ningxia renmin chuban she, 1992.

Shi Jinbo and Huang Zhenhua. "Xi Xia wen zidian 'Yin tong' di banben yu jiaokan" 西夏文字典"音同"的版本與校勘. *Minzu guji* 民族古籍. 1 (1986): 17–27.

Shu Xincheng 舒新城 et al., comps. *Cihai* 辭海. 2 vols. 1936–1937. Reprint (2 vols. in one). Hong Kong: Zhonghua shuju, 1947.

Sima Guang 司馬光 (1019–1086). *Sushui jiwen* 涑水記聞. Reprinted in *Congshu jicheng jian bian*, ed. Wang Yunwu, vol. 131. Taipei: Shangwu yinshu guan, 1966.

———. *Xin jiao zizhi tongjian zhu* 新校資治通鑑注. Commentary by Hu Sanxing 胡三省. Text criticism by Zhang Yu 章鈺. Reprint. Taipei: Shijie shuju, 1977.

Snellgrove, David. *Indo-Tibetan Buddhism: Indian Buddhists and Their Tibetan Successors*. 2 vols. Boston, Mass.: Shambhala, 1987.

Snodgrass, Adrian. *The Symbolism of the Stūpa*. Delhi: Motilal, 1992.

Sofronov, M. V. *Grammatika tangutskogo iazyka*. 2 vols. Moscow: Nauka, 1968.

Song dazhao lingji 宋大詔令集. Anon; ca. 1131–1162. Reprint. Beijing: Zhonghua shuju, 1962.

Soothill, William E., and Lewis Hodous. *A Dictionary of Chinese Buddhist Terms*. 1934. Reprint. Taipei: Ch'eng Wen Publishing Co., 1975.

Spence, Jonathan D. *The Search for Modern China*. New York: Norton, 1990.

Sperling, Elliot. "Lama to the King of Hsia." *The Journal of the Tibet Society* 7 (1987): 31–50.

Sponberg, Alan, and Helen Hardacre, eds. *Maitreya, the Future Buddha*. Cambridge: Cambridge University Press, 1988.

Stein, R.A. "Mi-ñag et Si-hia: Géographie historique et légendes ancestrales." *Bulletin de l'École Française d'Extrême-Orient* 44, no. 1 (1947–1950): 223–265.

———. "'Saint et Devin,' un titre tibétain et chinois des rois tibétains." *Journal asiatique* 269, nos. 1–2 (1981): 231–275.

———. *Tibetan Civilization.* Trans. J. E. Stapleton. Stanford, Calif.: Stanford University Press, 1972. Originally published as *La Civilization tibétaine* (Paris: Dunod Editeur, 1962).

Strickmann, Michel. Review of *Political Propaganda and Ideology in China at the End of the Seventh Century*, by Antonino Forte. *The Eastern Buddhist*, n.s., 10, no. 1 (May 1977): 136–153.

Strong, John. *The Legend of King Aśoka: A Study and Translation of the Aśokāvadāna.* Princeton, N.J.: Princeton University Press, 1983.

Sun Xiushen 孫修身 and Dang Shoushan 黨壽山. "'Liangzhou Yushan shifo ruixiang yinyuan ji' kaoshi" "涼州御山石佛瑞像因緣記"考釋. *Dunhuang yanjiu* 敦煌研究 3 (1983): 102–107.

Takakusu Junjiro 高楠順次郎 and Kaikyoku Watanabe 渡辺海旭. *Taishō shinshū daizōkyō* 大正新修大藏經. Tokyo: Daizō shuppan kabushiki kaisha, 1924–1934.

Tang Kaijian 湯開建. "Xi Xia shi zhaji" 西夏史札記. In *Zhongguo minzu shi yanjiu* 中國民族史研究 2, ed. Bai Bin et al., 186–200. Beijing: Zhongyang minzu xueyuan chuban, 1989.

Tang Kaijian and Liu Jianli, comps. *Songdai Tufan shiliao ji* 宋代吐蕃史料集. Vol 1. Chengdu: Sichuan minzu chuban she, 1986.

Tao, Jing-shen. *Two Sons of Heaven: Studies in Sung-Liao Relations.* Tucson: University of Arizona Press, 1988.

Teiser, Stephen F. *The Ghost Festival in Medieval China.* Princeton, N.J.: Princeton University Press, 1988.

Tsong-ka-pa. *Tantra in Tibet: The Great Exposition of Secret Mantra.* Trans. and ed. Jeffrey Hopkins. Introduction by His Holiness the Fourteenth Dalai Lama. The Wisdom of Tibet Series 3. London: Unwin and Allen, 1977; Reprint. Ithaca, N.Y.: Snow Lion Publications, 1987.

Tuotuo 脱脱 et al., comps. *Liaoshi* 遼史. 1344; reprint Shangwu yinshu guan Bona edition; reprint Beijing: Zhonghua shuju, 1974.

Tuotuo et al., comps. *Jinshi* 金史. 1344; reprint Shangwu yinshu guan Bona edition; reprint Beijing: Zhonghua shuju, 1975.

Tuotuo et al., comps. *Songshi* 宋史. 1345; Xinjiao edition. Zhongguo xueshu leibian. Ed. Yang Jialuo. Reprint. Taipei: Dingwen shuju, 1978.

Twitchett, Denis C. "The Khitan and the Liao Dynasty." In *The Cambridge History of China*, volume 6, ed. Herbert Franke and Denis Twitchett. Cambridge: Cambridge University Press, 1994.

Twitchett, Denis C., ed. *The Cambridge History of China*, volume 3: *Sui and T'ang China, 589–906.* Cambridge: Cambridge University Press, 1979.

Ui Hakuju 宇井伯壽, Suzuki Munetada 鈴木宗忠, Kanakura Yenshō 金倉

圓照, and Tada Tōkan 多田等觀, eds. *A Complete Catalogue of the Tibetan Buddhist Canons (Bkan-hgyur and Bstan-hgyur)*. Sendai, Japan: Tōhoku Imperial University and Saitō Gratitude Foundation, 1934.

Uray, Géza. "The Annals of the 'A-Ža Principality: The Problems of Chronology and Genre of the Stein Document, Tun-huang, vol. 69, fol. 84." In *Proceedings of the Csoma de Körös Memorial Symposium (1976)*, ed. Louis Ligeti, 541–578. Budapest: Akadémiai Kiadó, 1978.

Visser, M. W. de. *Ancient Buddhism in Japan: Sūtras and Ceremonies in Use in the Seventh and Eighth Centuries A.D. and Their History in Later Times*. Vol. 1. Paris: Librairie Orientaliste Paul Geuthner, 1928.

Wang Chang 王旭 (1725–1806). *Jinshi cuibian* 金石萃編. Shike shiliao xin bian *di yi ji* edition. Taipei: Xinwenfeng shuban, 1982.

Wang Cheng 王稱 (d. ca. 1200). *Dongdu shilüe* 東都事略. Reprinted in *Songshi ziliao cuibian*, 1, comp. Zhao Tiehan, vols. 11–14. Taipei: Wenhai chuban she, 1967.

Wang Jingru. "Xin jian Xi Xia wen shike he Dunhuang Anxi dongku Xia Han wen tiji kaoshi" 新見西夏文石刻和敦煌安西洞窟夏漢文題記考釋. In *Wang Guowei xueshu yanjiu lunji* 王國維學術研究論集, ed. Wu Ze 吳泽, vol. 1. Shanghai: Huadong shifan daxue, 1983.

———. 王靜如. *Xi Xia yanjiu* 西夏研究. Vol. 1. Beiping: Guoli zhongyang yanjiu yuan lishi yuyan yanjiu suo, 1930.

Wang Renjun 王仁俊 (1866–1913). *Xi Xia yiwen zhi* 西夏藝文志 (1904–1905). Appended to Huang Yuji 黃虞稷 (1629–1691). *Liao Jin Yuan yiwen zhi* 遼金元藝文志. Reprint Taipei: Shijie shuju, 1963. Also in Ershiwu shi kanxing weiyuanhui. *Ershiwu shi bubian* 二十五史補編 6:8029. Shanghai: Kaiming shudian, 1937.

Wang Yao 王堯. "Xi Xia Heishui qiao bei kaobu" 西夏黑水橋碑考補. *Zhongyang minzu xueyuan xuebao* 中央民族學院學報 1 (1978): 51–63.

Wechsler, Howard J. *Offerings of Jade and Silk: Ritual and Legitimation in the T'ang Dynasty*. New Haven and London: Yale University Press, 1985.

Weinstein, Stanley. *Buddhism under the T'ang*. Cambridge: Cambridge University Press, 1987.

———. "Imperial Patronage in T'ang Buddhism." In *Perspectives on the T'ang*, ed. Arthur Wright and Denis Twitchett, 265–306. New Haven: Yale University Press, 1973.

Whitfield, Roderick. "Esoteric Buddhist Elements in the Famensi Reliquary Deposit." *Asiatische Studien* 44, no. 2 (1990): 247–258, illus.

Williams, Paul. *Mahāyāna Buddhism: The Doctrinal Foundations*. London and New York: Routledge, 1989.

Wittfogel, Karl A., and Feng Chia-sheng. *History of Chinese Society, Liao (907–1125). Transactions of the American Philosophical Society*, n.s., 36 (1946). Philadelphia: The American Philosophical Society, 1949.

Wright, Arthur. *Buddhism in Chinese History*. Stanford, Calif: Stanford University Press, 1959.

———. "The Formation of Sui Ideology, 581–604." In *Chinese Thought and Institutions*, ed. John K. Fairbank, 71–104. Chicago: University of Chicago Press, 1957.

Wu Fengyun 吳峰云. "Xi Xia lingyuan ji qi jianzhu tedian" 西夏陵園及其建築特點. *Ningxia wenwu* 寧夏文物 1 (1986): 26–31; republished in Shi Jinbo, Bai Bin, and Wu Fengyun, eds. *Xi Xia wenwu*, 1–8.

Wu Guangcheng 吳廣成. *Xi Xia shushi* 西夏書事. Preface dated 1826. Reprint. Taipei: Guangwen shuju, 1968.

Wu Tianchi 吳天墀. *Xi Xia shigao* 西夏史稿. Rev. ed. Chengdu: Sichuan renmin chuban she, 1980.

Wylie, Turrell. "A Standard System of Tibetan Transcription." *Harvard Journal of Asiatic Studies* 22 (1959): 261–267.

Xi Xia wen zhuanhao 西夏文專號. Special issue of the *Bulletin of the National Library of Peiping* 國立北平圖書館館刊 4, no. 3 (May–June 1930; Jan. 1932).

Xiandai Hanyu cidian 現代漢語詞典. Ed. Zhongguo kexue yuan yuyan cidian bianji 中國科學院語言詞典編輯. Hong Kong: Commercial Press, 1977.

Xie Zhongguang 謝重光 and Bai Wengu 白文固. *Zhongguo sengguan zhidu shi* 中國僧官制度史. Xining: Qinghai renmin chuban she, 1990.

Xing Jun 行均 (fl. 997). *Longkan shoujing* 龍龕手鑑. Reprint. Beijing: Zhonghua shuju chuban she, 1985.

Xu Song 徐松 (1781–1848), ed. *Song huiyao jigao* 宋會要輯稿. Photographic rpt. Beiping: Beiping tushu guan, 1936. Reprint. Taipei: Xinwen feng chuban, 1975.

Xu zangjing 續藏經. Reprint of *Dai Nihon zokuzōkyō* 大日本續藏經. Ed. Yoneda Mujō et al. Kyoto: Zōkyō shoin, 1905–1912. Shanghai: Hanfenlou, 1923.

Yan Kejun 嚴可均 (1762–1843). *Tieqiao jinshi ba* 鐵橋金石跋. Shike shiliao congshu edition. Reprint. Taipei: Yiwen yinshu guan, 1966.

Yang Hsüan-chih. *A Record of Buddhist Monasteries in Lo-yang*. Translated by Yi-t'ung Wang. Princeton, N.J.: Princeton University Press, 1984.

Yu Qian 喻謙 (Wei'an 昧菴), comp. *Xin xu gaoseng zhuan siji* 新續高僧傳四集. N.p.: Beiyang yinshua ju, 1923. Reprint. Taipei: Liuli jingfang, 1967.

Zahler, Leah, and Jeffrey Hopkins, eds. and trans. *Meditative States in Tibetan Buddhism*. London: Wisdom Publications, 1983.

Zang Lihe 臧勵龢 et al., comps. *Zhongguo gujin diming da zidian* 中國古今地名辭典. 3rd edition. Taipei: Commercial Press, 1972.

Zeng Gong 會鞏 (1019–1083). *Longping ji* 隆平集. Reprinted in *Songshi ziliao cuibian* 1, comp. Zhao Tiehan, vols. 9–10. Taipei: Wenhai chuban she, 1967.

Zhang Guangda and Rong Xinjiang. "Les noms du Royaume de Khotan." In *Contributions aux études de Touen-Houang*, vol. 3, ed. Michel Soymié, 23–46. Paris: École Française d'Extrême-Orient, 1984.

Zhang Jincheng 張金城 (fl. 1776), comp., and Yang Huanyu 楊浣雨, ed. *Ningxia fuzhi* 寧夏府志. Qianlong 45 (1780) edition. Reprint. Taipei: Chengwen chuban she, 1968.

Zhang Shu 張樹 (1781–1847). *Liangzhou fuzhi beikao* 涼州府志備考. 3 vols. Wuwei: Wuwei shi shi zhi bianzuan weiyuan hui bangongshi jiao yin, 1986.

———. *Yangsu tang wenji* 養素堂文集. Donghua shuju kanben, 1837 (Daoguang 17).

Zhang Siwen 張思溫. "Gansu sheng Yongchang xian Houda si (Shengrong si) liu ti wenzi shike" 甘肅省永昌縣后大寺(聖容寺)六體文字石刻. *Xibei minzu yanjiu* 西北民族研究 2 (1989): 210–212.

Zhang Tingyu 張廷玉 (1672–1755) et al., eds. *Ming shi* 明史. Bona edition. Reprint Beijing: Zhonghua shuju, 1974.

Zhang Wei 張維 (1891–?). *Longyou jinshi lu* 隴右金史錄. Gansu sheng wenxian ji weiyuan hui, 1943.

Zhang Zhijun 張之浚, Zhang Qimei 張玘美, et al., comps. *Wuliang kaozhi liu de ji quanji* 五涼考治六德集全集, preface dated Qianlong 40 (1775–1776).

Zhiguang 智廣 and Huizhen 慧真, comps. *Mizhou yuanyin wangsheng ji* 密呪圓因往生集 (1200). T. 1956.

Zhipan 志磐 (fl. 1258–1269), comp. *Fozu tongji* 佛祖統紀. T. 2035.

Zhong Gengqi 鍾賡起, comp. *Ganzhou fuzhi* 甘州府志. Qianlong 44 (1779) woodblock edition. Reprint. Taipei: Chengwen chuban she, 1976.

Zhonghua da zangjing 中華大藏經. Taipei: Xiuding Zhonghua da zangjing hui, 1968.

Zürcher, Erich. *The Buddhist Conquest of China*. 2 vols. Leiden: E. J. Brill, 1972.

———. "'Prince Moonlight': Messianism and Eschatology in Early Medieval Chinese Buddhism." *T'oung Pao* 68, nos. 1–3 (1982): 1–75.

Index

Akṣobhya, 32, 190 n. 31
Aligu, xxiii–xxix, 75, 77. *See also* Qingtang
Amoghavajra (705–774), 22, 32, 89, 95, 186 nn. 54, 56
Anquan State Preceptor, 66–67
An Zhongjing (eighth century), 89
Army Board (H22), 131, 234 n. 138
Army Inspectorate (T2) *(jianjun si)*, 121, 220 n. 17
Aśoka (T6, H2, H16), 20, 63, 92–93, 112, 121, 126, 130
Audience Ceremonies (T27, H21) *(gemen)*, 126, 131, 229 n. 83, 233 n. 130
Auxiliary Palace Fiscal Commission (T24–25, H23) *(xinggong sansi)*, 101, 125, 131, 227 n. 67
Avalambana society *(yulan foshe)*, 109
Ayuwang Temple, 62–63

Badaling Stūpa, 48
baǧši (pakshi / baksi), 56, 199 n. 24
Bai Ashan (T26, H25), 125, 132, 151–152, 228 n. 81
Bai Faxin, 46
Baixi Qitejile, 55–58
Bai Zhiguang, 46, 66–67
Bai Zhixuan (T26, H24), 96, 99, 125, 132, 151
Ban Shu (H4), 127, 231 n. 108
Baobaoxi Jiduoji, 55–58
Baojue Temple (Wofo si), 80
Beidougong (Big Dipper Palace), 112, 114

Bijuzhi pusa yibaiba ming jing ("Sūtra on the One Hundred Eight Names of Bhṛkutī Bodhisattva"), 70, 203 n. 73
Birnbaum, Raoul, 21, 186 n. 54
"black-headed" (T19), 103, 124, 137, 144, 225 n. 57, 238 n. 23
bodhi (T14), 102, 103, 123, 214 n. 64
Boluozhi, xxi, 91, 210 n. 14
Bonin, Ch.-E., 109–110
Bowring, Richard, 31, 189 n. 19
Buddhism: ceremonies and rituals, xxv, 28; and community, 23, 26, 157; and East Asian state building, 4, 28, 29–31; Esoteric, 19, 29, 31, 32, 47, 62, 95, 226 n. 60; exchanges between India and China, 29–34; at Liangzhou (fifth century), 140; Liao patronage of, 34, 47–48; Song patronage of, 29–32; and sovereignty, 19–26, 53–54, 157; in Tang dynasty, 19; Tibetan, 18, 21, 23; and trade, 23, 187 n. 64; in Xia, 5, 47–49, 137–139, 157–160
Buddhist canon: Jiaxing (Jingshan), 33; Liao, 34; Song, Tangut requests for, xxi, xxii, 29, 31, 34, 36–37, 54, 58, 59, 62, 200 n. 42; Xia, 34, 38, 63–65. *See also* Saṅgha
Budong ("Xi Xia monk"), 32–34

cakravartin, 20–21, 22, 39, 47, 48, 102, 185 n. 47
Cao Guangzhi, 65, 68
Calendar Board (T2, H22) *(da heng li*

yuan), 120, 131, 219 n. 11, 234 n. 137
Capital Security Office (T17, H22) *(huangcheng si)*, 124, 131, 224 n. 52, 234 n. 136
Central Asia, 23, 186 n. 62
Central Secretariat *(zhongshu)*. *See* Secretariat
changzhu (H14) ("permanent endowment"), 129
Chengtian Temple, 52–55
chengzhi (T25) ("recipient of directives"), 125, 228 n. 70
Chinggis Qan, xxv
Chong E, xxiii
Chongsheng Temple (T25, H23), 94, 96, 125, 131
chujia tidian ("superintendent of monks"), 36, 193 n. 58
Cibei daochang chanfa ("Method for [Conducting] Repentance in a Ritual Site of Compassion"), 64, 67, 68, 70
Confucianism, 4, 18, 23–26
Confucius, xxiv, 24
Coral Forest *(shanhu lin)*, 115
couming (H23) (Tangut rank), 131, 235 n. 148
Crossley, Pamela K., 11–12, 22, 183 n. 24

Dacheng sheng wuliangshou jing (*Amitābha-vyūha*, "Sūtra of the Buddha of Limitless Life"), 73, 205 n. 92
Dafo Temple (Wofo si), 78–82
Dangchang, 59
Dangxiang, xiii, xxii, 3, 11
Daoism, 19, 21, 186 n. 52
Daoists: in Xia, 61, 200 n. 49
Da Yun (Ming), 107
Dayun Temple, 5, 87–91, 94, 97–98, 104–117. *See also* Huguo Temple
Desheng Empress Dowager (T10, T13), 122–123, 222 n. 36. *See also* Liang empress, second
Devéria, Gabriel, 119
dharmarāja, 39, 47
Dongzhan, xxiii, 59, 75. *See also* Qingtang
duda goudang ("court officials overseeing the duties of . . ."), 148, 233 n. 132
Dunhuang, 35–36, 55, 63, 193 n. 59
Durt, Hubert, 80

ethnicity, 14–15, 146–152, 159–160
examination system, 24, 187 n. 68

Faguo, 20
Fahu, 30
Fajin, 30
Fajing, 78, 81
Fa Jixiang, 31
Fan: Jurchen ban on use of term, 26; meaning Tangut Mi-nyag, xiii, xv, 41, 43, 69, 96, 98–99, 131 (H21); meaning Tibetan, 36, 98–99, 193 n. 61; meaning "Westerner" (foreigner), 113; paired with Han, 125 (T25), 129 (H14), 131 (H24), 146, 159; rites, xxiii, 60–61, 158
Fan Zhongyan (989–1052), 17, 44–45
Farquhar, David M., 19–20, 22, 185 n. 45
Fatian, 30, 188 n. 9, 203 n. 73
Faure, Bernard, 31, 39, 54, 189 n. 21
Faxian (Tianxizai), 30, 203 n. 72
Fiscal Commission (T24, H22) *(sansi)*, 100–101, 125, 131, 226 n. 63; Auxiliary Palace Fiscal Commission (T24–25, H23) *(xinggong sansi)*, 101, 125, 131, 227 n. 67
Five Constants (H1) *(wuchang)*, 126, 140, 230 n. 102
Five Liang. *See* Liangzhou
Forte, Antonino, 19, 10, 21, 185 n. 44
Foshuo Amituo jing (*Sukhāvatīamṛta-vyūha-sūtra*, "Smaller Sukhāvatī-vyūha Sūtra"), 67
Foshuo yueguang pusa jing (*Candraprabha-bodhisattvacaryāvadāna-sūtra*, "The Sūtra of Moonlight Bodhisattva"), 69
Four Graces (T13) *(si'en)*, 123, 222 n. 40
Four Profoundly Great Vows (T13) *(si hongyuan)*, 123, 203 n. 66
"four rivers" (T14) *(sihe)*, 102, 123, 223 n. 44
Franke, Herbert, 23

Ganling Mountains, 78–79
Ganquan (Ganzhou), 79, 207 n. 117
Gansu, 23, 36, 186 n. 62

Index

Gantong Temple, 95, 97
Gantong Stūpa (T1, T24, T25, T26, H23, H24), 62, 67, 70, 72, 73, 87, 89, 93–98, 125, 131–132, 213 n. 48; post-Xia history of, 103–117; restoration of, 100–103
ganying, 218 n. 1
Ganzhou, xxi, 36, 78–79. *See also* Zhangye
Gaotai Temple, 47
Geshu Han (eighth century), 89–90, 209 n. 11
Ge Zhang-ndindzio (T2), 121, 136–137, 145, 221 n. 20
government households (T16, H14), 123, 129, 224 n. 48
Great State of White and High, xiv, 3, 27, 140. *See also* Xia
Great Xia (H12, H17), 39, 41, 129, 130. *See also* Xia
Guo Doanu (T28), 126, 145
Guoqu zhuangyan qie qian foming jing ("Sūtra on the Thousand Buddha Names of the Past Ornamented Kalpa"), 46, 63, 66
Gusiluo, xxiii, 36, 200 n. 38. *See also* Qingtang

Han: as paired with Fan (Tangut), xv, 43, 96, 98–99, 125 (T25), 129 (H14), 131 (H24), 146, 159; rites, xxiii, 60–61, 158
Helan Mountains, 33, 35, 45, 52
Helian Bobo, 40, 42
Hexi, xiii, xxii, 8, 36, 80, 89
Holmgren, Jennifer, 17, 184–185 n. 37
Hongren Temple (Wofo si), 80
Hongyuan Temple (Dayun si), 91
Hongzang Temple (Dayun si), 88
Houda Temple (Shengrong si), 97
huai wo le, 72, 131 (H22), 150, 205 n. 89, 233 n. 134
Huang Chi-chiang, 31, 189 n. 20
Huguo Temple (H24), xxiii, 5, 32–33, 87, 94–98, 118, 131, 212 nn. 34, 36. *See also* Dayun Temple
Huizhen, 36
Hun-Weiming Yu (T27, H21), 126, 131, 136, 152, 229 n. 84

ideology, 25–26. *See also* Xia
incarnation, 21
Indian monks, 29–31, 34, 38, 39

Inner Palace Council (T2) *(neisu)*, 121, 220 n. 16

Jan Yün-hua, 29
Japan: Heian (compared to Xia), 12, 16, 18
jianpin (T24), 125, 227 n. 65
Jiaohe (Gaochang), 41
Jiayike (Baixi Qitejile), 55–58
Jietan Cloister, 45, 55–56
Jin (Jurchens), 8; conquest of North China, xxiv, 8; discussions on legitimate succession, 26; emperor Shizong, xxiv–xxv; relations with Xia, xxiv–xxv, 158
Jin Bohong, 82, 208 n. 128
Jin'ge Temple (Baomo zhenguo jin'ge si), 95, 212 n. 34
Jin guangming zuisheng wang jing (*Suvarṇaprabhāsottamarāja-sūtra*, "Sūtra on the Golden Light All-Conquering King"), 66
Jinshan princess (Tangut wife of Dongzhan), 76. *See also* Qingtang
Jinzongchi, 31–32
Jiuquan (Suzhou), xv
Jiu Zhibo (T27, H25), 126, 132, 145, 152
Jiu Zhiqing (T26, H24), 96, 99, 125, 132, 151, 228 n. 77
Jiwaiji Fazheng, 37, 193 n. 64

Kaibao canon. *See* Buddhist canon
Kaiyuan Temple, 21, 89–90, 186 n. 52
Kang Gouming (T28, H21), 126, 131, 230 n. 95
Kāśyapa (buddha of the past), 79, 208 n. 123
Kāśyapa Rulai Temple (Wofo si), 80
Kepping, K. B., xiv
Khara-khoto, 3, 181 n. 3
Khotan, 23, 76, 80
Kirkland, Russell, 31, 189 n. 23
Kokonor, xxi, xxiv; Song sources on, 182 n. 9; Xia relations with, 7, 36, 59. *See also* Qingtang
Kozlov, Peter Kuz'mich, 3, 181 n. 3
Kucha, 76
Kychanov, E. I., 24–25

Lanzhou, xxiii, 72
Liang empress, first, 50, 83, 157–158; authority and power of, 29, 51, 59, 143; Buddhist activities, 51,

59, 62, 202 n. 57; death, xxiii; marriage to Weiming Liangzuo, xxiii, 58; restoration of Fan rites, 60; titles, xviii
Liang empress, second, xxiii–xxiv, 83, 157–158; authority and power of, 29, 51, 71–75, 143–144; Buddhist activities, 51, 63, 67, 70, 202 n. 57; death, 28, 51, 74, 58; marriage to Weiming Bingchang, 204 n. 78; military activities, 72, 74, 127 (H6); titles, xviii
Liang Qibu, xxiii, 70, 72, 75
Liang Wudi (r. 502–549), 20, 70–71
Liang Xingzhenie (T16–17, H22), 72, 124, 131, 136, 147–148, 150, 234 n. 135
Liang Yimai, xxiii, 50, 58, 61, 70, 200 n. 48
Liang Zhihui, 68
Liangzhou (T7, T10), xv, xxi, 5, 36, 62, 122; Liao raid on, 52; under Northern Wei, 20; Xia imperial cult center, 40, 118; Xia military headquarters, 100. *See also* Wuwei
Liangzuo. *See* Weiming Liangzuo
Liao (Khitans), xxi–xxii, xxiv, 8; Buddhism, propagation of, 34, 47–48; embassies from Xia, 60, 77; emperor Xingzong, 47–48; empress dowager Jin'ai, 48; Khitan language (T27), 126; marriage alliance with Xia, xxii, xxiv; wars with Xia, xxii, 45, 48, 52; Xia requests for help from, 72, 74; Xia rivalry with, 44, 59
Li Deming, xvii, xxi, 34–35, 37, 40, 42, 192 n. 51
Li Fanwen, xvii
Light Voice Heaven *(guangyin tian)*, 115, 217 n. 98
Lijing, 55
Li Jiqian, xvii, xxi, 34, 40, 91
liming (H23), 131, 235 n. 150
Lingjie Chengpang (T25, H24), 96, 125, 131, 151–152, 228 n. 76, 235 n. 152
lingpi (T27, H21), 126, 131, 229 n. 82
Lingzhou, xxi, 61
Li Qing, xxiii
Li Ruyin (Qing), 115
Li Shougui, 55–57

Liu Gouer (T27, H25), 126, 132, 152, 229 n. 90
Liu Quliyai (H23), 101, 131, 145, 150–151, 235 n. 151
Liu Xiu (eighth century), 88
Li Yuan (eleventh century), 76
Li Yuanhao. *See* Weiming Yuanhao
Longcan, 75. *See also* Qingtang
"Lotus Sūtra" *(Saddharmapuṇḍarīka-sūtra, Miaofa lianhua jing)*, 46, 93, 101–102, 223 n. 45, 232 n. 121
Lu Guangzu (Ming), 107
lüjing (T24, H22, H23), 131, 154, 225 n. 53
Luohan Cloister, 48

Mai Majie (T24, H22), 100, 125, 131, 146, 148, 150, 227 n. 66
Maitreya (future buddha) (T20), 20–21, 62–63, 73, 79, 81, 124, 225 n. 55
Manchus, 11, 22
Mañjuśrī: cult at Wutai shan, 19, 21, 22, 35–36, 95; Ming emperor Yongle's designation of his father as, 186 n. 59; Qing emperor as reincarnation of, 186 n. 60
Mañjuśrī-nāma-saṃgīti (Wenzhu pusa [suo shuo] zuisheng mingyi jing), 32, 190 n. 25
Mannerheim, Gustav, 109–110
Mengshan, 32–33
Mi. *See* Mi-nyag
Miaofa lianhua jing. *See* "Lotus Sūtra"
Mingwang Qi'e (T2), 96, 121, 136–137, 145, 149, 220 n. 15
Ming Yingzong (r. 1435–1449, 1457–1464), 105–106
Mi-nyag (Mi-niah, Mi), xiii, 3, 103, 141, 231 n. 110
Mizang Etepang. *See* Mocang Epang
Mocang (clan name), 239 n. 27
Mocang empress, xxii, 45, 52–54, 55–58
Mocang Epang, xxii, 55–58
Mongols, xxv, 22, 23, 49, 105–106
Muyang Eyi (T25), 101, 125, 145, 150, 228 n. 72, 235 n. 149

"New Laws," 99, 214 n. 55
Nisimen, 41
nomads, 7–8

Northern Wei, 20, 138, 140–141; Tangut royal claims to descent from, 40–42
Nushe Eji, 41

Ordos, 3, 13, 15, 23

Pang Ji, 240 n. 42
Pāramitās, Six (T5, T13), 121, 123, 221 n. 27
Pulleyblank, Edwin, xvi

Qiang (T10, H6, H17), 122, 127, 130, 222 n. 35
Qiao, Lady, 55
qiejie (H22), 131, 235 n. 144
Qingtang (Xining, Kokonor), 55; absorbed by Xia, xxiv; Aligu, xxiii–xxiv, 75, 77; Aligu's son Xiazheng, 75–76; Dongzhan, xxiii, 59, 75; Dongzhan's mother Lady Qiao, 55; Dongzhan's wife, 76; Gusiluo, xxiii, 36, 200 n. 38; Longcan, 75; wars with Xia, xxii–xxiv, 122 (T10), 222 n. 35; Xia-Song rivalry over, 75–77
Qingtang lu, 76–77, 206 n. 106
Qingying Temple, 87, 109–117
Qubilai, 82
Quye River, xxii–xxiii, 57–58

"recipient of directives" (T25) *(chengzhi),* 125, 228 n. 70
"red-faced" (T20), 103, 124, 137, 144, 225 n. 57, 238 n. 23
reincarnation, 21, 22, 186 n. 59
Ren Dejing, xxiv, 158
Renduo clan, 74
Renjing Emperor (T10, T13), 122–123, 222 n. 36. *See also* Weiming Qianshun
Renwang huguo banruo boluomiduo jing ("Sūtra on the Perfection of Insight by Which a Humane King Protects the Country"), 95, 211 n. 32
Ren Yuzi (T28, H21), 126, 131
Richeng, 32
Right Wing (H22) *(youxiang),* 131, 227 n. 64, 235 n. 143. *See also* Southern Court

Śākyamuni, 28, 190 nn. 31–32
Samantabhadra, 32, 191 n. 35
Saṅgha (Xia Buddhist establishment), 28, 46–47, 51, 63–68, 75, 78, 81, 143, 158, 160, 200 n. 49; ethnic composition of, 67, 98–99, 147; officials of, 66, 120, 219 nn. 12–13
Secretariat (T16, H22) (Central Secretariat, *zhongshu*), 124, 131, 153, 224 n. 49, 233 n. 133
"seven treasures" (H10), 102, 128, 214–215 n. 66
Shazhou, 193 n. 59. *See also* Dunhuang
Shengrong Temple (T2, T24, H23), 94, 96–98, 118, 121, 131, 219 n. 13
Shen Kuo (1031–1095), 58, 200 n. 34
Shen Yong (Ming), 104–106, 107
Shi Jinbo, 24, 28
Shihu, 30
Shijing Empress Dowager (T8–T9), 122. *See also* Liang empress, first
Siduoduo, xxi, 91
Sima Guang (1019–1086), 14
Sima Yi (eighth century), 89
sinicization, 9–10
Sino-Tibetan languages, 11, 183–184 n. 25
Sofronov, M. S., xvi
Song: Buddhism, patronage of, 29–32; emperor Renzong, 29, 30, 40, 43, 240 n. 42; emperor Shenzong, xxiii, 14, 50, 62, 197 n. 2; emperor Taizong, 30; emperor Taizu, 30; emperor Zhenzong, 30, 42; emperor Zhezong, 50, 74, 232 n. 115; empress dowager Gao, 50, 232 n. 115; expansion in the northwest, 50–51, 72, 74, 82; factional struggles, 9; military, 14; relations with Xia, xxi–xxiv, 4, 9, 59, 62, 71, 73; succession and regencies, 16–17
Southern Court (T24) *(nanyuan),* 100, 125, 226 n. 64, 227 n. 67. *See also* Right Wing
state formation, 6–18, 22, 159; centralization, degree of, 51–52; military considerations, 8–10; Xia, early stages, 12–18, 35, 37
state preceptors *(guoshi),* 46, 66, 79, 81
stūpa: Aśokan stūpas, 80, 87, 91–94, 112, 116–117; cult of, 38, 87, 91–

95, 109–117, 128–129 (H11), 210 nn. 19–20, 232 n. 121; Liangzhou, at, 90; in 1050 inscription, 52–54; in 1672 inscription, 115; in 1038 inscription, 39; at Qingtang, 77; stūpa lamps, 114. *See also* Gantong Stūpa
Su Che (d. 1112), 14
Sui Wendi (r. 581–605), 20, 23, 93
Sui Yangdi (r. 605–616), 97
Sun Duer (H25), 132
Sun Kedu (T28, H25), 126, 132, 230 n. 97
Sun Rezi (H25), 132, 145
Sun Sike (Qing), 114–115
"superintendent of monks" *(chujia tidian)*, 36, 193 n. 58
"Sūtra on the Visualization of Maitreya Bodhisattva's Rebirth in Tuṣita Heaven" *(Guan Mile pusa sheng sheng doushuaitian jing)*, 225 n. 55
sūtra translation bureau (Xia), 64–67

Taiping Xingguo Temple, 30
Tang: emperor Daizong, 22, 95; emperor Taizong, 22; emperor Xuanzong, 19, 21, 89, 186 n. 52
Tangut: ethno-cultural identity, 5–6, 14–15, 69, 133, 137–144; ethnonym, xiii–xiv; literary styles, 133–135, 236 n. 2–3; names, 145–152; romanization, xvi; script, 15, 37–38, 41, 137, 194 n. 66, 236 n. 7; social-tribal structure, 15–16; titles, 72; translating, xiv–xv, 120, 153; transliterating, 153–155, 240 n. 42
Tantric Buddhism, 5; tantric texts, 31; yoga tantras, 32, 190 nn. 31–32; Vajrayāna, 39, 190 n. 32
Tao River, xxiii
Tathāgata, 20, 115, 121 (T3), 190 n. 31–32, 221 n. 22
Tatars, 41
Temüjin (Chinggis Qan), xxv
"The Text of the Penitential Offering to the Thirty-five Buddhas' Names" *(Sanshiwu foming li chan wen)*, 32, 191 n. 34
Thought Scorching Heaven *(yizao tian)*, 115

Three Realms (T4, T13, T20) *(sanjie, sanyou)*, 121, 123, 221 n. 23, 223 n. 41
Three Times (T19) *(sanshi)*, 124, 225 n. 56
Three-Wheel Body (T21) *(sanlun shen)*, 124, 226 n. 60
Tiancian, 88
Tiandu Mountains, 45
Tiansheng law code, 6, 24, 28, 52, 188 n. 4
Tianxizai (Faxian), 30, 203 n. 72
Tibet, 11, 23, 51; Qingtang Tibetans, xxii; Tibetan envoys to Liao, xxi; Tufan, 41, 77; Xi Fan, 99. *See also* Qingtang
tidian (T2) ("superintendent"), 121, 220 n. 14
tiju (T2, T24–25) ("supervisor"), 96, 120, 125, 212 n. 38, 219 n. 13, 227 n. 68
Transformation Body (T5) *(hua / ying shen)*, 121, 221 n. 25
True Body (T3) *(zhenshen)*, 121, 221 n. 21
Tufan, 41, 77
Tuoba, 15, 40–45
Tuṣita Heaven, 63, 73, 79, 81, 115
Tuyühun, 59, 126, (T27), 202 n. 62, 229 n. 84, 228 n. 81
Two Sages (H7, H10, H12, H19) *(ersheng)*, 127, 128, 129, 130, 232 n. 115

Uighurs: Alashan, 54; Ganzhou, 41, 55; Gaochang (Jiaohe), 41, 55; and Liangzhou, 90; monks, 34, 60; names, 202 n. 62, 203 n. 67; at Qingtang, 75–76; Shazhou, 54, 193 n. 59; in Xia Buddhist establishment, 47, 54–55
Uraqai (Wulahai), xxv

Vaiśravaṇa, 39
Vajrabodhi (Tang), 32, 191 n. 37
Vimalakīrtinirdeśa-sūtra. See *Weimoji suo shuo jing*

Wang Anshi (1021–1086), 14, 17, 62
Wang Chang (1725–1806), 88, 110
Wang Dan, 76
Wangna Zhengyu (T25, H24), 96, 125, 132, 150–151, 235 n. 153

Index

Wang Puxin, 46, 200 n. 32
Wang Shao (1030–1081), xxiii, 50
Wang Zhen (T28, H25), 126, 132, 230 n. 99
Wechsler, Howard J., 19, 182 n. 5, 185 n. 41
Weimi Liegui (Li Shougui), 55–57
Weimi Sineng, 79–82
Weiming Anquan, xix, xxv
Weiming Bingchang (Huizong), xviii, 60–61, 64, 65–70
Weiming Chunyou (Huanzong), xix, xxv
Weiming Dewang (Xianzong), xix, xxv
Weiming Liangzuo (Yizong), xvii, xxii–xxiii, 52–53, 55, 58–60
Weiming Qianshun (Chongzong), xxiii–xiv, 51, 68, 70–71, 78, 80–81, 204 n. 78
Weiming Renxiao (Renzong), xiii, xxiv–xxv, 28, 63, 67, 158
Weiming Restoration, 51–52, 158
Weiming Shan, xxiii
Weiming Xian, xix
Weiming Yuanhao (Jingzong), xxi–xxii, 36–49; birthday, 47; death, 45; enthronement, 27, 35, 38–40; legacy, 60–61; letter to Song court in 1038, 40–43; names and titles, xvii; reforms, 37, 41, 51
Weiming Zunxu (Shenzong), xix, xxv
Weimoji suo shuo jing (*Vimalakīrtinirdeśa-sūtra*, "The Sūtra Spoken by Vimalakīrti"), 68, 78, 124 (T21), 226 n. 58
Weimu empress, xvii, 36
Weinstein, Stanley, 19, 185 n. 42
Weiyaini, 41
Weiyi Yiyai (T28, H21), 126, 131, 230 n. 94
Wenhai (Tangut rhyme dictionary), 28, 188 n. 3
White Body Heaven *(baishen tian)*, 115
Wofo Temple (Dafo si), 78–82, 207 n. 115
Wopu Lingji, 41
Wo Qujie (T17, H22), 124, 131, 136, 146, 147–150, 224 n. 53, 227 n. 69
world-system perspective, 7, 9–10, 18, 182 n. 10, 183 n. 23
Wright, Arthur, 19, 21, 185 n. 40
Wu Guangcheng, 34, 47, 54, 58, 78, 80–81, 237–238 n. 18

Wu Modou (H23), 101, 131, 145, 150–151, 235 n. 149
Wutai shan (Mount Wutai), 19, 21, 35, 95, 192 n. 53
Wuwei (T7, H9), 97, 122, 128. *See also* Liangzhou
Wu Zhao (Empress Wu, Tang), 19, 20, 21, 88, 188 n. 11
wuzu, 37

Xia: administrative usages, 145–156, 160; Buddhist establishment, 28, 47; ethnic identity and imperial ideology, 5, 43–44, 48–49, 133, 135, 137–145, 159–160; female regents, 16–18; imperial tombs, 48–49; marriage politics, 16–18; military elites, 29; name, xiii–xiv; reign era titles, xvii–xix; relations with Liao, 44, 48, 52, 59, 72, 74, 75–77; relations with Song, 4, 7, 9, 153. *See also* Liang empress; Liao; Saṅgha; Song
xianhou (H6) ("former sovereign"), 127, 231 n. 111
Xianzai xian qie qian foming jing ("Sūtra on the Thousand Buddha Names of the Present Bhadra Kalpa"), 65, 67
Xiazheng, 75–76. *See also* Qingtang
Xiazhou, 13
Xie Zhixing (T27, H25), 126, 132, 145, 152, 229 n. 87
Xi Fan, 99. *See also* Tibet
Xingzhou (Zhongxingfu), xxi, 39
Xi Xia. *See* Xia
Xuanwu di ("Dark Emperor," Xuandi, Zhenwu), 107

Yandan *guoshi*, 79–82, 207 n. 118
Yang: 1038 inscription, 38; 1094 inscription, T28, H25
Yang Bo (Tang), 97
Yaonie Yongquan (T24, H23), 96, 100–101, 125, 131, 148, 227 n. 69
Yeli empress, xvii, xxii, 56–57
Yeli Renrong ("honored teacher Iri"), 37–38, 194 n. 67
Yeli Wangrong, 56, 240 n. 42
Yeli Yuqi, 45, 55–56
Yin Sun[?] (T28), 126, 145
Yongle fortress, xxiii
Yongning Temple, 93

Youlongbo, 91, 210 n. 13
Yuanfeng campaign, 61–62
Yuan Hongde (Ming), 113–114
Yulin caves, 55, 62
Yu Qian, 29, 31
Yuqie jiyao jiu a'nan tuoluoni yankou guiyi jing, 191 n. 37
Yuqie jiyao yankou shishi yi, 191 n. 39
Yushan (Liangzhou), 97

Zhang Fanyi (T26, H25), 125, 132, 145, 151
Zhang Gui (T7, H2, H16), 122, 126, 130, 140, 231 n. 104
Zhang Shu (1781–1847), 109, 110–111, 215 n. 75
Zhang Tianxi (T7, H3, H16), 88, 89, 91–92, 122, 126, 130, 231 n. 106
Zhangye (Ganzhou), xv, 41, 78
Zhang Zhengsi (T27, H21), 126, 131, 152
Zhang Zhi, 38, 194 n. 70
Zhao Wanbi (Ming), 107–108
zheng ("director"), 96, 212 n. 39
Zheng Sandui (T28, H25), 126, 132, 230 n. 96
Zhenling cheng Emperor (T9), 122, 222 n. 33. *See also* Weiming Bingchang
Zhiman (Japanese monk), 105, 107
Zhongxingfu (Xia capital), 35, 192 n. 55
Zhu Yuanzhang (r. 1368–1398), 21
Zuo Aling (T28, H25), 126, 132
Zuo Jiyi (T28, H25), 126, 132
Zuo Paner (T28, H25), 126, 132, 230 n. 98
Zuo Zhixin (T28, H25), 126, 132